John Miller

Suggestive Commentary on St. Paul's Epistle to the Romans

With an Excursus on the Famous Passage in James (Chap. II.: 14-26)

John Miller

Suggestive Commentary on St. Paul's Epistle to the Romans
With an Excursus on the Famous Passage in James (Chap. II.: 14-26)

ISBN/EAN: 9783337008970

Printed in Europe, USA, Canada, Australia, Japan

Cover: Foto ©Lupo / pixelio.de

More available books at **www.hansebooks.com**

Price, $1.50.

COMMENTARY

ON

PAUL'S EPISTLE TO ROMANS;

WITH AN

EXCURSUS ON THE FAMOUS PASSAGE IN JAMES
(CHAP. II.: 14-26).

BY

REV. JOHN MILLER.

PRINCETON, N. J.:
EVANGELICAL REFORM PUBLICATION CO.,
1887.

Mailed post-paid by this Company on receipt of price.

COPYRIGHT,
1887,
By JOHN MILLER.

Press of W. L. Mershon & Co.,
Rahway, N. J.

PREFACE.

I. There is a vast difference between the sentence "I will have mercy on whom I will have mercy" (E. V., Rom. 9 : 15), and the sentence "I will have mercy on whomsoever I can have mercy." It would be worth a life-time of an exegete to establish this rendering, especially if he added to it, "So, then, it is not of the willing, nor of the running, but of the mercy showing God" (v. 16), and also, "Therefore, one man whom He has a desire after (see Matt. 27 : 43), He shows mercy to, and another man whom He has a desire after, He hardens" (v. 20). This nest of proof texts which have done awful service for doubt, would sweeten the whole of Paul if they can give this bettered idea of Jehovah's sovereignty.

II. There is a vast difference between the sentence "obedience to the faith" (E. V., 1 : 5), and the sentence "obedience of faith." One favors the view of doctrinalism, or our believing our way into the kingdom. The other makes faith obedience, and itself a moral act, or the beginning of a better life.

III. There is a vast difference between the sentence, "justified by faith" (E. V. 3 : 28), and the sentence, "made righteous in the shape of faith" (*material dative*). One builds a doctrine not lisped of till the Reformation, and the other rests upon the atonement, and considers righteousness that imparted righteousness which Paul means by what we have already noticed in the "obedience of faith."

IV. There is a vast difference between the sentence, "for that all have sinned" (E. V., 5 : 12), and the sentence, "on Him at whose charges all did the sinning." We quit looking for an apodosis across a quarter of a chapter ; we put an end to the champion parenthesis of Holy Writ (E. V., vs. 13-17) ;

we unearth an orthodox sense; we shut up protasis and apodosis in a single verse; and we reduce this most baffling sentence of the ten (vs. 12–21) to a similarity to all the rest in its balanced signification, "Wherefore as by one man sin came into the world, so death by sin, and thus to all men death passed through on to Him at whose charges all did the sinning."

V. There is a vast difference between the sentence, "Until the law sin was in the world" (E. V., 5 : 13), and the sentence, "As far as there was law." One is thrown away upon a case that never happens, while the other is the soundest ethic. In proportion as there is law, men sin. And as all men have law, at least in an original conscience, all sin. Even the Devil has law. It is necessary to accountability. For, as this same apostle expresses it, Without law "there is no transgression" (4 :15).

VI. There is a vast difference between the sentence, "I was alive without the law once" (E. V., 7 : 9), setting men to dreaming when that could be, and the wholesome moral fact that sin is the punishment of sin. Paul is full of this conception of "death." "The wages of sin is death." "The strength of sin is the law." "Without the law sin is dead ;" and then the present verse following immediately after :—" I had been alive without the law at any time." That is, sin would be no cause of sin but for a law, and release God from the obligation of law, and no poor sinner would continue a moment under the power of sin.

VII. There is a vast difference between the sentence, "All things work together for good" (E. V., 8 : 28), and the sentence, God "works as to all things for good with them that love" Him. In the other way it is true, but irrelevant. In the literal way it agrees with prayer. Prayer, we have just been hearing (vs. 26, 27), is made prayer by God working in us and with us in intercessions otherwise unutterable; and Paul, wishing to complete the idea, adds, "And we know" that prayer is not peculiar in this concursus, "We know that He works as to all things for good with them that love God."

VIII. There is a vast difference between the sentence, "declared to be the Son of God" (E. V., 1 : 4), and the sentence, "determined on as the Son of God." One postulates an eternal Sonship, and that it is only "declared" in time. The other ranges itself with such expressions as "Mine elect;" it agrees with the account "by that man whom he hath ordained" (E. V., Acts 17 : 31, the same word, ὁρίζω, *determined on*); it agrees with Gabriel where he is satisfied with the word "be called" (E. V., Lu. 1 : 35); it agrees with Gabriel's reasons marked by his expressive "*therefore*," and with Paul's (see Commentary); and best of all, it agrees with the same root three sentences before (Rom. 1 : 1), employed as of Paul himself, and translated by King James, "separated unto the gospel of God."

Let our Preface deal with samples, therefore. We are content that way. If they are new, they should be watched. If they are true, they should be treasured. But if they are both new and true, that is not what has roused us to the work. These and a multitude of others are not simply new texts, adding, if they are supported by the Greek, new paragraphs to the Word of God, but they bring to bay a concerted system of mistakes. Protestantism has ascribed too little morality to God, and demanded too little morality of men. Paul has been the arch-priest of horrors, and the world is beginning to move. To sweeten Paul is not only hermeneutically right, but theologically the thing required, as the curse of the Reformed just now is, that they build Rome with a faith that has no works, and place at the top of their creed Sovereignty instead of Holiness.

JOHN MILLER.

PRINCETON, Oct. 16, 1885.

COMMENTARY.

THE EPISTLE TO CERTAIN ROMANS OF PAUL THE APOSTLE.

Paul does not call himself "*the apostle to the Romans*" (E. V.), for he had possibly never seen Rome. The like mistake is made by the Revisionists. It occurs in all his epistles. We are not to say "Apostle to the Corinthians," or "Apostle to the Hebrews" (E. V. and Re.), but "**Epistle to**" each of these different people. Moreover we are not to say, "*Epistle to the Romans*," but "*Epistle to Romans*," for it was written only to a few in Rome. Paul wrote to "the Church of God," or to "the saints," or to "the faithful in Christ Jesus" (Rom. 1:7; 1. Cor. 1:1; Eph. 1:1). Hence there is reason for the wording, "*The Epistle to Romans* (or **to certain Romans**) **of Paul the Apostle.**"

But these titles, writ as we may please, were not inspired; they are of uncertain date; they are different in different MSS.; they were sometimes changed; were not always necessarily correct; and, in the instance of the "Epistle to certain Hebrews," not necessarily to be relied on to authenticate that as an "epistle of Paul" (E. V. and Re.).

CHAPTER I.

I. Paul, a bondman of Jesus Christ, called to be an Apostle, having been set apart to a Gospel of God.

1. **"Paul;"** Paul's Greek name. It occurs first in the thirteenth chapter of Acts (v. 9) ; " Then Saul, who also is called Paul." Saul is Hebrew, and means *asked for ;* and Paul is Greek, and means *little.* All kindred Greek is transferred into the English in two syllables ; as, for example, Festus, not Fest, Justus, not Just, Gaius, not Gai. That *Saulos* should be rendered Saul is natural, for that is the shape of the word in the Hebrew language ; but that *Paulos* should be rendered " *Paul*," is probably to be accounted for by what is accident in this similarity of sound ; and perhaps to the same sort of accident of sound may be chiefly attributed the whole choice of the name. " *Paul*," moving about among the Greeks, did what was customary then, took a name from among that people, and called himself " *Paulus ;* " not necessarily because he was little (Augustine, De Spir. et Lit. 6, 7, vol. x. p. 207), nor probably in honor of Sergius Paulus, who is marked as his convert in the very same passage (Acts 13 : 7–9, see Jerome) ; but as Joseph was called Hegesippus, and Eliakim, Alkimos, because of the alliteration, or because of the affinity, of some sort, the one for the other. We may say with confidence that there is nothing practically discoverable that is of moment in the change. **" A bond-man."** Δοῦλος is from δέω to *bind.* It is a prime rule for exegetes to translate by the original meaning as far as possible. The force, too, of general usage should be felt in assigning a signification. We shall presently see that "*declared*" is a most vicious rendering in the fourth verse, because in the seven other places where the original occurs, it never once means *declared*, but always "*determined on.*" So "*but*" (E. V.) is a very vicious translation in Gal. 2 : 16 ; for

of the fifty-eight other places where the Greek ἐὰν μή occurs, not one will bear the meaning of *but*, and in no other case does our version imagine so. An attention to this rule alone would make a vast difference as against the prepossessions of translators. Δοῦλος is found a hundred and twenty-two times in the New Testament. "*Bondman*" will translate it always. It literally means a *slave*. But as it would be needlessly harsh to say, "Well done good and faithful slave" (Matt. 25 : 21), or " He sent and signified it by His angel to His slave, John" (Rev. 1 : 1), or, "These men are slaves of the Most High God" (Acts 16 : 17), we sacrifice the advantage where slave would be better, as, for example, " slave of sin " (Jo. 8 : 34), or "slaves of corruption" (2 Pet. 2 : 19), and translate everywhere *bondman*. That leaves the word διάκονος (*deacon*), which has grown technical in an office of the church, to mean a higher "*servant*," and to be translated in every instance in that way in its thirty passages. "*Paul*," then, "*a bondman*," bought with Christ's blood, and sealed forever to his service!

"**Of Jesus Christ.**" These names are of different languages, and one describes the God in our Redeemer, and the other the Man. "*Jesus*" was a corruption of *Joshua ;* and, though Gabriel assigned the name, yet it was a common name (often under the form of Jason) at this time among the Israelites. Joshua was a name given by Moses, (Num. 13 : 8, 16). Joshua's original name was Hoshea. Hoshea meant *one who saves*, Moses added the idea of *Jehovah's salvation*. And though the name fell back to *Jeshua* (Neh. 8, 17), and in the Greek to "*Jesus*," which means little more than *help*, yet, to a Jew's eye it had all its early significance, and the mere shrinkage by use did not blot out Jehovah's part of it. "*Christ*," on the contrary, meant *Anointed*. It was a translation of *Messiah*. And as God is not anointed, it is the title of the Man. "*Jesus*" is Christ's Godlike name as being the *Jehovah who saves*. "*Christ*" is a human designation, not simply as of one *anointed* to office, He being Prophet, Priest and King, but, as, what that unction means, anointed of the Spirit, not simply in all these respects, officially, but in all respects, and chiefly in unspotted holiness, and in a form hereafter to be explained of moral recovery (6 : 7). Paul, therefore, pictures himself as a slave of this unspotted God-Man.

"**Called to be an apostle.**" "*A called apostle*" would be more after the Greek, but then "*called saints*" in the seventh verse would be ambiguous, and might mean *named* saints. Therefore, to translate alike in so near a context, we say "*called to be*" (E. V. & Re.).

The word ἀπόστολος occurs but once in the Septuagint scriptures. "I am sent to thee as a hard messenger" (1 Ki. 14 : 6). Ἀποστολή, which occurs four times in the New Testament, and always means *apostleship* (E. V.), occurs ten times in the Septuagint, and has the wildest variety of meaning. It means "*pestilence*" (Jer. 32 : 36, E. V.) ; it means *gift* or "*present*" (1 Ki. 9 : 16, E. V.) ; it means "*plants*" (Cant. 4 : 13, E. V.) ; it means some sort of *missive* in some of the other places. It is clear that these words were of no technical use two centuries before Christ. Our only light upon their meaning, therefore, is in two facts : first, that Christ "chose twelve whom also He named *apostles*" (Lu. 6 : 13) to be eye-witnesses (1 Cor. 9 : 1) of His ministry and the first preachers and founders of His church (Eph. 2 : 20), and second, that, true to this origin of the title, a certain fourteen men, viz. Christ's original twelve, and one appointed in the place of one of them (Acts 12 : 26), and one miraculously appointed afterward, to wit, Paul, always appropriated this name ; and that in the eighty-one New Testament passages where it occurs, it is used of no one else, save once of Christ (Heb. 3 : 1), twice of "false apostles" (2 Cor. 11 : 13 ; Rev. 2 : 2), twice of Barnabas (Acts 14 : 4, 14), once of a man and woman probably (Rom. 16 : 7), twice of common messengers (2 Cor. 8 : 23 ; Phil. 2 : 25), once of Paul and two of his companions (1 Thess. 2 : 7), and once of "James the brother of the Lord" (Gal. 1 :19) ;* from all which we are to infer that "*apostle*," like *presbyter* (Acts 2 : 17 ; 1 Pet. 5 : 5) ; and like *deacon* (Jo. 2 : 5, 9),

---

* Perhaps it is not altogether certain that this James was not the son of Alpheus, and, therefore, from the first, one of the twelve.

and like *church* (Acts 19 : 32, 40), and like *spirit* (Lu. 8 : 55), and like *flesh* (Lu. 24 : 39), had not left their primary meaning and hardened altogether in the Greek into ecclesiastical terms, but that they had done so enough to be usually definite, and that Paul was "called to be an apostle" in the sense of being one of fourteen men designated by Christ to be "eye-witnesses of His majesty." In all other senses they were official "*elders*" (1 Peter 5 : 1), instructed by God to make elders of others (1 Tim. 1 : 6), but not instructed to make *apostles*, even though hundreds of men had seen their common Master.

"**Having been set apart.**" Commentators have lost much by not studying this word in connection with that translated "*declared*" in verse fourth. Ὁρίζω coming from ὅρος a *boundary*, means to *bound* off, or *fix a limit*. It occurs eight times in the New Testament, and in every case means to *determine* or *determine upon* (*terminus, limit*). The word is so important that we will quote every case. "The Son of Man goeth as it was determined" (Lu. 22 : 22, E. V.). "Him being delivered by the determinate counsel" (Acts 2 : 23, E. V.). "It is He which was determined upon (ordained E. V.) of God to be the judge of quick and dead" (Acts 10 : 42). "The disciples determined to send relief" (Acts 11 : 29, E. V.). "Hath determined the times before appointed" (Acts 17 : 26, E. V.). "A day in the which He will judge the world in righteousness by that man whom He hath determined upon (ordained, E. V., Acts 17 : 31). "Who was determined on as God's Son (declared to be the Son of God, E. V.) in power" (Rom. 1 : 4). "Again, He determines upon (limiteth, E. V.) a certain day" (Heb. 4 : 7). It will be noticed that it is translated (E. V.) but once *declared*, and that under an obvious theological bias, being never so understood in the Septuagint, and really without any warrant in the general usage of the language. And yet to say "*appointed*" would be too far from the meaning of ὁρίζω. A boundary is set *for reasons*. "*Appointed* the Son of God" would be too naked. "*Determined upon*" is the very word, and agrees with the speech of Gabriel,—" Therefore "—as though there were intrinsic reasons, apart from mere appointment—

"Therefore"—because "the Holy Ghost shall come upon thee, and the power of the Highest shall overshadow thee; therefore, also, that holy thing which shall be born of thee shall be called the Son of God" (Matt. 1 : 35). Let it be noticed farther that *predestined* (E. V.) is the same verb compounded with a preposition. *Determined upon beforehand* (προ) is the meaning. *Predestined* is a little too arbitrary, like *appointed*. " Whom He did foreknow, them He also did determine upon beforehand" (not *predestinate* E. V., 8 : 29). The word is a delicate one, and unites the ideas of appointment and of reasons for it, just as exist in the fixing of a boundary. Now it is this ὁρίζω, with a different preposition before it, viz. απο, *out from among*, or *away from*, that we are concerned with at present. It was fitting that Paul should have a different description from his Master. Christ " was determined upon as God's Son " at once (*aorist*), and without any calling out from among the wicked. Paul had been (*perfect*) απο *determined upon*, that is *bounded off*, or *set apart, called out from* very bad relations, and that not at a single stroke (like Christ), such as the *aorist* would express, but by successive fixings of his case (*perfect tense*), not only "from (his) mother's womb " (Gal. 1 : 15), where this word ἀφορίζω is also used, but under Gamaliel, and on the way to Damascus, and in successive stages of divine preparation. " *Separated* " (E. V.) would do very well, but it is awkward English, and still more awkward where it speaks of being " separated from my mother's womb " (Gal. 1 : 15). *Set apart* will answer everywhere. Set apart the righteous from the wicked (Matt. 13 : 49); set them apart from each other (Matt. 25 : 32); set apart the sheep from the goats (*ib.*); set you aside or apart (Lu. 6 : 22); set apart for me Barnabas and Saul (Acts 13 : 2); set the disciples aloof or apart (Acts 19; 9); be ye set apart (2 Cor. 6 : 17); he who set me apart from my mother's womb; put himself aloof or set himself apart (Gal. 2 : 12); these are all the nine instances of ἀφορίζω in the N. T. Greek, and answer perfectly to show that Paul meant that he had been " *set apart* " from other wicked men to preach the gospel.

"**A Gospel of God.**" We do not say "*a good message of God*," because the word had hardened enough into what was technical to make that awkward in many passages. "According to my good message" (2 : 16), or "the good message which I have good messaged" (1 Cor. 15 : 1), or "the good message of the circumcision" (Gal. 2 : 7), are sentences which show that the word had escaped from its original simplicity. "A gospel of God" means a gospel given by God (and not a gospel about God), as will appear in the succeeding verse.

2. As to which He announced Himself before by His prophets in holy scriptures.

"*Promised*" (E. V.) would do well enough were it not for the unhappy English. "*Glad tidings promised*" is not just the expression we would choose. *An annunciation before announced* is more what would come under a Grecian's eye, as the verb and the substantive are from the same ἀγγέλλω. But the verb is in the middle, and naturally means **announced himself.** As *announcing oneself as to a thing* which is of a promissory sort, is virtually to promise it, it is used that way (E. V.) thirteen times in the N. T. On the other two occasions of its use the word *professing* is brought in (E. V.), "which some professing have erred concerning the faith" (1 Tim. 6 : 21); "professing godliness" (1 Tim. 2 : 10). The compound with προ (before) which occurs but once, and that in the present passage, may very properly, therefore, be rendered ("the glad annunciation) *as to which He announced Himself before* (or which He announced for Himself before), **by His prophets in holy scriptures.**" That there should be no article before "*scriptures*" was not unnatural, for it was not every scripture that foretold the gospel. But we are to notice how the ample predictions which there were, are thus early announced, and everywhere brought out by Paul, to confirm his representations.

His book might be called, The Gospel of Christ proved out of the Old Testament Scriptures.

3. Concerning His Son, the Jesus Christ our Lord, who came into being of David's seed through flesh.

"**Concerning.**" Scripture is often ambiguous, and carelessly and purposely so when the ambiguity makes not the slightest difference (vs. 6, 17 ; 5 : 5, 17 ; 13 : 14 ; 16 : 2). The gospel "*concerning*" and the announcing of himself "*concerning*" would amount to the same thing. As the very Greek for *annunciation* (ἀγγέλλω) is found in both noun and verb, the question as to which the preposition belongs to is not worth settling, and the comments as between Lange and Meyer are based upon nothing, and could not touch a shade of the significance, even if they could be made certain either way.

"**His Son.**" This great personage Paul announces to be the sum of the gospel, and proceeds at once to give a definition the most complete in scripture. "**The Jesus Christ our Lord who.**" Now we ought to watch every word. For there is nothing like them in elaborateness as to the Son of the Father. "**Who came into being.**" He "*came into being*" then. Let us fix the meaning of that verb first of all. It is used seven hundred times or more in the New Testament. Therefore what we are about to announce is very decisive. In all these seven hundred instances, if associated with a nominative in the predicate, it means *became ;* as for example, "*the Word became flesh.*" If, on the other hand, it be the whole predicate itself, it means *originated ;* as for example "*the world came to be.*" Its primary meaning is not *to be born* (so say most lexicographers), or, if it is, that has long sunk into a least frequent meaning. The text, therefore, is very manageable, unless the words that follow in some way alter or specialize the sense, which, we may say beforehand, they do not do.

"**Of David's Seed.**" A common reader would understand that the "*Son of God*" came into being nineteen centuries ago as a descendant of David. If he had heard of the "*Eternal Sonship*," he might look into his concordance for other sentences that would trace farther back, and these he would never find.

All the words, "**Son,**" with a big S, centre about Nazareth. The only trace of what is otherwise is in Daniel (Dan. 3 : 25). It is from the lips of a heathen. It is without the article. It is not "the Son of God" (E. V.), but "a son of a god." The "gods" of Nebuchadnezzar had been quoted to him in the plural (E. V.), see the twelfth verse, but a few sentences before. There is not a single passage of the Old Testament Scriptures that asserts a "*Son*" then existing, or even alludes to such a person in all those four thousand years.

God was existing; and we long for the opportunity when we can explain this. And God became incarnate in the child of Mary. But God was not before incarnate, and therefore had no earlier "*Son.*" Or, rather (that we may not hasten anything), it appears by this third verse, that there came into being of the seed of David, nineteen centuries ago, "*the Jesus Christ our Lord,*" who therein and thereupon became "*the Son of God.*"

"**Through flesh.**" "*According to the flesh*" (E. V.) would answer very well, but it is more awkward than *through*, and is still less eligible when applied to the Spirit (v. 4). One sense of κατά is "*by virtue of,*" so says Robinson; though, as he represents, "the idea of accordance lies at the bottom;" as for example "through ignorance" (E. V., Acts 3 : 17). "Is it lawful for a man to put away his wife for (κατά) any cause?" (E. V., Matt. 19 : 3). "*Through flesh,*" therefore, means, that by His sinful mother He became the child of David, and "*through*" this fleshly origin came into being nineteen centuries ago.

Though there is no passage in the Old Testament that speaks of the "*Son*" as anciently existing, yet it is time now to say that there is a passage that speaks of the "*Son,*" and that a very celebrated one. It is quoted three times by the apostle (Acts 13 : 33 ; Heb. 1 : 5 ; 5 : 5). "Thou art my Son; this day have I begotten Thee" (Ps. 2 : 7). Here is a distinct assertion of a begetting at a certain time. All agree that it is a Messianic prophecy. Its prophet-guise *in situ* is quite spectacular. No one doubts that. Men have made endless efforts to get rid of this sentence. Some have said that "*begotten*" means exhibited or manifested (Calvin on Ps. 2 : 7). Some fly to two begettings, one eternal and one in Nazareth, imagining, therefore, two Sonships (Hodge, Syst. Theol., Vol. 1 :

p. 474). Some expound thus :—" Thou art My Son, this day I am Thy Father" (Alexander); others, " Thou art My Son; this day I declare it" (Calvin), making the begetting a mere asseverance. Some say that Acts 13 : 33 spoils the argument for a local and temporal creation (Meyer, Calvin), still another objector overthrowing this last by showing that the "resurrection" there spoken of is not the rising on the third day, but really the raising up or originating that we are now contending for (Hodge). Which comments might be pardoned if there were strong scriptures to make them necessary; but, as will be seen in the next verse, when the time might seem to have come to speak of the Spirit as distinct from the flesh, or an eternal Sonship as distinct from that in Galilee, the trend is the other way, and the very look of the English shows the violence of the steps against it.

V. 4. For example, ὁρισθεὶς does not mean "*declared*" (E. V.). When "*begotten*" (Ps. 2 : 7) is tortured into "*manifested*" (Calvin), just as "*except*" (Gal. 2 : 16) is strained into "*but*" (E. V.) in a case already mentioned, the very violence of the strain should turn us against the commentator. Ὁρίζω means *bounding off* or *determining*, and the very attempt to understand it as "*declared*" (E. V.) should awaken our full suspicion. The fourth verse thoroughly agrees with the third. For while the third announces that the "*Son*" originated, the fourth favors that view by announcing, not that He was "*declared*" (E. V.) what He had been ages before, or, to take in the whole view, not that He was born "*Son*" in one nature and "*declared*" Son in another, as though He had really been that from all eternity, but, according to the simple Greek, that He came into being such as He was by a fleshly birth, and was "*determined upon*" (Acts 11 : 29, E. V.) or "*ordained*" (Acts 10 : 42, E. V.) "*Son of God*," in certain ways or through certain agencies, as a thing happening in time, and justifying the language, "This day have I begotten Thee."

Ὁρισθεὶς, therefore, receiving this interpretation, and being refused the sense "*declared*" (E. V.), as being altogether too biassed, and of design,* there remain the other expressions of the fourth verse, which singularly agree with the idea of a "*determined upon*" or *appointed* Sonship.

4. **Who was determined upon as God's Son, in power, through a Spirit of holiness, by a rising of those dead.**

Before we discuss these words, let us say particularly what we imagine them to establish. They do not affect the question whether Christ is God. For, if the one personal Jehovah descended upon Mary, and was begotten into her Son, that is as much a Godhead as for a Second Person in a Trinity so to descend and be begotten. It would be fatal, of course, to a Trinity, and fatal to the use of the word Son before the incarnation. But the Deity of Christ, which is the great fulcrum of salvation, would be more rather than less. Let that be well remembered.

Moreover, we should not be departing from the general

---

* Olshausen has a very tell-tale note on this expression. "The choice of the word ὁρίζεσθαι, however, has led several ancient and modern commentators to understand the words in an entirely different sense. This word, in the language of the N. T., means 'to fix, determine, choose for some purpose' (Lu. 22 : 22 ; Acts 2 : 23 ; 10 : 42 ; 17 : 26). From this has been derived the translation, ' God has chosen, appointed Him to be the Son of God,' which would at once lead to the Jewish view of Christ's subordinate character, viz., that he was the Son of God, not in his essential being, but only by God's election (ἐκλογή) (Justin Martyr, Dial. c. Tryph. Jud. p. 267). In close connection with this stands another interpretation, which makes ὁρισθέντος identical in meaning with προορισθέντος, a word which Epiphanius has even admitted into the text. Accordingly the expression is translated '*prædestinatus est*, and referred to God's decree with respect to the incarnation (Iren. adv. haer. 3 : 22, 23. August. de prædestin. sanct. c. 15). But both views, to say nothing of the untenableness of the former, on doctrinal grounds must be rejected [!] ; because, from the connection, it is manifestly not the decree of God, but the proof before men of Xt's Divine Sonship that is here in question. No other course, therefore, remains but to take ὁρίζεσθαι in the sense to declare, to exibibit as something. * * * There is indeed some difficulty in proving that ὁρίζεσθαι is ever used in this sense. For ὁρίζω means originally to define the limits, ὁρίζεσθαι, to determine limits for one's self, *i. e.*, to determine. *No passage in which it means directly declarare, ostendere is to be found either in the profane or scriptural writings.*"

belief that Christ is not God in the sense that the man became transmutedly divine. Nobody believes that. Impossible infinitudes may be imputed to Christ's human nature (Swedenborg, Crosby, Beecher), but, looked at in front, no man says that the man becomes God. The uniform doctrine with us all is that the man is so united with the God as to become one person, and that this composite King blends the two natures into one Redeemer. It will be seen how carefully Paul talks of the notion of equality. He does not say, speaking of the man as he stood in Jewry, that he was "equal (ίσον) with God" (E. V., Phil. 2 : 6). This is a sad translation. Paul's language is very express. It ought to have been considered. He says, "Being in the form of God;" which at once refers to the human nature of Christ. And then he uses very peculiar characterizations of Christ's Deity. Why can not we in all fidelity preserve the strict speech? He does not say, "Thought it not robbery to be equal with God" (E. V.) ; for that man-part of Christ, which was "in the form of God," which could make itself "of no reputation," which could take on "a bondman's form," which could "originate in the likeness of men," and, "formed in fashion as a man," could be "humbled" and die and be "exalted," could not be said to be "equal (ίσον) with God;" and, therefore, Paul talks just as here in this fourth verse. There are certain "*respects*" in which he is equal, and so, in our present passage, he tells most definitely what they are :—"**(1) In power, (2) through a Spirit of holiness, (3) by a rising of those dead.**" So that most admirable is the wording of the apostle (Phil. 2 : 6) where he refuses to say ίσον, and says ίσα, or, to trace the whole careful inspiration, "Who, being in the form of God, thought it not robbery τὸ εἶναι ἴσα, that there should be equal respects with God," that is, precisely as our present passage renders it, that a certain born "*Son*" of the Father should be so begotten that the Father should be in Him, and that He should be hence "*determined on*" to be "*God's Son* (1) *in power*, (2) *through a Spirit of holiness*, (3) *by a resurrection of those dead.*"

CHAPTER I.

Before we consider these ἴσα or "equal things" respectively, let us see the amazing similarity of the speech of Gabriel. Angels are not verbose (Lu. 2 : 14), and it must be seen, therefore, in his short speech what abounding weight must be given to "*Therefore.*" "The Holy Ghost shall come upon thee, and the power of the Highest shall overshadow thee" (Lu. 1 : 35). This is his account of that great act, "This day have I begotten Thee,"—and then, as the result, "*Therefore.*" Paul has less rhetoric than the angel. But who can refuse us the result,—that then and there and "*therefore,*" that is, specifically, on that sole account, "that holy thing that shall be born of thee shall be called the Son of God?"

It will be seen that there are two questions imbedded in this discussion—one, whether "the Son" is a name of something of recent date, or of something born from everlasting; and the other, whether there is such a person, born from everlasting, as might have that or any other name. The former, of course, is not of so much moment.

It is like the questions already noticed (v. 1). What was Jesus the name of? We saw it was the name of the God. Or again, what was Christ the name of? We saw that it was the name of the man. And yet, what were they both the name of? They were the name of the God-man; in the one case of the God impersonate in the man, and in the other case of the man co-personal with the God: in either case giving no slender ground for the atonement, and for the name and for the claim of Deity.

And so in corresponding guise the "*Son*" is the name of the man. As Christ had to wait till a man was actually *Christos* before it could be a name; so the "*Son*" had to wait till a Son could absolutely "*come to be*" (v. 3), and till the King could give the name,—"Thou art My Son; this day have I begotten Thee."

The lesser and more trivial point, therefore, is, what must the "*Son*" be the name of?

But the other question transcends the mere name.

Christ, as the name of the man, could not affect the position that there was an eternal "*Son.*" But the "*Son*" as the name of the man destroys it totally. Once satisfy the world that the "*Son*" attained to the name on the plain of Bethlehem, and the figment of the Hypostasis would be miserably dissipated. Where else could we get it? Not from God where He says, " I will make him my first-born " (Ps. 89 : 27); not from Paul where he says, "*Determined upon as the Son of God ;*" not from Christ where He says, " He that hath seen me hath seen the Father " (Jo. 14 : 9); and where He really puts it out of the question, for He never so much as glimmers about a distinctive Person, but says, " I live by the Father " (Jo. 6 : 57): whereas " before Abraham was I am " (Jo. 8 : 58), it is because " I and my Father are one "(Jo. 10 : 30); and then, more articulately, " If he call them gods to whom the word of God came, and the scripture cannot be broken, say ye of Him whom the Father hath sanctified and sent into the world, Thou blasphemest, because I said I am the Son of God ? " (Jo. 10 : 36).

Yet Paul was not Socinus. For if the "*Son*" be God by reason of His union with the Father, that is just as much a Deity as that there be God by reason of a union with a Second Person. In fact it is more. And Paul is not to be impeached as failing of a Godhead for his Master, by anything that follows in the language of the text.

Let us proceed to that.

"*In power.*" Not "*powerfully declared*" (Alford, Beza, Tholuck), for the word "*declared,*" which would fit such an adverb, itself has to be given up. Ὁρίζω never means "*declared.*" Besides, where do we find even the adverb? Ἐν would naturally indicate the respect "*in*" which the man, made God, would be "*determined upon*" as the Deity. What more directly than " *in power ?* " Christ had a "*power*" which neither the God nor man, if separate, could wield or possess. First of all (1) a *power forensic.* God could not forgive, and man could not forgive, in any disjunctive relation ; but man laid on the altar, which God could not be, and God, blessing the sacrifice, which man could not do, constitute a " *Son,*" that is a God-man, such that the "*Son*" is really more potent than the Father, the Father dwelling in the "*Son*," and the "*Son*" containing more than the Father, viz., the Eternal God and a guiltless man, without whom there could be no remission. Again (2) there is *regenerative* power. Man could not wield it. Man could not even understand it. And yet God could not wield it without the man. It is the God-man that wins the possibility of salvation. And, therefore, God delights to give a determination to the man. "All power is given unto (Him) in heaven and earth "(Matt. 28 : 18). And see how He describes it : "As the Father hath life in Himself, so hath He given to the Son to have life in Himself" (Jo. 5 : 26), for "the time is coming and now is when the dead shall hear the voice of the Son of Man" (Jo. 5 : 25); for "as the Father raiseth up the dead and quickeneth them, even so the Son quickeneth whom he will" (Jo. 5 : 21). The man could not regenerate, any more than Moses could divide the sea ; and yet the man, even more than Moses, can summon the sea to open, and has a will, even as human, in the great work of the world's turning to God. Again (3) He is *sovereign*. Mark now with great distinctness His three attributes of "*power.*" "*Determined upon as the Son of God in power,*" and in these indispensable particulars, first, in *forensic* power, which the Father could not possess without Him ; second, in *regenerative* power, which sprang directly from forensic work, and, thirdly, in power as a *King*, travelling the length of the statement that "all things were created for Him" (Col. 1 : 16) ; endorsing the title of "head over all things, to the church " (Eph. 1 : 22), and making it signally the truth, and that even of the man Christ, that not a syllable of recorded fact, not even in the universe of worlds, could at all have been written down, except as it met the mind and gratified the purpose of Christ our King and our Redeemer.

So then for the first count in the Sonship, viz., *in "power."* But "*determining upon*" a "*Son*" required more than a mere decree. It did not do to say, (1) The man shall have such "*power*" in court, and (2) the man shall choose His saints, and

(3) the man shall rule the universe. The apostle hurries up with another specification. Christ had to be prepared. Incarnation was not itself an act in such a sense as that the God had to be transfused into the man. The scheme is impossible by which some men give God's infinity to the Son of Mary ; but, before the man could be one with the Father, the man himself must be prepared. Incarnation may be by mere decree. For God cannot be personate in man except by an ordinance of heaven, and an eternal oath that links the two natures into one. But man has to be lifted toward God. I need not tarry upon the secular gifts. Neither Gabriel nor Paul sees fit to notice them. Their enthusiasm is all for character. Christ with them is a lost man, I mean by heritage (Zech. 3 : 2; 9: 9). He is a child of Adam (1: 3 ; Lu. 3: 38). He bears upon His face the marks of " infirmity" (Heb. 5: 2). He is " tempted " (Heb. 4: 15), and, beyond all doubt, tempted to sin (Matt. 4: 1, etc.). The torture that this begets becomes our ransom (Heb. 5: 7); the victory, our retreat ; and Gabriel and Paul, therefore, put at the very front that marvel by which the man, curst by descent, is gotten ready for, as God, by a moral rescue from His state by nature. Look at both their speeches. Paul's is the least special, "**Through a Spirit of holiness** "; but Gabriel sounds it forth as plainly as it could be uttered, " The Holy Ghost shall come upon thee, and the power of the Highest shall overshadow thee ; therefore also that thing, begotten holy, shall be called the Son of God " (Lu. 1: 35).

Righteousness, contrary to the nature of Mary, is necessary to the person of Christ ; and, therefore, His struggle to maintain it is His great battle, and His being "*determined upon* " as " *Son* " is in reward, so the Bible often tells us, of " the travail of His soul " (Is. 53: 11), and His " obedience unto death " (Phil. 2: 8), and His overcoming to the very end (Rev. 3: 21). " Wherefore God also hath highly exalted Him and given Him a name which is above every name " (Phil. 2: 9). " It became Him to make the captain of (our) salvation perfect thro' suffering " (Heb. 2: 10). He " overcame and is set down with (His) Father in His throne " (Rev. 3: 21). This does not derogate from the incarnation, any more than our struggle to be saved derogates from our saintship which was decreed before the foundation of the world.

But, now, there is a third count. Not only was Christ determined upon first "*in power*" and, second, "through" that which made possible "*the power*," viz., His Christ-ship or anointment by the Spirit; but third, ἐκ or "*out* of " the results of all this, viz., the object of His Messiahship in "**a rising of those dead.**"

And here Paul sheds light upon that word as used often in Holy Scripture. When Peter says, "by the resurrection of Jesus Christ" (1 Pet. 3: 21), he means much more than His bodily rising. We would make the body a horrible idol if we treated it with all the sentences on the rising of the dead.

Therefore Paul, when he goes on to his third clause, "*Who was determined upon as God's Son* (1) *in power* (2) *through a Spirit of holiness* (3) *by a rising of those dead*" is infinitely far from merely treating of the "*resurrection*" (E. V.).

Christ, as Mary's son, would have been born dead (Eph. 2 : 3). There is no reason to suppose that He would not have inherited from His mother. The angel signalizes the grace in " that thing begotten holy" (Lu. 1 : 35), and Paul connects the action of the Spirit with the rising of the dead.

Now this agrees with the whole testimony of Scripture. Christ is said to be "a dead man according to the flesh (1 Pet. 3 : 18). We are "quickened together with Christ " (Eph. 2 : 5). He is spoken of as " redeemed " (Heb. 9 : 12) ; and, in explanation of it, as "offering for Himself and for the errors of the people " (Heb. 9 : 7 ; 5 : 3). He is said to be " the first begotten from the dead " (Rev. 1 : 5) ; to be " separated from sinners " (Heb. 7 : 26), and " to (be saved) from death " (Heb. 5 : 7). We are told that He was "tempted " (Heb. 4 : 15) ; that He "resisted unto blood "(Heb. 12 : 4), that He was "compassed with infirmity " (Heb. 5 : 2). We are informed in direct asseverance that He was " quickened by the Spirit " (1 Pet. 3 : 18). And we can put together but one consistent proposition, viz., that He was from Adam. Our Saviour was not a creature foisted in upon our family, but was a descendant of our race (Heb. 2 : 16), and therefore had to be generated "holy" (Lu. 1 : 35), or, as the Bible calls it, "raised from among the dead" (Rom. 6 : 4) ; and this agrees with all the wonders of the narrative. He must be "tempted" and "infirm" and have a horrible fight with wickedness. This tempting must be His torture, and He must come out of it unscathed. If He sin, we are ruined. That fight in the Wilderness, and the blood of the Garden, and the shriek of His last despair, must all be passed, and He must be "holy, harmless, undefiled" and entirely incorrupt. And, to make Him all this, He was born miraculously of a woman by the agency of the *Holy* Ghost. As we are regenerate by the Spirit, He was generate in the very womb. He was born having infirmity, and God gave Him no such supply of Himself as made it an easy victory. At times He was almost abandoned (Matt. 26 : 41 ; 27 : 46 ; Heb. 5 : 7). And this whole thing, including His body, is His "resurrection from among the dead" (Heb. 6 : 2 ; Phil. 3 : 11 ; 1 Pet. 1 : 3 ; 3 : 21).

Now when Paul says, " *Through a Spirit of holiness, by a rising of those dead,*" he is answering the question of the "*therefore*" of the angel Gabriel. "Determined upon as God's Son in power, through a Spirit of holiness;" and marked as having such power not simply by His own rising from spiritual death, but, more signally, by the raising of others :—" *The Son of God in power, through a Spirit of holiness, by the rising of those dead.*"

**5. By whom we received grace and apostleship for His name, in order to an obedience of faith in all the nations;
6. Among whom are ye, also, called ones of Jesus Christ.**

"**By**" (E. V.), causal as well as instrumental. He being God as well as man, the "**grace**" was "**by**" Him as well as through Him. "*Through whom*" (Re.), therefore, would be too narrow a sense.

"**We.**" Not "*we,*" all the apostles, nor "*we,*" all gracious persons, for Paul is speaking of a special embassage to Gentiles. But "*we,*" Paul, a change from singular to plural which may be seen in any language. "**Received.**" Both "**grace**" and "**apostleship**" with Paul were "*received*" *ab ictu*, and, therefore, explain the aorist on this occasion.

"**For His name**" (E. V.). "For the sake of His name" (see Revision) is too general. Ὑπέρ in its primary sense, means *over*. In its first metaphorical sense it means *over* in the sense of *defence* or *shelter;* then, *in behalf of*. That is its meaning here. Paul's apostleship was "*for*" Christ, and, to express it more definitely still, for his "*name*" or honor in the world ; a most thorough counterpart to which characterization is that earliest account by his Master, " A chosen vessel unto Me, to bear My name before the Gentiles, and kings, and the children of Israel" (Acts 9 : 15).

"**In order to an obedience of faith.**" Paul is noted for his single sentences. Of all the teachers of divinity he concentres the most. Of the gospel he just gives but one subject,—"*concerning His Son!*" (v. 3). Of salvation he has sought him out one careful expression, We "are justified by faith." In that dreadful chapter where election is to be vindicated (Rom. 9), he has but one reply, and when we come to examine it, it is the most perfect possible. And now in three vocables he is to tell the object of his apostleship. We must be very careful with such dense speech. It is not "*for an obedience to the faith*" (E. V., Alford). The margin of King James implies that this is doubtful interpolation. It is not "obedience as the result of faith" (Barnes, Stuart), for that could only be admitted through the default of the more simple rendering. But, like a crown of thorns, or a grove of trees, it is an obedience which consists of faith. Paul talks this way in other passages. He speaks of a "holiness of truth " (Eph. 4 : 24, E. V., *marg.*), which evidently means a holiness which is "truth in the inward parts." " A breastplate of faith " (1 Thess. 5 : 8), or "a shield of faith " (Eph. 6: 15), or "a hearing of faith " (Gal. 3 : 2, 5), or " a righteousness of faith " (4 : 13), all mean a breastplate or a shield or a hearing or a righteousness which consists in faith ; and this agrees with all the teaching of the apostle. There is a superstition of modern times which a false view of Paul vastly confirms, which makes faith, like sacrifice, like absolution by the priest, like the circumcision of the ancient ritual service, like the sacraments of our own time, a means of supplanting the "*obedience*" of the pious. Paul was loud in rebuke of this. He calls it "another gospel." Taking the form of it in his day, viz., circumcision, he traces it to an aversion to this very thing "*obedience*." "For neither they that are circumcised keep the law" (Gal. 6 : 13), but desire to have you circumcised "only lest they should suffer persecution by the cross of Christ" (Gal. 6 : 12). We do not sufficiently probe this passage (Gal. 6). It is not "for the cross" (E. V.), but "by the cross." The cross is the persecuting agency by whose smart and sacrifice we are scared away, and Paul adopts it in this sense; — "Circumcision availeth nothing, nor uncircumcision, but a new creature" (Gal. 6 : 15), and he says (not glorying in the cross as we would speak of glorying in the gospel, but glorying in the cross as a *cross*, that is as demanding painful and self-denied "*obedience*"), "God forbid that I should glory save in the cross of our Lord Jesus Christ, whereby the world is crucified unto me and I unto the world" (Gal. 6 : 14). So then "*obedience*" is that obedience of a changed nature which consists in "*faith;*" and as we shall have much to do with that, we may as well at once be entirely specific.

We have seen the tendency of Paul, nay of all the men who have been inspired, to wrap up a whole account of things in a single expression. A whole account of things in gospel changes would be thus : First, born in sin. Second, sin incurable. Third, angels, having no Redeemer, perpetual sinners. Fourth, men, blessed with a Redeemer, capable of salvation. Fifth, idiots and infants, dying in that condition, saved without faith. Sixth, others, never. Seventh, salvation, being moral, God pleased that that moral salvation shall begin in this world. Eighth, that moral salvation everywhere pressed, and called repentance, conversion, regeneration, justification, quickening, wakening and all the thousand names in which the work is shown in us or by us. But ninth, inasmuch as it is not causally by us, I mean in the higher sense of cause, forasmuch as a change of heart is like the creation of a heart in the beginning, God pleased only to create when we seek the work of Him ; and, tenthly, when we do honor to the work by seeking in the name of the Redeemer. This last may be very imperfect ; for Abraham and the awakened Peter must have known little of Christ ; but all the more therefore have we need of "*obedience*." Blessed is he who has the more "*obedience*," even if he has the less doctrinal training. For, like Cornelius, I may have never heard of Jesus ; yet if I believe in God, and without understanding of His methods, believe in Him as Himself a rescuer in my wickedness, who shall say I may not be pardoned ? It is not of works, for who ever by mere teaching worked his way into the kingdom ? It is not of grace in such a way as to answer for me without the cross of the Redeemer. It is not of nature in such a way that I can rise to it by human powers. But it is of seeking, and that not of myself, but as of the oak or the vine, by a power leading me to grope for maintenance in the soil provided.

This is a long story, and, as I say, the apostle makes it short. He tells all this by the word "*faith*." And we must pack the word as we would a trunk. There is a common faith, under which a million of times a sinner starts to ask and does not persevere. There is a saving faith, which simply tells the story when he does persevere, that is when this great act of "*obedience*," which consists in asking, seeking, does really begin to seek, namely, out of the true motive, penitence, and out of the true drawing, viz., by the loveliness of Christ, which then for the first time begins to dawn upon the mind. The faith, hence, that saves the soul is not that which resorts to Christ out of a selfish terror (though the Bible tries to wake up even such a faith, Jude 23, and that, persevered in, may lead to the other), but it is the faith which the soul attains when the lower sort of faith is striven in, so that it begins to work its effect on God ; when, therefore, a moral light enters the soul ; when, therefore, a whole group of other graces begin ; when seeking, which is but another name for faith, goes on from moral motives ; and when we are able to arrive at this conclusion, that, whereas seeking became the great thing commanded for the sinner, seeking or "*faith*" became the great "*obedience ;*" so that "*obedience*" is of the very nature of "*faith*" before it can be imagined at all to save. To put it plainly, faith must become moral before it can be considered a saving grace.

Now one caution before we leave the subject. Common faith is a grace ; that is, in a lower sense, it is the gift of the Holy Spirit. And in this commoner meaning it is a saving grace. For unless a man is stirred up by selfish terror to seek, he is not, as a usual thing, ever delivered. Ten thousand men who have had this faith have perished. Saving faith is that which saves. And though this other faith saves in a certain previous and prefatory sense, yet the man is not saved when he has it. All men have had it who were well raised. The faith that saves is that actual vision (2 Thess. 2: 10), which shares with love and patience the moral light of the regenerated man.

"**In all the nations.**" We call unchristian nations *heathen*, which is the Greek word for "*nations*" simply Anglicized. The Jews, looking upon this same word in the Greek, though it is the commonest word for "*nations*," rarely understood it that way, but understood it of their sort of heathen, viz., of men not Jews. The Latins managed the thing better. They took their word "*nations*," viz., *gentes*, and altered it a little, and called men not Romans *Gentiles*, and then the Romans, when they became Jews or Christians, took this word for those not so. And finally into our English, through Jerome and other translators, there came the word Gentiles, and the Greek word for "*nations*" is translated "*Gentiles*" all through the New Testament.

Nevertheless sometimes it is translated "*nations.*" This, impulsively, we might imagine a mistake. It is translated "*Gentiles*" just below (v. 13). But while the vast majority of sentences require the translation "*Gentiles*," the present text, for example, is justly different. Let us examine other instances. "Go teach all Gentiles" (Matt. 28: 19) would not do for a moment. " Before Him shall be gathered all Gentiles" (Matt. 25: 32) would be equally unhappy. While, on the other hand, to talk of "Jews and nations" (Gal. 2: 15), or of going to the nations (Acts 18: 6), or "being in time past nations" (Eph. 2: 11), would show with what exceeding fitness the same word has been translated differently, so long as we had the means of doing it. "*Among all the nations,*" therefore, is truer to the apostle's appointed mission than "*among all the Gentiles.*"

"**Called ones of Jesus Christ**" gives no inconvenient ambiguity. The genitive of possession and the genitive of efficiency are equally in place. Where both are true, the Holy Ghost would have little care to be particular about either. It is to these "*called ones*" that Paul now addresses his epistle.

7. To all the beloved of God, called to be holy, who are in Rome. Grace to you and peace from God our Father, and Lord Jesus Christ."

"**To all the beloved of God.**" "*To all who are in Rome*" (E. V.) is one of those slight errors of translation which we have already noticed in the inscription to this epistle. It is not The Epistle to the Romans, but The Epistle to Romans, that is, to certain men of that particular city. And now he tells to what men. "*To all the beloved of God, called to be holy, who are in Rome.*"

"**To be holy.**" We have already seen how the Greek for "*nations*" may have a distinct translation where the Latin or the English may furnish it. And so we have *Christ* for *Anointed*, and *deacon* for *servant*, and *Ghost* for *Spirit*, sometimes wisely, and sometimes, as in the last instance, without any very good effect. "*Saints*" (E.V.) in the present clause is but an adjective, the Greek for "*holy.*" It is the plural ἅγιοι, and once in the Bible is translated "*holy ones*" (LXX. Dan 4: 17). We are convinced that *saints* is an improvement, like *Gentiles* for *nations*, or *Christ* for *Anointed* ; that is, when a word hardens into what is technical (as διάκονος becoming *deacon*), it is better, when it comes into a fresh language, to give it a vocable by itself ; just as it is better to speak of " a collection for the saints," than a "collection for the holy ones" (1 Cor. 16: 1), or to speak of "the saints and widows" (Acts 9: 41), or of washing "the saints' feet" (1 Tim. 5: 10), rather than to insist upon the translated adjective. Yet when it appears merely as an adjective, without the awkwardness of "*the holy*" or "*the holy ones*," it seems better to preserve the simplest idea.

"**Who are in Rome.**" We fix a period here, not a colon. The sentence terminates. Paul finishes here the address of his epistle.

"**Grace to you and peace from God our Father and Lord Jesus Christ.**" This is a new paragraph. It is not of much importance, but even the Revisionists mistake the fashion of the East. John reveals it more perfectly (3 John 1). He gives the address without any salutation at all. And in his second epistle, by a better reading of the Revisionists, he gives it thus, "Grace, mercy, peace shall be with us." Neither grammar, therefore, nor the custom of the people, forbids the punctuation as we have given it. *Paul to certain Romans;* so far the address; and then "*Grace to you and peace*" as a self-contained and independent form of greeting.

"*Grace*," a usual word for mercy to sinners, though in a wider sense it has been vital to Gabriel as much as to the redeemed. "*Peace*," the *salaam* of the East; in those stormy times, a most expressive salutation. No wonder it has been borrowed into religion. "*Father;*" so obvious a title for God that Paul says that from Him "every fatherhood in heaven and on earth is named" (Eph. 3: 15).

This is the salutation, therefore. That before is the address. Then proceeds the epistle :—

8. On the one hand, first; I thank my God, through Jesus Christ, for you all, that your faith is published throughout the whole world.

"**On the one hand, first.**" The Bible becomes a different Bible if we reject every attempt to find mistakes in it. Paul has been wonderfully mutilated. Commentators, pressed into some strait, have not hesitated to say: This comes from Paul's employing an amanuensis (see also Tholuck, Meyer, Rom. 5:12), or, Such and such a protasis with no apodosis (Olshausen), or, as in the present instance, such and such a μέν ("*on the one hand*") without any δέ ("*on the other hand*"), sprang from Paul's heat and the thronging of his inspired teachings. Some of his noblest thoughts have been missed, and then buried by this dangerous treatment. How much better to imagine that the Holy Ghost meant entirely what he wrote. "*On the one hand, first*" and most important of all, Paul saw immense advantages to *others* in the faith of the Romans, and "*on the other hand*" (δέ), see verse 13th, "*I do not wish you to be ignorant, brethren,*" that I tried hard to get to you "*that I might have some fruit also in yourselves.*" The extra καί in this passage (v. 13) is the tell tale particle that is quite *de trop* except for this view.

"**I thank my God, through Jesus Christ, for you all.**" "**My God through Jesus Christ**" is the reading of some commentators (Glöckler, Koppe), that is, He who is "*my God through Jesus Christ.*" But Rom. 7: 25, where we read, "I thank God, through Jesus Christ our Lord," and Col. 3: 17, "Giving thanks to God and the Father by Him," and plenty of other passages, fix another meaning. Christ stands in a peculiar relation to His people; and as their worship is sin, not perfect, He offers it as from Himself, with hope and promise of its becoming perfect through His blessed intervention.

"*For you all.*" The English "*for*" answers capitally to the original ὑπέρ; "*for*" in every reasonable sense. "*For,*" *in behalf of*, as though "*you*" thanked him, and "*for,*" directly, as though "*you*" were the subjects of the thanksgiving.

"**That your faith is published.**" We object to the expression "*spoken of*" (E. V.). This particular Greek occurs seventeen times in scripture, and everywhere means *preached*. "Christ is *preached*," says this same apostle (Phil. 1: 18); and his death (1 Cor. 11: 26), and resurrection (Acts 4: 2), are *preached*, using this same word. It sheds light on the μέν ("*on the one hand*") of which we have just been speaking. "*On the one hand,*" he exalts the "*published*" benefits of their active "*faith.*", And, as Rome was the centre of the universe, he informs them, before he comes to speak "*on the other hand*" of their own interests, how incessantly he prayed for them, evidently with the apostolic consciousness of how much was to be gained by the "*published*" example of the metropolitan followers of Christ. This agrees better with the facts. They were not "*spoken of*" in the way of wide approval ; for when Paul actually did come to Rome, he was greeted with the statement, " As concerning this sect, we know that everywhere it is spoken against " (Acts 28: 22).

9. For God is my witness whom I serve in my spirit in the gospel of his Son, how unceasingly I make mention of you,

10. Always in my prayers making request, if by any means, now, at any time, I may, in the will of God, be prospered to come unto you.

"**For ;**" that is, in proof of this, viz., that I am keenly alive to the importance of faith at Rome. That he should pray every day for unknown Romans would seem an affectation, considering the number of heathen cities. Hence the oath,— God knows I do it. And this confirms the idea of the importance with the apostle of Christian examples in the imperial stronghold. "**God is my witness.**" Christ's commands are to be understood in their substance. He gives a philosophic reason for very many of them, and for none a more beautiful one than the command, " Swear not at all " (Matt. 5: 34). A Christian is to be so God-like as not to suspect himself of faithlessness, therefore why the oath ? And this is the " temptation " that we might fear to fall into (Jas. 5: 12), a doubt of our truthfulness. And yet God swore (Heb. 6: 17), and Paul swore, and that in other places (Gal. 1: 20). There is to be reason in our obedience. The grand principle remains. We are not to swear, because we are not to make light of our own veracity. " Let your word be yea, yea, nay, nay ; for whatsoever is more than these is of the Evil One."

"**Whom I serve.**" The word usually translated " worship " (προσκυνέω), is not this word, but means to *kiss towards*, that is to *kiss the hand to*, and is often imagined to mean such technical worship as belongs only to Deity. We have a fault of exaggerating such words; as, for example, the word *ordain*. We imagine that it means a ghostly consecration which establishes a minister. Now there is such a consecration; more, however, in the vote of the church than in the laying on of hands. And there is a *worship* that belongs only to the Almighty. It is well to remember that a man ought to be formally *ordained*, and that God should be exclusively *worshiped*. But it is exceedingly wise to state that there is a word for neither except now in our English. The word *ordained* as official in its meaning translates seven different words in Scripture (Mark 3: 14; Acts. 1: 22; 14: 23; 17: 31; 1 Tim. 2 : 7 ; Titus, 1: 5; Heb. 5: 1; 8: 3); and never the same word except in a single instance. *Kissing the hand* may be to different persons beside the Almighty (Acts 10: 25). Our sole caution is in respect to the words. There is a certain sort of *worship* (though after all we mean a certain sort of admiration and of means to express it), which belongs properly to Deity, and is but the bald recognition of what is unparalleled and supreme in the Most High.

"**In my spirit.**" Here is quite a different word. It *did* acquire a special meaning in the Greek. It is like the word "*flesh.*" *Flesh* means any of a dozen things. But it grew into the technical significance of all of a man outside of the "*new man*," or of the regenerating Spirit. Refinements of the taste, which were of the very best, were "*flesh*" in the language of Paul, if they were not of the new nature. It is not certain that πνεῦμα was ever used for *mind* (Jo. 3: 8), that is, in the New Testament. And it is rarely used for the soul as distinct from the body, or for angels either good or wicked. But it is usually meant for conscience or our moral part, and often for that new conscience which marks the special meaning of conversion.

When, therefore, Paul speaks of *serving in the spirit*, he carries us back to the Gospels (Jo. 4: 23). Our Saviour puts all this into shape. He tells us, " The true worshiper must worship the Father in spirit and in truth. Spirit is God." Such is the order of the Greek. Middleton, with his predicate rule, himself acknowledges the pertinent exceptions (Chap. 3: Sec. 4). "Spirit is God." That is, spirit is the God part of man. We are told distinctly so in Paul (1 Cor. 14: 25). "Will report that God is in you of a truth." He says (Gal. 2: 20), "It is not I that live, but Christ that liveth in me." Our Saviour is not rash, therefore. He is in analogy with scripture. "Spirit is God," and they that worship Him must worship Him in the God part, that is "in spirit and in truth." Paul *serves in the spirit*, therefore, when he serves, not in his unsanctified nature, but in that moral part which has become occupied with the life of God.

"**In the gospel of His Son.**" What this means the apostle has just been stating (vs. 1, 3).

"**How unceasingly I make mention of you.**" Perhaps it is more accurate to say, "*make memory of you*," or "*cause you to be remembered*" (see the Greek), and this agrees with the favorite punctuation. The English Version is probably wrong in running the two clauses together, and making them read, "*I make mention of you always in my prayers.*" There are two adverbs "*unceasingly*" and "*always ;*" and there are two verbs, "*make mention,*" and "*making request.*" This is the outfit for separate clauses. And it is probable that the pointing of the *Receptus* is correct. "*How unceasingly I remember you,*" and then in that noblest manner, of "**making request**" for you "**always in my prayers.**"

"**If by any means, now, at any time.**" This is the wording of a very busy man, who could not long beforehand predict when he could do anything ; moreover who recognized distinctly the leading, and, in that miraculous age, the very orders of Heaven (see Acts 8: 29 ; 16: 7 ; 21: 4). This makes "**in the will of God**" more expressive. God had a map for all things which was the *projêt* of His "*will.*" Paul was praying that he might "**be prospered,**" not "*have a prosperous journey*" (E. V.); the word means more generally "*prospered*" (1 Cor. 16: 2 ; 3 Jo. 2), or having *one's way opened,* and it was not so much having his journey prosperous after he had set out, as getting prosperously started, that Paul was praying for, and, in order to that, that his plan, as the only possibility of its being accomplished, might be "*in*" (not "*by*" E. V.) the *projêt* or "*will of God.*"

11. For I long to see you, that I may impart unto you some spiritual gift to the end ye may be set firm.

"**Set firm.**" This is a very important word. Let us study it thoroughly. It comes from the root στα, and is reflected in such words as *stake* and *stand*. Indeed it means to *set fast* primarily; as when we read, "He set the stone fast in the ground" (Hes. Th. 498). The Bible does undoubtedly teach that a man must be "*set firm*" before there can be any certainty that he will persevere. *Election* has nothing to do with it. There is an election unto life, as this same Paul instructs us; "for whom He did foreknow He also did predestinate" (8 : 29); but what has that to do with the question of perseverance? The Almighty has set His law;—" He that endureth to the end the same shall be saved." Of course if He elects He attends to that prerequisite. Nor has *redemption* any thing to do with the question. For men are deeply convicted and thoroughly evangelized in all preliminary ways as the fruit of a Redeemer, when no one pretends that they are even converted. Why may not conversion, before men are *confirmed* and *settled*—as our passage has it, "*set fast*"—be equally indecisive? Our Saviour says it is. "They on the rock are they which receive the word with joy, which for a while believe, and in time of temptation fall away" (Lu. 8 : 13). Ezekiel is treated with singular disrespect. He tells us plainly, "When the righteous turneth away from his righteousness, all his righteousness shall not be mentioned; in his trespass that he hath trespassed and in his sin that he hath sinned, in them shall he die" (Ez. 18 : 24). And Paul says, " Enlightened and tasted of the heavenly gift and made partakers of the Holy Ghost, if they shall fall away" (Heb. 6 : 4, 6). He speaks of himself as becoming a cast-away (1 Cor. 9 : 27). And in a sentence ruined by Italics (see English

Version) he just tells us *simpliciter*, "Now the just shall live by faith ; but if he draw back* my soul shall have no pleasure in him (Heb. 10 : 38). This shows the importance of the word στηρίζω. It occurs thirteen times in the New Testament. We are not to destroy euphony, but "*set firm*" will convey the idea in every instance. "He set His face firm to go to Jerusalem" ("steadfastly set, E. V., Lu. 9: 51). "Between us and you there is a great gulf set firm" ("fixed," E. V., Lu. 16 : 26). "When thou art converted" (Peter had been converted before) "set firm " (strengthen, E. V.) the brethren" (Lu. 22 : 32.) That is, try all of you to be lifted above apostacy by being "*set fast*" in moral strength. Again, this text, "To the end ye may be set fast." Again, toward the close of the epistle, "Who is of power to set you firm according to my gospel." Then to the Thessalonians, "to set you firm" (1 Thess. 3: 2) ; "to the end he may set your hearts firm "(v. 13); "and to set you firm in every good word and work " (2 Thess. 2 : 17) ; "who will set you firm " (3 : 3). Then James adopts the expression ;—"Set your hearts firm " (5 : 8) ; and Peter, using it once in each epistle, "After you have suffered a while make you perfect, set you firm (stablish E. V.), strengthen, settle you" (1 Pet. 5 : 10) ; "and are set firm in the present truth" (2 Pet. 1 : 12) ; John ending with the counsel, "Set firm the things that remain that are ready to die" (Rev. 3 : 2). This comes as near to being technical as we can easily imagine. And the doctrine that emerges has been much neglected. A tree may perish when it is a little sapling, especially if it "have no root," that is, but little root (Matt. 13 : 6), or grow "among thorns " (Matt. 13 : 22) ; but when it becomes a tree, the case is different. Paul evidently contemplates a time when there is no moral possibility of falling away. And though Solomon fell away, and David and Peter, and Peter had to be "*converted*" to resume his state, yet Paul tells the Philippians plainly, "Having begun a good work in you, he will finish it unto the day of Christ" (Phil. 1 : 6), yet he spoils it as a text

---

* The E. V. has it, "If *any man* draw back," putting what it interpolates in Italics.

for creeds, where it always stands first, by making it special and really reducing it to this thing of *setting fast ;* for he says, It is meet to think this of you all. Why? Because all men persevere? On the contrary, because ye have been specially confirmed ; "I have had you in my heart" (*ib.* v. 7), having "greatly longed after you in the bowels of Jesus Christ" (*ib.* v. 8) ; and because I, a discerner of spirits (1 Cor. 12 : 10), have this confidence of your soul's salvation.

Now this "*setting firm*" is not a thing for a man to be confident of, or to be often conscious of in his own condition ; but to be striving after. Men, undoubtedly converted, are to make their calling and election sure. The stout oak is in but slender danger, though humility is of the very sturdiness of its safety. Nevertheless, "God is not unrighteous to forget our work and labor of love" (Heb. 6 : 10). Paul got past the cast-away, and shouted his believing confidence : "I have fought a good fight" (2 Tim. 4: 7) ; "I know whom I have believed" (2 Tim. 1 : 12) ; "I am ready to be offered" (2 Tim. 4: 6) ; "Henceforth there is laid up for me a crown of righteousness, which the Lord, the righteous Judge, shall give me at that day" (2 Tim. 4 : 8).

Now, toward this being "*set firm*" Paul enumerates the instruments.

"**That I may impart unto you some spiritual gift.**" This of course was chiefly piety. Nothing else would *set them firm*. But we cannot say that it was not also miracle. All the "*powers*" went under this name of "*spiritual*" (1 Cor. 12 : 1 ; 14 : 1, 12). Moreover the imparting was of itself miraculous. And we have to go further and say, that piety was added to as a gift under the hands of the apostles (2 Tim. 1 : 6).

But this leaves us opportunity to explain how *all* miracles were done by men. When Moses brought water out of the rock, *he* did not bring water out of the rock : on the contrary, he was cursed for dreaming that he did (Num. 20 : 10). When Christ raised Lazarus, the man did not raise him, but the God. When Christ stood out of His grave clothes, so that His very turban lay where He vanished out of it, "wrapped together in a place by itself" (Jo. 20 : 7), it was not His soul that waked His body ; nor His body that rolled back the stone ; nor even His angels, physically, though they were said to *do it:* for we do not know where they got their bodies, or whether their God in the skies did not extemporize for them flesh, and move the stone by His own omnipotence. We really do not know. But there is an unnoticed passage in Timothy that sheds wonderful light on all miracle. Paul is speaking of the very thing covered by our text, viz., the imparting of gifts. And if we will examine the passage, we will find there was little more variety of gifts than Paul longed to impart to the Romans. " Neglect not the gift that is in thee " (1 Tim. 4 : 14). Now certainly that was pious (*ib.* vs. 18, 19), and miraculous (Acts 8 : 17), and everything else : and just as we begin to wonder that man could act so like God, and the "Presbytery," even in that miraculous age, confer such a thing as spiritual increase of grace, a sentence falls from Paul which blazes out with light back to the beginning of history. " Which was given thee *by prophecy!*" (1 Tim. 4 : 14). What does that mean ? What can be given to a man *by prophecy?* Now that Greek διά is an extraordinary particle. If we translate it "*by*" we often obscure everything. " This is He who came by water " (1 Jo. 5 : 6), might featly mean anything better than what the English could give as the idea. " By whom also He made the worlds " (Heb. 1 : 2). Why, Paul is speaking of Christ in his human nature ! Let us, therefore, plunge into the study of διά, and see what this particle can really do.

Among its numerous meanings it implies the substance of that which is done or said. As for example, " He spake by a parable " (Lu. 8 : 4). That simply means that " He spake in parables," or that " He spake parables." Again, " Nothing is common by itself " (14 : 14). There, by the bye, the English heaves into sight as having something of the same. Again, " Exhorted the brethren by many words " (Acts 15 : 32), where of course the words were the exhortation. But now, coming right up to the case in hand, διά sometimes means, not the substance, but in a way that can be very clearly stated, the *necessary accompaniment.* " This is He who came by water and blood " (1 Jo. 5 : 6). He could not come without. Remission and cleansing were the great substance of His errand. " We walk by faith " (2 Cor. 5 : 7). " Not by the blood of bulls and goats " (Heb. 9 : 12). " By the letter and circumcision dost transgress " (Rom. 2 : 27). In all these cases it is not " by the blood " or " by the letter " or " by faith " in any usual English, but *with* these as a *necessary accompaniment.* So of Christ it is said (Col. 1 : 15–18), first, that He " is the image of the invisible God," which must of course be talking of His human nature ; that He is the " first-born "—" the first-born from the dead," and " the first-born of every creature ; " that He was " before all things," not surely in time, any more than that in time He was " the first-born from the dead ; and, next, that in Him all things stood together " (*ib.* v. 17) ; then, coming to our particular particle, that " all things were created *by* Him and for Him " in the way of course of *necessary accompaniment.* " In Him all things stood together," because the God that was to be incarnate in Him arranged for that final sovereignty as each thing came to be. He builded the universe upon Him. " By Him," in the sense of *necessary accompaniment,* " all things were created." He was the " first-born," because nothing was born except " for Him," and nothing was new-born or " born from the dead," without Him. And He " is the beginning," as Augustine explains (see Aug. on Jo. 17 : Tr. 105, § 8) in the might of His " predestiny." He was the most conspicuous personage in heaven ; not simply for the predestined incarnation, but actually. He did more than any personage in heaven, though He was not yet born. He did it nobly and splendidly on the base of His intended advent. God framed His whole scheme upon Him. And, what cannot be challenged for a moment, millions were pardoned by the means of a sacrifice that had not yet come into being.

This will all be needed in another part of the epistle ; but, for the time being, it explains the *imparting* Paul is speaking of, and how it is done, and in fact the method of all miracles.

When Moses struck the rock what did he do to effect the marvel? Of course he had not the slenderest agency in the results that followed. When Christ healed the woman He said that " virtue had gone out of Him." If that was a sense in the man, distinct from the Most High, that was but another miracle. When Moses rolled back the waters of the sea, we are not to suppose that the man stood in the place of God, in such a sense as to budge a particle of the moving water. What did he do, therefore? He did exactly what the Presbytery did. He wrought "*by prophecy.*" Elijah *prayed* for rain (1 Ki. 18 : 42, 45) ; Jesus *prayed* for Lazarus (Jo. 11 : 42), and we are to add that in ; but the miracle was given "*by prophecy ;*" that is, before the man dared to act, the God must intimate the certainty of a Divine fulfilment. Elijah, with the priests of Baal (1 Ki. 18 : 19) would need a prophecy that God would work ; and even David would hardly have ventured against Goliath without doing it "*by prophecy ;*" that is, with the "*necessary accompaniment*" of an intimation from on high. Such would have been the case with Paul in any miracle for the Romans ; it must be wrought "*by prophecy.*" And he expounds this further, for he says :—" According to the prophecies that went before on thee, that thou by them mightest war a good warfare" (1 Tim. 1 : 18).

"*Impart.*" Μετά is a different preposition from σύν, and means *amid* along with the idea of *with.* Paul's word has the implication of *sharing*, therefore, or of imparting, as the Presbytery did, the like of what they had themselves.

12. But that is, that in you we may be helped forward together by the faith in each, both yours and mine.

"**But**" (δέ)—a very essential little particle. We are not to translate "**That is**" (E. V. & Re.), but "*But that is*," the force of the "*but*," being to keep the benefit just spoken of within the sweep of the words, "*On the one hand,*" which cover the thought of benefit to others. "**On the other hand**" he is about to come (v. 13) to the idea of "*fruit*" in themselves.

"**Helped forward together.**" "*On the one hand*" he wished bright faith at Rome that it might be "*published*" everywhere, and he longed to *set it firm* that this Pharos light might increase among the nations. Then, furthermore, he wanted it bright and steady for its effect upon himself. Paul hesitated not a moment to count his own frame of mind important to all the world. "*Comforted*" (E. V. & Re.). That is not the word. Παρακαλέω means to *call near*, to *summon*. It is the word which in the participial shape means the one *called near* or summoned, *i.e.*, the *Paraclete*. Now men are shouted to for a thousand purposes, and one of them is to keep up their courage. So the word has an inconvenient multiplicity of signification :—*Called on for help*, i.e., *entreated* (Lu. 15 : 28) ; *called out to to help themselves*, i.e., *encouraged* (Eph. 6 : 22); *called out to to be of good cheer*, i.e., *comforted* (2 Cor. 1 : 4) ; *called near to stand for us or defend us*, i.e., *to be our advocate* (1 Jo. 2 : 1) ; and, more rightly still, *called near to do for us generally*, or to be our *Paraclete*, i.e., to *help* us (Acts 28 : 20). This was the best sense for Paul. To be "*comforted*" was but a trifle. To be "*helped forward*" would be felt in "*all the world*" by its effect upon the apostle.

"**Together.**" The natural accusative before the infinitive would be "*you*," as found in the eleventh verse. The two infinitives follow consecutively. But the συν in the latter gives us a right to "**we.**" It is not necessary to say "**I**" (E. V. & Re.), for *I being with you "comforted"* (Re.) makes it necessary to supply two pronouns ; nor is it correct to say *I comforted together with you* (E. V.), for that throws out "**in you,**" a most important element. The E. V. supplies it in the margin. The most effective rendering is to be content with "*we*," and then everything is expressed. "*That in you we may be helped forward together* **by the faith in each, both yours and mine.**"

"**On the other hand,**" (δέ) the apostle goes to the other side of the result, that he may speak of their personal benefit.

13. On the other hand, I would not have you to be ignorant, brethren, how I often purposed to come unto you and was prevented hithorto, that I might have some fruit likewise in yourselves, just as also in the other nations.

"**Likewise in yourselves.**" This "**likewise**" tells the tale of the πρῶτον μὲν (v. 8), and of the δέ (v. 13) ; that is, "*on the one hand,*" and "*on the other hand.*" His first great zeal about Rome was its metropolitan example ; but his second, the fruit "*likewise also in themselves*, just as in other nations.**"

14. I am debtor both to Greeks and barbarians, both to wise and unwise."

This was the only sort of indebtedness that Paul acknowledged. He tells these same people, "Owe no man anything but to love one another," (13 : 8), which has been made ridiculous as forbidding loans : practically, forbidding capital ! Paul's imperative is but a strong indicative, as we shall see *in loco*. Meanwhile he acts upon the principle,—All a man can owe to others is love. And under this one debt he must preach to all men.

We might pause upon the fact that the spirit of the age made little of men not Græco-Roman, and not refined.

15. So as concerns my own eagerness, it is to preach the gospel to you who are in Rome also.

Not "*as much as in me is*" (E. V. & Re.), whatever we might infer from Rom. 12 : 18, but literally, "*the readiness according to myself is to preach etc. ;*" the reserve being that *he* is willing, but there may be a doubt about the Almighty ; for he has already told them that he must be prospered "*in the will of God*" to come unto them (v. 10).

"**In Rome also.**" Well, why not ? Reasons throng. First, it was a haughty capital. But then he was not "**ashamed of the gospel of Christ.**" Again, it was surfeited with new faiths. What could he hope for still another ? Much, confidently ; for his "*gospel*" was "**the power of God unto salvation to everyone that believes.**"

So now he is approaching the centre of his work :—

16. For I am not ashamed of the gospel of Christ; for it is the power of God unto salvation to everyone that believes, both to the Jew, first, and also to the Greek.

"*Ashamed.*" Practically the gospel was much despised.

Contemporaneous history hardly mentions Christ. The chief notices seem forged (Jos. Ant. C. 3, also Tacitus). Paul all along feels the absence of influence (Acts 17 : 12), and eagerly longs for metropolitan believers (Phil. 4 : 22). Yet the work was among poor saints (Jas. 2 : 5). And, under Nero's sword (2 Tim. 4 : 16), he went out into the darkness with the poorest hopes humanly which any great leader could have left behind him.

"Ashamed of Jesus!"

is a sort of mockery now-a-days. But in Paul's time it meant something.

"**It**" not "*he.*" "**The power of God**" is a strong title to give to a message, but it is explained in the next verse. It cannot be αὐτός (" he ") that is meant, for the gospel is called "*the power of God*" further on (1 Cor. 1 : 18). Instruments are called powers elsewhere (1 Cor. 12 : 29). The "*gospel,*" like Philip (Acts 8 : 10), " was the great *power of God,*" because it was "**unto salvation;**" because it was "**for every one;**" and because it was *for every one* **that believed.** The *potentiality*, the *universality* and the *gratuity* of the gospel, even though in itself it had no power, can discover plenty of meaning in calling it " *the power of God.*"

This great sentence, one of the most significant in all the epistle, finds its complete unveilment in the seventeenth verse. Before we pass to that let us touch an intermediate expression :—"**Both to the Jew first, and also to the Greek.**"

" Go not from house to house " (Luke 10 : 7) had meant that they were not to scatter their work, but begin at an acquired centre, and push their influence out from where it was the most. It is a prime rule. Paul always struck for the synagogue (Acts 17: 1, 2, 17 ; 18 : 4). And so did Christ (Luke 4 : 16). Moreover they frequented the temple, and made much of its holy services (Matt. 26 : 55). God had been building a cradle for two millenniums (Gen. 12 : 1). It had not been altogether a failure, vile as it was. And therefore it was told them that they were to begin at Jerusalem (Lu. 24 : 47). Accountability began that way, and was to be measured similarly, "of the Jew first, and also of the Greek;" and, furthermore, as the justest and most rational conclusion, Judaism was more hopeful than Paganism. Salvation would spread the faster from Jewish homes. At first it did do so. There was to be an "advantage of the Jew" and a " profit of circumcision" (Rom. 3 : 1). And, considering the fewness of Israel, more of that race were to be brought into the faith than of any other of the tribes of men. The rule of results therefore is to be,—"*Both*" (not forgetting the τέ, for Paul is everywhere throwing Jew and Gentile together) "*to the Jew first,•and also to the Greek.*"

17. **For in it is the righteousness of God revealed from faith to faith; as it has been written, The righteous from faith shall live.**

Under the sweep of this "**for**" come two important questions : (1) what is "*salvation?*" (v. 16), and (2), what has "*the gospel*" to do with it? for the forthputting has been very strong ;—The gospel is "*the power of God;*" and it is "*the power of God unto salvation;*" and there is held a monopoly by what is called "*faith ;*" for the gospel is "*the power of God unto salvation unto every one that believes.*"

(1) "*Salvation,*" according to this seventeenth verse, means, simply, to be made to **live.** Nor is this an uncommon metaphor. The Bible is full of it. When Adam sinned, he died. Death is our grimmest enemy, and life our comprehensive friend. Rhetoric has seized upon both of them. And the apostate man is "dead in trespasses and sins," while the saved sinner is "alive to God through Jesus Christ our Lord."

But this rhetoric takes on distinctness when we say what this "*life*" is ; and Paul answers it perfectly. He says "**the righteous** *shall live.*" It was unfortunate to say "*The just*" (E. V.), for those diversities shake the continuity of a sentence. "**The righteousness of God**" immediately precedes the mention of "*the righteous.*" We shall see their connection ; though now we are engaged about another thing. How can we be said to "*live*" when we have no righteousness? Who ever saw a perfect character? and whatever is not perfect is of the very nature of sinfulness. The very Devil has some character, and loves some things in a numbed way that are of the nature of virtue. The worst fiend has not reached certain degrees of wickedness. And, therefore, we can appreciate the sentence, "There is none righteous, no not one." And yet the Bible perseveres in talking of "holy brethren," and Christ himself looks the disciples in the face and says, "Now ye are clean through the words that I have spoken unto you" (Jo. 15 : 3). In this way we are prepared to understand the apostolic expression,—Those "*righteous* **from faith.**" We understand it perfectly if we make it absolutely simple. Sin is in its nature incurable. To overcome this nature, we need the power of the Holy Spirit. As a law of the kingdom we are to ask for it, and to ask for it with more or less clearness in the name of our blessed Redeemer. To do this of course requires belief ; else who would do it ? and when we do it earnestly, our prayer is heard, and the faith with which we are looking to the Redeemer becomes suffused with love, and, like any other grace, partakes of "*righteousness ;*" or, to express it in commoner language, becomes touched with moral light, like hope and love and all the graces of the Spirit. Why should it not be so, seeing that it is the fruit of regeneration ? If regeneration be a moral change, why should not faith be a moral faith ? and if crying out to God be the great duty of the sinner, why should it not be moral, like any other duty of the soul ? If "all (our) things (are to) be done in love" (1 Cor. 16 : 14), and yet cannot be, till we are converted, why should not faith be "done in love ?" and why should it not only then be *saving* when, like repentance or any other work, it becomes touched by a moral nature ?

This is surely the thought of the apostle. Abraham had no righteousness, but his "faith was reckoned to him for righteousness" (4 : 9) ; not that it was sure enough righteousness, but that it was the beginning of it. Even Phinehas had a righteous act "counted unto him for righteousness" (Ps. 106 : 30, 31) ; not that it was really righteous, but the beginning of it ; in other words it was the first fruits of a new-born nature. And not only so, but it was the *earnest* as well as the first fruits. It was the promise of more. And that now distinctly was the idea of Paul. "*The righteous from faith shall live.*" This is his exact description of "*salvation.*" Of course it is very condensed, but the whole story is told in other places. Christ, having borne our guilt, has put within our reach this sort of "*salvation*" (v. 16). We are to pray for it. While we pray for it, we are to attack sin all along the line. If we persevere in this we will be converted. In being converted there has beamed into us the moral light that wakens all graces. Among others our very prayer has been wakened. Prayer is but an exercise of faith. Our faith, if wakened up, is touched for the first time with moral light. In other words it has become saving faith; a genuine act of a new "*righteousness ;*" and we shall "*live*" thereby, not only in the degree that it is "*righteous,*" being itself a "*righteousness,*" but as the harbinger of more; just as a little sanctification is a harbinger of more (8 : 23), and a little cleanness of more (2 Cor. 7 : 1), and a little quickening of more (1 Jo. 5 : 4), fulfilling definitely the divine words, "Now the righteous from faith shall live, but if he (not *any man*, E. V.) draw back, my soul shall have no pleasure in him" (Heb. 10 : 38).

So much for the first question, What is "*salvation ?*" It is being made to "*live*" by becoming "*righteous ;*" not "*from*" a sure-enough "*righteousness,*" for that requires our being perfect; but "*from*" a dawning "*righteousness ;*" that is to say, *faith*, which is itself a beginning of a *righteous life*, but, what is more, the harbinger of one more righteous, on, on, to the purity of Heaven.

So much for the first question. (2) Now for the second. What has the "*gospel*" (v. 16) to do with all this?

The "*gospel*" is not the redemption of Christ, but the message of it. "*In it,*" we are told, something is "*revealed.*" What is that something? That is the most important question in all the epistle. "*In it the righteousness of God is revealed.*" What is "*the righteousness of God ?*"* Of course the simplest answer

---

* It will be noticed that "*power*" (v. 16), and "*righteousness*" (v. 17), and "*wrath*" (v. 18), are all without the article. This is significant; for

would be, Just what Gabriel's "*righteousness*" is, or anybody else's. As a general thing this is the safer understanding of words, and has, so to speak, priority. In the sentence before "*the power of God*" is spoken of, and in the sentence after, "*the wrath of God ;*" and so "*the righteousness of God*" has a right to be considered, if possible, that quality in the Almighty.

The "*righteousness of God*" is brought forward in ten passages of the New Testament scriptures. We will quote all of them ; and we will begin with those as to which nobody hesitates in their simplest meaning. "If our unrighteousness commend the righteousness of God" (Rom. 3 : 5). "The wrath of man worketh not the righteousness of God" (Jas. 1 : 20). With no dispute upon two out of ten passages the rest gather more right to the simpler and more usual signification.

But now another two : "To declare His righteousness" (Rom. 3 : 25) ; "To declare I say at this time His righteousness ; that He might be just, and yet the justifier of him who believes in Jesus" (E. V., 3 : 26). If any deserved to be unusual, these might seem to do so. And many of the Reformed seize them at once for what is a forensic significance. Dr. Hodge, strangest of all, does nothing of the kind. He adopts the sense "as of the general rectitude of God" (see Com. *in loco*). It "is recommended," so he tells us, by the consideration that such is "*the common meaning of the word righteousness.*"

The eight, therefore, are now reduced to six. And I submit whether the disqualification of these six for what Dr. Hodge confesses is the "*common meaning,*" is not still further fearfully diminished by the whimsical differences of the significations by which it is to be replaced.

---

if the two former had the article in the Greek it would be easier to attach superstitious ideas to " *the gospel* " as *the* only "*power*" and to " *the* " righteousness as something special and artificial in redemption. We do not say " *a* " righteousness, for that in English would look more special still ; nor " *righteousness* " simply, for that would be awkward in our language ; but we give this notice that the English in its present shape has no warrant from an article to be anything but usual *righteousness*.

Let us quote the six :—" Seek first the kingdom of God and His righteousness" (Matt. 6: 33). *"For in it the righteousness of God is revealed"* (Rom. 1 : 17). " But now the righteousness of God without the law is manifested ; even the righteousness of God which is by faith in Jesus Christ " (Rom. 3 : 21, 22). Let it be considered that this is really close by the other passages which Dr. Hodge gives up as having the " common meaning "). " Who, being ignorant of God's righteousness, and going about to establish their own righteousness, have not submitted to the righteousness of God " (Rom. 10 : 3). " He made Him to be sin for us who knew no sin ; that we might be made the righteousness of God in Him " (2 Cor. 5 : 21). " Like precious faith with us in the righteousness of God, and our Saviour, Jesus Christ " (2 Pet. 1 : 1).

Any fair minded exegete must admit that refusing the plainest interpretation could only be justified by the clearest agreement in an understanding the other way. That to say, The righteousness of God does not mean God's righteousness, when it is confessed that four times it does, is a gloss that we could only excuse if it were consistent with itself ; but, on the contrary, there is no agreement, and the debate is endless. One commentator will hold that God's righteousness is " God's method of justification " (Meyer, Bengel) ; another that it is the righteousness or justified condition that God bestows (Alford, De Wette) ; another that it is the righteous or right standing that is acceptable to him (Calvin, Neander). One actually goes so far as to say that the first " is most generally received," but that " the second seems to be again coming into vogue " (Hodge, Com. *in loc.*). Can any thing be more admonitory? We confess, men might be driven after this fashion if the usual sense were impossible. But, on the contrary, such a sense is of the very best. We will not try this in each case of the six, but adhere to one (v. 17), believing that the most thorough exposition of one in its most simple signification, will cover all the rest, and prepare us to understand at once the two which we meet afterward in this epistle.

"*In it;*" that is, in "*the gospel.*" The gospel is " the power of God," not *suo motu*, for "the letter killeth," but because it is His great instrument. No one doubts that He could convert by the ten commandments. He did convert by a very imperfect knowledge of the gospel. He does convert idiots and infants, with no gospel at all. But it pleases Him to employ the gospel, and that because, as a moral lesson, it is so suitably the very "*power*" of the Almighty.

Now let it be understood : We are not speaking of redemption. That is a thing of court. That is a thing vital to the salvation of a soul. Put that entirely away. We are speaking of its message. After mercy has been bought, the message of it God uses as his favorite "*power.*" And now why ? because "*in it*" a certain "*righteousness is revealed.*" That tells the whole story. If "*righteousness*" be "*revealed*" to a man, he is himself righteous, and that by its very light. How else could he be converted ? And the "*righteousness revealed,*" whose righteousness had it better be ? Not his own ; for that is imperfect. Not of a tree or a bird, for there is no such thing. Not Gabriel's ; for that is far away. But "*the righteousness of God,*" and that eminently in the gospel ; that finest case of righteousness, the salvation of the sinner ; that which is to feed Heaven (Is. 35 : 8); that which entered into the heart of Lydia (Acts 16 : 14); that which befell the Thessalonians who were to "receive the love of the truth" (Thess. 2 : 10) ; that which makes us like to Him, when we "see Him as he is" (1 John 3 : 2) ; and that which bedecks all saints when "God hath shined into their hearts, to give the light of the knowledge of the glory of God in the face of Jesus" (2 Cor. 4 : 6).

So much for "*God's righteousness,*" and Paul's calling the gospel the power of God because "*in it the righteousness of God is revealed.*"

This fits all the other sentences.

It is not a matter of ransom. That is forensic. It is not a matter of immediate regeneration. It is a tale only of the instrument. God, who frees us by the cross, and who lifts us by His power, makes the instrument of that power to be the message of the gospel. For, to lift us at all, we must have an idea of righteousness, and there is no righteousness that shines like God's, and there is no shining of God's righteousness half so bright, and, therefore, half so fitted to be instrumentally ordained, as that which shines in the cross of the Redeemer.

Now this links all these notices together. First, "the gospel is the power of God." Why? because it is the instrument of God's power in revealing righteousness. Second, "the power of God unto salvation," and why? Because revealing righteousness is itself salvation, discerning righteousness being nothing else than being righteous, and death the darkness of the sinner. Third, "*to every one that believeth.*" Why? Because the righteous lives by faith. He becomes righteous in the shape of faith. He must see righteousness by the eye of faith; and if the reason that the gospel is the power of God is that in it God's righteousness is shown, then it must be to every one that believeth, because believing is a sight of righteousness; that is, faith, when it becomes saving, must be moral faith; the boyish faith of our infancy must be suffused with light, (as the Catholics say, "infused with love"), faith itself becoming righteousness (Trent, Canon 12), that is, the newborn sight of a better nature. And here comes in the expression "**from faith to faith.**" It has been miserably thrown into waste. And yet it helps marvelously. Shedd reads it, "from one degree of faith to another." Hodge reads it, "entirely of faith." Meyer reads it, "for the increase of faith." McKnight reads it, "which springs from faith, and which faith receives." In so critical a passage we scorn anything general, and insist on an absolute meaning. "*In it;*" that is in the gospel, "*the moral excellence of God is revealed*," so that our poor souls see it and therein is conversion; but they see it not without God's making "the gospel" His "*power*" (v. 16), and bestowing on us "*faith.*" In other words our seeing it is "*faith.*" And now (more inwardly still), we see it "out of" (ἐκ) faith. Faith is that in the illuminations of which we get our ideas of righteousness. The God-given dawning of "faith" is that "out of" (ἐκ) whose very bosom we get the light to see the *righteousness of God.* Hence

Paul declares that "faith" is the "substance" and the "evidence" (Heb. 11 : 1) "of things hoped for" and "not seen." Grant that it is the dawning of our own righteousness, and of course it is the dawning of God's righteousness in any increased sense and warmer appreciation of it by the sinner. And this makes perfect the expression "*from faith to faith.*" Where else could the revelation come from, I mean mediately, except *from* faith ? And what else could it be made "*to*" except to faith ? The meaning is complete. Righteousness itself exhibits itself in our own young righteousness, viz., in our faith, and it exhibits itself to nothing else possible than that, viz., to our faith. And this like a sum in arithmetic proves itself all the way back to the beginning; for that the righteousness of God is just plainly what we have stated, viz., his superior excellence, has now confirmation from the sentence that it "*is revealed from faith to faith.*"

"**As it is written.**" We need have little difficulty now with all that remains. "*Live ;*" that we have already looked at as a name for "*salvation* (v. 16). "*The righteous shall live.*" Who else do live ? and in what else does life consist ? "The righteous *from faith* shall live." How else are they righteous, except dawningly so, and in the shape of "*faith ?*" Or how else do they live ? for it makes not the smallest difference whether this sentence from Habbakuk puts the "*faith*" in the one part of it or the other. " *The righteous from faith live,*" not simply "*from*" that wretched beginning, which is really nothing but less sinfulness, but "*from*" this as the earnest of a better, just as we are said to be *partakers of God's holiness* (Heb. 12 : 10); not that we are really holy, but less sinful ; and that there is dawning in our mind a faith that may proceed to perfectness.

And how great a "*salvation*" this is the apostle means now to picture by exhibiting the opposite : —

18. For the wrath of God is revealed from heaven upon all ungodliness and unrighteousness of men who keep back the truth in unrighteousness.

The most important word in all this sentence is the word

"truth." The most important idea in all this epistle is that a new sight, speaking on the side of man, or a new light, speaking on the side of God, is what constitutes righteousness, and that the access of it constitutes conversion. This new light is a moral light, or, as the sinner had some before, a renewed moral light, or, more simply still, a greater; the new moral sight is nothing more than faith, though that word is chosen because it includes in it a recognition of Christ, which comes very naturally, because the sight itself arises under the hearing of the gospel (Gal. 3 : 2, 5). The favorite word that Solomon uses is "*wisdom.*" He actually opens the Proverbs with the key, Wisdom *is* righteousness (1 : 1, 2, see Com.). Let us fortify ourselves for a most thorough consideration by remembering that light is all that is necessary for righteousness, and for all the graces of the Spirit. We can see this no more clearly than in the announcement, "When He shall appear we shall be like Him, for we shall see Him as He is" (1 Jo. 3 : 2). This, of course, is a full exposition of the last sentence, "In it," that is in the gospel, "the righteousness of God is revealed." This light being a moral light, and answering to a moral sight, and, of course, to a renewed or a regenerated conscience, is really a constituting fact in all the Christian graces. Having this moral light upon God, or, what is the same thing, a moral sight of His righteousness (having His "*righteousness revealed*" v. 17), is tantamount to loving him. Seeing the beauty of a picture and loving a beautiful picture are one and the same. Having a moral sight of Christ is the *differentia* between a common and a saving faith. Having a moral sight of ourselves is repentance in its very genuine self. And so a moral sight is the gracious ingredient of hope and diligence and all the virtues of the believer.

The great crime of the Protestant church, with all its splendid excellencies, was that it disturbed the Catholic definition. The Catholic definition of faith was that "*fides formata,*" or faith that was saving, was faith that was "infused with love." It was horrible to disturb that view. The Catholics disturbed it by imputing to faith perfectness and supererogatory merit. But the Protestants disturbed it by throwing it clean off its base. We have destroyed the very nature of faith. We make faith a clinging to Christ on the explanation of His plan. We make holiness a *consequence* of believing. Whereas believing *is* holiness. We lose all sight of Paul's careful sentence,—" In it (viz., " the gospel ") the righteousness of God is revealed," and " revealed out of (from) faith," faith itself being the thing in which better views of holiness for the first appear ; " revealed (therefore) out of faith unto faith," faith introspecting itself and getting in itself its first new enkindled ideas of righteousness;—and encourage a murderer, for example, to get a knowledge of a mere saving plan and squarely trust it ; beating down his better thoughts that penitence must come at the very beginning ; saying nothing about faith as itself a moral illumination ; and hence, as Jeremy Taylor writes, betraying the church into being saved by faith, when that faith is so bare in its idea that betterment is to come after ; exhibiting the baleful model of believing as a trusting in an explained Christ, with holiness as the effect ; having the trust, therefore, and sometimes not the holiness ; leaning heavily upon Christ with only clean cut views of His redemption, and never getting on to the result (since we are saved before it), viz., the actual eye for a thorough revolution in our living.

Faith, therefore, being this actual eye, and standing for that vision in the sinner when the righteousness of God has been savingly revealed, is the very salvation itself, and, now, the " for " with which our present verse begins, ennobles the salvation by showing just as distinctly the difficulty of the sinner out of which the salvation by faith the more strikingly appears. "**The wrath of God.**" Not his *resentment*. Sinfulness in God would be the same as sinfulness in man (1 Jo. 2: 8 ; 4: 16). Not his *vindicatory justice* in the sense of some of the Reformed (Hodge, C. 5, § 12). God has nothing moral primordially, save (1) benevolence and (2) a love of holiness. To put *revenge* in such a place is blasphemous and wicked. God hates sin, and unspeakably loves its opposite. This is the primordial affection. *Vengeance* is its consequence. *Vengeance*, therefore, is not an original lust, but a derivative obligation. Punishment is a constitutional device, and God necessarily follows it. But he hates it as a bitter need (Lam. 3: 33 ; 2 Pet. 3: 9). Moreover he does not hate the culprit (Matt. 5: 45). He hates him as we are enjoined to hate him (Ps. 139: 21) ; but He loves him in every other sense (Jo. 3: 16). And "*the wrath of God*" is a convenient trope for saying all this as to His awful administrations.

"*The wrath of God* is **revealed.**" Not like His righteousness at all (v. 17). That is revealed savingly. "*The wrath of God is revealed*" to the damned. It "*is revealed*" to all of us. It "*is revealed*" not "*from faith*" (v. 17), but "**from heaven ;**" and how it "*is revealed*" Paul tells us in certain other verses (vs. 19, 20).

But now he is engaged upon the subjects of the wrath. These are not **the ungodly and the unrighteous.** If they were, there could be no gospel. Paul is about to utter the most distinctive evangel. "*Righteousness*" is a thing "*revealed*" (v. 17). It is revealed in the shape of "*faith.*" When I have a revelation of righteousness, I become righteous, by all the increase of the moral vision. This revelation of righteousness is made to faith. And as faith itself is a vision, it is in faith, or, as Paul expresses it, out of faith, that I discern the right. The righteousness of God, therefore, is revealed to faith out of faith, and it is in the weak beginnings of faith that I begin my heavenly vision.

Now why do not all men begin it ?

It is in expounding this that Paul shows what is "*ungodliness,*" or what that "*ungodliness*" is on which "*the wrath of God*" preeminently descends.

All men have "*truth.*" Paul is about to show where they get it (vs. 19, 20). Most men have saving "*truth.*" "*Truth*" is a wide word. The "*truth*" in art means more than shape or color, for, most of all, it means beauty. And so in Christ men have all measures of the "*truth.*" "*Truth*" most worth the name is precisely that "*righteousness of God*" which is revealed from faith to faith. As a man can't paint divinely till he knows that "*truth*" which consists in beauty, so a man can't live divinely till he knows that "*truth*" which consists in righteousness. But then all men know this to some extent. Even the devils have a decaying character.

Paul recognizes the fact that this knowledge of the "*truth*" urges and presses. The Quaker and his "inward light" undoubtedly are of this nature. Paul pictures the idea of truth-enough-to-convert-us. Undoubtedly he favors the fact of light enough for every one, *if he would follow it*, to bring him out into the Kingdom (v. 20), and, therefore, his lost ones are but of a single class, viz., the ungodly and unrighteous among men, "**who hold back the truth in unrighteousness.**"

Let me be careful with all this. I do not mean an "inward light" that would save a man without the Spirit; I mean one that would save a man *if he would follow it*. No man *will* follow it. By the works of the law, that is, works engendered by any form of "*truth*" left simply to teach, no man is made righteous. He would be made righteous if he would obey; but there is the very mischief. Evil has the upper hand, and drives the sinner to "*hold back*" the truth; and that is the only sort of impenitency and ruin.

"*Hold back.*" Κατέχειν never means to "*hold*" (E. V.), that is, in the New Testament. It may in the classics; but, scripturally, it always conveys an intensity of meaning. We are commanded to "*hold fast* that which is good" (1 Thess. 5: 21). We hear of *holding hard* to the land (Acts 27: 40), of *holding* him *hard* not to go from them (Lu. 4: 42). If κατέχειν meant simply to *possess* (E. V.), this would be its only instance. They that buy are to do so as not *holding hard* (1 Cor. 7: 30). They are to *hold fast* the traditions (1 Cor. 11: 2). "As having nothing, and yet holding all things hard" (2 Cor. 6: 10). The Revisionists are right, therefore, in translating it here as *holding down* (Re.). "*The truth*" is *par excellence* moral, as where Christ appears "full of grace and truth" (Jo. 8: 44; 2 Cor. 4: 2). The devils, even, have the working and the striving of the "*truth.*" *Holding back* that "*truth*" which is ever pushing for the supremacy, is just the feature of impenitency, and is just the sin and the curse "*upon*" which "the wrath of God is revealed."

It will be noticed that the apostle says "*upon*"(ἐπί). The translators render it "*against*" (E. V. & Re.), and they may appeal to Homer (Il. 13: 101; 5: 590); though even in Homer we gain by speaking of making war "*upon.*" In Paul every syllable is to be counted in. If Paul said "*against,*" the view would be commonplace. But as he says "*upon,*" we are led to connect the sentence with all the rest of the epistle. "*Salvation*" (v. 16) consists in "*righteousness*" (v. 17), and it consists in having it "*revealed*" (ib.), and it is "*revealed*" in the embryonic condition of believing (ib.). Damnation consists in wickedness; in pain, to be sure, additionally, but above and aback of that, in wickedness. Therefore the philosophic text that "*wrath*" is "*upon*" the wickedness. It is "*against*" it as well; but, more than that, "*upon*" it. It descends in that very shape; and where the law strikes the man, may be eminently in the point of pain, and in the shape of torment, but, far above this, in the shape also of sin. Therefore the man is "*given up,*" to use the language of the apostle (vs. 26, 28), or, to express it as above, "*The wrath of God is revealed from heaven upon,*" that is in a very curse upon the thing itself, deepening it and making it more bitter, for the very crime of *holding back the truth*, and that *by the very means of* (ἐν) the "*unrighteousness.*"

19, 20. "**Because.**" The apostle now adds two verses to show that they "*hold*" the truth, and then twelve verses more to show that they "*hold*" it "*back*":—

19. Because that which is known of God is manifest in them, for God made to them the manifestation; 20. For the unseen things of Him from the creation of the world are deeply seen, being perceived by the things that are made, even His eternal power and Godhead, so that they are without excuse.

"*That which may be known*" (E. V. & Re.) is classical,

CHAPTER I. 61

and might sufficiently answer, but it is ominous of what is best that it would not answer in any other of the fourteen instances of τὸ γνωστόν in all the Testament. There is a vast deal unknown. If Spencer had confined himself to that, he would have done very well. Then there is a vast deal "*known;*" and Paul ennobles that when he calls it the "**the eternal power and Godhead.**" He calls these, "unseen things," and so they are; so signally so that a man like Spencer can deny them. In other words God is silent and invisible, so that an atheist, without visible absurdity, can deny any such being. And yet these "*unseen things* **are deeply seen.**" Paul, to bring out the paradox, uses the same ὁράω. They "*are deeply seen,* **being perceived by the things that are made.**" Of course before "**the creation**" there was nothing to see. But, after the creation, that is "**from**" or after "**the creation of the world,**" things were in such a plight, that when man came (the King was still invisible; everything about Him personally was still an "*unseen thing,*" but) He was to be known of in His works. We were so constituted as that we must have found Him out, and, therefore, Paul says, He was *manifested in ourselves.* And, choosing attributes that are bravely comprehensive, viz., His "power" and also His "Godhead," and affixing a word that carries them back to everlasting, he says, what is very expressive, that "**God made the manifestation;**" that is to say, that our Creator had such fidelity as that He took care that we should know His "*eternal Godhead.*" And Paul could say this without risk; for the Romans need but step to their own Pantheon, to see how the knowledge of a God was to be found all over the earth.

But the idea is, that all men, thus possessing this knowledge of God, were choking it, and *keeping* it *down* (v. 18) all the time. And he develops this to three degrees: First, they fought it off, so that it should not increase and save them (v. 17); second, they fought it back, so that it should decrease and darken (v. 21); and third, they were "*given up,*" so that they should fall into utter folly (v. 22), and into utter shame and bestiality of living (v. 24 etc.). This is the way that the apostle illustrates his idea that the entrance of moral "*truth*" or light was faith and righteousness and salvation (vs. 16, 17), and that the *keeping back* of moral "*truth*" was that which constituted the "*wrath of God*" directly "*upon*," and in the shape of, the world's "*unrighteousness.*"

21. Because, when they knew God, they glorified Him not as God, nor gave thanks, but were made vain in their reasonings, and dark as to their senseless heart. 22. Asserting themselves wise, they were made fools, 23. and changed the glory of the incorruptible God in the likeness of an image of corruptible man, and of birds, and of four-footed beasts, and of creeping things.

The "*because*" previously (v. 19) covered only their knowledge, and how they were "*without excuse*" because "*they knew.*" The "**because**" now covers their use of knowledge, and how they abused it and *kept* it *back*. One idea follows endlessly. "*Salvation*" is *life* (v. 16). *Life* is "*righteousness*" (v. 17). "*Righteousness*" is "*faith*" (vs. 16, 17), at least the small beginnings of it in the regenerate sinner. Regeneration is by the "*power of God*" (v. 16). And the "*power of God*" makes such a favorite instrument of "*the gospel*," that the apostle calls that "*the power of God.*" And the thing *in* "*the gospel*" is "the light of the knowledge of the glory of God" (2 Cor. 4 : 6), or, as the apostle expresses it, "*the righteousness of God*" (v. 17). When that is "*revealed,*" viz., God's moral excellence, the man becomes morally excellent. Every man understands that (even God) " as he thinketh in his heart so is he" (see Com. Prov. 23 : 7). Let a man see "*righteousness,*" and he is "*righteous ;*" and he is "*righteous from faith.*" " *The righteousness of God is revealed from faith to faith.*" That is, "*faith,*" when man has been busy seeking God, though the driving force may have been terror, and the "*faith*" quite the common "*faith*" of selfishness, yet, when it becomes responded to by the Almighty, has opened into its very bosom a revelation of "*righteousness.*" That is, a man's conscience becomes quickened, and in the revelations of this moral eye God reveals Himself. Hence the meaning of the sentence, " *The moral excellence of God is revealed from faith.*" Where can I resort for any cognizance of excellence, if I do not look for it in upon my faith. And as taste in a man is that which uncovers beauty, and the taste of a man must resort, in order to understand beauty, to his taste, so the apostle makes the genesis of conversion very complete. It is "*the power of God*," in the grand instrument of "*the gospel*," making the central figure of "*the gospel*," viz., God, to be "revealed" in His *excellence*—that *excellence* "*revealed*" (in the very act of prayer) in the very bosom of the praying man's "*faith*"; so that the common faith breaks out with the light of conscience, and so that it is there that a man gets his view of righteousness, and so, in his very "*faith*," becomes "*righteous*," so that the revelation "*to faith*" is made "*from faith*," and the "*faith*" so engendered is imputed to a man for righteousness (4: 22, 24), and becomes actual righteousness in a sense that shall be complete when it becomes lost in sight (2 Cor. 5: 7), and perfect (1 Cor. 13: 12) in the kingdom of the blessed.*

So much for the one side of the apostolic statement. But they "that are contentious, and do not obey the truth, but obey unrighteousness," have just the opposite history. The one man is saved in his very faith; the other man is damned in his very sinfulness. His fault is that he "*keeps back the truth*." Therefore he is cursed in this very shape; the truth is darkened to him. The apostle divides his reasoning. First, there is the possession of the truth. That is made sure in the verses that have gone before (vs. 19, 20). **"They know God."** Let us hope the aorists may be noted. He was not a some-

---

* The whole thing is stated in different language in Second Thessalonians (1: 8):—" Taking vengeance on them who know not God." What is there in God to know except His "righteousness?" Knowing His power or knowing His wisdom would not save us. Knowing His spiritual wisdom, or knowing His moral excellence, is what we achieve in being converted. And to justify Paul's awful threats (vs. 8, 9) against so helpless a thing as not knowing, comes the explanatory sequel—"and obey not the gospel of our Lord Jesus Christ." The very " gospel," according to Paul, is that in which "*the righteousness of God is revealed*." And the crime of not knowing Him (2 Thess. 1: 8) is signalized by the wickedness of not yielding the least to the simple directions of the gospel.

thing that "*may be known*" (E. V. v. 19), but τὸ γνωστὸν *i. e.* a something actually "*manifest.*" The apostle goes further, and says, He was "*manifest inside of them ;*" and, further, that "*God made the manifestation.*" Then, secondly, that this "*manifestation*," which was not "*the gospel*," but, as Paul expresses it, "*from heaven*," and which "*being perceived by the things that were made*" was no less a truth than an "*Eternal*," with "*power and Godhead*," they stifled. And Paul illustrates this as of the most wilful shape. They saw plentifully His gloriousness, and did "*not glorify Him*," and they used plentifully His power, and did not thank Him; and so the third truth came out, that what truth they had was dazed. They **"were made vain in their reasonings, and dark as to their senseless heart."** This was a judicial sentence. "*Made vain.*" Liddell has the plausible idea that ματαιόω is linked with the Italian *matto* and the English *mad;* and certainly μάταιος in its six instances in the New Testament, would give its meaning better by being translated *crazy* than translated "*vain;*" but in all the classics μάτην especially, and some of the compounds, seem to demand the sense of *futile* or *to no effect.* "**Dark.**" We adopt this reading simply for euphony. The literal reading is "*their foolish* (or senseless, Re.) *heart was darkened*" (E. V.). "**Asserting themselves wise.**" The very roar of some great metropolis thunders this out upon the air. It is a singular mixture, however; for the mass of the impenitent, boldly as they turn to cavil, will admit in quiet moments their own foolishness. "**Changed.**" It is important to notice the particle "**in.**" It is not "*into* (E. V. and Re.) **the likeness of a man**," but "*in the likeness of a man.*" And this is a nice description. It is repeated in the twenty-fifth verse. If I charge a man with making an "**image of God**" and *changing* "**the incorruptible God**" *into* the *image*, or even *into* the "*likeness*" of "**four-footed beasts,**" he will repel the charge with indignation. He will tell me justly that he does no such thing. And the second commandment was intended, not to forbid any such thing as this, but just that which the man will confess, viz., that he makes a certain something to *represent* God. The hideous little idols in the eye of a Hindoo are not God, but something that stands for God ; and indeed, as he is a Pantheist, in his particular case they are, as taken at random, a part of Him. All idolaters profess in their more learned class a unitary Deity. But God forbids such representations ; and now Paul gives the reason for it. Men change the truth of God "*in*" the false thing (v. 25) ; or, as it is expressed here, they change "*the glory of the incorruptible God*" (not "*into*," for scholars with singular unanimity agree that ἐν never means "*into*," but) "*in the likeness of the image*" of such degrading objects, viz., "**of corruptible man and of birds and of four-footed beasts and of creeping things.**" That is to say, the practical result as shown in history is, that God gets "*changed*" in such representations ; and as "*the image*" must have been chosen for some sort of "*likeness*," they change God "*in*" that "*likeness ;*" that is, they are "*made vain in their reasonings*" from the twist given by such a representation.

24. **Wherefore also God gave them up in the desires of their hearts unto the uncleanness of having their bodies dishonored between themselves.**

"**Also.**" A very nice distinction seems made by the position of καί. It belongs to "**wherefore.**" For the same great reasons God gave over their "**bodies**" (v. 24) as well as their minds (v. 23). It does not mean "*also* **God**" (E. V.) ; nor are we willing to see it obliterated as by a various reading (Re.) ; for the MS. testimony is not sufficient. It is needed just where it is. It does not belong to "*God*," for it does not mean that "*God also* (E. V.) **gave up** *their bodies*," when they themselves (v. 23) had given up their minds. The giving up by God is of the whole, and from the very beginning. And here is just the time to announce four realities. First, a man saves himself. The first motions of a change are by the man. As far back as conviction the first cloud of seriousness passes over a man's own spirit. A man is never saved till he " stirs up himself to take hold on God" (Is. 64 : 7). It is vital to know this ; otherwise men may trifle according to the prophet by saying, " Let Him come near and hasten His work that we may see it " (Is. 5 : 19). Because, secondly, the first motion of a change is by the God. God saves a man ; and saves him from the very beginning. The very motions that are most our own are motions of the Almighty. There is no difference in the periods. God begins with a believer at the bottom of his unbelief. The influences are upon our will ; and therefore it seems as much our will at one stage of our sanctification as another. If the gospel is the power of God, it shows itself in *our* power ; and if it proclaims His righteousness, it shows itself in *our* righteousness. And if we give God thanks, it is from an outside revelation that reveals to us that it is God that worketh in us, even when we are conscious that we are working out our own salvation with fear and trembling. This is the reality on the one page of the apostle. Now on the other it is exactly the same in regard to sin. It is always our sin. For, thirdly, it is not true that we first sin wilfully, and then God *gives us up* so that it is less our agency than it was before ; for, fourthly, He gives us up from the very beginning. All these puzzles are due to the fact of the nature of the will. " *God gave them up* **in the desires of their hearts."** We are not to say, " I can begin the work of reading and prayer, but when the gracious moment comes God must act ; " or, " I can begin to trifle and reject, but when the judicial moment comes, it is God that gives me over." It is God that gives me over from the very first. He must rule me from the very beginning of my history. There is never a moment but I must act myself ; and never a moment in which I am not acted in by the God that made me. " *In the desires.*" This is the key to the whole paradox. In either damning or saving God acts in and with our "*desires.*" "**The uncleanness of having."** It might be read, " *unto uncleanness so as to have.*" But the infinitive rather has a right to be governed if there be a proximate noun. " *To dishonor* " (E. V.) will not answer ; for there is no instance of a middle in ἀτιμάζω, and the passive capitally expresses all that could be desired.

25. As being men who changed the truth of God in the false, and worshiped and served the creature rather than the Creator, who is blessed forever more. Amen.

Not "*who*" (E. V.), for the οἵτινες means more than that. In the sixteenth chapter it is three times repeated. "Salute Mary" (not "*who*," E. V., but) "as one who" bestowed much labor on us (v. 6). It gives the reason for the special salutation. "Salute the beloved Persis as one who labored much in the Lord" (v. 12). And again "salute Andronicus and Junia as being people who are of note among the apostles" (v. 7). By the use of this pronoun Paul terminates the passage by summing up the specific charge against the impenitent.

"**Who changed,**" The idea is again presented of changing not "*into*" (E. V.), or "*for*" (Re.), but changing "**in.**" They "*changed* **the truth of God in the false.**" Indulging in idolatry, which used images of God not truly descriptive of Him, they colored God in the picture. "*The truth of God*," which really included his "*righteousness*" (v. 17), they got all besmirched. And changing the true "*in the false*," they lost God in the very pretence of worship. And, sliding from the one to the other, they "**worshiped and served the creature rather than the Creator.**" Paul's holy horror at which breaks out in the doxology, "**Who is blessed forever more.**"

26. Wherefore, God gave them up unto dishonoring passions; for their females changed the natural use into that which was aside from nature. 27. In like manner, also, the males, leaving the natural use of the female, were inflamed in their lust for each other, males with males, accomplishing shame, and bearing away in themselves the due reward of their error.

"**Wherefore.**" This word confirms the view just given. "**God gave them up,**" in no way to destroy their responsibility. It is in man's "*desires*" that the mischief works ; and as long as it is "*desire*" that "hath conceived" (Ja. 1 : 15), the progeny must be "sin." There is no difference in man's acts as to their voluntariness, from the first dawning of accountable being. "*Vile affections*" (E. V.). Literally, "*passions of dishonor.*" In more perspicuous English, "**dis-**

honoring passions." "Females." That is the Greek, and Paul may have shrunk from the nobler epithet of "*women*" (E. V. and Re.). "**For their** *females.*" Not "*for even* (E. V.) *their females.*" Τε never means that. It might mean "*for, for example, their females,*" or "*for, on the one hand, their females,*" (and there is another τε to keep up the balance in the following sentence). But τε is not strong enough as a copulative to make much notice of it necessary. We mention it at all because "*even*" (E. V.) is an unhappy expression. "*Females*" were not so sacred that an Eastern pen would be apt to say "*even*" in exposing horrible iniquity. "**Into that.**" Please observe that when Paul really means *exchange* or change *into*, εἰς is the word, and not ἐν as in those previous verses (vs. 23, 25). "**Aside from.**" This is the meaning of παρά.

28. And as it was not their judgment to keep God under close acquaintance, God gave them up to a mind without judgment, to do things not fit.

Our authorized version reads "*as they did not like.*" We can say with great boldness δοκιμάζω never means to "*like*" (E. V.) ; and, putting the negative to it, it cannot be rendered "*refuse*" (Re.). It has an undetermined derivation, but, by its usage simply, its meaning can be sufficiently identified. Of its twenty-three instances in the New Testament, King James gives eight renderings, and the Revisers four ; but the word *judge*, if we take it, not in the sense of a court, but in the sense of making an estimate, might admirably fill the place of every one of them.

"**Without judgment.**" The word ἀδόκιμος occurs eight times in the whole Testament, and King James translates it with three words, and the Revisers with two ; but in neither version is the word *judge* or *without judgment* applied either to verb or adjective. We hesitate therefore. And yet even one passage in the Testament makes very awkward this steady omission of the commoner meaning of the word. "Prove (δοκιμάζετε) your own selves ; or know ye not your own selves, that Jesus Christ is in you ? unless indeed ye be reprobate (ἀδόκιμοι). But I hope that ye shall know that we are not reprobate (ἀδόκιμοι). Now we pray to God that ye do no evil; not that we may appear approved (δόκιμοι), but that ye may do that which is honorable, though we be as reprobate (ἀδόκιμοι)" (E. V. 2 Cor. 13 : 5-7). Show an atom there of consistent sense! What has Paul's being a "*reprobate*" to do with what he was saying? But substitute the word *judge* and *judgment*, and every thing comes into place. "Try your own selves whether ye be in the faith; judge your own selves. Know ye not your own selves how that Jesus Christ is in you—unless indeed ye be without judgment. But I trust that ye will know that we are not without judgment. And I pray God that ye do no evil; not that we may appear as having judgment, but that you may do nobly, though we be as without judgment." And we might take other instances. "Men corrupted in mind, without judgment (reprobate E. V.) concerning the faith" (2 Tim. 3 : 8). "As to every good work void of judgment" (Titus 1 : 16). Not that we need insist that the words can not be more idiomatic; but only that *to judge* and to be *without judgment* are the sufficient meaning, and that those are the words which most often prevent an entangling or discordant interpretation.

"**Close acquaintance**," (ἐπιγνώσις). Notice the ἐπί. It creates a meaning stronger than γνῶσις. "**As it was not their judgment;**" that is, since they made no such estimate as that they should "**keep God under close acquaintance.**" God did what has been repeatedly described; that is, to those who sought this ἐπιγνώσις, and urged a prayer for it, his righteousness was revealed (v. 17); but in those who made no such practical "*judgment*," what "*judgment*" they had was darkened.

29. Being filled with all unrighteousness, maliciousness; full of envy, murder, strife, deceit, malignity, whisperers, 30. Accusers; hated of God, insolent, haughty, boastful, inventors of evil things, disobedient to parents, 31. Without understanding, covenant breakers, without natural affection, unmerciful; 32. Being such persons as that when they had close acquaintance with God's manner of making matters right, since they who practice such things

are worthy of death, not only do the things, but have a complacency with those who practice them.

"**Full.**" Different Greek from "**filled.**" *Stuffed* or *gorged* would be the figure literally, the adjective being from the verb *to eat*. "**As persons who.**" The apostle sums up at convenient intervals by this word οἵτινες (see v. 25). In each case it covers the cream of their iniquity. "**Close acquaintance ;**" again the word ἐπιγνώσις (see v. 28). "**Making right.**" We will waive our comment upon this till the next chapter (vs. 13, 26). It is a very important word. It is not God who makes these things "**worthy of death.**" They are so in themselves. Therefore "**since**" is the meaning of ὅτι, not "*that*" (E. V. & Re.). "**God's mannner** *of making things right*" is, to give men what they deserve, not to create the feature of ill-desert. "*When they had a close acquaintance.*" How real this is, can be seen in bloody sacrifices. The lost have more thought of terror sometimes than the saved. Nevertheless, with this agony upon them, they not only commit atrocities, but, what is strangest of all (συνευδοκοῦσιν), have a sort of "**complacency**" in them, along "**with those who practice them.**"

CHAPTER II.

1. **Wherefore thou art inexcusable, O man, whosoever thou art who judgest, for wherein thou judgest another, thou condemnest thyself; for thou that judgest practicest the same things ; 2. And we know that the judgment of God is according to truth upon them who practice such things.**

"**Whosoever.**" A most inexplicable criticism has been always making the first chapter an address to the Gentiles, and the second to the Jews. It ruins every thing. In the first place there is not a tittle of text for it. From the very beginning Paul addresses Romans, and, as a class among the Romans, converted people or saints. Jews and Gentiles being both at Rome, and both among the converts, he addresses both of them; and, in fact, makes no discrimination, except that he uses both to illustrate his doctrine. In the first chapter he is describing, not Gentiles, but men, in the result, under the righteous judgment of heaven, of *keeping "back the truth in unrighteousness"* (v. 18). This was not the result to one class only, except as they had sinned more or longer in keeping back the truth. But Pompeii shows in that very age that it was the result to Gentiles, and the prophets showed that it was the result to Jews (Ps. 14 & 53; Is. 1: 4, 9, 21–23. Paul sketches *all* impenitence, and paints, what he would not charge upon all, but what all are on the highway to, sooner or later. He shows the gospel as a means of opening afresh the moral eye, and sin as a means of closing it; and of closing it more and more till it darkens into inexpressible transgression. That is his sole object. And in the second chapter he varies it by showing that wakefulness in condemning others, enhanced rather than mitigated iniquity. His teaching here is signal. He does not say, "**Thou who judgest another**," if thou "**practisest the same things, condomnest thyself.**" That of course. Just here in the epistle we must prepare ourselves for profounder depths. His doctrine is much stronger. His burden is that the gospel is the power of God for revealing moral excellence to men, that, in that moral light, they also may look and live. He holds this forth as that which must be the life of all men. If, therefore, a man refuses this, but still insists upon being a judge of others, Paul does not say that then, if he commits the same things he condemns himself, but, much more signally, that he will commit the same things; that sin is the same pest everywhere; that its deep reaches are the same; that its helplessness and incessant growth are universal; and that if a man imagines himself clean when he is unclean, he parts with still more of his excuse, and adds another to the score of his iniquity. We do not deny that Paul might have been thinking of Jews. Doubtless he was; and in the seventeenth verse he actually uses them for illustration. We do not question but that he may picture his worst Sodomitic practices from the heathen. If he did not, he was forgetting that heathenism was farther on toward damnation than what, till lately, had been the only religion in the world, viz., Judaism. We only say that Paul, speaking to Jews as well as Gentiles (see v. 7 ; 2 : 9, 10), did not specialize his drift, but used the one as well as the other for illustrating the consequences of *keeping back the truth in unrighteousness.*

"**According to truth.**" This of course merges all into one grand theatre of inspection. "According to thy fear so is thy wrath" (Ps. 90 : 11). Show me exactly God's "*fear*," that is, how much He is to be loved, and then show me exactly how far I have departed from this standard of "*truth*," and I will measure to the last ounce the weight upon me of the wrath of the Almighty.* A neighboring text does indeed say "*of the Jew first*" (v. 9), but that is only because the Jew is the more responsible. Show me the heart of a man, and I do not care for his hue, or his blood, or in what form he bends his knee, or in what tongue he utters wisdom. Those are terrible texts: "According to thy fear" (Ps. 90 : 11), and "*according to truth.*"

"*Against*" (E. V. and Re.). Better say "**upon**" (ἐπί.) God pities the condemned, and will say, " Friend " (Matt. 22 : 12), and " Son " (Lu. 16 : 25) in the very act of inflicting vengeance.

3. But canst thou be calculating upon this, O man who judgest those who practise such things and doest the same, that thou mayest escape the judgment of God? 4. Or despisest thou the riches of His goodness and forbearance and long suffering, not knowing that it is the goodness of God that is to lead thee to repentance?

---

* This point is finely illustrated in Prov. 15 : 11 (see author's Com. on Prov.) : " Hell and destruction are before the Lord, because also the hearts of the children of men." That is, hell will be measured in its severity by the heart in its corruption. The sinner who leaves the world with a certain measure of sin, will begin his perdition with pain and sin of a corresponding grade. No feature of this is lightened because the word is " *Sheol.*" The grave means Hell just as fittingly and just as often as death means ruin. They are corresponding physical emblems for eternal giving up to sin. (Prov. 5 : 5 ; 7 : 27 ; 9 : 18 ; 15 : 24 ; see Com. Prov.).

CHAPTER II.

"**Canst.**" The subjunctive certainly (see also "**mayest**" below) should have some distinctness. In Matt. 23 : 33, the E. V. translates the similar part of the verb, "How can ye escape the damnation of hell?" This will become very important in the ninth chapter (v. 15).

"**Judgest.**" This (see also v. 1) is κρίνω, like a "**judgment**" in court, not δοκιμάζω, *to make an estimate of*, as in the last chapter (v. 28).

"**Despisest.**" Man, looking upon Christ, and seeing the enormous sacrifice that God's "**goodness**" is making to save even a remnant, and then "**calculating**" that in some indifferent way he may "**escape**," does most insolently *despise* the "**forbearance**" and "**longsuffering**" and the terrible expedient of God in the ransom of our spirits. Where God is "*calculating*" so closely, what an infamy for men to be "*calculating*" to run the venture!

"**Not knowing.**" If we could mix the idea of not *considering* also, we would cover the Greek. "**That it is the goodness of God.**" That is, of this grandly pains-taking awfully soul-coveting Redeemer. "**That is to lead thee to repentance.**" This not simply ends the idea, but adds to it. Luther, splendid as was his service, did no little damage. If we open a Catholic book this sentence would be largely emphasized. If we open a Protestant book it is almost ignored. It is more striking below. The text, "*every man according to his deeds*" (v. 6) Protestants hardly notice. So, deeper still, "*by patient continuance in well doing*" (v. 7), or the sentence that follows, "*To every man that worketh good*" (v. 10); and then more particularly the summing up, "*For not the hearers of the law are righteous before God, but the doers of the law shall be made righteous*" (v. 13). These are not Protestant sentences; and the Romanists, in their "*perfect*" righteousness, destroy them as Catholic sentences. Let us be very careful as they occur in place. They all blend in the apostolic gospel. We are already getting the key. Salvation is a giving of life to a man by revealing to him in the gospel by the power of God the moral excellence of God, so that the man himself, through that moral vision, becomes personally a better man (Rom. 1 : 16, 17), which is the apostle's own hermeneutic for his teaching that "*The goodness of God is that which is to lead thee to repentance.*"

5. But through thy hardness and impenitent heart treasurest for thyself wrath in a day of wrath, and of a revelation of a righteous judgment of God?

This is the rest of the question. "**Through;**" a meaning for κατά that is remarked upon earlier: "*through flesh;*" "*through a spirit of holiness*" (Rom. 1 : 3, 4). "**Hardness**" is that by which a man "*keeps back the truth*" (1 : 18) and therefore salvation. But, failing of life, he *accumulates* death, that is, adds to it. "**Treasurest**"—coin by coin of penalty. "**In a day of wrath.**" There is much significance in this word "*in.*" "*Against*" (F. V.) is not the preposition. Moreover the want of the article has its significance. It is not *the* "day of wrath;" else all the commentators might be right in saying that it was the "judgment." "*The great day of His wrath*" is of the Apocalypse (Rev. 6 : 17), though even there it does not mean the last day. The apostle has been speaking of "*wrath*" being "*revealed*" (1 : 18), and of the bad man's knowing this very thing, "**a righteous judgment of God**" (1 : 32); and of this "**revelation**" and of this knowing making him specially *inexcusable* (*ib.* v. 20), and becoming a great occasion of his being *given up* (*ib.* vs. 24, 28). And now, undoubtedly, the apostle is returning to this thought, and means *to-day* as the "*day of revelation;*" i. e. fixes upon *now* as of all others the time when the anger, being despised, is treasuring itself up in the transgressor.

6. Who will render to every one according to his works.

"**Render.**" Not necessarily *give back* (see Lu. 4 : 20), or *recompense* (12 : 17). If that idea enters, it must be from the context, and not from the preposition ἀπό. If we were to translate κατά "*through*" (as in 1 : 3, 4), we would not go far

CHAPTER II.

from the sense. If a man sins, God *gives* him his sinfulness as his most horrible perdition. If a man believes, God endows him with his faith, nursed and furthered into sight. In either case he rewards him "*through his works.*"

But as κατά oftenest means "**according to,**" let us give a wider significance to our comment. There are two species of award : one to the lost, and that we have already explained. There is a recompensing to every man "*according to his works.*" If there be any riddle, it must be on the salvation side in the judgment. And yet how *will* it be with the saved? Certainly, in a grave sense, according to their works. If I die good, I will be admitted into heaven. If you die better, you will be admitted higher. I need not break up the question, and expound how a man's "*works*" indicate his character, or go further and show that the sum of his "*works*" form his character : all this is understood. It is mere altering of the rhetoric, too, that all character must be of record, and that every act that shapes it must pass into the account. All this is obvious. But then the real question, What do I mean by character? brings up the solecism at once. When I speak even of Paul's character, I mean bad character. When I speak of any saintly works, I mean evil works. How reward me if every imagination and thought of mine is only evil, and that continually? Let us draw close to the apostle. With the finally lost man, judgment will be simple. " Every transgression and disobedience shall receive a just recompense of reward " (Heb. 2 : 2). But with the saved man it will be peculiar and gracious. Some saved men have had more sins than some lost men. And how could heaven be according to our works, when our works have been shameful, and nothing but sin has marked our acceptance with the Father? The key is a mode of speaking which is rife in our present epistle. A man is "*righteous*" when he is less sinful. The clue is found in the facts. A man is pardoned when he is touched with grace ; and grace is of this very nature : it is amendatory, but not perfect. The sinner is always worse ; the christian is always better. The better man is the righteous man in Bible language. "Wherefore, holy brethren" (Heb. 3 : 1), is an address, not to the holy, but to the sinful. It is in the measure in which they are less sinful that they are called holy. And as each act that is less sinful, makes the sinful saint by promise better, that tells the whole story. God keeps his books practically upon our hearts ; and our acts, though sinful each one, if they be less sinful, are kept as our account ; and we shall be rewarded thus intelligibly "*according to* (our) *works.*"

Rewardableness, which the scriptures undoubtedly speak of (Mar. 9 : 41 ; 1 Cor. 3 : 8 ; Heb. 11 : 6 ; Rev. 11 : 18 ; 22 : 12), the Romanists have treated under the name of "*merit,*" laboring to efface the mischief by two sorts of *merit,* one like the guilt of the wicked strictly according to law, or, as of Adam, should he have continued innocent, and the other, *not* of *condignity,* as they call this, but of *congruity,* that is grace of the Almighty leading to a certain measure of "*works,*" and regulating thereby, as what He calls a "reward" (Matt. 5 : 12), the distinctions of glory in that world that we are to meet hereafter.

The misery of the Catholic is that he confounds the two, and makes the merit of the saint too dangerously perfect.

7. To those who through patience in well doing seek for glory and honor and incorruption, eternal life.

"**Through;**" not "*according to*" or "*by*" (E. V. and Re., see 1 : 3, 4). "**Patience;**" the only virtue that actually *pledges* pardon. Christ says that it gets possession for us of our souls ; for that is His language, "In your patience get possession of your souls" (Lu. 21 : 19). "Ye have need of patience, that, having done the will of God, ye may receive the promise" (Heb. 10 : 36). Unless we are confirmed (στηρίζω) by perseverance (Acts 16 : 5 ; 1 Thess. 3 : 13), there is no promise, after conversion, that we may not fall (Heb. 6 : 4 etc.; 10 : 26–38). The verb that answers to ὑπομονή (patience), is employed in the only promise :—" He that endureth (ὑπομένω) to the end, the same shall be saved" (Matt. 10 : 22). "**Incorruption;**" not "immortality" (E. V.). Adam and Lucifer had neither of them "*incorruption,*" even when they were perfectly holy : nor have we, for we may possibly fall ; but, "*through patience in well-doing,*" we may "*seek for*" it, and there is reason to believe we may attain it, even in the present life.

8. **But to them who are selfishly in opposition, and do not obey the truth, but obey unrighteousness, anger and wrath, 9. Distress and anguish, upon every soul of man that works evil, both of the Jew first, and also of the Greek.**

•**"Selfishly in opposition."** Not from ἔρις strife, but from ἐριθεύω, *to hire out, to act the hireling*. It came then to mean to *be mercenary*, and, finally, to *be of a party:* the implication being that it was for gain, or at least for selfish opinion's sake. Ἔρις is twice used in the same text with ἐριθεία (2 Cor. 12 : 20 ; Gal. 5: 20). **"Do not obey the truth;"** rather *keep it back* as we have seen (Rom. 1 : 18). **But obey unrighteousness;** how singularly real ! Men impatient of Christ, will absolutely *slave* for Satan. "*Truth,*" endlessly cavilled at, might look with envy at the weight which the sceptic will give to errors. **"Jew first;"** most righteously, for being most responsible for wickedness.

10. **But glory and honor and peace to every one who works good, both to the Jew first, and also to the Greek ; 11. For there is no respect of persons with God.**

11. **"For."** This is rather an odd sequel for the expression **"to the Jew first."** **"No respect, etc.,"** because, "*to the Jew first!*" The remedy is to hold the "*for*" as belonging to the whole sentence. "*No respect etc.,*" because, indiscriminately of race, there is **"glory and honor and peace to every one who works good."** But then, on this very rule, "*to the Jew first,*" because, while "*indignation and wrath* (shall be) *to the Jew first,*" because "*he that knew* shall be beaten with many stripes" (Lu. 12 : 47), so "*glory*" shall be "*to the Jew first,*" because what is hereditary in faithfulness breeds the strongest christians. Bible readers will be "*first*" in hell, but, in reward of faithfulness, "*first*" in heaven. Bushmen lost will be beaten with few stripes ; but Bushmen saved, *tantis pro tantis,* shall have little "*glory.*" In the world to come (as a general rule at least) the highest and the lowest

will be those who stood the highest in hereditary knowledge.

12. For as many as sinned without law, shall also perish without law; and as many as sinned under law, shall be judged by law.

"**For.**" The apostle now gives his most philosophic arguing. "*God is no respecter of persons*" because he will judge every man according to the light he has. "Sin is not imputed where there is no law" (5 : 13); but this is only an imaginary case. Idiots and infants might come up to it. But the lowest Bushman has "*law;*" otherwise there could be no punishment. When Paul writes "**without law,**" he is writing Orientally. The Bible is full of such exaggeration. When Christ says, "Ye had not had sin" (Jo. 15 : 22), He means, Ye had not had near so much sin. When Paul says, "Sent me not to baptize"(1 Cor. 1 : 17), he meant, chiefly, or not near so much. And so in the present text. All the laws of the Jews were helpful and precious, and hence, of course, increased their responsibility. Therefore we are simply taught, the more law the more punishment. The crazy notion that because "thou hast taught in our streets," therefore, of all reasons in the world, "Lord, Lord, open unto us" (Matt. 25: 11), meets here a signal refutation. The "*law*" we did not have we will not "**perish**" for, and when that "*law*" contains the gospel, as the whole "*law*" from Sinai undoubtedly did, we will not "*perish*" in that sin which Christ talks of as though it swallowed all other sin (Jo. 15 : 22), if we were without the gospel; but only in that "*law*" we had, viz., that γνωστὸν θεοῦ which is the appanage of every sinner (1 : 19).

13. For not the hearers of law shall be righteous before God, but the doers of law shall be made righteous.

"**For.**" The apostle very naturally goes on to reason, If any other rule prevailed, a man might get to heaven by *hearing law* instead of *doing* it. He illustrates by the case of the Jew. He is about to press that case (v. 17). For though the epistle is catholic, and addressed to cosmopolitan saints, he seizes upon Jews as a very extreme illustration. "*If thou*

CHAPTER II.

art called a Jew" (v. 17). As though he would say, Take the worst case. Undoubtedly he was glad to reach that nation, for the Rabbins snared them fatally. No Jew, they taught, if circumcised, would ever perish. Of course he would benefit that nation. But dialectically they were his mere case in point. He would show the folly of false confidences, and the Jew, as betrayed into them most, he could hardly leave out in such reasoning. "**Righteous;**" in the way we are about to show. "*Righteous* **before God.**" This is wonderfully frequent throughout the Bible. Hezekiah was righteous before God (2 Ki. 20 : 3). So was Zacharias (Lu. 1 : 6). So was Elizabeth. Righteous before men a man may be, and be very unrighteous. The Jews were in that condition. "*Before*" anybody means in his sight, or in his opinion. "The earth was corrupt before God." It is a Hebraism, and Paul devotes his logic to show how mortal man can be made really just, or, to use his own idiom, how the sinner can be "**made righteous** *before God.*" "**Made righteous.**" This is a key to the whole epistle. It is Paul's critical expression; and yet, perhaps, it would not be, if men had not warped it since the days of Luther. Δικαιόω, let us distinctly think, was a plain word to the eye of a Greek; and not a foreign word. It was bred in the language itself. Moreover it was not changed by the Hebrew; for the Hebrew equivalent, as more simple, was quite direct. The Hebrew was the Hiphil of the verb to be righteous, and of course meant to make righteous; and the Greek was a verb in οω, from an adjective in ος. What that means all linguists will know. Ἀξιόω means to make ἄξιος. Νεκρόω means to make νεκρός. So δικαιόω in the present instance, means to make δίκαιος (or "*righteous*"). Now there is one difficulty, and that can be easily explained. Who is ever to "*make*" anybody "*righteous?*" The word hence is rarely used in the classics, and ἁγιάζω (to *sanctify*) is never used at all. Therefore, in scripture, neither could be used, except in a very accommodated sense.

Nevertheless, as both are used, and δικαιόω also in the classics, it offers itself to the same literary dissection as any other predicate. And, at the very outset, among many other meanings, it offers two that are just the opposite. How are we ever to decide? Δικαιόω to *hold righteous* (Hdt. 1 : 89, 133), and δικαιόω to *condemn* (Thuc. 3 : 40) are notorious in classic learning. The same word in the Greek eye is to mean one thing here, and flat the opposite over yonder. What are we to do? Why things like this are really keys to unlock, not facts to embarrass, linguistic difficulties. They tell a story, just as men do who are comrades on the opposite sides of an impassable arm of the sea. We make an inference at once— One or the other forded where the stream was near its spring. So now of δικαιόω. It is foolish in Robinson, and worse, classically, in Donnegan, to come down the stream and choose a meaning as of the fountain head, which makes it necessary to suppose that just the opposite is across the gulf, and the ford practically impossible. Such has been a dreadful habit of interpreters. Instead of saying δικαιόω originally meant to *count righteous* (see Robinson), is it not better to go high up the stream, and ask, What does δίκη mean? insisting upon a traceable signification? Then δίκαιος, which is next below, would be the adjective, evidently, from the noun δίκη. Then δικαιόω would be the verb, creative of the condition implied in the adjective. Just as ἀξιόω means to make ἄξιος, so δικαιόω would naturally mean to make δίκαιος, whatever the adjective from δίκη would naturally imply. Δικαίωμα would then come in as the resulting effect, and δικαίωσις as the substantive act, and δικαιοσύνη not as the same as δίκη, but as the condition of the man or the thing that possessed the δίκη. This now is as smooth a laying down as of any possible tracings of sense, marred only by the fact of the horrible scarcity of subjects; for in heathen history where was the enrighteouser? and, either in church or temple, where was the instance of the enrighteousment in any actual sense of one being, in this world, by another?

Still, to see how to *count righteous*, when it came to that, could change in the end into *condemn*, let us trace the thing fairly down by beginning at the head. What does δίκη mean?

Originally, every body agrees, it meant *custom*. Δίκαιος would then mean *customary* ; and, sure enough, we read in Homer of persons (δικαίους) "observant of custom" (Od. 3 : 52). But as what is *customary* among a settled people must, for mere State preservation, be principally *right*, δίκη as the *right* soon got a final footing. And let us disabuse it of all mixtures. It meant *right in esse.* There is no doubt about that. It was used to mean the intrinsically noble, morally excellent, or *semel ipso* virtuous or divinely right thing. Δίκαιος, now, meant simply the adjective for that, and, hurrying on to our conclusion, δικαιόω meant simply to make a man or a thing after the character of that adjective. The world would get back to that sense after exiles under a thousand Luthers.

But now, the necessary variations. Δίκη undoubtedly meant *the right*. Δίκαιος meant *right* in the adjective sense, and could be applied either to persons or things. Among persons God can receive the title without perplexing us, for he is "*righteous*" just as the sky is blue, or the ocean beautiful. Gabriel and Christ are unequivocally *right*. But man is not. And we are to consider the variance by which we call him so. And the grandest simplifier is to look at other words. How is a man "clean" (Jo. 15 : 3)? Why do we call him " holy " (Mar. 6 : 20)? This is a helpful part of our study ; for we have nothing to do but to press that question. Why should we go off into sophisms and say, to *make righteous* means to *count righteous*, unless we say, to make holy means to count holy? We are "*quickened*." Precious little ! *Set free*. Alas, alas ! There are plenty of words in which a whole story is spared the reader. Unless we are willing to say *counted clean* wherever that word is to appear, we have no right to say *counted righteous;* for the motives of the two things are precisely similar, and either would do harm, as tending to obscure incipient sanctification. A *righteous man*, therefore, is called a *righteous man* in scripture when he is less sinful by the grace of his Redeemer, and when that young righteousness, which is really not righteousness at all (just as it is not holiness), is the earnest of more and better daily and in the life to come.

So much for δίκαιος. Now for δικαιόω. It means to *make right*. First, as to *things*. A man stabs a man. A chief autocrat, looking on, says, I'll make that right. How can he? Why, of course, by punishing. This is the way the comrade crossed the water. He crossed it high up. To *justify* a man, and to *condemn* a man, would come strangely out of the same word, if the word primarily meant *count righteous* (Robinson); but let it mean to *make right* (Liddell), and the divergence easily occurs. If I see a man robbing a cripple, and say, I'll make him all right, or see a man nobly defending him, and say, I'll make *him* all right, my meanings are directly opposite; and yet they are not opposite at all. I mean in either case I'll see the thing righted; and in Scotland justifying a man means to hang him (see Liddell).

There is no reason, therefore, why δικαιόω should not be translated to *make righteous*. If it is said, Men are not *righteous*, I answer, Neither are men *holy*. Unless you are willing, therefore, to abandon *sanctifying* or *making holy*, and *cleansing* and *setting free*, articulately you are just as reasonable when you say "*made righteous.*" If you say, Justifying is used putatively, I say, So is sanctifying. "The unbelieving wife is sanctified by the husband" (1 Cor. 7 : 14). If you say, Undoubtedly the one is used of pronouncing or declaring righteous; I say, So is *cleansing*. The priest, upon certain marks, was to *cleanse* the leper, and upon certain other marks, was to *foul* him (Lev. 13: 3-13), which King James' men very properly translated to "pronounce clean" (Lev. 13 : 13), or to pronounce unclean (*ib.* 5 : 3), according to the state of the leper. But if, keen for the Lutheran justification (which, let me remark here had no syllable to teach it for fifteen centuries*), you say, God is said to be justified (Lu. 7 : 29)—

---

* This is a very remarkable fact. Luther has been celebrated above other achievements of his history for his doctrine of Justification by Faith. Luther invented it. There is not a line of it in the world before him. Augustine, whom the modern world makes foremost in the faith, gives the natural sense to justification. "Who has wrought righteousness in a man, but He who justifies the ungodly; that is, by His grace makes a righteous and men are said to be justified who are notoriously wicked (Is. 5 : 23), I say, Such usages are in every language. I murder my victim if I do it in buskins on a stage. I crush my opponent, when he is laughing at me, and taking notes to crush me immediately afterward. Men *justify God* (E. V. Lu. 7 : 29) just as we sanctify Him, or pray, " Sanctified be Thy name." And men make the wicked righteous (Is. 5 : 23) when they pretend to, or, to slide off into more unusual language, just as they "take away the righteousness of the righteous from him " (Is. 5 : 23).

Men are sadly in error when they speak of their own doctrine as purely *forensic*. It is not only not forensic, but no counterpart of any word spoken among men. It is a favorite assertion that δικαιόω in this constrained sense, has the enormous predominance of approved usage. It is time to take note of the fact that it has no usage at all, unless we make an exception to this in the usage of these very men themselves.

A *forensic* justifying is a pronunciation by a judge that a man, because he is not guilty, is actually righteous. A jury, from this nice distinction in men's minds, do not " make " a verdict, but " find " it. When I justify God, I find Him righteous actually. When I justify the wicked, I assert the same thing. When wisdom is justified, she is found righteous ; and when the publican is more justified, he is subjectively a better man than the hollow-brained Pharisee who is arraigned against him. These are all subjective findings, or makings out, while, heaven-wide from this, the Lutheran idea is factitious and nothing of the kind. **" The hearers of law," therefore, " are not righteous before God ; but the doers of law shall be made righteous."** That is, sweeping all the contents of law into

---

man of an impious man ? " (Ps. 118, vol. 8). " Justification here is imperfect in us " (vol. 5 , p. 867). " When our hope shall be completed, then also our justification shall be completed" (vol. 5, p. 790). Chrysostom, Anselm, Jerome, Aquinas, Justin, and all the Apostolic Fathers, made justification mean sanctification, with none other than a picturesque or mere illustrative distinction. They knew no other. Why are we not informed of this in the History chairs of our seminaries ?

one, (and that will include the "obedience of faith," 1 : 5 ; 16 : 26, as well as every other obedience), the *hearing* of such a law, instead of making a man more righteous, may make him more wicked ; but the *doing* of it is itself righteousness. If it were perfect it would be righteousness like God's. It may be very imperfect, and yet "exceed the righteousness of the scribes and Pharisees ; " and if it is a righteousness risen at all above the condition of growing worse, it is a saving righteousness, just as fitly as there can be a saving repentance (Acts 3 : 19) ; and it is a conversion and a rising from the dead (Jo. 5 : 25), and a new life (6 : 4), and as of a clean heart, (Ps. 73 : 1), and of that regenerating and sanctifying power which begets a moral change, and shows itself in ever increasing righteousness.

14. For when it may happen that Gentiles who have not law, do by nature the things of the law, such men, having not law, are a law unto themselves, 15. Being persons who exhibit within the work of the law written in their hearts, their consciousness agreeing in the testimony, and their reasonings making accusation or excuse the one to the other

"**For.**" He gives now the reason why it is "*the doers of law* (that) *shall be made righteous* " (3: 13). The parenthesis into which these texts are thrown (E. V.), is for purposes of special pleading. The words are to be understood as they stand. Nothing could be more simple naturally. "**When.**" This is a very contingent *when*. Ὅταν means *when rarely*, or *when possibly*, or "**when it may happen that.**" "**Gentiles.**" Ὅταν indicates that he is not speaking of all Gentiles, or of many Gentiles. The article is left off. "**Who have not law:** " in the sense before explained (v. 12) of those who had little "*law ;* " like as those of whom Christ speaks as having "no sin " (Jo. 15 : 22). "**Do by nature.**" That does not mean, as in our theological language, " do in their state by nature." The word occurs but fourteen times in all the Testament ; sometimes of beasts ; rarely of character ; once of God ; and never so as to be of service critically. In fact our technical adjective (*natural*), so far as the New Testament is concerned, comes from ψυχή (1 Cor. 2 : 14, 44-46) oftener than from φύσις.

Men are said to be Jews by nature (Gal. 2 : 15) ; surely not "in their natural state." And so "*when Gentiles who have not law, do by nature* **the things of the law,**" they do them in the circumstances of their birth (φίω) and not in the more artificial circumstances of having heard "*the law.*"

"**The things of the law** "; that is, the gospel, along with all the other "*things.*" The most dreadful law is the gospel, the most cruel infinitely to them that disobey (Matt. 21 : 44 ; Jo. 16 : 9). Sinai thundered that with its most terrible denunciations. We must either imagine that it was mocking Israel, or else, when it said, Do this and thou shalt live, we must remember how much of Sinai revealed a Redeemer. It reeked with sacrifices and bloody rites. And it gendered to bondage, not because those that followed its teaching were not saved ; thousands were saved ; but because the " old covenant," which it exhibited, had to become a " new covenant," and to be " written in ;" that is, the revelation made on Sinai had to be in-wrought. What Moses said with a veil upon his face, Christ had to say, having stripped off the veil ; He being "the prophet like Moses," but turning the outward into the inward, taking the old covenant and turning it into a " new covenant," simply by having it submitted to, that is, by writing it on the heart (Jer. 31 : 33). Now what do we want of Christ precisely ? That will explain our text. (1) First, all His sacrifice is necessary ; and that more (and more positively) than we can speak of or imagine. Without the shedding of blood there can be no remission (Heb. 9 : 22). But then the whole world has that. Why then might not all heathen be saved ? Because, (2) second, He must convert. It lies with Christ not simply to redeem but to convert the sinner. Why then may He not convert the heathen ? Because, (3) thirdly, He requires the truth, and this of course ranges with the passage where " the power of God unto salvation " is declared to be the uttered " gospel."

So much is settled.

But now a question remains which is quite unsettled,—How much truth ? (1) Ransom is indispensable. (2) Conversion is of vital force. But these are provided by the Redeemer. The question is (4) How much truth must be provided? And there is much in the word of God to lower rather than to heighten this demand for the saving of the sinner.

Hardly has Paul asked "How shall they hear without a preacher?" before he thunders forth, "But I say, Have they not heard?" (10 : 18), and then plunges into that great answer,—"Their sound has gone out into all the world" (Ps. 19 : 4). This was an old teaching (Col. 1 : 6, 23). To these very Romans he has supported our text by a previous position :— "For that which was known of God is manifest in them ; for God made the manifestation" (1 : 19); and then he says, "They kept back the truth" (1 : 18). Now we have only to ask, Does that truth, thus wilfully kept back, never assert itself? We must be carefully understood. (1) Redemption is necessary ; but that is a work done. (2) Regeneration is just as vital ; and that too must be by the power of the Redeemer, (Jo. 5 : 21). (3) And he must regenerate by the truth (1 Pet. 1 : 23), at least we know of no other method. (4) But query, how much truth? Is not that really the only point in the difficulty? The heathen has vast truth, and it has been shed upon him by revelation. He knows of God. He knows of grace. He knows of sacrifice. He has a distant shadow of pardon and redemption. He has images of prayer. How much more had Abraham? (Gen. 15 : 8). Yea, Peter? (Matt. 26 : 56). When John verily thought that he might be an *attaché* to the throne, how much more had Salome? (Matt. 20 : 21). No hint can be gathered that Cornelius had knowledge of Christ, and he is a snare unless he can be converted without it. We do not doubt that "*the gospel is the power of God*" (Rom. 1 : 16), for that we have just been interpreting ; but query, how much gospel? Undoubtedly a man is saved who is better morally, for that is the repentance with which the Bible rings. The question is only, then, Were these men better? and with all that remains of the text we would say, Decidedly they were.

"**May.**" Notice the subjunctive. The thing imagined to

"**come to pass**" might come so rarely. Paul is urging the gospel, and would not be likely to exaggerate our chance without it. But it was of his mind to show that hearing was not doing; and it made that more intense to intimate that doing might sometimes be without hearing, that is without so much hearing as the Jews might boast of in "*the oracles of God*" (3 : 2). "**Such men.**" There is a change to the masculine. "**As persons.**" We have remarked on οἵτινες before (1 : 32). "**Exhibit within.**" The ἐν should have its emphasis. "**The Law;**" with the article. "**The work of the law.**" Put all these peculiarities together. Not "*law*" in its vaguer generality, but "*the law*," just as though they had heard the noblest teaching of the Law-giver. Not law, in theory espoused, but practically, "*the work of the law*." And not that "*work*" prescribed by "*the law*," doctrinally submitted to, but *exhibited within*; and definitely, to crown the representation, "**written in their hearts,**" a clause impossible to satisfy, without the idea of inward conversion (see Prov. 3 : 3 ; 2 Cor. 3 : 2, 3 ; Heb. 8 : 10 ; 10 : 16). "**Consciousness.**" Not "*conscience*" (E. V.). When Paul says, "I have lived in all good conscience before God until this day" (E. V. Acts 23 : 1), he was infinitely far from claiming a good moral sense. Συνείδησις had not become so definite. When Paul said he had "a good consciousness," he meant that he was sincere. When he directed people "to keep a consciousness void of offence," he was bidding them be honest. And Peter, when he says that "baptism" (which is his name for conversion, just as "circumcision" is, a few sentences below, vs. 28, 29) is "not the putting away of the filth of the flesh," means that it is, like "*righteousness*" here with Paul, a very imperfect cleansing. "Putting away the filth of the flesh" means perfectness, not at all bodily washing. And Peter says, Baptism (conversion) does not pretend to that, but is "the inquiry of a good consciousness after God" (1 Pet. 3 : 21).

"*Consciousness,*" therefore, in the present text, means their honest actual conviction. These convictions hold court, so the text proceeds to fancy, and make "**accusation or excuse the one to the other.**"

But when? Before we add a syllable, any usual reader would say, Undoubtedly in this world. But let us proceed.

16. In a day when God judges the hidden things of the men through my gospel by Jesus Christ.

"**In a day.**" That means any day in which the "**gospel,**" which in a few sporadic cases men have been saved without, happens to reach "**the men.**" Take Peter. He was a saved man before the scene on the Sea of Tiberias (Matt 4 : 20). Yet what did he know of the "*gospel?*" Why, afterwards, months and years, he imagined it an earthly kingdom ! We ought not to mock the facts by supposing that he was an intelligent believer. Yet he was a Christian. So was John. So was Mary. So, afterward, was Cornelius. Now, suppose "*a day*" when some Philip mounts into the chariot and explains the way of God more perfectly. What is the result ? Why, all which this beautiful text expresses. First, it is "*a day*;" not "*the day*" (E. V.). King James took this translation from a text that had not the article. And, though some MSS. supply one, the authorities are very balanced (see Alford) ; and the reason for copying one in might easily be imagined in the universal haste to write upon the thought of the apostle as though he were speaking of the Day of Judgment. But examine him further. Not only is the *textus receptus* "*a day*," but it joins a sentence which must be plainly understood of this world. The E. V. prefixes a long parenthesis (vs. 13–15), but it is plainly to defeat the inference of which we speak. And not only so, but the other terms, "**the hidden things,**" for example, and the word "*judge*" exactly suit the facts with a man like Cornelius. Let us bring his case into the question. "There was a certain man in Cæsarea called Cornelius, a centurion of the band called the Italian band." There is not the slightest evidence that this heathen captain, landing from Rome, had ever dreamed of the Nazarene. In an inspired book, would not the opposite have been noted ? He was just such a man as that Peter shrank from seeing him ; and it took a miracle to overcome the prejudice. And yet he was "devout, and one that feared God, gave much alms to the people, and prayed to God always." Now, what would naturally happen upon Peter's visit? First, there would be a "*judgment*," and let us trace the use of that word in other sentences. See just below in the present chapter : " Shall not the uncircumcision, if it fulfil the law, judge thee, who, with the letter and circumcision art a transgressor of the law ?" As though a man should say, Does not this peasant with his splendid taste, though he has never seen an easel in his life, judge thee who, an idiot in taste, hast nevertheless been painting nearly all thy days ? And then a more marked case : " But if all prophesy, and there come in one that believeth not, he is convinced of all, he is judged of all : and thus are **the hidden things** of his heart made manifest " (1 Cor. 15 : 25). Here we are helped forward to this second expression. Now, to sum all up. What does Cornelius encounter when he encounters the gospel? If he has "*hidden things*" of righteousness, as the account assures us he had, or, as Peter expresses it, "the hidden man of the heart " (1 Pet. 3 : 4), and not " the hidden things of shame " (2 Cor. 4 : 2), or "the hidden things of darkness " (1 Cor. 4 : 5), then, **"by Jesus Christ** *through the gospel*" his "*hidden things*" will be *judged;* that is, that dawning " *righteousness*," which is neither law-satisfying righteousness, nor down-tending, increasing, impenitent wickedness, will be found out or get a *judgment*, and will be found to have been made possible by the redemption of Christ, wrought by His grace, and in this way "*judged*" joyfully when it meets " *the gospel.*" This is a grand text, incapable of any allusion to the Last Day; illustrating as the γάρ implies, how, even in extreme cases, " *the doers of the law will be made righteous*," (v. 13) ; and illustrating that grand fact, that though a man may get repentance very rarely without a pretty extensive knowledge of Christ, yet he may and does, sometimes with very little, and *that if he does, no matter how he gets it, he has been born again ;* that is, if any man becomes a better man, when all impenitent men steadily grow worse, he has in some way got hold of God, probably like Cornelius, by praying to God daily ; and how little " *law* " this requires no mortal knows. If, like Sinai, it includes the gospel, a man, like Abraham, may have but little "*law*," and yet emerge as the very "father of believers."

"**But if.**" We need say nothing of the various reading here, Ἴδε (E.V.). Paul seems to have written εἰδὲ.

17. **But if thou art by name a Jew, and restest upon law, and boastest thyself in God, 18. And understandest the will, and judgest between things that differ, being instructed out of the law, 19. And art confident about thyself that thou art a guide of the blind, a light of them who are in darkness, 20. A corrector of the foolish, a teacher of babes, having the forming of the knowledge and of the truth in the law, 21. Then, the teacher of others, teachest thou not thyself? the preacher that there must be no thieving, dost thou thieve? 22. Thou who sayest that there must be no adultery, dost thou commit adultery? thou who hast disgust for idols, dost thou strip temples? 23. Being a man who boastest thyself in law, by the transgressing of the law dishonorest thou God? 24. For the name of God is blasphemed among the Gentiles because of you, just as it has been written.**

"**But.**" This apostolic "*but*" means to say, If, in addition to *judging* (v. 1), and in divers manners holding thyself above the sweep of the general condemnation, thou hast, either by birth or proselytism, the "**name**" of "**a Jew**," then pretensions, if false, are naturally more insidious, for "**thou restest**" and "**boastest**" and "**art confident**" in divers ways which he describes. He begs to know if **teaching** does not imply *doing* (v. 21), even more than *hearing* does (v. 13). The whole argument is cumulative, but does not depart from being general. If he mentions the "*Jew*," he accomplishes side purposes, of course, but not for an instant by abandoning his thread. The Jew is his intense illustration; and in the hub of the universe, which was then Rome, he wishes to start upon his gospel with "all the world guilty before God" (3 : 19). "**Understandest the will.**" If Paul meant "*of God*" (see E. V. & Re.), why did he not say so? If a man thinks he should interpolate "*his*" (E. V. & Re.) into the English, why was it absent from the Greek? We know very little of the psychology of Paul, but if he meant exactly what he has written, and meant to attribute to the Rabbis theoretic teachings about "*will*" (and Paul knew, for he had sat at their feet), it would be a fine prelude to what immediately succeeds; for, discussing the proper choices of "*the will*," that is, **judging between things that differ**, was a great stroke in the casuistry of Israel. 'Thou who makest the nicest moral distinctions for the direction of the will, why dost thou flout them by all iniquity?' "**Art by name.**" The verb means to *add a name;* and that is exactly what Paul does. He adds the consideration of being a Jew to others previously stated. But unfortunately for this nicety of speech, the word means simply to *name* in other places (LXX. Gen. 4 : 17, 26). "**Law**" and "**the law**" are distinctions strictly kept up throughout the passage. "**Forming.**" Μόρφωσις is not the same as μορφή. Δικαίωσις (5 : 18) is not the same as δικαίωμα (5 : 16, 18). Δικαίωσις means *the act of making righteous.* So μόρφωσις means the "*forming*" or *throwing into form.* That the Jews had the "*form*" of "**knowledge**" was true. But that they undertook the "*forming*" of it by **teaching and correcting** opens them still more to the attack of the apostle. "**The** *knowledge* **and the truth.**" We must observe the article. "**In the law.**" All "*knowledge*" and all "*truth*" was "*in the law*," even, as we have seen, "*the knowledge*" of the gospel. The scribes and Pharisees sat in Moses' seat. If they could inwardly have "**instructed out of the law,**" they would have saved every body. But they could only accomplish the μόρφωσις. They could *form* the truth, and throw it into theory. And Paul is about to show them (v. 28) that "he is not a Jew who is one ἐν τῷ φανερῷ (that is, in a way that can be exhibited in speech); for he has just been saying (v. 27) that there were those **who, along with the letter and circumcision, were transgressors of law**; but that he is a Jew who is one ἐν τῷ κρυπτῷ (see "*the hidden things*" spoken of above, v. 16), "**and circumcision is of the heart, in spirit, not in letter** (not in any way that men could "*form*" by instructing in the truth), **whose praise is not of men, but of God.**"

"**Strip temples.**" We know nothing about this. Σύλη was by the law of reprisals, and in maritime language was the forfeiture of a ship. Ἱερόσυλοι were those who took some such step against temples; but how, or why, or for what uses, we are utterly uninformed. "**Correctors of the foolish**" would naturally have "**the name of God blasphemed**" if they stripped one sanctuary to adorn another.

25. For circumcision indeed profits if thou dost observe law; but if thou be a transgressor of law, thy circumcision has become uncircumcision.

Paul has a wholesome horror of undervaluing Judaism. Sixty years before it was the only religion. In the chapter below he is to discuss that subject: "What advantage hath the Jew? and what profit is there of circumcision?" (v. 1). He had already announced the gospel as being to "the Jew first and also to the Greek" (1: 16). And though he had observed the same order of priority for the curses of the gospel (v. 9), he had been very careful to repeat it as to the blessings (v. 10). There is no mystery. The trained man is most cursed, and, in the other event, most blessed. In the world, at the time, most were Jews who were of the number of the disciples. Peter swept three thousand of them into an acquaintance with the Redeemer. At the same time they were the most cursed. God forbid that we should disparage training. It is the recruiting school of the Redeemer. But God forbid that we should deny that Daniel Webster is more responsible than Sin Fong, and must do better than mere "*forming the truth*" (v. 20), or else perish with a two-fold penalty. "**Thy circumcision.**" Just like thy "baptism" (6: 4; Heb. 6: 2). These words became beautifully inclusive (Col. 2: 11; 1 Pet. 3: 21). "**Has become uncircumcision;**" and, as we have seen, the most hideous form of it.

26. If, therefore, the uncircumcision observe the righteous-making provisions of the law, shall not his uncircumcision be reckoned for circumcision? 27. And shall not the uncircumcision, which is by nature, if it fulfil the law, judge thee who, along with the letter and circumcision, art a transgressor of law? 28. For not one who is so in what

is apparent, is a Jew, nor is that which is so in what is apparent in the flesh, circumcision. 29. But one who is so in what is hidden is a Jew, and circumcision is of the heart, in spirit, not in letter, whose praise is not from men but from God.

"**The uncircumcision;**" all those who have not had the advantages of the Jew (Rom. 3 : 1 etc). "**Righteous-making provisions.**" Δικαίωμα does not mean "*righteousness*," but any "provision" or ordinance that was to *make righteous* either a person or an act. Let us repeat the tracing of our meanings. Δίκη means *what is right*. Δίκαιος means *right*, and is applied to persons or to things. The English usage translates it "*righteous*" when applied to persons, and hence, not necessarily, but often, when applied to acts. "Righteousness" (δικαιοσύνη) is the noun from this adjective. Δικαίωσις is the noun for making either a man or thing *right* or *righteous*. And δικαίωμα is the thing or act or process gone through with to that regard. There were two covenants, one "the old covenant" which *enjoined* the gospel and all other ordinances of the law (Heb. 8 : 9), and the other, "the new covenant" which added to this, effectual or actual grace. One wrote out the law and thundered it from Sinai, gospel and all, and it was "*righteous-making*" in this, that the soul that hearkened would live thereby (Deut. 11 : 27). Moses constantly said so, (Lev. 18 : 5); and millions did live, because the "new covenant" was active also in that day. "The old covenant" gendered to bondage (Gal. 4 : 24) because, taking one of its commands, for example, "Believe on the Lord Jesus Christ and thou shalt be saved" (Acts 16 : 31), it was perfectly inoperative unless the new covenant came in with its operative grace. Still the old covenant was honest. Men would be saved if they would hearken and turn (Deut. 4 : 30, 31). And therefore, all through the Old Testament, δικαιώματα was a favorite word (LXX.) for "old covenant" demands. "Statutes" they are often translated. Still oftener, "ordinances." It will be seen that our Revisionists say "*ordinances*" here. Zecharias was represented as "in all the δικαιώμασι of the Lord blameless"

(Lu. 1: 6). Still the "*righteous-making*" idea should be kept. It was not a sure enough "*righteous-making.*" When Moses said, "This do and thou shalt live" (Lev. 18 : 5 ; Lu. 10 : 28), he was not, indeed, mocking the impenitent ; nor was he saying that they could "*do*" without grace, or that they would "*do*" perfectly or meritoriously *with* grace ; but he was declaring that all that was promised would be complied with ; that all that was necessary to life was thundered out of the mountain ; that the manna and the rod and the tables were summaries of the gospel ; that any who listened would be saved (and many who listened *were* saved) ; but that "the old covenant" must have the benefit of "the new covenant," and that these "*righteous-making*" demands should write them on the heart, that God might be our God, and we genuinely and ἐν τῳ κρυπτῳ, not "**in letter**" but "**in spirit**" (Jo. 4 : 23), His believing people. This is the mystery of "the two covenants," so hideously abused as to have given a name, and that a mistranslated one, to the older and younger parts of our inspired Bible. "**Be reckoned for;**" that is, *be* or *stand for*, just as Abraham's "faith" was actually "righteousness," that is, the germ or dawning of it (Matt. 17 : 20 ; 2 Cor. 5 : 7). "**Which is by nature**"(φύσις from φύω, see v. 14). "**If it fulfil the law ;**" that is, incipiently so, and with the earnest of better, as with any Christian. The word is not πληρόω, but τελειόω. Job was called (LXX.) τέλειος ("perfect") ; though poor Job was any thing but perfect. The meaning is, *reach its end*. The gospel may *reach its end* when it is any thing but perfect in the mind of the sinner. "**Judge thee.**" Paul has brought the case completely round. Now it is the despised Greek that "judgeth" (vs. 1–3), and that in this case rightfully, the contemptuous Pharisee. "**Along with the letter and circumcision.**" This is one of the known uses of διά. "*By*" (E. V.) is a mistranslation. "This is he who came by (E. V.) water and blood" (1 Jo. 5 : 6) means *with* it as a signal accompaniment. So "*by* (E. V.) prophecy" (see Comment. 1: 11 ; also 1 Tim. 4 : 14). "**In what is apparent.**" "*Outwardly*" (E. V. & Re.) is not enough. Ἐν γράμματι ("**in letter**") is more than *outward*. Paul has been admitting deep pretensions. Though I have all knowledge, he says in another place (1 Cor. 13 : 2). *Knowing the will, and judging things that differ, instructed out of the law*, having the "*forming of knowledge*," and being *teachers* and *preachers* and deep *readers* in religion, following "*the letter*" with the most painstaking hope, "*outwardly*" is too light an expression. They were Jews ἐν τῷ φανερῷ, and close up to that sense. We would better translate literally. They were Jews to *all* appearance, not only to other eyes, but *inwardly* (E. V. & Re.) to their own. And, therefore, Paul makes a much higher exaction. He is a Jew who is one **"in what is hidden"** (just the expression he uses of some heathen, see above, v. 16). Circumcision is not that which is **"in what is apparent in the flesh; but circumcision is of the heart"** (just as baptism is: see this often repeated— Deut. 10: 16; 30: 6; Acts 1 : 5), **"in spirit** (that is, in the God-part of man, Jo. 4: 23, 24, meaning his conscience), **not in letter"** (for "the letter killeth ;" yea, though " I have all knowledge I am nothing," 1 Cor. 13: 2) : **"whose;"** probably a neuter : "*circumcision*" is feminine, and Ἰουδαῖος is too far off : neuter in all probability for the whole character as stated ; **"whose praise is not from men, but from God."** Probably no dozen verses of the Bible (unless it be 1 Cor 13) describe a counterfeit where " *in what appears*," both outward and inward, there is a closer resemblance to piety. **"The hidden things"** (vs. 16, 29) are what Paul insists upon : not that our life ought not to shine forth, but that counterfeiting is too deep an art. What a man really is, "the Day will declare" (1 Cor. 3 : 13). It is "the hidden man of the heart" (1 Pet. 3 : 4). And sin so obscures our piety, that, with the best of us, for the most part, our "life is hid with Christ in God" (Col. 3 : 3).

CHAPTER III.

A man's being a Jew being no certainty that he is a believer, and in Elijah's time, to all appearance, much the other way; and "anger and wrath, distress and anguish (being) to the Jew first,"

1. What then is the advantage of the Jew, and what the profit of the circumcision? 2. Much every way: for, as the very first thing indeed, the fact that the oracles of God were believed. 3. For what if some did not believe? Shall their unbelief make the faith in God utterly in vain? 4. Be it not so! But let God turn out true and every man a liar, as it has been written:

That thou mightest be made righteous in thy words,
And triumph when thou art judged.

"**What then is the advantage?**" The twelve baskets that were *left over* were described by this same word (Matt. 14:20). It means *surplus*, or what *flowed over*. "Where sin abounded, grace did much more abound" (περισσεύω). He had made "the Jew first" in everything, so that, under the severities of the last chapter it became well to know what the περισσὸν or *abounding over* consisted in. "**Oracles.**" Λόγος means *word*, but λογία ("*oracles*") means something more ecclesiastical or sacred. "**Were believed.**" It will not hurt to resume the thread of the apostle, and to do it often. It is of wonderful effect in binding this Greek together. *Righteousness* is a noun answering to *righteous*, and *righteous* is an adjective answering to δίκη, what is *right*. This *right* is moral, and never wanders from a moral signification, except as *holiness* does, or *cleanness* does, or, notoriously, any word may, in well-understood rhetorical aberrations. When I say, The priest shall make him clean (in a case of leprosy, Lev. 13 : 13), I understand, *make him out clean*, or "pronounce him clean" (E. V.). "Thy name be made holy" is not a *thought* that I stop or hesitate upon in the Lord's prayer. So, then, when I read of *righteousness*, as applied to men, I remember *holiness* and *cleanness* as applied to the same erring creatures, and it balks me but little to affix the necessary limitations. *Righteousness*, as applied to Eve, would be perfect ; but *righteousness*, as applied to Seth, would really be *less sinfulness*, just what Seth's *holiness* would be, along with all the ideas of its being an earnest of more, and badge of that pardon of sin which has procured it, in eternal mercy. It is for this reason that we are said to be "*made righteous* in [His] blood" (5 : 9). But what breeds *righteousness ?* or, coming still closer to the fact, what *is righteousness ?* It is a new moral light. "This is life eternal, to *know* thee" (Jo. 17 : 3) ; "The eyes of your understanding being enlightened" (Eph. 1 : 18) ; "God, who commanded the light to shine out of darkness, (having) shined into our hearts ;" and so we are to understand the genesis of the Christian. We may get rid of Oriental speech and say, It is having a better conscience. But when, in answer to prayer, this better conscience appears, or when, convinced that I am a sinner, I ask God for moral light and He gives it to me, a favorite expression of the whole is that He gives me "*faith*." It is sometimes described by saying that He gives me "repentance" (2 Tim. 2 : 25), and sometimes that He gives me "obedience" (16 : 26 ; 1 Pet. 1 : 2). The fundamental fact is that He hath *made me righteous*. But as this *righteousness* is very imperfect, and rather a seed or seal of what is to be, than anything but sinfulness, Paul calls it "faith." It is an epitome of history. It is isogonous with repentance. It is isometric. It is, in the grace of it, identical. It is "*righteous*" for the same reason, viz., its possession of a moral light. It is the fruit of a moral change. And, therefore, it is a favorite word for "*righteousness*." Instead of "*righteousness*" being its result (or *holiness* either, Hodge's Syst. Theol. vol. 3 : p. 108), except as one degree of holiness is the result of another, it is itself "*righteousness*," and so splendid an account of it that when Abraham performed that wonderful act of faith in offering his son, we are told in terms, that his "*faith*" was reckoned "*righteousness*," and would have been just that perfectly but for the same imperfection by which "righteousness" itself is a name for *less sinfulness*.

Of course this is not to forget that faith is faith, and has in it the element of believing ; any more than that hope expects, and love dotes, and joy has the element of pleasure, yet neither of these is saving till it is holy. We cannot be saved except by seeking God. But we cannot seek God, except as the impenitent do, who only thereby bring themselves nearer to grace till grace actually flows in, and then hope and joy and faith, and all the exercises of righteousness are simultaneous gifts, bestowed upon common faith, and in answer graciously to the prayer of the impenitent.

" *What advantage then has the Jew !* " Why Paul fairly leaps to an answer ! "**Much every way.**" He has an *embarras des richesses*. And after saying, " First and foremost," his zeal exhausts itself upon that. "**What profit of circumcision ?**" Why, this profit, Paul declares (and lo ! with what wonderful sight he touches the blessing), that, while the whole world was lying in wickedness, millions of the Jews repented and "*believed.*" What other blessing was there ? The meaning of the apostle, therefore, is that "**the advantage of the Jew**" was that millions of them became " *righteous,*" or better men, and that the shape of their betterment was the same as with Abraham, and that their faith, dawning with moral light upon themselves and upon their Maker, was reckoned for just what it was, an incipient righteousness. But now certain confessions ! First, we stand alone in this English ; but that makes little difference, for the appeal can be only to the Greek. Second, "*oracles*" are plural, and neuter plurals usually call for a singular verb. Third, "*were entrusted with*" (Re.) or "*had committed to them*" (E. V.) is a repeated idiom of Paul. " I have been entrusted with a dispensation" (1 Cor. 9 : 17). " I have been put in trust with the gospel" (Gal. 2 : 7). "" Which was committed to my trust " (1 Tim. 1 : 11). " To be put in trust with the gospel " (1 Thess. 2 : 4). Fourth, it is an idiom that makes sense. Now, therefore, it is just there that we start our reply. And we say, first, that it does not make *much* sense. Considering that Paul gave density to everything, he did not give much when he said that they had the "*oracles.*" What is that greatly more than saying that a *Jew* is a *Jew*. Second, "*were believed*" is plural, "*the Jew*" is singular. Therefore, thirdly, "*were believed*" may have been made plural for the very purpose of distinction. Had it been made singular it might necessarily be connected with "*the Jew*." Whereas, as a neuter plural, plenty of exceptions warrant the other reference. Neuters that are massed, agree with the singular ; but neuters that are individual, and seem separable in their make, claim a plural ; and in fact these idiosyncrasies in grammar allow no end of freedom. Fourth, the sentence "**What if some did not believe?**" is almost unmeaning unless for this plainer sense. Fifth, this commoner sense occurs likewise with Paul in other writings. "Our testimony was believed" (2 Thess. 1 : 10, E. V.). "Believed on in the world" (1 Tim. 7 : 16). And sixth, the οὐ πάντως ("*not all together*"), of which we have much to say below (v. 9), loses infinitely there but for this simpler expression. Our understanding, therefore, makes out this significance for Paul,—That "*the Jew*" had great "*advantage*" because millions of them will be found in heaven. "**For** *what if some did not believe ?*" That of course is the proper question if the other is the proper beginning of the context. "**Shall their unbelief make the faith in God utterly in vain?**"

We cannot understand this till we are informed of their Rabbinical conceits. They had this quaint teaching : "No drop of Abraham's blood can come within a billion of miles of the Great Gehenna, be there only lawful circumcision." This was Paul's "other gospel" (Gal. 1 : 6). Hence the reason of his cry, "Circumcision availeth nothing" (Gal. 5 : 6). Hence their "endless genealogies" (1 Tim. 1 : 4). And hence the reasoning of Paul.

Their "*faith in God*" carried with it the idea that all would pull through, with some chastisements no doubt (Ps. 89 : 32), whether they believed or not. And Paul does not stop just now to take up the unsoundness of their "*faith*," but grapples them just here, Is God to be "*true*" or they ? Undoubtedly God spoke of apostate and damned Jews. They themselves turned men out of their synagogues. There must be a false thinking somewhere; and he boldly taxes it upon them, "*For what if some did not believe*" (and therefore according to their own Scriptures perished, Ps. 95 : 11) "*shall their unbelief make the faith in God*" (that is, the proper confidences in which Moses had steeped the nation) "*utterly in vain?* **Be it not so! But let God be made out true and every man a liar, as it is written—**

That Thou mightest be made righteous in Thy words, And triumph when Thou art judged."

It is not the "*faith*" (E. V.) or "*faithfulness*" (Re.) *of God*," but that "*faith of* (in) *God*" which is expressed by the same language in another place (Mar. 11 : 22). Paul could scarcely have imagined that the Jews believed that all of Abraham's circumcised children should certainly be saved, but he denounced their "*faith*" as only satisfied by that, and then he denounced that as glaringly against the oracles of God. "**Be it not so.**" "*God forbid*" (E. V. and Re.) obliterates the "*but*" in the next sentence, and substitutes "Yea" (E. V. and Re.). But "*but*" (δὲ) is the language of the apostle. "*Let God turn out true.*" This is characteristically Hebrew. It is a Hebraistic use of the Greek in two particulars. In the first place it is intense prediction in the shape of an imperative. When Isaiah says, "Make the heart of this people fat" (Is. 6 : 10), who will understand it as a command? And in the second place, it is *making* God true or God's *becoming* true (γινέσθω) in the sense of his *turning out* or being *shown* to be. The last of these particulars is to be noted where Christ commands his disciples to say, " Hallowed be (ἁγιασθήτω) Thy name " (Matt. 6 : 9).

The Hebrew will deceive us, however, unless we erect a guard. When the priest *cleansed* the leper, King James wisely translates it, " pronounced him clean ; " when he *fouled* him (for that is the Hebrew), he "*pronounced him unclean*" (E. V., Lev. 13 : 3). Solomon is intense in this half-wild rhetoric. He speaks of the Almighty, " I saw under the sun the Place of Judgment," and then he has absolutely blinded us to the sense by saying " that wickedness was there!" for indeed the Orientals were not afraid of such things; "and the Place of Righteousness that iniquity was there." Solomon recovered himself by saying, "God *shall* judge" (Ec. 3 : 17), and Paul correspondingly says, "*He shall become true*" (γινέσθω)! or, as the next clause words it, "*that thou mayest be made righteous in thy words, and triumph when thou art judged.*"

Hort and Westcott are more ornamental. They read νικήσεις, throwing away the subjunctive; "*That thou mightest be made righteous in thy words, and then*" (the καὶ is quite sufficient for that), "*thou wilt triumph when thou art judged.*" Their authority, being only A, D, ℵ, is not sufficient, however.

So much for one of the intermediate cavils before we come to the more important matter in the ninth and twentieth verses. Now for another.

If sin breeds this "*triumph*," why punish it? Paul simply recites this sophistry, and leaves the answer to itself. In fact the Jews had hurled this very taunt at the doctrine of the disciples (v. 8).

Let us translate :—

5. But if our unrighteousness make complete the righteousness of God, what shall we say? Is God unrighteous who inflicts the wrath? I speak as a man. 6. Be it not so! For then how shall God judge the world? 7. Yet if the truth of God abounded more in my lie to His glory, why still am I also judged as a sinner? 8. And why not (as we are slanderously charged, and as some affirm that we say), Let us do the evil things that the good things may come, being persons whose damnation is just?

"**Our unrighteousness.**" The manifest subjective character of this "*unrighteousness*" shames commentators into a like subjectiveness in what immediately follows. But why is this? If "**the righteousness of God**" is forensic almost everywhere, why vacillate? Fluctuations under a theologic stress are the bane of anti-Papal interpretations. "**Make complete.**" "*Commend*" (E. V. & Re.) is a narrow sense.

It springs in this way,—because a note of *commendation* brings people *together*. The wider significance is,—*Cause to stand together* (as though the verb were transitive, see Robinson). Hence in the Scriptures themselves, to *frame*, to *throw into order*, to "*complete*" is a usual sense. The passive (*Anglice*) serves as a translation of the active in two very striking texts : They are the following :—" The earth framed together out of the water and by means of the water " (2 Peter 3 : 5) ; " And in Him " (viz., in Jesus of Nazareth), " all things were framed together " (Col. 1 : 17). In Jesus Christ, originally and before He was born, the universe was framed together, so that without Him it would have been useless and incomplete. Paul borders on the same idea in respect to sin. What would "*truth*" be without it ? The devil had some sparks of light in the very darkness of the " tree of knowledge (Gen. 3 : 5). "*Made complete ;*" not absolutely. "*Made righteous*" (v. 4), rhetorically or declaratively so, just as "*come to be true*" (v. 4) is not to be taken absolutely, but in the way we have already explained. The belles-lettres sense is perfectly intelligible, and means an *abounding* or *welling over* ($\pi\epsilon\rho\iota\sigma\sigma\epsilon\upsilon\omega$) in a way, man-ward, thoroughly evincive of "**His glory.**" "**What shall we say**" then ? "**Is God unrighteous who inflicts the wrath?**" Never ! Paul retorts ; for then, if that be dreamed, universal monarchy is at an end. But the cavil presses, Why ? Explain the difficulty. "**If the truth of God abounded more in my lie to His glory, why still am I also judged as a sinner?**" With startling summariness Paul manages the challenge thus :—If men really sin, they must be punished, or else what governs the world ? (v. 6). If sin "*completes*" the Almighty in the sense of His largest "*glory*," either this must be a mere incident, and men go on to be punished, which is what the apostle would aver, or else sin is no sin at all. We are to esteem it very highly in love for its work's sake ; and Paul evolves the consequence in so disgusting a shape as to need no further setting back.

This argument is good enough if moderns would leave the conditions of it alone. But, unfortunately, things more disgusting than Paul would use to drive us back are put into the very bosom of God's Providence. Under such treatment Paul's appeal perishes. That God damns the wicked for display, silences all appeal to mere disgust on the other side. Better no punishment than such a punishment as that. Nor has there been the least reason for such a gloss. That God builds Tophet for "*His glory*" is true, so long as we give "*glory*" its literal sense of *weight* or *excellence*. That He punishes the wicked to do right, a little child might accept as sufficiently complete. That He even curses the wicked for *display* is true, if we make the end intermediate and secondary (Ps. 79 : 9 ; Rom. 9 : 23; 2 Cor. 3 : 18); but that He torments the wicked simply to exhibit anything ; or to state it in theologic phrase, that His chief end is to glorify Himself, is horrible, and might well defy disgust at no punishment at all as a mere platitude on the part of the apostle. Such thoughts have been a brutal trait in Reformed theology. A certain Providence is *right*. It may be boldly said that there is but one such Providence for all the universe. God has spied it out. Part of this Providence is Hell. God builds Hell in spite of His pity. But His motive is simply *right* (δίκη). A lesser end may be to display all this ; and why? Because "*therein the righteousness of God is revealed.*" Making "*the wrath descend*" is a necessary discipline. All this is true. But when, untying from the main idea that the thing is *right*, we make the main idea to be the display,—shame upon such a following of the Almighty. Philosophers laugh at it (Mill, Ex. of Ham., Amer. Ed., Vol. 1, p. 221), and justly denounce it, and only unjustly when they do as we do, and call any such thing divine. We make the enemies of God to blaspheme. To show God's own "*glory*" illustratively to be the end of His creation is to brutalize His work, and to forget His glory itself, I mean His unspeakable "*righteousness.*"

9. Why then do we not win the advantage for ourselves all together? for we laid it down as the pre-occasion, that both Jews and Greeks are all under sin ; 10. As it has been written,

There is none righteous, no not one.
11. There is none who understands, there is none who seeks diligently after God.
12. They have all turned aside; they are together become useless;
There is none that does useful things; no, not so much as one.
13. Their throat is an open sepulchre;
With their tongues they have used deceit;
The poison of asps is under their lips.
14. Whose mouth is full of cursing and bitterness.
15. Their feet are swift to shed blood.
16. Destruction and misery are in their ways;
17. And a way of peace have they not known.
18. There is no fear of God before their eyes.
19. But we know that what things the law says it speaks to those who are under the law, that every mouth may be stopped, and all the world come under penalty to God. 20. Because by works of law shall no flesh be made righteous in His sight; for by law is the fuller knowledge of sin.

This whole chapter has been beset with riddles. Dr. Hodge far back in its paragraphs, stops at a certain text and complains, " This verse is very difficult " (v. 3). Προεχόμεθα (v. 9) in the track of the expositors, looks like a spot in the road where a hay wagon has been overturned, muddied with feet and littered with the hay that has run to waste. Our English Version has it, "*Are we better?*" and supplies "*than they*" to promote the sense. The Revision is just the opposite ! " Are we in worse case than they?" Wetstein reads, " Are we surpassed " (by the Jews)? (Ecumenius, " Are we surpassed " (by the Gentiles)? Reiche, " Are we preferred " (by God)? Wahl, "What can we bring forward" (as excuse)? Godet, "Are we sheltered?" Kindred trouble surrounds οὐ πάντως ("*No, in nowise*," E. V. and Re.). Van Hengel, says Winer (Am. Ed., p. 555), " despaired," etc., and concluded there must be unnoted corruption textually. " Meyer even finds himself obliged to abandon his philological rigorism " (so says Godet *in loco*), and is actually driven to a " second " and scarce defensible sense. When such things occur, one maxim all will encourage—to abandon speculation, and come right down to the letter of the Greek. What does it radically mean? Προεχόμεθα : what is that? It occurs but once in the Testament, and is made up of προ and ἔχω. Προ means *before*, and ἔχω means to *hold* or *have*. If a man uses a shield, it is proper to say, *He holds it before*, προέχει. This word is either passive or middle. We can take our choice. If middle, it means, *We hold ourselves before* or *get ourselves into the advance*. How could we come more honestly by a sufficient meaning? " *Why then do we not get ourselves into the advance*," or "**win for ourselves the advantage?**" Let us trace the grammar first, and Paul afterward. That is a safe course, and will have the prevailing right over different expositions. Οὐ πάντως never means "*not at all*." If it does, show the instance. Πάντως οὐ would be that, and would give us the right for "*No, in no wise*" (E. V. and Re.). Οὐ πάνυ has been thought to give a color that way in a certain passage (see Meyer), but even there there may be supposed an irony (see Schoemann, ad Is., p. 276), just as *Not quite!* is an ironical stroke for saying *Never!* So then, according to the Greek, οὐ πάντως must, in some fashion, be woven in as meaning *not all together*. But how can that be done? Meyer, in excuse for the violence that he confesses, holds out that it cannot be. But let us look at that. What if, as in many such cases, the tabooed idea should be proved to be the very best?

What has Paul been speaking of? He has begun with the question, "*What advantage hath the Jew, and what profit is there of circumcision?*" (E. V., v. 1). The reply is, "*Much every way.*" Then the specification of the "advantage"—that the "*oracles*," of course including the gospel, made many Jewish believers. Then comes the cavil. What if some did not believe? And then, built up upon that, that other cavil, If, not believing, they glorified God, why punish? Paul cuts his way through all this jungle, and comes out upon a still higher inquiry. What higher inquiry could there naturally be? Repeating nothing, such as by saying, "Are we better than they?" (E. V., Behlen), and confusing nothing, such as by saying, "*Not at all*" (E. V.)

to the question "*Are we better?*" (E. V.), or to the question, "Are we worse?" (Re.), or to the question, "Do we surpass?" (De Wette, Alford), when he had said already, We had an "*advantage,*" and described it as "*much every way,*" a question arises which no exegete seems to have noticed, viz., Why, if all are sinners, "**Jews and Greeks,**" and one of these classes, viz., *Jews*, have the enormous "*advantage*" of possessing "the law," and of having that "*law*" include "*the gospel;*" and, furthermore, of having that *gospel* thundered out on Sinai, and of having it impressed by painful ceremonials, why, when many *helped themselves forward* (προέχομαι) unto life, or, as Paul expressed it, "*the oracles were believed*" (v. 2), *did not all help themselves forward?* or, returning to the Greek, "**Why then do we not win the advantage for ourselves all together?**" Paul is going to make this attack all the intricacies of salvation. He throws into a parenthesis (vs. 9–18) what will make it stand naked. We all start fresh, "*Jews and Greeks.*" We all start sinners, utterly condemned. The Jews have the law which includes the gospel. Millions "*believed*" and snatched an "*advantage great every way.*" Now why did not all believe? that is the point of the passage. Having the same blessed "*law,*" why did it not convert every body? It is a question for all time. And what was there to blunt its edge, or to make it diverse, or to make it partial, or to keep it back from the uniformity that "all (should obey) the gospel (10 : 16)?" "**Because**" (the reply afterwards gives the solution) "**out of works of law shall no flesh be made righteous**" (v. 20).

Here a wonderful confirmation is found in διότι; though again comes up a struggle of the commentators. Διότι is never illative in the indirect sense. The sequence "*Therefore*" has marred the passage (E. V.). The linguists stop and look at this (Alford, Meyer), as Meyer stopped and looked at οὐ πάντως (3 : 9); and when the Revisionists amend, and translate "*because,*" and reduce this verse to a confirmation of the last, they not only daze the reader by an imperfect sense, but they discredit Paul; for so great a dialectician would hardly enter so grand a sentence by so side a door.

Throw out the poem (which, by the way, is shaped into one mainly by Paul), and throw out the remark (v. 19), that essential parts of it, being from *the law* (Ps. 5 : 9 ; 10 : 7 ; 14 ; 36 ; 53 ; 140 ; Isa. 59 : 7, 8), were meant for **"those under the law,"** and we have this grandest answer to an emphatic text, " *Why then do we not win the advantage for ourselves all together ? Because, out of works of law shall no flesh be made righteous in his sight.*" "*No flesh.*" Alford makes something of the fact that the Greek reads "*all flesh.*" "*Out of works of law all flesh shall not be justified,*" i. e., as he expresses it, All flesh are in the condition *not justified*. But there seems no value in this, for the Hebraism that lodges this in the Greek has no such particularity (Mar. 13 : 20 ; 1 Cor. 1 : 29). We may notice however how the word "*all,*" starting from the ninth, besets all the verses. "*Flesh.*" It does not say *spirit*. For the *conscience* (spirit) of a man, left to itself with the gospel, would turn to it at once. "*Made righteous.*" We need add nothing more. "*Made*" actually "*righteous*" in that incipient degree which makes up in its very nature as love (Matt. 22 : 40) the *differentia* of saving faith.

But now we arrive at the new phrase. Only Paul uses it. He has used it before, but in the singular number, " *Who exhibit within the work of the law written in their hearts* " (2 : 15). He uses it nine more times, and always in the plural ; and he uses it only in two of his epistles, and we can quote him easily in every instance. The first three cases are from this same epistle. " We reckon that a man is made righteous by faith, aside from works of law " (3 : 28). " Not by faith, but, as it were, by works of law " (9 : 32). (Here law is thrown out by the Revisionists). Three of the remaining cases are in one verse to the Galatians, " Knowing that a man is not made righteous by works of law except by faith in Jesus Christ, we also believed in Christ Jesus, that we might be made righteous by faith in Christ, and not by works of law ; for by works of law shall no flesh be made righteous " (Gal. 2 : 16).

"Received ye the Spirit by works of law, or by hearing of faith?" (Gal. 3 : 2). "He, therefore, that ministereth to you the Spirit, and creates active powers in you, doeth he it by works of law, or by hearing of faith?" (Gal. 3 : 5). "As many as are by works of law are under a curse" (Gal. 3 : 10). If we can find out distinctly what **"works of law"** mean, we have greatly promoted our entire exposition.

What do *works of light* mean? There is no such scripture; but what would it naturally mean? Works begotten from a man by moral light. "Works of darkness" (13 : 12) are works that darkness sets forth from its seat in our nature. "The work of faith and labor of love" (1 Thess. 1 : 3) are the literal thing, what faith works and what love works. "The works of the flesh" (Gal. 5 : 19) are the like; and so, "of God" (Jo. 6 : 28, 29), and "of the Devil" (1 Jo. 3 : 8). They are works which a man does, but which no other principle or power or part of him does than that of which they are said to be the works. "The old man and his works" (Eph. 4 : 22), "and the works of the body" (8 : 13), are of a like significance. There is a wonderful unanimity; and therefore the analogy is entire by which "*the works of the law*" distinctly arise into our view. What "the old man" can do when it is all that one has; what "the body" can do when it masters "the spirit"; what the Devil can do when he reigns; or God has done when we believe; what "darkness" or "faith" or "flesh" or "love" can be said to do when man acts under their influence; that "*law*" can be said to do or to have as its "*works*" if the thunder and imprint of the law is all that one has to depend upon to cleanse him or make him righteous. This is a critical sentence. When profoundly seated in a man, as "*law*" was with the Jew, and when warmly boasted of by the man, as Paul was quick to picture (2 : 17); when thoroughly understood by the man, as it critically was; and made to take in the gospel, as it undoubtedly did; if it and nothing more gracious inspired its "*works,*" then by "*works of law shall no flesh be made righteous.*" It is repeating only in different phrase that about "the letter and the spirit" (2 : 29).

But let me be distinctly understood. Faith is incipient holiness. I hold that "*law*" cannot produce faith as one of its "*works.*" And I hold that it can produce nothing, as "light" can, and "faith" can, and "love" can, and as the Giver of all these, viz., God can, except that which is abreast of itself, viz. "**knowledge;**" and though I have all "knowledge," as Paul says, "I am nothing" (1 Cor. 13 : 2). Men cannot be *taught* righteousness. Therefore the "*work of the law*" is only a higher responsibility, or, as Paul declares it, "**the**" ἐπίγνωσις (v. 20), or higher "**knowledge of sin.**"

Going back therefore to our passage, each text lies in smooth consistency with this significance. The great end of religion is to "*make* (men) *righteous.*" For this, Christ was raised up. "Christ is the end of the law for righteousness (holiness) to every one that believeth" (10 : 4). His very name is the token of His work, viz., to "save His people *from their sins.*" Now, the distinctions we are aiming to establish can perhaps be additionally noted by a return to the "covenants." The "old covenant," was full of the gospel. It contained nothing else. It was the gospel entire, because it was built upon a redemption entirely achieved. Its watchword was, "Do this and thou shalt live" (Lu. 10 : 28). And what the sinner was to do, was, not to keep the whole law. He was "a debtor to do the whole law" (Gal. 5 : 3) only if he broke the covenant. It was indeed said, "Cursed is every one that continueth not in all things written in the book of the law to do them" (Gal. 3 : 10); but that is said still. In the eye of grace that is still demanded. We are to repent of "all" sin, and obey "all" righteousnesses; not perfectly : that is never said : but incipiently. We are to be born again. The change was to reach all our faculties. And what the old covenant did was to thunder that out. Along with the decalogue, and as a needed part of it, was this—"Believe on the Lord Jesus Christ, and thou shalt be saved" (Acts 16 : 31). No statute breathed fiercer (Jo. 16 : 9 ; Mar. 16 : 16). And what was the "new covenant?" Something more than the "new song" (Rev. 5 : 9), and better than the "new commandment" (1 Jo. 2 : 8), or the "new wine" (Matt. 26 : 29); for those were brighter and better instances of a thing with no advance upon its nature. But the "new covenant" had as precise a difference as we can imagine. It was the "old" covenant" *plus* grace to obey it. Not a shred more did it possess. Honesty was complete in either. Grace was the foundation of both. The "old" had sufficient for its maintenance, for it had provided that Christ should die. It lacked but one thing, not to make it honest, but to make it serviceable, and for that lack it "gendered to bondage" (Gal. 4 : 24). Not one Israelite employed it, and all who were saved stepped over into that other "covenant," which is the sole dependency of ungodly men. Now let Jeremiah describe that needful difference. "I will make a new covenant; not according to the covenant I made with their fathers, which my covenant they brake; but this shall be the covenant, I will put my law in their inward parts, and write it in their hearts, and will be their God, and they shall be my people" (Jer. 31 : 32, 33,. Paul speaks of them (Gal. 3 : 16; Heb. 8 : 6), as both having "promises," the "old covenant" ἐν γράμματι ("in letter," 2 Cor. 3 : 6). He elaborates Jeremiah, and makes him plainer. The "old covenant ;" was the whole gospel with one thing yet to be supplied,—power to keep it. The "new covenant" was all the "old" with the fatal necessity supplied, not, now, that there were such formal "covenants" in different periods of time, but that this was the rhetoric of grace intended to describe just the points that we would now make clear. "*Works of law*" are what could be accomplished by "the old covenant," in point of grace just nothing at all. Nay, more comprehensive than that, for "*works of law*" differ from *the works of the law* ; for this latter would include the gospel. But the former might never hear of Sinai ; and as Paul includes "*Greeks*" as well as "*Jews*" his sentence is universal. No light of law without grace to "write it on the heart" is any more than γράμμα (letter), and cannot reach ἐν τῷ κρυπτῷ (2 : 29) into the inward spirit.

Now let us survey the instances (the ten given above).

"*Who exhibit within the work of the law written in their hearts*" (2 : 15). That is plain enough. It is the picture of poor Gentiles who, when favored Jews could not be "made righteous by works of law," because nobody can, are "*made righteous*" as "*doers of law*" (2 : 13) through rare grace in having "*the work of the law*" (that is, just such work as "*the* law" which they had never heard of, by grace produces) "written," just as Jeremiah describes, "inwardly" upon the heart. Hence the importance of that word "*except*" (Gal. 2 : 16), which was so long omitted. That was a rare wrong in exegesis. It occurs fifty-nine times in the N. T., that expression ἐὰν μη, and always means *except*. Lo, for two centuries and over, it has stood "*but*" (E. V.) in an important sentence. The Revisionists restore it, but timidly, "A man is not justified by the works of the law, save through faith in Jesus Christ" (Re.). Why not say boldly "except," and not put "*but only*" in the margin,* especially as ἐὰν μή *never* means "*but only?*" "A man is not made righteous by works of law, except by faith in Jesus Christ." That is, "law," even if it include the gospel, never can convert a man unless "mixed with faith in them that hear it" (Heb. 4 : 2 : for "the letter killeth" (2 Cor. 3 : 6). But when its works are written on the heart" (2 : 15), then a man is converted, and that covers the exception in the text, "except by faith in Jesus Christ" (Gal. 2 : 16).

The remaining texts in Romans we will leave till we reach them. In Galatians we have what is appended to the last treated sentence : "That we might be made righteous by faith in Christ, and not by works of law" (of course, from what we have already seen) ; "for by works of law" (repeating the sentence that we are now discussing), "shall no flesh be made righteous" (Gal. 2 : 16). "As many as are by works of law" (that is, as many as are what they are by what works unaided law can work in them) "are under a curse" (Gal. 3 : 10): and who doubts it? or who doubts a still heavier curse, if that

---

* Our American committee favored the retention of "*but*" (E. V.), and requested it to be marked in their exceptions to the work of the British ! (See Appendix, Re.).

" law " happen to include the gospel (Ps. 81 : 7–13 ; 105 : 1–10 ; Jo. 15 : 22) ; for the " gospel " must be made " *the power of God*," and has been so made by " effectual calling " to *every one that believes* (1 : 16). Then follow two sentences which seem to settle the whole thing. " Received ye the Spirit " (what has that to do with Lutheran "*justification*" modernly so called ?). " Received ye the Spirit " (what is that but, Were ye made holy, *righteous*) ; or, sweeping in the next instance, " He that ministereth to you the Spirit, etc., etc., (doeth He it, E. V.) by works of law or by the hearing of faith " (Gal. 3 : 2, 5)? These are all the cases in the Bible of that Pauline expression.

Now to resume. "**Laid it down as a pre-occasion.**" This is an aorist. The πρό does not refer to what " *we before* "(Re., see also E. V.) did, but to the *condition* or *occasion* or, if we please, *accusation precedent*, which makes us all alike. If out of this dead level of condemnation (ἔνδικος), many who had the law escaped, why did not all ? "**Written.**" Well, much of this was never written before, but, "**as it has been written,**"— that is true literally. "**Seeks**" (v. 11). The ἐκ before ζητῶν ought to have its influence ; for many do "*seek*" (Lu. 13 : 24) who do not *seek* "**diligently.**" Paul is full of such delicate particularities. "**Useless.**" Bentham, if he would supply a moral sense, would be a good measurer of piety (Matt. 13 : 23 ; 1 Jo. 3 : 7). See "**useful things**" just afterwards. "**Blood**" (v. 15). Two reasons account for this strong language, first, that the most modest sin as measured by human eye, in the divine eye is cruel (Ps. 90 : 11 ; Prov. 12 : 10 ; Hab. 1 : 13), and second, that these are the reaches to which sin will advance, and to which it is constantly arriving even in this world. "**Under penalty.**" (Ἔνδικος, v : 19) ; a word but once used by Paul. "**By**" (v. 20). It might be stronger to say "*from*" or "*out of*," for the word is ἐκ, not διά, and in all cases the difference is intentional (1 : 17 ; 3 : 30 ; 4 : 16 ; 1 Cor. 8 : 6) ; but translators avoid changing, because the words might be ambiguous. If I say " *made righteous from works* " it jingles sadly like *away from* works, and if I say *out of*, that sounds like *aside from*.

Let it be only understood that ἐκ means that a man can not even begin a holiness *out of* such "*works*" as "*law*" by itself can inspire.

21. **But now, aside from law, the righteousness of God has been manifested, being borne witness to by the law and the prophets, 22. But the righteousness of God by faith in Jesus Christ unto all them that believe, for there is no difference; 23. For all sinned, and are short of the glory of God, 24. Being made righteous as a gift by His grace, through the redemption which is in Christ Jesus;**

"**But now.**" Always, indeed, "*but now*" with a manifestness giving less room for mistake. "**Aside from law.**" "**Righteousness**" never can be *aside from law*" in most senses, for one is but the fulfilment of the other ; but that great light of "*righteousness*" in the soul of a sinner has to be revealed by God, and can never be revealed by "*law.*" Our task is becoming easier, for this is but a repetition of another sentence (1 : 17, see comments). "**Manifested;**" equivalent to "*revealed*" as above (1 : 17). "**The law and the prophets.**" Here, at length, our idea is caught up. " *The law* " (not anarthrous) includes the gospel. "**Borne witness to by.**" The gospel (*scripturæ omnes*) cannot save, but it can bear witness to itself, and becomes the instrument of saving by "*the power of God*" (1 : 16). "**But**" (v. 22). We must not neglect the δὲ. " *The righteousness of God* " is very little " *manifested* " even to (εἰς) the very most eminent saints. Therefore Paul qualifies, and interposes "*but,*" and repeats a part of his sentence. " *The righteousness of God* (is) *manifested*," and that is our inward light ; "*but*" it is alas ! a faint manifestation. It is "**the righteousness of God**" (and how well this one of the ten cases (1 : 17) agrees with " *moral excellence* " !) through that weak thing, "**faith.**" And the manifestation is not made ἐκ νόμου, though, indeed, it takes "*the law*" in its most extensive sense to preach and teach it; but it is made " *through faith* in Jesus Christ;" and it is made to whom? not to "*all,*" which was the point of the apostle's question (v. 9), but "**to all them that believe.**" And here Paul repeats his "*pre-occasion*" (vs. 9–18),—"**for there is no difference.**" But still he has not quite answered. " *To all that believe?* " Yes; but that is the very question. " *To all that believe.*" Yes; but what makes them "*believe?*" " *What advantage hath the Jew?*" Why, that many believed (v. 2). But this question has come since :—Why do we not all win for ourselves the blessing? (v. 9). The gist of the rejoinder, therefore, is in the Greek that follows,—"**Being made righteous as a gift by His grace through the redemption which is in Christ Jesus.**" "*Freely*" (E. V. & Re.) might have other meanings than δωρεάν, which means simply after the manner of a δῶρον ("*gift*"). Here then is an unbounded answer. " *Why do we not all get forward?*" (v. 9). For a most obvious account. " *Getting forward is a gift.*" " What the law " (with the gospel in it, vs. 21, 22) " could not do, in that it was weak through the flesh," God chose to do ; and He does it under fixed rules. And He does it not wilfully (9 : 16), or sovereignly (9 : 15), or, as the last teleology of the case, to display his glory (see com. on C. 9), but He does it *ex necessitate rei*, from the fiat of what is right ; and He does it, not according to the geography of the law, but hither and thither as He may, for both " *Jews and Greeks.*" "**For all have sinned.**" That is the condition-precedent of which He has already spoken (v. 9). All start equally there. '**And are short.**" All sin is a deficiency. The command is, Thou shalt love God, and, Thou shalt love thy neighbor. Even devils have the obscure remainders of these affections. But they are to be perfect. We are to love God with all our powers, and our neighbor as ourselves. He that is "*short*" by nature is an apostate. Now "**the glory of God,**" or, as the Hebrew meant, His *weight* or His *excellency*, is the norm of all our righteousness. Conversion consists in revealing this excellency to us inwardly by the Spirit (1 : 17). But *perfectly* it is never revealed in this world. " In glory," as we call it, " we shall be like Him, for we shall see Him as He is." But here there is an ἔνδειξις (showing) of " *God's righteousness,*" that is, His moral excellence (see the next two verses), and that, along with its recognition of the Redeemer, is called "*faith ;*" but the whole is very imperfect. All men in this world are still sinning, "*and are short of the glory*" (that is *the full holiness*) "*of God ;*" "*being made righteous,*" that is incipiently or germinally so, "*as a gift by His grace through the redemption which is in Christ Jesus.*" "*Redemption.*" No word has been emasculated more than this by the labors of our Protestant Reformers. Fifteen hundred years made it the great feature of the gospel ; rightfully so ; for the Bible makes it the whole of our forensic safety. Augustine knew no other ; nor Chrysostom, nor Bernard, nor Anselm, nor the whole host of ante-Lutheran theologers. This is a marvel of fact, that fifteen centuries should have read the Bible with precision in a certain way, and then that a German monk should suddenly change it, and the world be so little sensitive to the change that had been made. Before, "*redemption*" was every thing ; and articulately just here, let it be said what "*redemption*" was. Men had sinned. The curse of sin is death. Death means incurable sinfulness. There are added ideas of torment ; but those are consequential and administrative. The head curse is continued sinfulness. The devils, falling into the same estate, realize the incurable malignity. But, for reasons of which we are utterly unaware, man may have a better destiny. It is provided by an incarnate Redeemer. That is, God chose to unite Himself with a creature, the man Christ Jesus, and bargained with the man, "compassed with infirmity" and bloody with temptation (Lu. 22 : 44 ; Heb. 12 : 4), that if, as Adam was to have done, He, the second Adam, would fight the battle for His race, and do what Adam failed to do, that is, never sin, His torment in the doing (being undeserved by Him) should be imputed to His race, and should stand for their deservings ; provided, however, that in this world, and as a fresh probation, they should turn from their evil ways, and by earnest seeking to their Maker in reliance more or less distinct) upon this ransom work, they should accept the offer made in the gospel. This is "*redemption.*" It has many strange concomitants. It is slow and tardy, and may not reach a man for eighty years. Though provided for all our race, it misses millions. Though provided for all our time, it arrives tardily. Though provided for all our sins, it extinguishes them slowly. And though provided for all our pains, we breathe our first breath in pain, and breathe our last often in horrible anguish. But what does this matter? It is as it is; and we learn what it is, fact by fact, as we survey the gospel. "*Redemption,*" therefore, strictly and in every sense it certainly is not. The Redeemer did not pay what we would have to pay; only, being God, He paid enough. He did not pay for one set of men exactly with the good results with which He paid for others. He damned some men more desperately. Therefore it was not a redemption at all in any thing like an ordinary sense, and an attempt to make it so has bred the doctrine of *a definite atonement*, and other figments that have scandalized the church. It was not any one thing of human boundaries. It was not a "*sacrifice*" in any such sense as that God was resentful. God has no such trait. He has but two moralities, a love for the δίκη (*right*), and benevolence for His creatures. Mediæval theology, in its worst shape, was uppermost when men dreamed of Vindicatory Justice as by the side of Benevolence. The severities of Hell are real, and vindicatory justice exists, and is just as terrible as they have said; but it is not *what* they have said. It is the fruit of higher moralities; and God's love of holiness is the adorable fountain from which have originated all the divine administrations. Men err, therefore, when "*propitiation,*" or "*expiation,*" or "*atonement,*" or "*substitution,*" or "*ransom*" are pushed beyond the intention of the apostles. The very multiplication of the terms shows the labor of the inspired to let in side lights. And, therefore, when men proceed to extremities, and represent God as angry in such a sense as to need placation, when the very plan is from Him; or the Son as pleased in such a sense as to be in a fit frame to placate and soothe the Father, when He is the very begotten of the Father, men ruin every thing. "*Redemption*" is a great plan, which we can but little fathom; the sure feature of which is that it is *necessary;* which has wholesome elucidations in these names for it by the apostles; but which, like the Fall, is beyond reason; and is best described by Christ where He says, "It behoved Christ to suffer" (ἔδει, Luke 24 : 46). That is the wisest word yet. It was necessary; why, we shall never know. It was the directly essential thing, for some cause that we must leave to God, "for eternal salvation to all them that obey Him" (Heb. 5 : 9).

But, now, we mortals, having that which the devils never had, what is the result? Why, the cure of our sinfulness. We are constantly laying emphasis on hell-torment. If we are pardoned, what does pardon amount to? Would it be anything if it left the head-curse? This was what rung in the brains of the earlier Christianity. What is the great curse? Sin. What is the great grace? Ransom. What is the fruit of ransom? Pardon. What must be the effect of pardon? Heaven, indeed; but, as the great foretaste of heaven, a diminution of our sinfulness. This, in their different poses, is conversion, regeneration, cleansing, a new creation, or whatever you choose to call a betterment of character. Now, the Reformers stripped "*redemption*" of a part of its effect, and carried it over to a new conception. If I am pardoned, what do I need more? If I am pardoned, Tophet will be shut, but, as the more exalted part of the effect, sin will be diminished. What is the diminution of my sinfulness but a creation of righteousness? It is not really righteousness, for it continues sinful; but it is called righteousness so as to avoid telling the story over again. Luther would agree in that, for "holy brethren" (Heb. 3 : 1) certainly did not mean holy brethren. Now, continue pardoning me, and continue sanctifying me, and what do I need more? What do I need of Christ's righteousness? Christ's righteousness made my ransom perfect, because it left Him innocent, and handed over to me His otherwise unjust sufferings. But what do I need further? Luther dishonored our redemption when he tore from it its plenary results, and built up another story to the work, namely, the transfer to us of another's righteousness. Let us not be misunderstood. We build everything upon Christ. We emphasize to the very last that "without the shedding of blood there is no remission." But we emphasize the doctrine further, that *with* the shedding of blood there may be every remission; and that remission would be a farce if it did not take away our sinfulness; and that if it takes away our sinfulness, that means that it "*makes* (us) *righteous ;*" and that if it "*makes* (us) *righteous,*" we do not need the righteousness of Christ, except to lean on as giving His sufferings free, and to pattern after as our Great Redeemer. The whole *justifying* idea as taught in modern times has lessened the morality of the people. It is true we build upon Christ as much as *it* does, and make as entire the helplessness of the sinner ; but, blotting out a whole round of texts that mean that *I* am to be righteous, and lessening by that number the appeals for my own personal purification, cannot but act disastrously ; and hence the exceeding importance of just such a text as this :—"*Being made righteous as a gift by His grace*"—infinitely not by a borrowed or transmitted righteousness : I do not need that if I am forgiven ; but, as the fruit of my forgiveness, a righteousness of my own ; that is, what the devils are denied, an incipient cure within ; very imperfect, but yet dignified (as all admit in some texts) by the name of "righteousness" (2 Cor. 9 : 10), and, in the sinner's case, wholly of "*grace,*" and as the fruit in its very highest attainments of the Great Redemption.

25. Whom God proposed to Himself as a propitiation through faith in His blood, to show His righteousness on account of the passing over of the sins that had been previously committed in the forbearance of God; 26. More immediately to show His righteousness in the present time, that He might be righteous, and yet make righteous him who is so out of faith in Jesus.

"**Proposed to Himself.**" There has been a strange disposition to translate this, "*set forth*" (E. V. & Re.), or by some equivalent expression. The verb is middle, and means most radically to *set before one's self*, and, hence, to *propose*. Such is its meaning in classical authors. In the New

Testament it occurs twice elsewhere, and in each instance in this sense. "I purposed to come unto you" (E. V., Rom. 1 : 13). Again, Paul being still the speaker, "Having made known unto us the mystery of His will, according to His good pleasure which He hath purposed in Himself" (E. V., Eph. 1 : 9). Paul, therefore, uses the verb three times ; and he uses the noun seven times, in fact only six, if we exclude the Hebrews, and the latter number is half of all the instances in the New Testament Scriptures. Of the remaining six, four relate to the shew-bread, "the loaves προθέσεως, of the setting out" (Matt., Mr., Lu.), or, in the Hebrews, "the setting forth of loaves" (Heb. 9: 2). The two others are just what we speak of, viz., a purpose, "with purpose of heart" (E. V., Acts 11 : 23), and, in the same book, "they had obtained their purpose" (E. V., Acts 27 : 13). And then the six instances, which are certainly of Paul, are these :—" According to His purpose" (E. V., Rom. 8 : 28). "The purpose of God" (E. V., Rom. 9 : 11). "According to the purpose," and "according to the eternal purpose" (E. V., Eph. 1 : 11 & 3 : 11). "According to His own purpose" (E. V., 2 Tim. 1 : 9). "Doctrine, manner of life, purpose" (E. V., 2 Tim. 3 : 10). The arrangement, therefore, of which He is about to speak is a matter of God's *purpose*, however important the *setting forth* idea may be before the close of the sentence. "**Propitiation.**" The word is from an adjective (ἴλαος) that means *mild* or *clement*. Our word *hilarity* traces to it. The idea is a very simple one, and means any certain something that *makes clement*, or secures "*propitiation.*" "**By faith in His blood.**" The Revisionists, catching the feeling that "*propitiation*" cannot be "*through*" (Re.) "*faith*," have attacked the punctuation. Their idea is that "*propitiation*" is gloriously sufficient ; that "faith," as added to it, is utterly unscriptural, and so it is. "*Propitiation*" is a clean work by itself, and "*faith*" is only necessary to it to secure its benefits. In fact "*faith*," in itself considered, is the very "substance" (Heb. 11 : 1) of its benefit. They, therefore, point in this fashion :—" Whom God set forth to be a propitiation, through faith, by His blood."

Now, the difficulties of all this are, first, that it remedies nothing. Making "*faith*" parenthetical does not remove it sufficiently. What is it still but " propitiation through faith ?" Second, why did not Paul attend to the matter ? A Greek clear of the mistake could be constructed easier than by parenthesis. Third, how better than just this way could a meaning be constructed which we are about to dilate upon? Διά, as we have seen (1 : 11 ; 2 : 27), has the sense of *accompaniment*. " This is He who came by water and blood." " Neglect not the gift that is in thee that was given thee by prophecy" (1 Tim. 4 : 14). " Who by the letter and circumcision "etc. (2 : 27). " By Him were all things created " (Col. 1 : 16). This like *běth essentiæ* (Prov. 3 : 26) is a peculiarity that we neglect at our peril. The idea is of *necessary accompaniment*. As God " created all things by Jesus Christ " (Eph. 3 : 9) in the sense that all was naught without Him as an accompaniment, so He "*proposed to Himself a propitiation*" with this inexorable link, that all was naught without faith ; that just as the universe required Christ, or Christ's errand required blood (Heb. 9 : 12), so this " propitiation," in its turn, should require faith as its *necessary accompaniment*," and that, too, the "faith in (the) *blood*" of the exacted sacrifice. " *Propitiation*," therefore, is a desirable word except in certain particulars, first, that it does not *make clement* except where it has given "*faith*," and, second, that it does not *make clement* at all in the sense of God's personal estate, in as much as He was previously *clement* in the very act of *proposing to Himself* the blessed gospel. " *Blood*," I need hardly say, means all suffering from the manger to the ascension into heaven.

We come next to the special uses of the passage in carrying out Paul's projêt from the beginning :—" I am ready to preach the gospel to them that are in Rome also " (Rom. 1 : 15). And he described what the gospel was. It was " the power of God unto salvation to every one that believeth." And he gave the general reason, " Because therein the righteousness of God is revealed," and revealed to " faith," and revealed in so internal and moral a way that men " live " thereby (*ib.* v. 17), that is, seeing this noble exemplar of "righteousness," they become "righteous," and "righteous" inchoately in the shape of "faith," fulfilling a quotation of the apostle taken from Habbakuk, "The righteous by faith shall live."

Now, having taken the gospel to pieces, he takes each part of it and explains how *showing it* (as, for example, in this instance, the "*propitiation*" feature) is a *showing* of "*the righteousness of God.*" And when the showing is ἔνδειξις, an inward showing, it amounts to inward "*faith.*" What God προέθετο He had to propose *for Himself* in order to satisfy justice; but, having *proposed it to Himself* as what ἔδει, that is, was the thing required, He expounds it to His people; and uses what was a necessity in court, as a necessity a second time for the moral illumination of the sinner. "*Whom God proposed to Himself as a propitiation by faith in His blood*, **to show His righteousness.**" The word is ἔνδειξις which always means an inward showing. It is never applied to outward objects, but always to inward; that is, in the few cases in which it occurs, it means to show "wrath" (9 : 22), or to show "power" (*ib.* : 17), or "the work of the law" (2 : 15), or "faith" (Ti. 2 : 10), or "meekness" (Ti. 3 : 2), or "diligence" (Heb. 6 : 11), or "boasting" (2 Cor. 8 : 24), or "many evil things" (2 Tim. 4 : 14), with such a result upon the inward eye as the necessities of the passage would lead us to imagine.* Now, Paul shows a lesser and a deeper *showing*; and he also states an earlier and a more immediate end. "*To show His righteousness;*" now, in what particular? First in the lesser particular of "**passing over sins previously committed.**" This had been a scandal in the universe. The "*propitiation*" explained how God could slumber so when men were cursing Him. This was the earlier exigence, and is expressed by εἰς; and then comes the more **immediate purpose** (πρὸς, a particle more urgent than εἰς), "**to show His righteousness in the present time, that He might be**

---

* When Alexander, the coppersmith, "showed (Paul) many evil things," of course it did not sanctify Paul in the way that it did to show him the righteousness of Christ. The result must be in the thing shown.

righteous and yet make righteous him who is so out of faith in Jesus." Paul, as his custom is, carries everything along in the torrent of his speech. He drags after him in one breath two unspeakable sequences, one that God may be able to do a certain thing, and the other that He may have actual subjects to do it on. The failure to disentangle these has caused some of the embarrassments about the word προέθετο. God προέθετο, that is "*proposed to Himself*," the ἱλαστήριον, to make it possible to remove the sinfulness of men. It was "the requisite for eternal salvation." But then, as it was bound inexorably to "*faith*," He must have His way of producing "*faith ;*" and He chose most practically to do it by *showing* this very "*propitiation ;*" that is by *showing* inwardly and savingly, and in the shape of "*faith*," and in such a shape of "faith" as shall be through moral light and itself a *righteousness*, the *righteousness of God*," as gloriously exhibited in a plan by which always sin could wait for its punishment upon the operations of the gospel, and by which now sin can be forgiven, and God make better men those "**who** (are) **so by faith in Jesus.**" "*Him who is so*" is not vital to the meaning, but it makes it plainer ; and the warrant for such filling out of texts can be found in many a sentence (5 : 12 ; 16 : 27 ; 1 Cor. 2 : 9 ; 2 Cor. 4 : 6 ; see Winer, Am. Ed., p. 168).

Two inferences remain, first, that **"boasting"** is out of place, and second, that there is no **"God of Jews,"** except in the aspects stated (v. 2), who is not the God of all nations ; and that, by throwing over board the Israelitish claims, there is nothing really taken from **"the law,"** but much confirmed.

27. Where is the boasting then? It was shut out. By what sort of law? Of the works? Nay, but by a law of faith. 28. We reckon, therefore, that a man is made righteous in the shape of faith aside from works of law. 29. Or is He the God of Jews only? Is He not also of Gentiles? 30. Aye, of Gentiles also. If indeed God is one, being such a one as out of faith will make righteous the circumcision, and by means of faith the uncircum-

cision. 31. **Do we then bring law to nothing by faith? By no means. On the contrary we set up law.**
"**The boasting.**" That which Paul has been arguing down in other passages (2 : 17 etc.). "**It was shut out:**" that is (aorist) a long time ago, through all dispensations. "**By what sort of law?**" The Jews, in "*boasting*" of law (2 : 17), of course appealed to it. Now, "*what sort of law*" justified boasting? Not even a law " of works," especially of "*the works*" such as the Jews themselves professed, which were full of sacrificial gospel. But eminently not another sort of law. A second covenant added to the first; that is a new "*law*" added to the old, and was strictly "**a law of faith;**" which new law not simply demanded "*faith*," for that the old law did, but afforded grace for its bestowal, and more than ever, therefore, "**shut**" *boasting* "**out**" ("*excluded*" it, E.V.); for by the very nature of the "*faith*" Abraham, as we afterwards learn, could not boast "*before God*" (4 : 2).

"**Made righteous in the shape of faith.**" "*By faith*" (E. V. & Re.) is a most injurious English. It appears in all our translations. Sometimes "*through*" is substituted for it ; rarely anything else. It is a key point in all our theologies, and this is a good moment thoroughly to discuss it. The preposition "*by*" (E. V. & Re.) is made to express in English four conditions of the Greek—either, first, of this where there is no preposition at all, but simply the dative case ; or, as occasion comes, of that where there is either of three prepositions, ἐκ, διά and ἐν. This general rendering by "*by*" is often mourned over, and men are ready to complain of the poverty of the English ; indeed, with all his nice distinctions, Paul is not only stripped of them in our tongue, but, alas, for his main point ! has it completely blurred, and, in fact, altered, in the hands of the Reformed. Justification "*by faith*" has been a different thing since the days of Luther. In a way that impaired redemption (see com. v. 24), the doctrine that Christ's sufferings were imputed to us has been added to by the idea that so was also His righteousness. Δικαιόω, to *justify* (E. V. & Re.), has, therefore, received the meaning of this transfer. No earthly writing uses it in a kindred sense. I justify myself, but I pretend that I deserve it. I justify God, but I know that He deserves it. I justify the wicked, but I lie in doing so, for I make pretend his innocence. If I translate δικαιόω of a transference of righteousness, I do that which has no warrant in any human language. If it became necessary to coin a sense, we would not object; but that is not the outgiving. The pretension is that *justify* naturally translates δικαιόω in the sense of imputed righteousness. We have already shown that δικαιόω means to *make righteous* (2 : 13). We have traced it to its root in δίκη, and we have further shown that, as that word means the actual *right*, so the verb means actually to *make righteous*, only with the same reserve with which to *make clean* or to *make holy* are used for incipient believers. This being so, faith, in the Greek, unfolds an easy teaching. Paul means differently by all his prepositions. When he says, "*Made righteous by faith,*" he means, that when a man, driven by terror, cries out to God, and in the light of his boyhood's faith appeals to Christ for his deliverance, and God, as He has promised, hears him and regenerates his spirit, the light in which that new birth consists, enters his "faith" as it enters his love, and as it enters all his repentance, and it becomes saving "faith," and therein, just there, it is his essential righteousness. A man, therefore, is not justified by faith in the sense of having Christ's righteousness transferred to him on the condition of trusting Him, but he is *made righteous by means of faith* (choosing now the word διά), when his common "*faith*" is touched by the Spirit and becomes coeval with repentance, and becomes a fruit of regeneration, and hence moral in its nature, and hence an actual righteousness in its germ and earnest. All the sense of διά is not exhausted by the idea that "*faith*" *is* the righteousness. It is a means as well. That is, it is that grace which has the further promise of life and help if we continue in the seeking. And now, "*made righteous out of* (ἐκ) *faith*" (5 : 1): What is that? It is a stronger expression, that "*faith*" is of the very essence of the righteousness. "*In*"

($ἐν$, Gal. 2 : 20) is still stronger. But then, coming close to my text, the dative ($πίστει$ or $τῃ πίστει$) is strongest of all. It really places "*faith*" in apposition to *righteousness*. It is "the dative of material" (see Jelf, Ox. Ed., § 610). It means "**righteous in the shape** (or form) **of faith,**" and so we have translated it; and it has oceans of precedent in this same apostle.

Let us dwell upon this a little. (Where is there anything more vital?) In the very call of this apostle we have this language, "Sanctified by faith (E. V., $πίστει$) that is in me" (Acts 26 : 18). "Sanctified," it will be noticed; not justified; destroying Luther's right to separate justification from other subjective words; and "sanctified" in the shape of faith (*dative*), plainly meaning that the sanctification consisted in the faith. "The hand-writing" consisted in the "ordinances" (dative) beyond a doubt, as Paul wrote to the Colossians (2 : 14). Abraham was "weak in faith" (dative), or "made strong in faith" (dative), when his weakness or his strength equally consisted in his faith, I mean as weak or strong (4 : 19, 20). *Standing by faith* (2 Cor. 1 : 24), *abounding in faith* (2 Cor. 8 : 7), *purifying by faith* (Acts 15 : 9), all datives, mean that the *standing* or the *abounding* or the *making pure* were all essentially the faith; that is, that they consisted in it. The genitive is used with like effect where it speaks of "the righteousness of faith" (4 : 11). What is that but faith? And $ἐν$ (*in*) often amounts to the same; as for example, "salvation in sanctification of spirit, and faith in truth" (2 Thess. 2 : 13); indeed a double example; for if salvation consists in sanctification, why not also essentially and subjectively (as here in the same category) in "faith in the truth"? "**Wo reckon, therefore, that a man** *is made righteous*" by being made to believe graciously and as a gift, the "*faith*" being itself moral like all the other graces of the Spirit, the "*faith*" becoming, therefore, itself his righteousness; "**aside from works of law,**" because "*law*" cannot produce such "*works,*" simply from being thundered at us; any more than "body" can (7 : 24; 8 : 13), or "flesh" can (8 : 3), or "darkness" can (13 : 12), or even Christ can (Jo. 5 : 30), without His Godhead achieving it for Him (Jo. 14 : 10).

To suppose that, as a gospel for the Jews, He should deny its freeness, and plan to save them in trampling the gospel, would be audacious. **"Is He God of Jews only?"** Appeals so plain as to be *nil* logically, are warm in the hands of Paul. **"If indeed God is one."** Why, of course He is one. Well, then, **"being such a one as"** (see the force of ὅς, Jelf, also Winer, Am. Ed., p. 168, and comment., 5 : 26; also com. 5 : 12) has made a rule, and a very gracious one, that is, to **"make circumcision righteous out of faith, and uncircumcision by means of faith,"** how possibly can circumcision either glory or complain? The sentence is strangely keen. If you are the genuine "*circumcision,*" and of a line with Abraham, then, of course, you believe, and "*out of faith*" (notice the preposition ἐκ) God is *making* you *righteous*. If you are not the "*circumcision*," but either "*by nature*" (2 : 27), or sin (2 : 9), are become "*uncircumcision*" (2 : 25), God "*by means of faith*" will yet "*make*" you "*righteous;*" that is will answer your prayer, and give you graciously the holiness that is in believing. "*Do we then make void the law by faith*" (E. V.)? **"By no means."** It is to re-establish the law. "For what the law could not do in that it was weak through the flesh;" that is, what the old covenant could not do simply by promise and gospel speech, God did. He wrote the law on the heart, and gave the gospel an imprint upon the sinner.

CHAPTER IV.

Paul, having prepared the way, for the first time introduces Abraham. It is a master stroke. The Jews trusted to Abraham. One drop of Abraham's blood, with circumcision, was crown and castle. If Paul illustrated by Israel (9 : 6), he must include the Patriarch. This he does signally in the present chapter. There are divers differences in the MSS.; none of them very vital. We choose by the usual criteria of claim, but without comment :—

1. What shall we therefore say that Abraham, our first father, found through flesh?

Paul reaches the very core of the Jew's prejudice. He does not attack what the Jew could **find** from "**Abraham**," but, infinitely worse, what "*Abraham*" could *find* for himself. His catapult is flat against the citadel. "**Therefore,**" if we are to "*set up law*" (3 : 31), then "*Abraham!*" What are we to say of him? "*According to*" (E. V. & Re.). We translate "**through**" as more English, and for other reasons detailed in a previous case (1 : 3, 4). This expression, "**through flesh,**" is a key to the whole epistle. It means that *through the flesh* a man cannot be "*made righteous.*"

This is the omnivocal truth. "*By works of law shall no flesh be made righteous.*" Why? Because by the heralding of the gospel (to take the "*law*" at the very strongest) no mortal man can be converted. He needs something more, viz., the inward application of "*law,*" thus thundered forth. "Believe in the Lord Jesus Christ" is uttered to that which is dead. Paul explains this, "For what the law could not do, in that it was weak through "**the flesh,** God, etc., etc." (8 : 3); and still more extensively just afterward. The apostle expounds the apostle. What "*according to the flesh*" (E. V.) did he find? Why, nothing. "'They that are after the flesh do mind the things of the flesh; but they that are after the Spirit, the things of the Spirit; for the minding of the flesh (*marg.*) is death, but the minding of the Spirit (*marg.*) is life and peace; because the minding of the flesh (*marg.*) is enmity against God, for it is not subject to the law of God, neither indeed can be. So then they that are in the flesh cannot please God." There is no mystery in this thing. "*Works of law*" are "*works of flesh ;*" that is, if the law which is to produce them in the soul has nothing to depend upon but to herald out its commands to our σάρξ ("*flesh* "), when stronger than our πνεῦμα ("spirit "). For though our "spirit" is the abode of God's Spirit, yet He must increase its light before it is moved savingly by "*law* " or gospel. This makes the passage very complete.

2. For if Abraham was made righteous by works, he has whereof to boast, but not toward God by what the Scripture says; 3. But Abraham believed God, and it was reckoned to him as righteousness.

"**For.**" There follow a series of arguments to show that "*Abraham through the flesh found*" nothing.

"**Works.**" He uses this expression as a word by itself for the first time. And we see, he falters. "*Works of law*" (3 : 20 etc.),—that can be positive. "*Works*" that "*law*" can produce by the mere γράμμα or heralding—that we can dispose of brusquely. But "*works!*"—that will answer for terseness, but must be understood with vast explanation. And, therefore, before Paul launches himself upon that free use, he takes care that he be understood. "**Was made righteous by works.**" He does not say "*were*" (E. V.). He discards the subjunctive altogether. Nor does he say "*would have*" (*subjunctive* with ἄν); but he says "*hath*" (E. V. & Re.), whereby we understand that Abraham "**was** *made righteous by works,*" and *did have* καύχημα, or "**whereof to boast.**" Nor need we be uneasy for the gospel; for Paul says that thing over and again. He says, "A man is not made righteous by works of law, *except* by faith in Jesus Christ " (Gal. 2 : 16). And now for our general comment: To say that "*a man is not made righteous by works*" would be very much like saying that he is not made bad by sin, or made fat by bodily substance. The folly of this guards Paul's tersenesses of rhetoric. He has said "*works of law*" till the thing could be understood, and has explained himself in so many ways as to venture now the more terse expression. Think of men who sang, "Oh, how love I Thy law!" being taught that by "*works*" no man was "*made righteous*"! And, therefore, Paul had explained himself all the way along. "*The work of law,*" even, would save a man under certain gospel circumstances (Gal. 2 : 16). "The doers of law" would alone "be made righteous" (2 : 13). They were to be judged "every man according to his works" (Rev. 20 : 12). And John was not more earnest that "he that doeth righteousness is righteous" (1 Jo. 3 : 7), or Christ that men must *do these sayings of His* (Matt. 7 : 24, etc.), or James that we must be "doers of the work" (Jas. 1 : 25), than Paul, that it must be "by patient continuance in well-doing" that we are to " seek glory, and honor, and immortality, eternal life" (2 : 7). That it is not "*works*," therefore, that *make* us *righteous* is absurd. They actually grade all the extent in which we are "*righteous*" (Rev. 20 : 13). But that we are "*made righteous*" in this world in any but the very incomplete sense of being less sinful, or that we are "*made righteous*" ever in the sense of satisfying for the sins of life, or that we are "*made righteous*" (now, as the chief point) by starting out to be so in the strength of "*the flesh*," and under thunders from "*the law*," are equally impossible, and Paul aims to teach that we have been redeemed by the sufferings of Christ, and had bought for us (as the devils never had) the influences of the Spirit,—that we may seek and find ; and that we may have in this dawning "*faith*" the beginnings of a righteousness.

"*If,*" therefore, "*Abraham was made righteous by works,*" as, of course, he was, for who by the possibilities of ethics can be made righteous in any other form ? "*he has whereof to boast,*" and Paul, when men were concerned, did much of this rightful boasting. He cries, "I have fought a good fight" (2 Tim. 4 : 7). He declares, "I labored more than they all" (1 Cor. 15 : 10). He boasts, "I am not behind the chiefest of the apostles" (1 Cor. 15 : 10). He uses this very word (καύχησιν), "that whereof I may boast through Jesus Christ" (Rom. 15 : 17). And, if he had hesitated, he need but turn back to an older date ; for the saddest of the prophets cries out, "Thus saith the Lord, Let not the wise man boast (LXX, καυχάσθω) in his wisdom, neither let the mighty man boast in his might ; let not the rich man boast in his riches, but let him that boasts boast in this, that he understands and knows me, that I am the Lord who exercise loving-kindness, judgment and righteousness in the earth" (Jer. 9 : 23, 24). If, therefore, "*Abraham was made righteous by works*" (as indeed all must be in the more natural and usual sense), "*he has whereof to boast*" (Neh. 13 : 14), for he greatly excelled in righteousness (Heb. 11 : 17) those about him; "**but not toward God**" by any warrant that the Scriptures give. "*But*" (v. 3). This word (δέ) is not in the Septuagint. The Seventy have καί ("*and*"). But δέ also appears in the Epistle of James (Jas. 2 : 23). We cannot explain it there. But here it has seemed to be connected with the particular shape of the clause preceding. That clause scarce answers to the English, " For what saith the Scripture?" (E. V. & Re.), because the ἡ γραφή is before the λέγει (see 11 : 2, Gal. 4 : 30), and such things, under so careful a pen as Paul's, should be carefully noted. Τί ("*what*") as τί *indirect* (see Matt. 10 : 19) would give greater room for "*but*," or, even if we had to discard it as interrogative (as perhaps we ought to do in certain other Scriptures), it is better to imagine moderns to be false in the accent, than Paul himself as not careful of the order of his speech. Γάρ often tinctures with this sort of *soupçon* of a reason; and the meaning of the apostle might naturally be, " *not toward God by* " (meaning *for the reason of*) "*what*" (or "*anything that*") "the Scripture says," "*but*" (giving free room to introduce the δέ before the actual quotation) :—"*but* '*Abraham believed God and it was reckoned to him as righteousness.*'" It is possible, however, that all this is unnecessary, and that there was a reading of δέ in LXX MSS. (see Meyer). There is neither καί nor δέ however in the Epistle to the Galatians (3 : 6).

Thus then is introduced a sentence that seems to have had a broad horizon in the mind of the apostle. Of all other texts in the Bible it ought not to be considered as rendering less subjective—"**righteousness.**" " By *faith* "—and here let it be noted that that dative all through the most marvellous chapter in the Hebrews (11) is without the preposition, and therefore, means that essential "substance" (see first verse) of piety which each case quoted brings into view (*see com.* 3:30)—"By faith Abraham, when he was tried, offered up Isaac" (Heb. 11 : 17). All our study of Abraham should convince us that his faith was new-bred holiness, as imbuing and characterizing, just as it might love or alms-giving, the pious act by which he trusted the Almighty. All holiness expresses itself in exercise ; and if seeking and trusting are just that exercise which God commands to the sinner, it is perfectly just to say that when he obeys the command out of holiness, just as he would that of love or alms-giving, it becomes saving, and it becomes the method of more and more holiness ; and who can profess, then, not to understand how "*Abraham believed God, and it was reckoned to him as righteousness ?*"

It will be noticed that we scarce quote from James. James has strong texts in our English Bibles (E. V. & Re.). He is made to say, "By works a man is justified" (2 : 24) ; and to ask, "Was not Abraham our father justified by works" (v. 21) ? "and was not Rahab justified by works, in that (Re.) she received the messengers, and sent them out another way" (v. 25) ? This was the great Jamesian subjectivity that made Luther speak of a "straw epistle." But just where the English (E. V.) comes in to help our view of Paul, we are obliged to give it up. We are obliged, in honesty, to understand James differently. We understand from the order of the Greek that he was asserting a fact ;—"Abraham" (and in the like case "Rahab ") "was not made righteous by works ; " and in the twenty-fourth verse he was asking a question, "Do ye, indeed, see that a man is made righteous by works, and not alone by faith ?" So that James is more Pauline than Paul. And yet, though we know that till some day we can treat * separately of this criticism, and rob it of its improbable look, our repute will suffer, yet we insist upon bringing it forward. If it is false, the more whimsical it seems the better. If it is true, it will work its way. And it ought to be so evident that,

---

* See Excursus at the close of the book.

"*Abraham—the—father—of us—not—of works—was made righteous*," does not mean a question, and that no sentence like it can be found that does mean one, that it should win respect, as the physicians say, " on the first intention."

But though James gives away "*righteousness by works*," technically so spoken of, and joins Paul, yet he is even stronger than Paul in asserting the righteous essence of faith. He says that though " Abraham was not made righteous by works," so that we need abandon Paul's ground, or forget that works, gendered without grace, never saved any man, yet that faith was the intimate working principle of works ; faith was the intimate inner worker along with works or inside of them (συνήργει, Jas. 2 : 22), "and by the works was the faith made real (ἐτελειώθη)." He insists upon the faith, and he insists upon it by the quotation of this same passage, "*But Abraham believed God, and it was reckoned to him as righteousness*" (*ib.* v. 23). With this testimony of James that "the faith, aside from the works, is dead" (*ib.* v. 20), and with the testimony of Paul that " faith aside from works of law makes (us) righteous " (3 : 28), we are fetched quite up to the necessary sense :—that (as to the getting of "*righteousness*" subjectively, or to our becoming less sinful) works stirred by preaching, or which are set out upon under the thunders of the law (that and nothing else), make no man righteous ; but that faith (which is the great commanded work, and which owns by its very nature* the insufficiency of the flesh) when it " comes by hearing " (10 : 17), and is the gift of the asked for efficiency of the Spirit, is itself our "*righteousness*," and that this was what Phinehas had when " he believed God," and when a righteous act, full of grace, was " reckoned to him as righteousness " (Ps. 106 : 31).

4. **But to him that works anything out, the pay is not reckoned of grace, but of debt; 5. But to him who does not work the thing out, but believes on Him who makes the ungodly righteous, his faith is reckoned as righteousness.**

---

* James has this idea. " Faith, if it have not works, is dead according to its very self " (2 : 17).

To go back (3 : 24) :—"*Redemption*" was a total purchase, to which man owes as much his deliverance as though the substitution were made twice, and man were blessed with the twofold transference, first, of his guilt to Christ and, second, of Christ's righteousness to him as his obedience. In fighting against this last, and condemning it as a myth conceived by Luther, we are in danger all the time of being imagined to lessen the Redeemer. Let us be always going back :—Sin at the first stroke is helpless. Like a stone loosed from human hand, it gravitates endlessly. The tall archangel, when he sinned, fell into a pit literally bottomless ; and nothing can arrest the law as he goes on perpetually downward. It is a horrible idea. And there it is that our religion should have taken hold more of our thought. To make us righteous is deliverance itself. To save us torment is more, in our view, but less, in the eternal redemption. "How shall man become righteous with God" (Job 9 : 2) ? is the great problem of the gospel. It belittles this to divide the plan of mercy. We had a great curse. The devils sank under it. Redemption came to remove it. And Christ, in order to put it away, endured sufferings which He did not deserve, and they were imputed to us. Of course we ennoble everything if we consider that sufficient. Christ's righteousness we do not actually need if He has bought for us a plenary pardon. For let us look at that once more. If He pardon, taking His own time to the work, could He leave us sinful ? For that is the very curse. And if He leave us not sinful, but in His own gradual way make us righteous,* what did Luther do but emasculate that triumph ? for if the good God pardon me to the very last of my transgression, what do I further need if He gradually complete my righteousness ?

To do this, He drives me to "*faith.*" That is, He makes no promises unless I seek Him, and He counsels me to seek Him,

---

* As Augustine says, " Beginning to be justified, and to receive the power of doing right " (ad Simp., vol. 4, lib. 1), by a " justification here imperfect i: us" (vol 5, p. 867), such that " when our hope shall be completed, then our justification shall be completed," (ib. p. 790).

recognizing as distinctly as I can the work of my Redeemer. Why this is necessary I cannot distinctly say. **" Now to him that works the pay is not reckoned of grace, but of debt."** If I, without *"grace,"* either from scorning it or knowing little about it, set out to be a better man, just as Satan might set out to lift himself from hell ; even though we differ from Satan and have redemption ; and even though we differ more than that and have the gospel, and have the law of it thundered from Sinai ; yet if we reject the gospel, and spurn the grace of it, and refuse the prayers of it, and in our strength undertake to obey its laws, we are neglecting the whole spirit of God's administration ; we are treating the thing as though it were to be *wrought out* in the way of wage and payment ; we are forgetting the insufficiency even of the righteousness of the saint ; and we are altogether losing sight of the fact that by believing deference to a Redeemer we have entered a school of *grace*, which does by contrast little now, but incomparably much as time rolls away.

6. Even as also David speaks of the blessedness of the man to whom God reckons righteousness aside from works ;—

7. Blessed are they whose transgressions were put away, And whose sins were covered over ;

8. Blessed is the man whose sin God will not reckon.

The adverse criticism that, because these two latter verses seem forensic, therefore, the result must be, can now be easily answered. The effect of pardon must necessarily be holiness ; otherwise the pardon is nothing. And as to saying that a forensic pardon cannot show itself in a subjective righteousness, that would be to forget that a forensic condemnation does show itself in a subjective sinfulness (1 : 24, 26, 28 ; Mar. 3 : 29, see var. lec.), and that the great curse forensically is, to be abandoned to sin as the result of previous wrongdoing (Hos. 4 : 17). David, therefore, is a strong ally to Paul in teaching that though Abraham was righteous, and righteous in a very remarkable faith, and most righteous, so that he could glory before his fellow men, yet that he had no cause of boasting "*before God*," because he had not earned his righteousness as a workman does his pay, but had heired it, and in a most imperfect state through the forgiveness of the Redeemer. "**Reckons.**" This word puts before us plainly the putative character of our "*righteousness.*" Because it is not Christ's righteousness,—that does not make it less necessary to show its putative cast. It is putative in that it is wholly sinfulness. Sinfulness-grown-less is the whole of a Christian's righteousness. And it is putative also in its promise, which the Bible strikingly puts before us where it says, " We, in the Spirit, by faith wait for the hope of righteousness" (Gal. 5 : 5). "*Righteousness*" is therefore *reckoned* where it really does not exist (v. 6), and sinfulness refuses to be reckoned where it does (v. 8) ; and yet the "*sin*" and the "*righteousness*" are both now subjective in the way that we have distinctly explained.

"**Put away**" does not mean, solely, "*forgiven*" (E. V. & Re.) ; but we do not wish to disturb the main point. The pregnant use of ἀφίημι might be a subject of separate discussion.

9. Was this blessedness, therefore, upon the circumcision, or also upon the uncircumcision? for we say, Faith was reckoned to Abraham as righteousness. 10. How was it then reckoned? When he was in circumcision, or uncircumcision? Not in circumcision, but in uncircumcision.

Not even in his "**faith**" was "**Abraham**" to show a monopoly for the circumcised ; for Paul remembers that he was himself uncircumcised when he achieved his faith.

11. And he received a sign in circumcision, a seal of the righteousness of the faith which he had when uncircumcised, that he might become a father of all those who believe, though they be not circumcised, that the righteousness might be reckoned to them ; 12. And a father of circumcision to those not of circumcision only, but who also walk in the steps of the faith of our father Abraham, which he had when uncircumcised.

This is very Zwinglian. "**Circumcision**" was "**a sign,**" therefore. Instead of being relied upon as even Reformers have relied upon baptism, it was but an instrument for making impressive what had been achieved already. It was a "**seal;**" that is an impressed token of fidelity to a "**faith**" had before hand ; and a *sacrament ;* an occasion for an oath which was to bind, in case it was fulfilled, God and the believing "*Abraham.*" He was "**a father**" about as Tubal Cain was (Gen. 4 : 22). The devil (Jo. 8 : 44) and God (Matt. 23 : 9) and Christ (Is. 53 : 10) and the church (Is. 49 : 20, 21 ; Gal. 4 : 26) are parents in a much more intimate way. As "Jabal was the father of such as have cattle" (Gen. 4 : 20), so Abraham "**of all them that believe,**" viz., as the great exemplar "**of the righteousness of the faith,**" that is of that "by courtesy" or putative "*righteousness*" which consists of "*faith*" at first, till it grow unspotted (Eph. 5 : 27) in the garden of the Lord. "**Though they be not circumcised**" (δἰ ἀκροβυστίας). This is that use of διά, as meaning *a necessary accompaniment* (see comments 1 : 2 ; 2 : 27) ; a very important and a very unobserved Greek usage ; and in the case of the text, "Neither with (διά) the blood of goats and calves" (Heb. 9 : 12), or of the text, "By (διά) whom also He made the worlds" (Heb. 1 : 2), decisively crucial in its elenchtic determinations. "**And a father of circumcision;**" that is of the true "baptism" (Gal. 3 : 27) which the "*uncircumcision*" may become (2 : 26), even if it is never "*circumcised,*" if it "**walk in the steps of the faith of Abraham which he had when**" an "**uncircumcised**" Gentile.

13. **For not by law was the promise to Abraham, or to his seed, that he should be heir to a world, but by the righteousness of faith. 14. For if they who were of law were heirs, the faith has been made void, and the promise utterly in vain.**

"**By law**" would have abundant meaning if it were said that "*law*" did not *make* "**the promise to Abraham,**" for the "*law*" made no such "*promise.*" On the contrary it made an adversative threat. But "**the righteousness of faith,**" that is, a betterness of moral behavior, taking its seed and original "substance" (Heb. 11 : 1) in "*faith,*" did. "*Abraham,*" waking up in answer to his prayers to a new moral light, did find in that illumination a "*promise*" of everything. Agar gendered to bondage, for it simply commanded the gospel without imprinting it ; but the "new covenant" was altogether different. It inscribed the law, and this inscription inwardly, which is the "*righteousness of faith*" (by which is meant that "*righteousness*" which is "*faith*") makes "*the promise*" without an *if*, and without the alternation of any threatening. This would do, therefore, if this were the only verse ; but the next verse creates a difference. **"For if they who were of law were heirs."** *Were heirs*, therefore, must be the idea ; not were promised heirship. "*By law*," therefore, must be like "*by uncircumcision*" in the eleventh verse, which we had to translate "*though they be not circumcised.*" It has the διά of *vital accompaniment.*" "*Not by law was the promise to Abraham*" in such a sense as that because he had the "*law*," therefore he had the promise. What would be the meaning then of the adversative threatening ; for we are to see presently that **"the law works wrath"** (v. 15)? But "*by a righteousness*" that never "*works wrath*," that is, a betterment of his moral nature, coming to him and consisting in a gigantic "*faith*"—"*by*" that, in the sense of a *vital accompaniment* (διά), the "*promise*" did come, and that in the most splendid possible amplitude. **"Heir to a world."** "In thee and in thy seed shall all the families of the earth be blessed" (Gen. 22 : 17). "God gave our father Abraham possession of the heavens and earth" (*Tauchuma, Commentary on the Pentateuch*). **"Faith made void."** What would be the sense of a "*promise*" conditioned on "*faith*," if men enjoyed it without the condition, and the rule were that all "**who were of law were heirs,**" that is, who heard the "*law*," or who were of "*the seed*" to whom God sent it? Besides, the "*law*" had other and deeper uses, and even some contrary to those to which it had been put by superstition ;

15. For the law works wrath, but where there is no law, there is no transgression.

So exceedingly opposite to Phariseeism was "*law*," that, instead of working life, it worked death. Each gift of "*law*" implied a deeper sentence. "**But.**" So fine is this δέ (I mean so delicate) that only our Revisionists retain it. The E. V. has "*for.*" So has the *Receptus :* though there is no strength for that varied reading. The authority is with δέ, and δέ never means "*for.*" Insisting upon "*but,*" there does appear this adversative significance. "*Law*" cannot save a man any more than the plea, "Thou hast taught in our streets." In fact the more street-teaching, the more curse upon unbelief. "*But*" there is one deliverance in the direction of law, if it could possibly be shown forth. That is, where it entirely keeps away, and has no trace of itself in heart or conscience, as in a born idiot, who never in any arena of life has a moral idea, there, of course, there can be no "**wrath,**" for there can be "**no transgression.**"

16. **Wherefore it is of faith, so that it is through grace; so that the promise is sure to all the seed; not to that which is of the law only, but also to that which is of the faith of Abraham (who is a father of us all; 17. As has been written, A father of many nations have I made thee), in the eye of that God whom he believed, who gives life to the dead, and calls the things that are not as though they were.**

"**It;**" that is the *heirdom*, or this whole effected blessing instead of an offered one. "**Is of faith.**" It is promised to "faith" under the "old covenant," and consists in "*faith*" under the "new." It is in its very "substance" (Heb. 11 : 1) "*faith*" considered as a beginning, and is promised to "*faith*" in its continuance and completion. "**So that it is through grace.**" First, because it is built upon a redemption. No such "*faith*" can be bred in Satan. Second, because it is not really righteous. It is only an illuminated sight, making us less sinful. Nevertheless, thirdly, it is spoken of as righteous, and rendered acceptable in the beloved (Eph. 1 : 6) ; and, fourth, it grows, and unless we quench it by apostasy (Heb. 6 : 4–6), it becomes a light shining brighter to the perfect day. It is in no sense by works, except in that great sense that it is itself a master work. But it is of all things else a "*grace.*" It is the grace of all graces. It is that which acknowledges "*grace*" in its very act. For, beginning away back where it was not saving, it sought God; and how can a lost wretch seek the Almighty without, in the name of some hoped-for redemption, appealing to the simplest "*grace*" for a moral return to life? "**So that.**" Paul is speaking of what things are, not what they were designed to be. This must affect both ἵνα and εἰς. It is not "*to the end that*" (E. V. and Re.) or "*that*" (*ib.*) in the intentional sense, but "*so that*" in the way of consequence. Some men deny this as possible in the Greek; but the slenderest bunch of sentences will settle it (Jo. 9 : 2 ; Rom. 11 : 11 ; 5 ; 20). "*Faith*" is not what it is *in order that* it might be of "*grace ;*" for how could it be different? But it is so with this plain *result*, that if it is a penitent and humiliated trust, and, as such, of a moral nature, it admits grace by its very act, and counts in every thing upon a forensic propitiation. "**Seed.**" The true seed undoubtedly. Not that which is "by blood" (Jo. 1 : 13), or physical generation, but "**that which is by the faith of Abraham,** who **is a father of us all.**" "*That only which is of the law*" (E. V. and Re.) is therefore a dreadful error; right athwart all from the very beginning. *That which is of the law* was to have no chance. The position of μόνον ("*only*") is dexterously significant. "*Not only that which is of the law*" (E. V. and Re.), would mean that while *that which is of the law* would be saved, so might something else; but "**Not that which is of the law only**" would mean that, while multitudes who were "*of the law*" might be saved, they could not be if they were "*of the law only*," that is, if their only plea or chance had been that they had "*the oracles.*" "**But just.**" "*But also*" (E. V. and Re.) would throw us back upon the old mistake. We would be saying that there are two classes of heirs, *they that were of law*, and *they that were of faith*, whereas the distinct meaning is that *they that were of law* might be saved, but not on that account, but that they and all others must be saved by being "*of the faith of Abraham, who is a father of us all.*" We will not stay to consider that being "*of the law*" might alter its sense for the occasion, and that they which are "*of faith*" might mean outside men who had only "*the faith*" and not the "*law*" of Abraham. Such changes do happen (2 : 14 ; Gal. 2 : 15 ; Eph. 2 : 3), and are grandly important. But here there is no such special necessity. We should be straining the grammar if we ignored the place of μόνον ("*only*"), and did not observe that, by strictly marking it, we hold everything to the sense of the apostle. "*But just*," or "*but indeed*," or "*but really.*" To say that καί ("*and*") can not have such a meaning, especially after ἀλλά ("*but*"), and after a former clause with οὐ μόνον ("*not* only") is a mistake. "Not only so, but we even (or really) glory in God" (5 : 3, 11) occurs but a few paragraphs further on. "Not only so, but even they who have the first fruits of the Spirit, even (E. V. and Re.) we ourselves groan within ourselves" (Rom. 8 : 23). "**In the eye of that God.**" "*Faith*" is among the things ἐν τῷ κρυπτῷ ("*hidden ;*" see 2 : 29). It must stand "*the eye*" of the Almighty. The parenthesis has been fixed differently. Some (E. V. and Re.) make the spiritual fatherhood to be that which confronts God (κατέναντι), or is to be judged of "*in his eye.*" It makes little difference. Often a text would be understood if there were no parenthesis marked out. The sole criterion is "*faith.*" It is the sovereign test either for Jews or Gentiles. And being such a pivot for the whole, we must be sure of its nature as "*righteousness*" (v. 13), and the only outside judge is the *eye* of the Almighty. "**Who gives life to the dead.**" This eulogium just here is nobly pertinent. The old grazier, when he was pointed to the stars, and called upon at his time of life to believe that he was to be the "*father*" of innumerable princes, surely had need of some such idea of Deity. "**Against hope ;**" of all other men, he was called upon "**to believe upon hope ;**" and, therefore, just such a "*God*" must appear to this old shepherd's vision ; a God who can quicken the dead, and call "**things that are not as though they were.**"

18. **Being a person who against hope believed hopefully, so as to become a father of many nations, according to that which had been spoken, Thus shall thy seed be. 19. And, not**

being weak in faith, he considered not his own body, now deadened (he being about a hundred years old), nor yet the deadening of Sarah's womb ; 20. But, as to the promise of God, he doubted not in unbelief, but was made strong in faith, giving glory to God, 21. And being fully persuaded that what He had promised He is able really to perform. 22. Wherefore truly it was reckoned to him as righteousness."

"**Being a person.**" Ὅς has that condensed sense as a pronoun (see comment on 3 : 26 ; 5 : 12) that reminds us that if the Greek had simply meant to say "*who*" (E. V. & Re.) it might have employed a participial method, and not the pronoun ; and therefore, in beginning a new assertion, it is well to give it a greater amplitude in the English. "**Against.**" Παρά rather means *aside from*. There being no possible "**hope.**" Ἐπ' ἐλπίδι rather means "*upon hope*," and "*believed upon hope*" would not be altogether vague ; but if we change it to "*in hope*," it might be better to make it plainer by saying "*hopefully*." We do not *believe in hope*, but in God "*hopefully*." " He that plows ought to plow "*hopefully*" (1 Cor. 9 : 10, "*in hope*," E. V. & Re.). "**So as to.**" Alford insists that ἵνα and εἰς *always* mean *intention*, throwing to the winds such cases as these (Jo. 9 : 2 ; Gal. 5 : 17 ; Lu. 8 : 10 ; Jer. 44 : 8, Sep.). He hardly can maintain himself. It is more broadly true that Abraham, out of the spontaneity of his own goodness, believed God, than that either God or he cultivated the faith *in order that* he might " **become a father of many nations.**" " **Not being weak in faith—but was made strong in faith,**" present us again the subjective nature of the dative. The weakness would have been the "*weak faith*," and the strength such as it was, was undoubtedly the "*faith*." And therefore where ἡ speaks of being "*made righteous by faith*" (*dative*, 3 : 28), or " purifying *by faith*" (dative, Acts 15 : 9), the "*faith*" must be the subjective righteousness. Δυναμόω to *make strong*, ἀξιόω, to *make worthy*, νεκρόω, to *make dead*, and δικαιόω, to *make righteous*, all have subjective rights, and it must be a strong reason that shall turn aside any of these words in οω. "**Considered not.**" "*Not*" is absent from many MSS., and is given up by the Revisionists. It makes little difference. If we are to erase it, then it would mean that Abraham fully considered these things, and yet (v. 20) believed. And if we are to retain it, then it means that he did not regard or care about them. "**Deadened;**" the past participle of the verb to *make dead* (νεκρόω, see above). "**Deadening.**" Νέκρωσις, the act or fact of "*deadening*" bears the same relation to νεκρόω, to *make dead*, that δικαίωσις, a *making righteous* in the verse below (v. 25), bears to δικαιόω, to *make righteous*. "**Doubted not in unbelief,**" and, once more, "**made strong in faith.**" These are again instances of the dative (see above v. 19). The "*unbelief*" was the *doubt*, and the "*faith*" was the *strength*, and why not, in corresponding grammar, "*the faith*" also "**the righteousness**" (v. 22)? "**Really**" and "**truly.**" "*Also*" (E. V. & Re.) in either of these cases (vs. 21, 22) would be miserably unmeaning. καί, with Paul, has the strongest Hebraistic tendencies, and we should watch them. *Vav* (Heb.) is more versatile than the classic καί.

23. **But it was not written for his sake alone that it was reckoned to him, 24. But also for our sakes, to whom it will be reckoned when we believe upon Him who raised Jesus our Lord from the dead; 25. Who was given over for the sake of our offences, and raised for the sake of making us righteous.**

It is fearful exegesis that makes this refer to the body. If Christ had never died (we mean physically), and God had tormented Him, as indeed He did, in other and more life-enduring ways, and if Christ had never risen, but after sufficient sacrifice in pain had been carried like Enoch to Paradise (it would not have done so well, or else that would have been the plan), but it would have done just as well, as far as we have any knowledge. We run wild with mere rhetoric. Because the Bible tersely talks of our Saviour's "blood," we take that particular secretion, and think it actually did bear a central part in our Lord's atonement. The cross is equally colored up. God may have never seen a cross, and yet, incarnate in a man, could have carried Him through greater torments (as He did), and just as sufficient, as far as we can divine. It is shameful that all the passages about *rising* should be attributed to that adventure at the sepulchre. That was a great event, and was often alluded to (Acts 10 : 41 ; 1 Cor. 15 : 4), and was a glorious evidence (Acts 1 : 22 ; 4 : 33), and was a great soteriological occurrence, for it restored the whole man to life, and sent Him presently to the glory of His kingdom. But it is a shame even to speak of it in this present text. **"Given over"** (διά, *with accusative*, "*on account of*") **"for the sake of our offences."** This was the whole broad account of our Saviour's sacrifice. To dream of it as happening with Pilate, in any sense but as an insignificant part of it, is to turn the whole scene into a superstition. "*Given over*." Christ was a man descended through His mother from the first apostate. Christ was God, entered at His conception by the one personal Jehovah. Christ as man would have inherited from His race actual sinfulness, for the Bible tells us that He was "a dead man according to the flesh" (1 Pet. 3 : 18), that He was "a saved one" (Zech. 9 : 9, see the participle), that "He offered for Himself as well as for the people" (Heb. 9 : 7), that He was the first begotten from the dead (Rev. 1 : 5), and that, though He was pure from sin for reasons that I am about to state, yet that He had "infirmity" (Matt. 26 : 41), nay, that He was "compassed about with it (Heb. 5 : 2), and that "He was tempted in all respects as we are, yet without sin" (Heb. 4 : 15). But Christ as God revolutionized all these calamities. He **"raised"** the sufferer. That is the almost constant meaning of the "resurrection" (4 : 24, 25 ; Eph. 2 : 6). He entered the mother. He *overshadowed* her. He put the "power" of God upon her. By sheer strength He kept that cursed offspring from ever enduring sin. He kept Him from scarce anything else of curse or misery. He knew no sin ; neither was guile found in His mouth. And, as being God impersonate, if "infirmity" had been all, we might conceive of Him as enduring pain enough for a personal expiation, and soon summoning "twelve legions of angels" to translate Him to His heritage. But that was not what He was created to accomplish. He was, therefore, "*given over*," as our text expresses it, for our mountains of transgressions, as well as for His own lighter implication in His parentage. His struggle was made difficult. His temptation became immense. It came on Him in great maelstroms of trial, till He cried out in fear of sinking. It came upon Him in the wilderness, when the dead fast of forty days was allowed to unman Him horridly for the trial, by its clammy and livid sinking upon His spirit. It broke out in blood among the olive trees (Lu. xxii : 44) ; and just at the last, when death seemed alone all that was possible to save Him, He shrieked out, as if lost, as though God had at last forsaken him—all this positively without sin. " Who in the days of His flesh, when He had offered up prayers and supplications with strong crying and tears unto Him that was able to save Him from death " (certainly not physical death, for then He was not saved at all) "and was heard in that He feared ; though He were a son, yet learned He obedience by the things that He suffered ; and being made perfect, He became the author " (E. V. and Re.), better, the ground or reason, the *sine qua non*, the thing forensically required, for " eternal salvation unto all them that obey Him " (Heb. 5 : 7–9). " Given over," therefore, means "*given over*" to this horrid implication more than His own birth-nature would have required ; and "*raised*" loses all its narrow connection of His rising from the grave, and means "*raised* **from** (among) **the dead** " (*plural*, ἐκ νεκρῶν), that is, that He fought a good fight, and when the sins of the whole world were laid upon Him, and accordingly when He was exposed to a temptation whose mortal anguish (to the very last undeserved through His strange success in the battle) would be an equivalent for all our curse, that He was "*raised*" out of this horrible pit, and brought safe to His eternal dwelling. **"For the sake of making us righteous."** Here it is, distilled down to its exquisite finality. Sin is the great curse. A spark of sin would have exploded all the magazine of mercy. Christ shut it out, but with **an** agony of self-deliverance. "He learned obedience," as trial became stronger by its previous throes (Heb. v. 8). And through anguish as a man, and by sheer omnipotence as a God, He was "raised" out of our horrible race (ἐκ νεκρῶν), and, needing no penalty Himself, bought "righteousness," that is, an escape from sinfulness, for us miserable transgressors. "*Making us righteous.*" This δικαίωσις, *enrighteousing*, which bears the same relation to δικαιόω (to *make righteous*) that νέκρωσις, a *deadening* v. 19), does to νεκρόω (to *make dead*), occurs but once besides in the New Testament, and that in the next chapter (v. 18). The phrase there is "*a making righteous of life*," the meaning being "*a making righteous*," or a making holy in such a way that " life " shall consist in it. That passage is so near, however, that one may easily turn to its page, and we need not repeat the exposition.

CHAPTER V.

1. Wherefore, having been made righteous by faith, let us keep possession of a peace with God through our Lord Jesus Christ. 2. Through whom, also, we have kept possession by faith of the entrance given into this grace wherein we have been standing, and let us exult over a hope of the glory of God.

"**Wherefore.**" Because the things just referred to were not written for Abraham's sake alone (4 ; 23, 24), but for ours who imitate Abraham in "*believing on Him who raised Jesus our Lord from the dead*," we ought to make Him our model in all respects, and especially in His endurance (ὑπομονήν, v. 4), and in His hoping against hope (4 : 18). "**Having been made righteous by faith,**" which is just the thing that has been declared of Abraham, "**let us keep possession of a peace with God through our Lord Jesus Christ.**" This implies the possibility of our not keeping possession ; for though we might be willing to imagine that Paul was considering that that would never happen, and was warning against it for the very purpose of preventing it, yet when we pile all the Scriptures together which bear upon such a question, they make the certain "perseverance of the saints" fatal to a consistent revelation (see comments on 1: 11; 8: 33–39; also Lu. 8: 13; Ez. 18: 24; Heb. 6: 4, 6; 10: 38). "**Through whom also we have kept possession;**" again the natural remark to make if apostasy be possible. "*Let us keep possession of a peace with God through*" that very same "*Lord Jesus Christ through whom*" we have been keeping possession of what he calls the "*introduction*" (προσαγωγή) or, as we translate it, "**the entrance given**," literally the *bringing into*, that is the *incipiency* of "**this grace wherein we have been standing,**" and then as a further counsel built upon the precariousness of this first "*entrance into grace*," let us "**exult**" or "*boast ourselves*"—now, in what? A certainty? Or in a full gospel fruition? Not at all. But "**over**" just what Abraham had, that is "**a hope**"(4: 18), and "*a hope*" of exactly that which we should imagine; not of "*righteousness*," for that in a dim way we have already— that lessened sinfulness which consists in faith; but of "**the glory of God;**" that perfect righteousness, which, as faith comes by looking at it (see 1: 17), so light will come by the same means, "the light of the knowledge of the *glory of God* in the face of Jesus Christ" (2 Cor. 4: 6), the entrance into which gives us "*faith*," and the full result of which gives us our final blessedness; just what John speaks of when he says, "When He shall appear we shall be like Him, for we shall see Him as He is (1 Jo. 3: 2).

Godet complains : "No exegete has been able to account satisfactorily for this imperative" (ἐχωμεν, "*let us have*," Re., or "*let us hold fast*") "occurring in the midst of our didactic development." But give up "perseverance," and give up Luther's "justification," and nothing can be more untrue. Load on those theologic weights, and we grant everything; but what is that but saying that authoritative Greek works mischief with both those older rationalisms.

Patriarchal "*righteousness*" was a "*righteousness of faith*" (4 : 13); and the genitive signifies a "*righteousness*" that consists in "*faith.*" To throw that into a fuller shape, it was a "*faith*" so bred morally by the Spirit as to be "*reckoned*" to the patriarch "*as righteousness.*" Let it be understood, however, it was only "*faith ;*" and therefore, though moral and answering to a condition of diminished sinfulness, yet it did not fulfill the law, but only began to. It gave "*peace with God,*" that is a cessation of enmity (8 : 7), because it is the earnest of what is perfect, and the pledge, even in its feeblest beginnings, of what grace will add. But it must be kept up. "Abide in me, and I in you. As the branch can not bear fruit of itself, except it abide in the vine, no more can ye, except ye abide in me" (Jo. 15 : 4). "*Possession,*" therefore, must be "through our Lord Jesus Christ ;" and Paul urges us, in view of what "*for our sakes was written,*" to "*keep possession*" through this same Christ, just as we have been *keeping possession* thus far of what he characterizes as the "*introduction*" or "*entrance given*" into the "*grace*" of the Redeemer ; still more, to "*keep possession*" boastingly, as Abraham did ; for he was "a person who against hope, hopefully believed" (4 : 18), answering thoroughly to the counsel, "*Let us exult* (boast, καυχώμεθα, see 4 : 2 and comment) *over a hope of the glory of God.*"

When, therefore, Meyer says that the old reading of the *Receptus*, ἔχομεν, "*we have peace*" (E. V.), which even the Revisionists give up, "is to be retained," and gives as his reason that ἔχωμεν ("let us, etc."), "though very strongly attested, is here utterly unsuitable" (!) ; and when Shedd says, "We retain ἔχομεν ("*we have*") upon dogmatic grounds (!), although the subjunctive ἔχωμεν ("*let us have*") is by far the most strongly supported ;" and when Alford, strangest of all, bows to the text and says, "It is impossible to resist the strong manuscript" evidence, "for, indeed, this may well be cited as the crucial instance of overpowering diplomatic authority," and, then, after all, rebels, and comments differently, we may well despair. If the Reformed did give a twist to orthodoxy, how are we to mend it, if they may now give a twist to Scripture, and where glosses otherwise fail, then overset the text that they may trample upon the more troublesome revelation?

3. But not only so ; let us even exult in the tribulations, knowing that the tribulation works patience, 4. But the patience probation ; and the probation hope ; 5. And the hope makes not ashamed, because the love of God has been poured out in our hearts by a Holy Spirit given unto us.

Paul abides singularly close to the point at issue. We are to "*exult in hope*" (v. 2). Then, by a most unexpected turn, he tells us that we are to *exult in trouble*. That might appear to be a very opposite exultation ; but see how he brings them together. "**Tribulation works patience**" (ὑπομονή ; literally, "a *remaining under*," that is to say, "*endurance*") ; "but" (δέ, for there is a slightly adversative idea in these sentences as they seem to unite such apparent opposites), "**the patience, probation.**" Like the fable of the faggots, now that the great apostle unties his bundle, each stick is easily managed. *Sorrow, patience.* Why that, of course. What else could it work, as long as the sufferer "*keeps possession*" (v. 2) ? *Patience, proof.* Equally, of course. For that is what God perpetually aims at, *the putting us to proof.* The word is from δοκιμάζω, which means to *prove*, like ores. The word is δοκιμή, the result of that trial. *Sorrow*, like a fierce heat, works *patience*. *Patience*, like the gold in ore, exhibits *proof*. And then the rest easily follows : A man's "*proved condition*" (δοκιμή), demonstrated to him by his "*patience*," breeds "*hope*," and so the apostle comes round to a strong inducement for the required exultation (v. 2).

But now he has a stronger. "**Love**" is the great antidote to fear ; and the absence of fear is, to "**hope**," what the absence of sin is, to righteousness. Another apostle has said, "Perfect love casteth out fear" (1 Jo. 4 : 18). Paul is full of this grand consummation. He seems to think that love and fear are antagonisms. " God has not given us a spirit of fear, but of power and of love and of a sound mind " (2 Tim. 1 : 7). In ecstasy at God's love pouring itself out and radiant in ours, he scoffs at fear. "Who is he that condemneth? It is Christ that died. Who shall separate us from the love of Christ? For I am persuaded that neither death nor life, nor angels, nor principalities, nor powers, nor things present, nor things to come, nor height nor depth, nor any other creature shall be able to separate us from the love of God which is in Christ Jesus our Lord" (8 : 38, 39). He half tears himself away, therefore, from lesser considerations, and suddenly announces, that "**the hope,**" that is *this* "*hope*"—the "*hope*" of Abraham and of every believing sinner—"**makes not ashamed**" (the favorite Old Testament expression, Job 6 : 20 ; Ps. 34 : 5 ; Is. 20:5). And why? He scorns the *patient* track through which he has been arguing his way, and bursts out into one overwhelming reasoning. "*Ashamed!*" Why not? Because of "*love*." But mark the completeness of the reason given. First, because of "*love*." That itself is a great consideration. Because the "*hope*" is mixed all up with that undoubting, unreasoning, unfearing principle of affection. That might be ground enough. But mark the dexterous terseness. Second, "**the love of God.**" This has become Pauline now. "*The glory of God*" (2 Cor. 4 : 6 ; Rom. 9 : 23), "*the righteousness of God*" (1 : 17), "*the name of God*" (9 : 17) ; these are all things for ἐνδείξεις or showings, and we learn to read them as such as we meet them anywhere. The apostle bursts upon us with the most express of all ; for, thirdly, he makes "**the love of God**" to be "**poured out in our hearts,**" and leaves no doubt of his meaning, for he says it is "**by a holy Spirit given unto us.**" This has stood, "*the Holy Spirit*" (Re.). But the Revisers themselves sometimes doubt (as also does the E. V.) and give the small s (1 : 4 ; 1 Cor. 2 : 12 ; see also Rev. 11 : 11), and notice, too, the absence of the article. It makes not the slenderest difference. A holy spirit is given (Acts 6 : 10), and a Holy Spirit gives (1 Cor. 2 : 13), and which positively should be printed in the text it is, many times, unnecessary to ask, and just as often impossible to determine.

6—11. And now, with this fine beginning, Paul, in six more verses, goes on to ennoble "*the love*" and, therefore, "*the hope,*" in two separate particulars. And it is important to see how this passage has been made difficult by an interwrapping of these different reasonings when they are utterly diverse. Let us mention them. One is that "*the love*" which is to be "*poured into*" ours, or, to speak more after the pattern of previous chapters, which is to be " revealed," like any other trait of " God's righteousness, from faith to faith," is so phenomenal as therefore to be well suited to produce wonderful "*love*" in us, and, therefore, wonderful "*hope;*" but, secondly, and on rational grounds, that that "*hope*" is wonderfully promoted, because such an amazing "*love*," so deep, that "**while we were yet sinners, Christ died for us**" (v. 8), now that He has died, and the whole expense has been gone to, and we are actually "**made righteous,**" and, as Paul truthfully reports it, "**in His blood,**" that is, through the great effect of His redemption, "**much more**" may justify "*hope*" and embolden it as it plumes its wing. (1) The essential buoyancy of "*love*" is helped by (2) the rational confidences of " *hope*," as it assures itself that such a "*love*," having "*made* (us) *righteous by His blood*," will save us " from wrath through Him."

But let us translate :

6. For when we were yet weak, Christ, through an opportunity for it, died for the ungodly. 7. For scarcely for a righteous man will any one die; (for for the good man some one might, perhaps, dare to die); 8. But God enhances His own love towards us in that while we were yet sinners Christ died for us.

"**Enhances His own love.**" That, of course, swells ours. For if the conditions are complied with, that is, on God's part, the gift of the Spirit, and, on man's part, the resultant faith, God's love is the provocative of ours ; efficiently, by being " poured into our hearts " (v. 5), and instrumentally by being set before our eyes, so that by ardent "*love*," "*hope*" may burn its very brightest, and we may even "**exult in God through our Lord Jesus Christ**" (v. 11). "*Without strength.*" That is the common rendering (E. V.), and it answers well enough, but "**weak**" is the literal word : and we keep it because of another passage. "What the law could not do in that it was weak through the flesh" (8 : 3). This is a thorough comment. When we were left to the flesh; when we were like the devils; when we belonged to that melancholy company who, as the apostle marks them, being "in the flesh, cannot please God" (8 : 8) : when we were "*weak*," therefore, in a way that precluded any other relief, "**Christ through an opportunity:**"—We seize here a chance for a very useful emendation. The devils had no "*opportunity.*" Christ could seize none for them. He could not have "**died for us**" but for a rare chance in the administration of the heavens. Paul seizes the same idea where he calls Christ the αἴτιος (what happened to be the *required thing*, the *thing charged upon Him*, αἰτιάομαι, the judicial or logical *cause* or *ground*) "for eternal salvation" (Heb. 5 : 9). "*Christ, through an opportunity,*" made His advent, and became the αἴτιος. And as to our right to the words, look at the vapid character of any thing else. "*In due time*" (E. V., "*season*," Re.)! What has that to do with this wonderful affection? The word is καιρόν, meaning "*just measure.*" It is usually translated as of time, for "*opportunity*" marks a time, and is necessarily always of a specific date. We speak in English of an *occasion* from much the same habit of thought. But sometimes the Greek asserts itself. Paul speaks of "serving the καιρός," meaning evidently that we are to *obey the opportunity* ("serving the Lord," E. V., is from a varied reading, 12 : 11*). And in the Epistle to the Hebrews (11 : 15) we read of men having "an opportunity to have returned" (E. V.). There is no doubt about the sense. Paul commands us to "seize (our) opportunity by purchase" (Eph. 5 : 16). And, in classic Greek, the proof would be still more plenty. "**Died.**" Of course not by crucifixion, except as included in His sufferings. He might have been beheaded, or, as we have seen (4 : 23-25), He might have not died at all. The wages of sin are far darker than *death*, except as *death* betokens them. All His

---

* And may probably be the true one. See the comment *in loc.*

humiliations are uttered under that most dismal syllable of rhetoric. "*Died* for." "*In the place of* " would be true, but "*for* " is broader. "Scarcely for a righteous man will any one die." The difference between "*a righteous man*" and "the good man" are not usually well declared (see the different commentators). The "*righteous man*" *is* a "*good man*," and "*righteousness,*" it ought to be kept in eye, is *all moral goodness ;* but our writer, having let μόλις ("*scarcely*") slip from under his pen, stops for an apology, and hence the "for," rather awkward in its sound, which seems established in the text. "*Scarcely for a righteous man will any one die*" (I say "*scarcely* " not to rob the glory of the Master, "*for* " really "for the good man," for that sweetest phase of moral righteousness, "some one might even dare to die"); "but God enhances συνίστησι, (see 3 : 5) His own love towards us," that is, *makes it stand together* in incomparable completeness, "that while we were yet sinners, Christ died for us."

9–11. Let it be understood, therefore, that the utmost "*love*" of the Almighty, exhibited in this extreme shape, and by the Holy Spirit "*poured out in our hearts* " as its reflexive influence (v. 5), gendering, therefore, a "*hope* " only short of that which through "perfect love casts out fear " (1 Jo. 4 : 18), is now to be added to by those *rational* confidences which these extreme thoughts reveal. He who loved me when I was a vile wretch, " much more " will love me when I have been incipiently "made righteous."

9. Much more, then, having been now made righteous in His blood, shall we be saved by Him from the wrath. 10. For if while we were enemies we were reconciled to God by the death of His Son, much more, having been reconciled, shall we be saved in His life. 11. And not only so, but even with exultation in God through our Lord Jesus Christ, by whom now we have received the reconciliation.

"Shall." The full salvation is future. "Made righteous;" only by that tincture of betterness which a slim faith begins. Nevertheless, it is "in His blood ; " for, barred of that, even beginnings of righteousness are impossible. We shall be saved from the wrath, first, when our righteousness shall have become complete, and, second, when our perseverance has become certain, for there is but one promise, "He that endureth to the end the same shall be saved" (Matt. 10 : 22). **"Saved in His life."** Had Christ died in any graver sense, that is, had He met the fate which He cried out against with strong clamor and tears (Heb. 5: 7); that is, had He succumbed to His infinite temptations, we would have been lost. And He said this to His disciples. He warned them in that paroxysm under the olive trees, "The spirit truly is willing (that is my human spirit), but the (my) flesh is weak" (Matt. 26 : 41). He cried out at their failure, and seemed to Himself the more imperilled for their desertion : "What, could ye not watch with me for one hour?" And then—a fearful figure of a man all clotted with the blood of His self-resistance—He cries out as though He would shake at them the finger of the most earnest warning of His risk, "Watch ye and pray, lest ye yourselves enter (by the fate of a failure) into (the results of this my) temptation" (Matt. 26 : 41). "*Saved by His life*," therefore, means *saved by His not dying*, that is not meeting with that dreadful "*death*" (Heb. 5 : 7) which would have followed if He had been beaten by temptation. No wonder Paul **exults** (v. 11), and that he *exults* "**through Christ,**" and that he counsels us to "*keep possession*" also through Him, and that He does " all things through Christ that strengthens (him);" adding, as he presently does again, that favorite adverb, "*much rather ;*" having borne the baptism of Kedron, "**much more**" will He go on to help. "**For if, while we were enemies, we were reconciled to God by the death of His Son, much more, having been reconciled, shall we be saved in His life.**"

It ought not to be necessary to add that the "**reconciliation**" is in both directions, of God to us, and of us to God.

12. The apostle is to go more deeply now into this πολλῷ μᾶλλον or "*much more*" idea as a foundation for *exulting hope*.

12. Wherefore, as by one man the sin passed into the world, so also the death by the sin, and thus the death

passed through unto all men on to Him at whose expense all sinned.

"Wherefore, as by one man the sin passed into the world." Of course it did ; for "*one man*" began the sinning. "So also the death by the sin." Of course it did ; for the threatening against "*the sin*" was "*the death*" (Gen. 2 : 17). If Adam had no progeny, this much would have been fulfilled. The transient act of a single "*sin*," which one might think of as perishing on its very stem, did no such thing, but bred "*death ;*" and millions of sins would have been born increasingly in these two transgressors. So far the sentence might stand by itself, but Paul hurries the results. "*Death*," planted in Adam, "passed through," and the sequence was entire ; "*passed through* unto all men ;" all were affected alike ; and then, rounding out the whole belief, "*passed through unto all men* on to Him *upon whom*" (that is, *at whose charges* or at whose expense) *all did the sinning*." "Wherefore ;" literally "*on account of this*." By "*this*" would then be intended nothing about Adam, for of our relation to that first pair this verse is the first to speak. The force of the illative has to do with this passing through unto Christ. "*On account of this*" refers first to the reconciliation" (v. 11), and, second, to its being accomplished "*by the death of* (the) *Son*" (v. 10) ; and before he can carve out for himself another of these exulting expressions, πολλῷ μᾶλλον ("*much rather*"), he seeks now a base for it in tracking the "*death*" back to its original seat in the history of Adam. He had said before, "*much more, being reconciled*," the easier part will follow. Now he takes another leap. He goes back to where death "passed in," viz., to the sin of Adam, and his reasoning is to be, If sin is so terrible an evil that "by the offence of one the many died," how "*much more*" glorious the grace whereby millions of offences, any one of which might have propagated sin, were swallowed up by one man's obedience. "*Passed into the world*." Eve's sin was the first known on the planet. "So also." This is a translation of the conjunction καί ("*and*") ; and that it is a proper one, take this from the very highest authority. It, καί, is also used "before the apodosis, and connecting it as a consequent with its protasis as its antecedent * * * where the apodosis affirms what is or will be done *in consequence of, because of*, that which is contained in the protasis, e. g., *and so, and therefore,* for example Acts 7 : 43, ' Yea, ye took up the tabernacle of Moloch, and the star of your God Remphan, figures which ye made to worship them : and (so that) I will carry you away beyond Babylon,' quoted from Amos 5 : 27 " (Robinson's Lex. ; see also Robinson upon ὥσπερ, and refer to Math. 25 : 14 and 2 Cor. 8 : 7.) Here then is the much desired apodosis of this critical passage. Some (Clericus, Wolf) have imagined that καὶ οὕτως began it, ("*even thus*"), but οὕτω καί means "*even thus,*" and the whole logical apodosis is more thoroughly gathered up if we gather into it *all* the consequences of "**the sin.**" These were, first, the death of Adam ; second, the death of all men, not even excepting Christ, and, third, the *passing through to Christ*, for the purposes of the "reconciliation" (v. 10), of that "*death*" (v. 6–8) which he endured for the redemption of the sinner. The order then was first, "*sin*," that is Eve's sin ; then "*death*," that is Eve's "*death*" and Adam's ; then "*death*" passing through to "*all men,*" that is sinfulness and all forms of "*death ;*" then "*sin*" in all, as a consequence of sinfulness ; and then "*death*" to Christ, a "*death*" deep and awful, but not sinful ; a "*death*" passed over to our Substitute, "*on whom,*" with a force not unusual to ἐπί, or "*at whose expense*" all did the sinning. "*On to him on whom*" seems a great deal to put into ἐφ᾽ ᾧ, but it is not at all too much even in classic literature. Ὅς has this sort of ricochet of sense very continually. The expressions we have already seen, "*as being one who*" (3 : 30 ; 4 : 18) are kindred in their make. Luke talks "*of those things which*" (E. V.), when all is expressed by ὧν (Lu. 9 : 36). The thief talks "*of those things which* (we have done) " Lu. 23 : 41 ; still nothing but ὧν. Paul has the same expression, ὧν, "*of those things which*" (E. V., Rom. 15 : 18) ; and again in Corinthians, " Did I make a gain of you by any of them (ὧν) whom I sent unto you ?" (2 Cor. 12 : 17). But still more to our purpose, he has this very exact speech ἐφ'ᾧ, and twice in other parts of his epistles. Let me say, however, first, that Luke has it :—" Took up that whereon " (ἐφ'ᾧ, Luke 5 : 25). Paul has it in the plural, "*in those things whereof*"—all expressed by ἐφ'οἷς (6 : 21). And then in the singular, "*that for which*" (ἐφ'ᾧ) also I am apprehended " (E. V., Phil. 3 : 12) ; and again, "*where in*" (ἐφ'ᾧ, or, " *as to that in which* ") " ye were also careful " (E. V., Phil. 4 : 10). The warrant of a translation could hardly be more established. The polemic aspects of this reading (which, however, are not doctrinal at all, for it is fairly on the orthodox side) would carry us too far. We can shorten our book by mere positive explication. Other renderings give their reasons ; and though our version might often be propped by a comparison with others, yet it is expensive as to time, and, perhaps, we should have clearer views if each exegete fenced himself off chiefly to his own exposition. The fixings of this verse are legion. The great thorn that besets its explication is the want of an apodosis. Our common Bibles stride over five verses to obtain one ; and when they reach the eighteenth verse, what have we ? One little more in the shape of this literary need than any of the five which have thus interrupted, most improbably, Paul's wonderful density and subtlety of speech. Then when we roll off the pestering question, and have our shorn protasis to ourselves, what can we do next ? 'Εφ'ᾧ has had a century of meanings. If we translate "*in whom*," we violate the preposition. Paul would have said " *in whom*," and not " *on whom*." Again, the grammar. Adam is far back. Plural nouns would interpose to defeat the pronoun. Again, we throw endless questions into the theology. What is meant by sinning in Adam ? It would be ἅπαξ λεγόμενον. We die in him (1 Cor. 15 : 21) ; but where do we ever hear that we sin in him ? Some think that we were actually present, and, in the loins of our father, ate, *quoad* a legality of ill-desert, the baleful sorrow. Others deny this. It is a turning point of infinite strait. And though it is flatly certain about Adam that we know no more than two all sufficient realities, first, that it is by *nature* that a bad father should produce a bad son, and, second, that it is *just* (though of such high administrations we can argue in our own light literally nothing), yet this passage has started another theory, viz., that though it would be ridiculous that we sinned in him in any actual thereness at the time, yet that we sinned federally, a covenant having been made with Adam, not only for himself but for his children, when there is not a word of the covenant in print, and we have not the slenderest ground of any such conception in the history. A bad acorn makes a bad oak. A fig tree does not produce olive-berries. And since man is not a fig tree, there must be another fact in the heredity, and that is sufficiently revealed, viz., that it is *just* in God, and, therefore, we may say necessary, to let this law of the universe extend to His sensitive creation.

But not only has the translation "*in whom*" created debate, but the *conjunction*-rendering of the words has been still more unsettling. "*For that*" is the rendering of our versions (E. V. and Re.). Well now, how "*for that?*" "Death passed upon all, for that all have sinned" (E. V.). But *why* "for that" or "because?" It is common to say, They die because they sin. But this is not so. They die for Adam's sin, and if there is anything personal to be considered, we must turn the sentence the other way. Either they sin because they die, or, what is more vitally to be considered, they are "dead in sin" (Eph. 2 : 1), just as we are "*righteous in faith*" (dative), that is "*in the shape of faith*" (3 : 28). In other words death and sinfulness are, in the main point (that is leaving off the other evils of death), interchangeably the same great evil. If, on the other hand, we take the Revision view, and read "*for that all sinned*" (aorist), Dr. Shedd is ready to say that we were *there* according to his subjective view of the Adamic imputation, and Dr. Hodge to re-open the debate, and insist upon the federal inness or oneness in the original transgression. Giving ἐφ᾽ᾧ an understanding which brings an apodosis to the first clause, and making ἐπί mean "*on*," and restoring it to its proper signification, we draw the lines back to where they cease to be polemic, and we exhume a sense in which all Christians are at one, and which is about all that has been taught to us of our apostasy in the Garden of Eden.

Making ἐπί mean "*upon*," which is its straight-out and most necessary signification, would be enough for our purpose, for "*upon*" Christ in the most literal sense men have been loading down their guiltiness. But ἐπί so distinctly means more (Lu. 12 : 44; 9 : 49), and so specially means *to a man's account* or *at his hazard*, or, as we would say in trade, *at his charges* (Dem. 822 : 10; Lu. 4 : 4; 9 : 49; Acts 2 : 38; 9 : 17, 18), that we have not hesitated to give immediate facility to the sense by this form of interpretation.

13. For as far as there was law, sin was in the world; but sin is not imputed where there is no law; 14. Yet death reigned from Adam to Moses, and over those who did not sin after the similitude of the transgression of Adam, he being a person who is of the pattern of the Coming One.

Barnes says of all this (vs. 12–21) : It "has been usually regarded as the most difficult part of the New Testament." But let us take it all carefully to pieces. Paul has been helped amazingly by Jewish quotations. Of enrighteousment by faith he has fine support in the sentence, " The righteous by faith shall live." So he has reaped much from the Patriarch ; and much from the Patriarch's eulogy—" His faith was reckoned to him for righteousness." But, wishing to celebrate "*the gospel*," which he had pronounced to be the subject of the Epistle (1 : 1, 15), and, therefore, to make much of the sacrifice of Christ, "*one man*" for millions, he is naturally drawn to extend his base over that other man's foundation, and to say, If "*one man*" could ruin the world, "*much more*" has another man saved it. But now, by a singular fatality, there is precious little Scripture about that other "*one man*," and no great text like that about the believer and about Abraham. There is a mention in the narrative in Genesis, and no mention again in all the Hebrew. The facts were so patent that they required no mention. That very obviousness was the exact stand for Paul. It will be seen that he demonstrates nothing. But the structure of his speech is a mere terse appeal to the facts that were unchallenged. He had said, "*Death passed through to all.*" He quotes nothing, for there is nothing to quote. And for that very reason, because the results of Adam's sin (except in the Apocrypha, 2 Esd. 3 : 21; 7 : 11, 12, 48; Eccles. 9 : 1), had not been thrown into shapes of their synagogue speech, he goes back to first principles in the matter, and makes ready, by a skilful word, for the use of the first man as **"of the pattern of the Coming One."** How could he show that "*death had passed through to all* (v. 12)? That all were sinners he could quote, and had quoted with more than usual decision (3 : 10, 19). But how all came to be sinners was another affair, and he traces that in a chronological way, and lays it at the door of the original transgression. **"As far as there was law sin was in the world."** That he lays down at once. He had already taught that all had sinned (3 : 23). But he was willing to go back, and make things more sweeping by a challenge. He was willing to admit that men were not sinners who had **"no law."** That is a plain truism. And he mentions it only to assume it. If I have nothing to teach me righteousness, I have nothing to breed me "*sin.*" There is no mystery in this. It is a plain, every-day thought which the apostle had previously noticed (4 : 15). But he adds to it. **"Sin is not imputed,"** that is, can not be reckoned or punished, **"where there is no law."** If a man is punished, it is a sign he has both "*law*" and "*sin ;*" and, thus reasoning backward, he carries us through all the passage. **"Death"** not only existed, but it absolutely **"reigned."** And it "*reigned*," not only in common times with which they were all familiar, but in times of less law, or, in Oriental exaggeration (see comment on 4: 15, also 1 Jo. 3: 4), of no law at all, such as those **"between Adam and Moses;"** and not only in times of "*no law,*" comparatively (just as our Saviour speaks of no sin, Jo. 15 : 22, and Paul of not being sent to baptize, 1 Cor. 1 : 17), but when they **"had not sinned after the similitude of Adam's transgression,"** that is, as standing for a race, with the awful heinousness of sinning away a world, and with the horrid criminality of plunging into sin out of a condition of light and righteousness. These are the simple reasonings of the apostle ; "*Death has passed through unto all,*" because all show it ; and that not in physical "*death,*" but in a thousand other symptoms. And as "*sin is not imputed where there is no law,*" and "*death*" can not be inflicted except as a reckoning for sin, it follows from the universality of pain, that there is a universality of sin, and, therefore, a universality of law, and, hence, from the whole picture of the facts, a need of tracing the history to an original transgressor.

It must be distinctly marked, however, how the Bible keeps diligently in view sinfulness as the punishment of sin. Just as Christ's great grace is righteousness, that is holiness, and it is sad that we have frittered it away into a forensic justification, so Adam's great curse was sinfulness, and we have frittered it away into "*death*" with a less radical sense than that imputed by the words of the apostle, "the wages *of sin is death,*" that is, more sinfulness, the undoubted agonies of wrath being only the nimbus around the great essential substance of the punishment. "In the day thou eatest thereof, thou shalt die." See how closely Paul follows the reality. "*Sin*" he couples instantly with "*death,*" and we find he gives no countenance to any thing but this : that our great curse in Adam is just what a fig-tree might inherit—character. Paul seems to think that enough. I get from Adam character. That is "*death*" in its very essence. To feel any thing painful I must have both law and sin. "*Law*" I certainly do have in my natural conscience, and "*sin*" all men show ; and "*death*" is nothing more than "*sin,*" except as there go with it temporal and eternal sorrows.

"*As far as.*" This is almost the original sense of ἄχρις. Ἄκρος means *to the utmost edge of.* Ἀκραχεῖρ means *to the end of the hand.* Ἄχρις usually means "*until*" (E. V. & Re.), a very natural sequence from the other meaning. But Xenophon says : "As long as (ἄχρις) they do not hunger " (Conv. 4 : 37). Luke says : " For (ἄχρι) five days " (Acts. 20 : 6), and we read in the Hebrews : While (or *as long as*) it is called to-day " (3 : 13). It is a preposition singularly philosophic in describing just how great sin is. It is sin just as far as it is against conscious "*law*."

Other and adverse renderings would fill a volume by themselves if we attempted to reply to them. They are positively numberless. In the throes of difficult exposition such as Barnes speaks of, it is astonishing how good men forget themselves. Like a woman in her agony, they say things that they could not be forced to utter in moments of ease. This, for example—it is from the grand work edited by Ellicott : " Strictly speaking, there could be no individual sin till there was a law to be broken. But in the interval between Adam and Moses, *i. e.*, before the institution of law, death prevailed over the world ; which was a proof that there was sin somewhere. The solution is, that the sin in question was not the individual guilt of individual transgressors, but the single transgression of Adam " (*in loco*).

Here, really, is where we should push, to force the necessity of some more reasonable rendering. Nearly all the commentators side with Ellicott. The theologizing is really dreadful. Egypt could build Cheops, but did not know that to rob widows was wicked ! Wait till some other page, and these same men will be extreme upon the perdition of the heathen ! We sometimes think passing by a sentence would be wise. It would ennoble an exegete sometimes. ' This paragraph puzzles me, and I pass it.' For surely it must injure the undevout when critics put hand to every sentence, and are manifestly dazed into a reading which makes the whole world for twenty centuries ; with Enoch in it, who walked with God ; with Noah in it, who was a preacher of righteousness ; with Abel in it, who obtained witness that he was righteous ; with Nimrod in it, a great founder of empire ; with Abram in it, before the giving of the law ; and with a world in it before the flood given up to wickedness ; yet, in all that time, simply guilty in Adam ; as Ellicott sanctions it, " without a law to be broken," and, therefore, with no individual guilt of individual transgressors ; the flood, of course, drowning no sinners, but only hapless heritors of the guilt of our great mother !

We base every thing upon the fall of Adam, but that every thing is in the chief part sinfulness, and sin can not be reckoned for where there is no law. And we base every thing upon the sacrifice of Christ, and that every thing is in chief part our own righteousness, very sinful indeed at first, but gradually growing more righteous, as Augustine represents,* and which can not be realized except under fresh law and under fresh probation. It is under these parallels "*of the one man,*" and "*the one man,*" that Paul introduces the sentence that the first man "**was after the pattern** (not *a type,*" E. V., simply, or, least of all, "*a figure,*" Re., simply, but "*after the pattern,*" that is, *in a kindred position*), of "**the Coming One.**"

15. **But not as the offence so also is the grace: for if in the offence of the one the many died, much more did the grace of God, and the gift in grace which is of the one man, Jesus Christ, flow over to the many.**

Godet complains that "this passage (vs. 15–17) has exhausted the sagacity of commentators." The "three verses," he adds, " are among the most difficult of the New Testament." His account of other authorities is curious and suggestive. " Morus holds that in vs. 15–19 the apostle merely repeats the same thing five times over in different words; Rückert supposes that Paul himself was not quite sure of his own thoughts ; (while) Rothe and Meyer find in these scenes traces of the most profound meditation and mathematical precision. Notwithstanding the favorable judgment of the latter it must be confessed that the considerable variety of expositions seem still to justify to some extent the complaints of the former." (!)

Let us, however, observe two rules, and watch their efficiency. The one is, not to imagine that the apostle is designing to say more than he actually says. We are constantly confused by mixing the ὅτι with the διότι. Paul is simply saying that if

---

* " Justification here is imperfect in us " (Vol. v. p. 867). " When our hope shall be completed, then also our justification shall be completed " (Vol v. p. 790).

"**the offence**" ruined us,* "**much more**" will "**the grace**" save us. Is not that true? And if you answer, yes; but before we can see that it is, we must see the reason; that brings us to our second point, that we daze ourselves by imagining one reason. Paul could give many reasons, too many to put into the verse. And, therefore, we must expound in that way. "*But not as the offence, so also is the grace*, for "— This "*for*" is the *for* of statement, not of explanation. "*The offence*" differs from "*the grace*" in this, not because of this; and the respect or modus of the difference is simply thus, that if the one damns, "*much more*" may the other save. Now the real fact is that the reasons are endless, and the multiplicity of the list is partly that which has confused our thinking. Paul, let it be remembered, is inflating our hopes (v. 5) with all sorts of joy and boasting (vs. 2, 3) in the Gospel. For this cause he has gone back to our apostasy, and, clearing up in a sentence or two our ruin, he wishes to show how much more triumphant "*grace*" is in our escape, than sin ever was in effecting our downfall. That then is our second point, that the reasons are many, and Paul did not attempt to put them in a list. In the first place, grace is the more welcome principle. God loves it the best, and will be sure, if it be safe, to prefer it. "He that spared not His own Son, how shall He not with Him freely give us all things?" (8: 32). Paul has been insisting upon this in the chapter previous (vs. 15–17). Again, "*grace*" actually wins. In the experience of all the saints ruin attacks all, and "*grace*" comes in and conquers it. It has the last hand; and if we would listen to its voice, it would save every one of us. Once more, it **overflows**. This is the respect that is most suggested. That word which Paul here only for the second time employs (see 3: 7) he seems to enjoy heartily hereafter. And what can it mean? However Christ was implicated, undoubtedly he *was* implicated in the sins of the whole world. We believe that he was implicated person-

---

* We must observe the "dative of material." "*The offence of the one*" was not merely the instrument, but the very "material" of our death. We therefore say "**in**," not "*by*" (E.V. & Re.).

nally in Adam, and, as Peter expresses it that " He was a dead man (unless ' saved ', Zech. 9: 9) according to the flesh " (1 Pet. 3:18). But all agree that He needed "*grace*" (Ps. 45: 2; Jo. 1:14) and if He needed "*grace*" in His human nature, it must *overflow* beyond Himself if any "*grace*" is to reach the world. This *overflowing* thing is " *the gift in grace which is of the one man Jesus Christ.*" But now, not only, as we have stated, must it *overflow* beyond Christ, but it must *overflow* beyond all the uses of the world. The primal curse lighted—every ounce of it ; but the final grace *flowed* over and to spare. Bad men feel every atom of the blight, but good men simply bathe in an *overflow*. The ocean of "*grace*" would not cease to " *abound*" (E. V.) if all had been wise, and the whole world were steeped in its glorious baptism.

We discard "*free gift*" (E. V. & Re.), which is a good enough word for χάρισμα, and aptly translates it, in order to keep near to χάρις ("*grace*"). χάρισμα is " *the grace*" bestowed, while χάρις is the principle of " *grace.*" The two words ought to be translated alike in the same sentence.

But now more specifically :

16. And not as by one that sinned, the gift; for the judgment was from one to condemnation, but the grace was from many offences to a making righteous.

"**Gift;**" not χάρισμα in this instance, but δώρημα, the simple word for "*gift.*" Χάρισμα occurs below, obviously with intended difference, and we translate it " **grace.**" On the contrary, " **from one to condemnation** " and " **from many offences to a making righteous,**" employ the same preposition, and the E. V. deserts the common ἐκ, and alternates it as "*by*" and "*of.*" Obviously the ἐκ should be retained. And though the idea modifies itself as between the one clause and the other, yet the very reaching for the connecting link clarifies the passage. Sin in each case was the occasion. In the one case it bred curse, and in the other "*grace ;*" in the one case by the law of the empire which bred " *death,*" and, in the other, by the law of the same empire, which gave life if the justice of Heaven could be satisfied in our salvation. Now, the whole object of the passage is—another " *much more* " exultation. For if *one offence* was so stingingly complete as to work mischief to millions of a race, how gloriously abounding must that " *grace* " be that can take a million of Adams, with millions and millions of trespasses, and counterwork at this late date what has been seating itself by increase for thousands of years. How thoroughly this illustrates the text (v. 20), "Where sin grew greater, grace flowed over in greatness." **" To a making righteous."** This is the word already remarked upon (1 : 32 ; 2 : 26). It is the noun from δικαιόω, to *make righteous*, which means, according to Greek structure, an instance of δικαιόω, that is " *a making righteous.*" Protestant expositors, of course, say "*justification*" (E. V. & Re.), yet it cannot be translated so in most cases, (Lu. 1 : 6 ; Heb. 9 : 1, 10 ; Rev. 15 : 4), and even that Latin word to *justify*, by nature means to make righteous. As " *one man* " makes us sinful, the Other Man *makes* us *righteous*. Of course the significance is complete, and, for the point greatly insisted upon (Alford, Meyer, Fritz), that it stands opposed here to "*condemnation*," that proves too much. Sanctification is opposed to " condemnation " (Gen. 4 : 7 ; Heb. 10 : 10–14 ; 13 : 12); and so is cleansing (Lev. 14 : 18, 29 ; Job 11 : 15 ; 1 John 1 : 7, 9) ; and so is any other fruit of the Spirit (1 Jo. 4 : 18). Such reasonings should not be resorted to. In many a large theology the very same covers of a book enclose the same author, fencing by the same method, in flat opposite direction in the use of kindred passages. If one sin debauched our race hereditarily, how much more grand " *the grace*," when the poison has spread into myriads of sinners, that can get hold of all that will obey (yes, and get hold of "*many*" and make them obey), and make them righteous in spite of their iniquity !

17. **" For."** Now the apostle will sum the previous verses (15, 16) together :

17. For if in the offence of the one death reigned by the one, much more shall they who receive the overflow of the grace and of the gift of the righteousness, reign in life by the one Jesus Christ.

The only advance in this verse, as it gathers the last two into one, is in its tone and in its fuller sentiment of boastfulness. What in the fifteenth verse is *dying*, swells out in this seventeenth verse into a wilder triumph, for Paul calls it the **reign of death.** What in the fifteenth verse was in the past, advances now into all the glory of the future. And what before was our poor souls reaching the *overflow of grace* and being saved by it, is now the " **reign** " of grace, when it shall take entire possession, and, what is more, the " *reign* " of " **life**," and, what is more still, of that " *life* " of which he has already spoken— that *enrighteousment which constitutes life* (1 : 17), *that living which consists in being righteous* (8 : 6), or, to go no further than this text, that *receiving* of " **the overflow of the grace and of the gift of the righteousness** " which shall constitute a *reign* in the shape of glorious " **life through the one man Jesus Christ.**" We speak with more emphasis of this subjective sense because ἐν ζωῇ ("*in life*") lies ambiguously between *receiving* and *reigning*. Like many another sentence, it is to be considered as making no difference whether we read *receiving in the shape of life*, or *reigning in the shape of life*. We have a right to either, and, therefore, to both. No mortal can choose ἐν γράμματι ; just as it makes not the slightest difference whether we say (1 : 17) " The righteous shall live by faith," or " Those righteous by faith shall live." In the language of the Spirit those are Providential forms ; and that is a stone of Sisyphus that men are heaving, when opposite creeds attempt to wrestle with but half-denied and, perhaps, wholly meant ambiguousnesses (1 : 3, 6 ; 5 : 5 ; 16 : 2).

18. Therefore then as by one offence there came that for all men which was for condemnation, so also by one righteous-making there came that to all men which was for enrighteousment of life.

Paul gathers himself back, now, for a general conclusion. Every time he asserts the parallel, he brightens it by some new feature of its truth. " **Therefore then ;**" that is, gathering all these lights together. " **By one offence.**" We have been accustomed to the reading " *by the offence of one* " (E. V.), and might set it down as a harmless ambiguity (see last verse). The thing is repeated, "*By the righteousness of one*" (E. V.). We would translate it, "*by making one righteous,*" and our meaning would be that "*by one enrighteousment,*" that is, by "*the righteous making*" of Christ, He was lifted out of the grave of death (1 Pet. 1 : 3), and was able to impute His sufferings to His people. It will be seen that "*by one enrighteousment*" or "*by the enrighteousment of one,*" makes not the smallest difference in the sense. We choose "*by one offence*" rather than "*by the offence of one,*" because, simply in the grammar, we are in doubt whether there is any ambiguity at all. An adjective with a noun, if they be in the same case, have probably the chiefest right to be understood together. What rule could there be for separating them? Grammar, like electricity, takes the shortest cuts, and though strong reasons in the sense might justify a divorce, yet here the reasons are the same. Paul is wending towards his end, and, therefore, the terseness of "*one enrighteousment,*" that is, one Adam *made righteous* to balance one Adam become a sinner, is just that neat phrase which Paul, in his magic of speech, would be very apt to bring into his reasoning. "**There came that.**" King James fills this gap from the sixteenth verse, and reads, "*judgment came*" in one clause, and "*the free gift came.*" But these large italics are a sort of reflection upon Paul. In many such cases a more rightful and idiomatic provision was intended. Paul delights in what every body must see and yield to; and, therefore, making his craft as sharp as he can upon the water, he utters that which every body must concede, namely, that there was *something* in the one offence that was for condemnation, and that such was the something in the one enrighteousment. At any rate, it is a capital rule, as we have seen already (see 3 : 9), not to supply italics, even when, with a still greater number of words, we can keep within the lawful meaning of what is written. "**Righteous making.**" King James has it "*righteousness.*" The Revisers, driven by the Greek, give us "*act of righteousness.*" *Ex necessitate theologiæ* beyond a question. Δικαίωμα, it is safe to say, never means "*righteousness ;*" and though there may be lexicons that say that it does, yet they are Protestant lexicons, not classical. And yet "*righteous act,*" except in the narrowest significance, is still more unmanageable. A sinful act ruined us, but what "*righteous act*" ever saved us? What exactly do the Revisers mean? If they mean some act of God, that would depart entirely from our parallel. And if they mean some act of "*the one,*" prythee what act? How much more satisfactory the sense if we can get back to the usual meaning of this form derived from ου? Here were "*one man*" and "*one man.*" One of these men sinned, and by the confession of almost every Christian "*there came that* **for all men which was for condemnation.**" The other man belonged to this "*all men,*" and would have come into this "*condemnation*" but for grace and power of His incarnate Godhead. As it was, He was "infirm" and desperate in His "temptations," and this, not by any theory of ours, but by the express words of accepted revelation. He is not so now, but has been "made perfect," and it was in "being made perfect" that He became the αιτιος, that is the *required ground* of eternal life to all them that obey Him" (Heb. 5 : 9). What is this *perfectness?* He calls it *being sanctified* (Jo. 17 : 19). It is called *learning obedience.* (Heb. 5 : 8). He is spoken of as "*begotten from the dead,*" and, constantly, as "raised up" (8 : 11). And we have the most glaring evidence that desperate moral temptation was the secret of His suffering, and the battle that He fought for our soul's deliverance. Now, no mortal imagines that His winning was human. He was "*made righteous,*" and that by the Deity, one within Him. He never sinned. He was spotless from the very beginning. But He was weaker (Jo. 17 : 19) in the beginning than at the end ; and the change between, is what is called "*being made perfect.*" He was eminently "*made righteous ;*" for the Most High, who overshadowed Mary, would have left Him to be sinful if He had not *made* Him to be *righteous.* And this enrighteousment continued. With the Almighty it was a stinted holding up. With the man it was an awful struggle. With us it was our great salvation. And as by one offence we all were damned, by this "*one enrighteousment*" there came that to us which might be for our own "**enrighteousment of life.**"

Not much remains to be explained. Δικαίωμα means *the thing* or *act* or *subjective occurrence that makes righteous.* Δικαίωσις means the act of making righteous. A nice sense will appreciate the difference. The former, in the Old Testament, is most frequently translated "*statute*," because a statute makes right either by being obeyed or by bringing punishment. Δικαίωσις is rarely employed (in the New Testament only twice, 4 : 25 ; 5 : 18). We infer not the smallest difficulty in the present text. If we may coin the word "*enrighteousment*," which explains itself, the meaning is, that as by one sin there resulted to many condemnation, so by one enrighteousment (not quite so narrow as the sin, because it was wrought out in many acts, and lasted for thirty years) many were made righteous.

"*All.*" There should be no danger of Universalism in this word, even if Paul had not said what he had about faith (4 : 5, 9). The terseness comes in as guard. He does not say that all men were made righteous, but "*there came that to all men which was for enrighteousment of life.*" "*Life*" occurs here as elsewhere (Jo. 5 : 29). It is the genitive *essentiæ*. The meaning of the whole is that "as by man came death, by man came also" that sort of resurrection in which the "*life*" is, in its chief substance, *righteousness.*

19. For as by the disobedience of the one man the many were made sinners, so also by the obedience of the one the many shall be made righteous.

This seems to require no notice. It is all that has gone before, clarified into the sense we have been distilling. Its beauty is that it is more express. The last clause projects us into the future. We are really not righteous here, but "**by the obedience of the one many shall be made righteous.**" It is only in this way that the truth can be final. "**By the disobedience of the one**" we were "**made**" (E. V. and Re.), not *reckoned to be*, but actually *constituted* sinners, so, of course, if we take the thing in its most rightful argumentation, "*by the obedience of the one the many shall be made* (that is *constituted*) *righteous.*"

20. But, side by side, law came in so that the offence grew more and more ; but where the sin grew more, the grace overflowed the further, 21. So that as the sin reigned in the death, so also the grace would reign through righteousness unto eternal life, through Jesus Christ our Lord.

Paul does not teach us that men sinned without "law," any more than they were righteous without law. The presence of law was necessary to both sin and righteousness. Nevertheless sin and law could be looked at apart, and that in a very essential way. A man would be a sinner if he came out of the loins of Adam, and yet he could not be a sinner without conscience and a law. The verb, therefore, is a very striking one : "*entered along*," or "**side by side.**" Nothing could be more real. The very same man we get our sin from, we get our conscience from. Our moral nature comes down to us in our descent from Adam. It would not be hard to state the two facts together. An imperfect conscience, that is an imperfect sense of law in its inner principles, is itself our sinfulness ; so getting an imperfect conscience from Adam unites the two facts of sin and law. Nevertheless law enters endlessly afterward. Sinai added to it. And each lesson in our duties is a new entrance of law. Now the law enters, not *in order* "*that*" (E. V. and Re.). This ἵνα is endlessly misused. It is the expression of *result* (Gal. 5 : 17). We are to keep clear of the other idea. God never sent the law *in order to* damn us. Paul is going deep into his facts and teaching us the nature of our ruin. The law came in along side (παρεισῆλθεν) of our descent from Adam, and each increase of law increased our sinfulness. In fact, we could have no sin without some law, and the law comes further in *with the result* of adding to our iniquity. And now with this fresh start from our misery in the Fall, Paul makes corresponding boast of the overflow of the gospel. "**But side by side law came in so that the offence grew more and more ; but where the sin grew more the** grace overflowed the further." These are not the same words. "*Grew more*" is from the word πλειων (*more*), whereas "*overflowed the further*" is a term of the sea, and means *hyper overflowing*, or, as we would turn it into Latin, *superabounding*. It is well to hold different words to their distinctiveness. Grace surges over any mountain, even of the most intelligible and law-defying increase of sin. "**So that as the sin reigned in the death,**" still the idea of the very nature and subjective character of the *reign*, "**so also the grace would reign.**" "*Would*," not "*might*" E. V.). He is still speaking of the result (see 4 : 18), for the two clauses should balance each other. "**Through righteousness.**" That ends the chapter. That fills this epistle. That is the key-thought of all these sentences together. Faith is the seed-germ of our glory. We are made righteous by our faith. Not that it is so very righteous, but that it is the dawning of a new moral nature. It is the richest act of human obedience. No wonder that it was reckoned for righteousness ; and no wonder that Paul, in these grand comparisons, when he came to speak of its results, should speak of it as a "*reign*," and as a "*reign*" of "*grace*," and as a "*reign*" of "*grace*" "*through righteousness ;*" that is, the very substance of the "*grace*" being that "*righteousness*" which is itself "**eternal life by Jesus Christ our Lord.**"

CHAPTER VI.

1. What shall we say then? May we continue in sin, and the grace be the greater? By no means. As men who died to sin, how shall we yet live therein?

"**Then.**" The illative idea here is, that inasmuch as "*where sin grew to be more, grace did overflow the further*" (5 : 20), the query might be worth answering : "**May we continue in sin, and the grace be the greater?**"

There are four of these queries, and they entirely engross

this and the next chapter. It will brighten our track if we recite them at once. This first ends with the idea, "*Ye are not under law but under grace*" (6 : 14). The second takes that point up. "*What then? May we sin because we are not under law but under grace?*" (v. 15). A reply to this, sweeping on through the rest of this chapter and through six verses of the seventh, ends with the expression, "*We have been brought to nothing as to the law, having died to that in which we were held.*" This breeds very naturally the third query : "*What shall we say then? Is the law sin?*" In treating this he utters the third provocative, and is ready for the fourth question. The law is not sin, he argues ; nevertheless "*I had been alive*" (that means I would have quitted sin) "*at any time*" but for the law (7 : 9). Sin, taking occasion by the commandment, deceived me and by it slew me, yet "*the commandment is holy and righteous and good.*" That, of course, leaves one more query to be listened to : "*Did then that which is good become death unto me?*" (7 : 13). One-eighth of the epistle, therefore (chaps. vi. and vii.) is occupied with these four successively self-suggested interrogations.

"*May we continue?*" Authority, as among the various readings, lies with the subjunctive. The contingency expressed by that mood may be of any nature, and "*may,*" *can, or shall* may be supplied. Either would do in the present instance ; but "*may*" is perhaps the best. If "*where sin abounded grace did much more abound* (E. V., 5 : 20), *may we*" avail of such an abounding, and sin the more, to increase the overflow of the graciousness. Paul replies,—not that this would be *shameful*, and not that this would be *unlikely*, and not that this would be an enterprise in which we *ought not* as Christians to engage. All that would be true but weak. The apostle's position is that the thing would be impossible. "*May we continue in sin*" with a certain result? It is idle for Winer to say that ἵνα always means *intention*. Paul is full of the opposite in this very epistle (4 : 18; 6 : 6; 8 : 4). And how is it in the

CHAPTER VI.

epistle to the Galatians? "So that (ἱνα) ye cannot do the things that ye would" (Gal. 5 : 17). Paul's argument, therefore, is, May we do a certain thing with a certain result? And he replies on the spot, not that we ought not, but that we cannot ; and his single reason is, **" As men who died to sin, how shall we yet live therein ? "**

"*As men who.*" This is but giving the proper force to οἵτινες. "*Died to sin.*" The meaning of the apostle in this whole verse has much light shed upon it by the surrounding passages. The verb is in the aorist, and the noun is in the dative case. The verb has nothing to relieve it from the idea that the persons intended "*died*" (aorist) on a certain occasion ; and the noun is in such a form (dative) as might mean, in common instances, the substance or essence of the death. Therefore a few (but a very few indeed) have translated the language, "*Died in sin.*" " How shall we who died in sin live any longer therein ? " That glaringly would be absurd. Still fewer read, "*died for sin*," and fancy we did so in the person of Christ ; but the mischief there is that Paul's demonstrative appeal would be lost. Those forensically safe might be just the persons to abuse their rescue. It is not difficult to centre upon one generally accepted sense. Nor need we quite reject the dative of *essence* or *material* (Jelf, Gram. §. 610). The very thing that "*died*" is "*sin.*" Recollect sin is a part of our moral nature. We may continue to live in *taste*, and live only the more keenly in *mind* or *knowledge*. What the apostle says we died "*to*" or "*as to*" is that intimate thing within us, our sinfulness. Now this agrees with all the language of the apostle. A little further on we read that *Christ* "*died to sin*" (v. 10), and that is cleaner cut in mental contemplation than our dying. Christ died utterly. He never sinned. But He was tempted shockingly. Sin for a third of a century was His desperate torment, and He writhed under it as the essence of His sacrifice. He was " made sin for us " in ways which show why "*sin*" was written instead of "*sin offering.*" He was brought close to sin, as much as mortal could be without committing it ; and, to stir the fires, God deserted Him often, and, bereft of His Godhead in such a measure as to make His temptation exquisite, it is perhaps this same apostle who paints Him as in "strong crying and tears unto Him who was able to save Him from death" (Heb. 5 : 7). So that we are at no loss to know when He "*died to sin*" (v. 10). But we, alas ! like our righteousness (Is. 64 : 6), and like our holiness (Acts 3 : 12), and like our cleanness (Jo. 15 : 3), had but a meagre dying. Yet we "*died ;*" and we "*died once,*" giving the full force to the aorist ; and that we are saying so with reason comes out with more force in the following chapter. There we are said to be "*dead to the law*" (E. V., 7 : 4). And the death happened on a certain occasion ; for the verb is in the aorist ; and it happened to a part (so to speak) of ourselves, for the noun is in the dative. It happened to "*the law.*" Law in a corresponding sense is as near to us as "*sin.*" I had not known "*sin*" but for "*the law.*" I could not do "*sin*" but for "*the law ;*" and that in the shape of conscience constitutional within us.

It may be well to remark that Paul is chary of the speech that the law is dead. He does not hesitate in the speech that sin is dead. But when it comes to the law he remembers that it does any thing else but die even in the cross of the Redeemer. He delights in the expression that we die, that is to the law in its curse. And that moulds his handling of the incoming metaphor (7 : 12). Let us anticipate a little. In the English, "*man*" in the first verse (7 : 1) and "*man*" in the other verses seem the same. But in the Greek the women may be included under the word ἀνθρώπου in the first of the passage. Let us avoid "*man*" (E. V.), therefore. "*Or are ye ignorant, brethren, for I speak to persons knowing law, that the law rules its human subject as long as he lives.*" Now, the last word in this sentence is perhaps designedly ambiguous. Is it "*he lives*" or "*it lives.*" There are scholars who say "*it*" (Origen, Erasmus, Bengel). If we say "*it*" it might seem to answer better, for Paul seems to be aiming at the doctrine that the law is dead. But if we say "*he,*" it is more respectful to the law, for the law really never dies, and Paul seems to shape his metaphor (vs. 2-4) so as to allow it to be said that the woman is "*discharged*" (Re.), or is "*brought to nothing*," or "*becomes dead*" to the law of her husband. Let us glance at the whole passage: "*For the woman under marriage to a man has been bound to the living man as law*" (notice the dative), *but if the man die she has been brought to nothing as to the law of the man.* * * * *So then, my brethren, ye also have become dead as to the law by the body of Christ.*" Instead of meaning that *we* are dead, which would spoil the comparison between man and wife, it means virtually that *the law* is dead as to us, or, availing of what is really in the idiom, that we are dead as to the law's constitutional claim, just as the woman might be said to be dead, though it were really the man, if she were said to be dead to the law of her husband, or, if you please, dead to her husband, if he were taken away by death ; and even our English Version seals all this, for it departs from the actual Greek (v. 6) by translating, —"*that being dead wherein we were held*," when the Revisionists adhere to the idiom, and come just to the side of "*dead to sin*" and "*dead to the law*," for they say: "*Now we have been discharged from the law, having died to that wherein we were holden, so that we serve in newness of spirit and not in oldness of the letter*" (Re.).

If the law, therefore, which is "the strength of sin" (1 Cor. 15 : 56), and which gives me over to my sinfulness, so that Paul cries out " I had been alive without the law at any time," could die, that is, could cease to curse me with my sinfulness, that would be my dying as to the most troublesome constitution of my history. On a certain occasion, therefore, we "*died to law*" (7 : 4), just as on the same occasion we "*died to sin*" (6 : 2), and that this is the meaning of the apostle flows conspicuously from the surrounding passages. We "*died to sin*," just as we "*lived to God*" (6 : 10, *material dative*). The God-part of our nature acquired life, just as the sin part of our nature began to perish ; and this, as we shall presently see, thoroughly agrees with the account of where we get that life (vs. 3, 4), and of how we got sin "*planted*" where it became stricken with decay.

Now one sentence more, and we shall be ready for those next verses. "**How?**" The appeal is this. Not, ought we to continue sinning, but can we? The whole is dimmed by that miserable fact that we do continue sinning. Christ is the only man who "*died to sin*" entirely. He not only never sinned, but at a given date he shook off his horrible temptations. But how is it with us? The apostle's argument is thoroughly achieved *tantis pro tantis*. Just so far as we "*died to sin*," it is impossible for us to live in it. And as we positively did die, and that at a certain date, and, moreover, in a way that promises a continued dying, Paul's argument is complete. Either we "*died to sin*" in part, or not at all. If we "*died to sin*" at all, we have caught the true sight of it as the great Sinai curse, and at any rate cannot live in it, or else the premise is undone that it died within us.

3. **Or do ye not know that as many of us as were baptized into Christ Jesus, were baptized into His death?**

"**Or.**" This is a deft rhetoric. Paul quietly implies that they ought not to require this explanatory sequel. "**Do ye not know.**" They ought to know. Paul thus daintily expresses it that he comes to the heart of their own religion. "*Baptized.*" Four theories are possible for this: First, that the rite was Paul's mere illustration (They had all been baptized. Now, what did that imply?); or, second, that baptism was the *opus operatum*, or, more, the means of their actual liberation; or, thirdly, that it was but a pregnancy, like "circumcision" (Col. 2: 11) expressing a whole change, or, fourthly, that it was this and the first thing all together: that Paul called conversion baptism in order to embrace in the word pregnant and telling elucidation. Ritualists might adopt the third, but the last is, of course, the most forceful and all comprehensive. "**Baptized into Christ.**" Converted or new-born morally. "**Were baptized into His death.**" Physical "*death*" was one of the smallest parts of His undertaking. Christ's "*death*" began by His taking our nature at all. It was loaded with corruption. In spite of

His Godhead and of God shadowing Mary in His very conception, the man was born "infirm" (Heb. 5 : 2); and though "separated (κεχωρισμένος) from sinners" (Heb. 7 : 26), He had to be that very thing—"*separated;*" and, having penalty to endure, I mean for His whole race, Himself and His people (Heb. 5 : 3; 7 : 27; 9 : 7), that penalty was horrid torment (Matt. 26 : 38), and that torment was awful tempting (Lu. 22 : 44; Heb. 12 : 4), and that tempting must cover His race (Matt. 26 : 41; Heb. 2 : 10), that is to say, He had to endure a desertion by His Godhead which left Him barely sinless (Heb. 5 : 7 ; Matt. 27 : 46), and oppressed by awful snares, through which He cut His way in most fearful agony. This agony saved the world. "It pleased the Lord to bruise Him" (Is. 53 : 10). He not only resisted sin by the help of His Godhead enough to carry Him along sinless, but enough to fight over again Adam's battle ; and, while Adam died in sin from a condition of righteousness, Himself to die "*to sin*" from a condition of inherited "infirmity" (Heb. 5 : 2). This now is what our Saviour did. He fought through a terrible struggle, and finally died to so much of self as tempted Him. Sin ceased to assail. And when those syllables floated over Jewry, "It is finished," this tenth verse was realized. He "*died (aorist) to sin once*," and never again had He a touch of this so-called "infirmity."

Now the thought which the apostle builds upon, and which he assumes that the Romans ought to know, is that we share in that death. And He calls the history by which we become the sharers, *baptism ;* just as on another occasion he calls it *confession* (Rom. 10 : 10). It makes very little difference what he calls it. Only in calling it *baptism* he gives fine occasion for the picturesque. Just as baptism occurs and is over, so at a certain time (aorist) believers "**were baptized into Christ.**" And Paul reminds them that they "**were baptized into His death;**" that is, as His whole struggle ending in His being made perfect" (Heb. 5 : 9) is called His death, and involved the last agony of it, viz., His dying "*unto sin,*" so they "*were baptized into*" this very thing, that is, stripping the figure, they "*died to sin*" the moment they became united to Christ, and enjoyed in this way the benefit of His sorrow.

Nothing more of difficulty remains.

4. Therefore we were buried with Him by the baptism into the death;

These are all aorists. And the meaning now is quite intelligible. And our Baptist brethren believe that the figure becomes very close. We were actually "**buried,**" when converted, by a spiritual "**baptism**" into His "*death*," so as to share the deadening influence which He won against sin.

4. That like as Christ was raised from among the dead by the glory of the Father, even so we also might walk in newness of life.

"**Raised from among the dead.**" We can no longer degrade this into mere bodily rising, any more than the death into mere physical dissolution. "*From among the dead.*" Was He not one of us? Peter calls Him a man "who had been given over to death (θανατωθείς) according to the flesh" (that is in respect to what His flesh would have made Him but for His Godhead), "but quickened by the Spirit" (1 Pet. 3 : 18). Paul says we are "quickened together with Christ" (Eph. 2 : 5). He repeats this many and many a time (Col. 2 : 13 ; Rom. 8 : 11, see comment.). There must be meaning in it. Christ is called "the first begotten from among the dead" (ἐκ τῶν νεκρῶν) ; and though there is no real difference between *dying to sin* and *living to God*, and one is but explanatory of the other, yet they are very joyful explanations. Just as "*we were buried with* (Christ) *by the baptism into the death*," so, at the same moment, we were "*raised*" with Him by "*the baptism*" into a better "*life.*"

Now, what made Christ win? First, His Godhead, in giving dignity and price-availing value to what He paid for His people ; and, second, His Godhead, again, in giving Him "*power*. He was "determined upon as the Son of God in power" (1 : 4). His courage would have snapped like a silly reed but for the presence of His Godhead. "It spake roughly to Him, and said strange things to Him" (Gen. 42 : 7), yet it stood by Him to the last. It never did really "*forsake*" Him, even in the last agonies of that bloody crucifixion (Matt. 27 : 46). It not only sustained Him, but it enlightened Him, poured **"glory"** into His mind. Just as the gospel saves by a moral revelation which Paul calls "*the righteousness of God*" being "*revealed*" (1 : 17), so the "*glory*" of God being revealed to Him, saved Christ. And, therefore, in two ways, by *dignity* and by *moral illumination*, that is by two forms of grace, *forensic* and *effectual*, in *court* and in *the man Himself*, our text is answered to and Christ is **" raised from among the dead by the glory of the Father."**

Let it be understood that Paul presses his argument. This is not the ἵνα of *intention*, but the ἵνα of *result* (see Com. 6 : 1). He does not mean if "*baptized into*" Him we have the privilege of rising with Him, but what he means by "*baptism*" is our actually doing it. *May we continue in sin and grace grow greater ? Impossible. How shall we who have actually lost sin* (of course he means in measure) *go on with it besides ?*

The next verse is even more positive. Christ "*was raised* (entirely) *from among the dead.*" We are not quite so fortunate as that, but still "*raised*" already, so as to **" walk in newness of life."**

5. For if we have been bred in with Him in the likeness of His death, on the contrary also we shall belong to His resurrection ; 6. Knowing this that our old man was crucified with Him, so that the body of sin should be destroyed, that we should no longer serve sin.

We "*were baptized* (aorist) *into Christ*" at a given time, viz., when we were converted and partook in that way of the benefits of His dying. But we **" have been bred in with Him."** The apostle lapses into the *perfect*. He speaks of a **"likeness."** We were "*baptized*," not into the "*likeness*" of death, but into His very dying. But "*we have been bred in with*" (Christ) variously, and perhaps on that account He changes into the perfect. We "*have been bred in with*" (Christ) in being bred at all, for our horrible curse He participated in by His descent from Adam. We were bred in with Christ, and that in a nobler way, when we were converted, and if that were all, it might be put in the aorist. But, again, and more perhaps in the mind of the apostle, we have been bred in with Christ into His horrible temptations. This was the essence of His "*death.*" And as long as the word "*likeness*" is employed here, the portrait fits. Christ's sufferings were entire, and we were baptized into them (when we repented) as our complete redemption; and yet Paul speaks of filling up "that which is behind of the afflictions of Christ" (Col. 1 : 24). Perhaps this word "*likeness*" is as good a solvent for such a sentence as we could possibly employ. In respect of ransom we are baptized entirely into another man's death, and He is our entire deliverance, but in respect of discipline, we die in the likeness of His death. **"Our old man was crucified with Him."** When He was nailed to the cross we were. Not only were we nailed there in the shape of a court deliverance, but our old man was nailed there, so that when we became "bred in with Christ," our crucifixion should begin, and we should begin to writhe and agonize and wrestle with our iniquity. **"So that the body of sin should be destroyed."** We read elsewhere of "*the flesh of sin*" (8 : 3), very properly translated "*sinful flesh*" (E. V.). These verses bring the whole subject before us. Crucifixion is not death. On the contrary, it is horrible, feverish, agonizing life. "They that are Christ's have crucified the flesh" (Gal. 5 : 24). And Paul means just that here. We are infinitely far from having destroyed it. But we are destroying it. And Paul's argument is just this. Sin being our original curse; and Christ having borne it; and having borne it not by succumbing under it, but in having been tormented by it in horrible temptations, we are baptized into Him in two respects, one final in having been bought off by grace, and one daily, being "bred in with Him in the likeness of His death," that is, nailed to a perpetual cross, and, like "the Captain of our salvation," made "perfect by suffering."

"*Bred in with.*" The word is from φύω, not from φυτεύω. **"On the contrary."** We are to give ἀλλά its force. Death, where it consists in torture, is very different from life when the victory is achieved. "**Belong to.**" "*Shall be also of*" (E. V.) would be much nicer. The difficulty is that it is ambiguous. "*If bred in the likeness of His death, we shall be also of His resurrection*" (E. V.) would be the literal Greek ; but it would inevitably read as though it meant "*we shall be bred, &c.,*" whereas it is the "*be*" of independent assertion. "We shall be of His resurrection." We translate it, therefore, "*belong.*" "**Resurrection ;**" of course out of "*death,*" the wider and the darker death, viz., our sinfulness. And here consists the argument of the apostle. If we are baptized into His death, we actually die, that is die to sin. "Our old man has been actually crucified." "**So that.**" Again it is *resultant*, and not *intentional* (see v. 1). "The body of sin" has actually been destroyed, "**that we no longer serve sin.**" And though the apostle can not always be saying that this is only partial, and that crucifixion does not kill at once, yet he reminds us that it kills all the time. And the gist of his argument is that we can not make grace abound by the perpetration of that which grace, if it exists at all, makes us hate and fight and be crucified to at the very time.

7. For he who died has been made righteous from sin."

We should suppose that this meant Christ, if it did not say, "**with Christ**" instead of "*with Him*" in the next passage. We must understand, therefore, a general proposition ; and in that event it means any man, and, of course, Christ as well as His people. "**He who died**" (aorist) ; that is, who has put death behind him as a thing that has actually been achieved and finished. To patter about physical death, and to say that the apostle argues that a dead man is out of the reach of law, is contemptible. To think of a man stopping to say that in a discussion grim with spiritual dying ! The very commentators who say it, believe (wrongfully no doubt) that a man passes by death at once into the hands of the law. We trifle by such interpretations. But all sense here is given by the aorist. Let a man have actually died, so that the great spiritual catastrophe can be put into the aorist form, and be entire in the past, and "*he dieth no more.*" Paul presently uses that language (v. 9). He "*has been raised* (aorist) *from among the dead.*" The curse has burned out. And as this same passage expresses it, "*Death hath no more dominion over him.*"

Now let us make this very plain. "The wages of sin is death" (Rom. 6 : 23), or, as all men agree, the original and only denunciation was, "In the day thou eatest thereof thou shalt surely die." This is the only curse, and so exclusively one, that if death could cease, that is if sin, which is death, could burn out in the soul, that second thing would stop, viz., eternal torment. This all men would admit. And the misery is, that sin will not cease, but feeds upon what it practices, and men grow worse in iniquity, and that by the law of God, and by the law of their own nature. If a man could die and get into the aorist, that is get it to be in some way the fact that he had endured spiritual dissolution, and actually exhausted it, and run it out as a spiritual penalty, then, according to our passage, he would be "**made righteous from sin ;**" but David, in a badly translated psalm, says that this is impossible. Let us render the simple Hebrew : "None of them can, by any means, redeem a brother, nor give to God a ransom for him, and a precious payment for their soul, and then cease forever, so that he still live forever, and do not see corruption" (Ps. 49: 7–9). This is an unnoticed text, and holds that, for one's self or for one's neighbor or brother, no man can buy off guilt' so as to finish and cease, and thereafter then still live forever, and not see corruption.

Now, what no sinner could do (that is die in the aorist tense, and get it finished) Christ did. He "finished transgression, and made an end of sin" (Dan. 9 : 24). And what we have said half figuratively, He made almost literal in fiery temptation. He actually burned out His weakness. He endured innocently fearful pangs which bought us off before the law ; and He endured, practically, fiery battles, by which he was "*made perfect,*" the Bible tells us, and by which at least He got the whole death behind Him, so that He at least answers to the

Greek, "*He died to sin*" (6 : 10), and to this neighbor passage, put in the form of something universal, "*For he who died has been made righteous from sin.*"

And we see, too, at this stage how Christ may be said to be "*made righteous.*" He never was made wicked. And yet He is said to be "sanctified" (Jo. 10 : 36), and to "sanctify" Himself (Jo. 17 : 19). We are told very early in the Bible that He was to be "saved" (Zech. 9 : 9), and He entreats that God may save Him (Heb. 5 : 7). Moreover, He was "*raised from among the dead*" (1 Pet. 1 : 21), and in this respect, not in time, but in sequence, he was "the first begotten" (Rev. 1 : 5). That He should be said to be "*made righteous*" is a light difficulty, after all these stronger expressions. If a man is tempted, and tempted to the very death, and so tempted in a peccable nature as to be said to "have infirmity" in the very language of the Holy Ghost, then to cease all this, and to become restfully and gloriously righteous, not painfully and strugglingly so, and to take His place, as we shall one day do, in the glories of a most spontaneous obedience, answers to all the expressions of our chapter. Such a man has "*died to sin*" finally and in the very letter, and such a man has been "*made righteous,*" no longer in the agonies of a perpetual fight, but as "being made perfect" (Heb. 5 : 9) ; as having "learned obedience" (Heb. 5 : 8); as having "(entered) into glory" (Lu. 24 : 26), and as being, what we will one day be, delightfully and without a fight, peacefully and by a new nature, obedient.

Now, how could this be universal? In a way altogether different. Christ could literally complement the Psalmist. He could redeem His own cursed humanity, and do literally as David asked : that is, He could pay the precious ransom, and "*cease,*" that is, in this God-like aorist sense, do the thing and finish it, and then do what the song boldly announces as impossible for any sinner, that is, "still live forever and never see corruption." And this is the way Christ puts it on the road to Emmaus : "Ought not Christ to have suffered, and to enter into His glory" (Lu. 24 : 26).

So he saved Himself (Zech. 9 : 9). And now Paul is busy with our share in this aorist *ceasing*. Christ broke the bars of the pit by bearing innocently the penalties of the law. We broke them when "*we were bred in with*" Christ. "*He who died has been made righteous from sin.*" Christ "*died*" when He finished His sufferings; and we "*died*" when we took a share in them; that is, when we were grafted into Christ (6 : 5); when we were circumcised (Col. 2 : 11); when we were baptized into His death (6 : 3); when we believed (13 : 11); when we repented (Matt. 12 : 41); when we were washed in His blood (Rev. 1 : 5); when we took up His cross (Matt. 10 : 38); when we discerned His body (1 Cor. 11 : 29); when we confessed Him before men (Matt. 10 : 32); or, when (abandoning all the rhetoric of the gospel), we turned from sin to holiness by the power of the Almighty asked for through Christ's redemption.

It must not go unsaid how this text, which even King James' men are shy of in their indifferent translation (for δικαιόω never means to *free*, E. V.), sustains the doctrine of anti-Lutheran enrighteousment.

8. But if we died with Christ, we believe that we shall also live with Him, 9. Knowing that Christ, having been raised from among the dead, dies no more; death no more has dominion over Him; 10. For in that He died He died as to sin once, but in that He lives He lives as to God. 11. Likewise reckon ye also yourselves to be dead indeed as to sin, but alive as to God in Christ Jesus.

We have shown that ἵνα (vs. 4, 6) was a ἵνα of result, and that Paul was arguing, not what they ought to do, but what they did do if they were Christians. If they were baptized into Christ, they were baptized into His death, and if they died with Him, it did not only follow that they ought to live with Him, but that they actually did live with Him, else they did not die. He now goes further, and adds another round to his ladder by claiming that they **believed** all this. "*May we continue in sin and grace grow the more? By no means*" (v. 1), because ye yourselves, who might carelessly utter such a speech, "*believe*" the opposite. For "**If we died with Christ, we believe that we shall also live with Him.**" Nay, ye know it, "*knowing* that Christ, having been raised from among the dead," that is "*from among*" the spiritually "*dead*" by a wonderful battle, itself a horrid death, in which His Godhead enabled Him to continue sinless, "**dies no more,**" that is, writhes no more in that frail and tempted nature; but lives the victor, sin's awful snare no longer shutting him about. What He reached, therefore, we are reaching if "*we are bred in with Him*" (v. 5). "**In that He died He died as to sin once for all.**" We have explained all that. "**In that He lives, He lives as to God.**" That is the same thing differently put. He that is dead to sin lives to God. Though this dative still deserves a thorough clearing up. It is the "*dative* of *material.*" If a man "*died to sin*" (aorist), there came a time when the sin-trait in his nature perished. In Christ's case this was complete. When He cried "It is finished," it perished altogether. But it never was a sin-trait of absolute sinfulness; it was only horrible temptation. Christ died to sin on losing that. But we died "*bred in with*" Christ. Ours was actual sinfulness; but alas! it did not die: it was only crucified. Our sin was set a-dying. Yet that happened at a definite date (aorist), and was the harbinger of an entire sanctification. "*In that He lives.*" Now this is the other statement. It will be noticed that we change the particle. If we say "*He liveth unto God*" (E. V. & Re.), it would seduce us as it does the other commentators. It does not mean that Christ lives to God in the sense of serving Him. That would be obvious, and would destroy the paragraph. Dying to sin means dying "*as to*" sin; that is, the sin part of the man dying. Living to God must have some kindred sense, and therefore we translate living "*as to*" God. We die "*as to*" sin when sin dies, and we live "*as to*" God when God lives, that is when He is our life, or as Paul expresses it (Gal. 2: 20), when it is not we that live, but He that lives within us. Paul then draws his inference, If this be so of Christ, and you were "bred in with Him," and what happens to Him, not ought to happen, but actually does happen, *cæteris paribus*, to yourselves ; and above all if ye "believe" this, and "*know*" this, then go on knowing and believing, or, as he expresses it, "**Likewise reckon ye also yourselves to be dead indeed as to sin, but alive as to God in Christ Jesus.**"

Paul's logic, however, does not forbid, but actually encourages entreaty. He does not relax an instant in the verses we have finished, but confines our minds to an iron sequence of results. "*He that died has been made righteous from sin.*" It is impossible, so he argues, to be both alive and dead. And so of Christ. If He "*died to sin*" by force of the Godhead that is within Him, He lives to that Godhead, or, as we have expounded that dative, "*as to*" it, or in that essential essence of His life. All that is plain. If Christ be glorified, He cannot at the same time be tried. And we who are planted with Him meet with the same necessity. If we be dead to sin, we must necessarily live to something else. And if we are dead imperfectly, that explains our miserable stupidity of speech. Just so far as we are dead, just so far and no farther are we sinless. And continuing in sin in order to quicken grace, could only be a thought conceived of by men who had far too little grace, inasmuch as, if we have grace at all, the very essence of the gift is a shrinking and a deliverance from our sin.

Paul, therefore, having finished one argument, stops a moment for entreaty.

12. Let not sin, therefore, reign in your mortal body in an obedience to its desires; 13. Nor through sin give over your members as weapons of unrighteousness; but give yourselves over unto God, as though alive from among the dead, and your members through God as weapons of righteousness. 14. For sin shall not have dominion over you; for ye are not under law but under grace.

There are six things that must be kept in view all through this epistle : First, that the great curse of sin is sinfulness. This we have a strange liking to forget ; and in every nation torment and the rougher consequences of the Fall come up before men as their perdition. Second, it is the law that works this sinfulness. I mean by that it is the law that gives us over to our sins. Nothing can be more revealed. It was the original threat, Eat and thou shalt die. Paul continues it in a maxim, "The wages of sin is death;" and in a philosophy, "The strength of sin is the law;" and in an inspired conviction, "I had been alive without the law at any time." We cannot be too rooted in this in understanding the epistle. This is why our own righteousness is insisted upon by Paul; for our being made righteous in the shape of faith is the beginning of our whole grace and hope and final glory in the Redeemer. Men think it safe to praise Christ as our whole righteousness in court, but it is Paul's way to praise Him for our ransom, and to build on that our own righteousness through the gospel. Third, it is the law that has to be satisfied, and when the law is satisfied, we cease to be sinful. Fourth, it is satisfied by Christ. It is satisfied, as Paul declares, by that life of agony which Paul calls His death. And it is satisfied for us when we are baptized into His death, that is "bred in with Him" into His sufferings, and become entitled thereby to our share of His blessed redemption. Fifth, this is what is meant by **our not being under law** (v. 14); and, sixth, our redemption (Eph. 4:30) is so imperfect, I mean in its results, and our pardon and our enrighteousment so incomplete, that we are sinners to be reasoned with, as well as saints to be divinely comforted; so that Paul turns from the argument that he that died to sin cannot live in it, to remind us that, though we died to sin, still we *are* living in it, and to imply that we were only crucified with Christ; that so far as the cross has worked, we are dead to sin; but that in immense degrees it has not worked; that this is the demand for the exhortation (v. 12), and that, like the inspired apostle, we are to carry about "in the body the dying of the Lord Jesus, that the life also of Jesus might be made manifest in our body" (2 Cor. 4:10). These relations of "*the law*" are the staple on the part of the apostle of this, and also of the following chapter.

"**Reign;**" either, first, in taking entire possession, or, second, in capturing the will. In neither of these respects can the Christian admit sin. Sin cannot "*reign,*" for he is crushing it, and he cannot be wilful in his wickedness, for that is utterly inconsistent with his warfare with it. "**In your mortal body.**" Sin is altogether privative. Of course it is so, or whence the command? The sole command of the Almighty is "Thou shalt love" (Matt. 22 : 37). We need not pause upon this. There are really two affections, but this does not disturb their nature. Paul boldly declares the emotional nature of our duty, and challenges any rival. He serves up half the decalogue, and with a wave of the hand says, "If there be any other commandment;" and then most anthoritatively puts it in the declaration, "Love is the fulfilling of the law." Hence the "*body*" is the throne of "*sin.*" If there be not conscience enough in our dead nature, that is, not love enough, other appetites take possession. Hence it is wrong to say "*lusts*" (E. V. & Re.). The apostle's word is "**desires.**" It is the simplest Greek for that innocent affection. It is no harm to desire money. All the appetites of the body are innocent impulses of our nature. The "*flesh*" which Paul constantly condemns, is all of our constitution as men, outside of the Holy Ghost. Let a man have the most exquisite tastes, they are of the "*flesh*" according to Paul. And these fleshly "*desires*" are our sins. What else could they be according to Paul? "*What I do I know not*" he says in another chapter (7 : 15). And how could he know it? Knowing my sin when it consists in a want, would be like knowing holiness in measures that exceed my conscience. Like the neck of a man whose sinews have been cut on the right, the crookedness occurs on the left. "*Desire*" pulls over the sinner. And what would be innocent, balanced by virtue, grow monstrous when, in the absence of love, they become the great exercises of our sinfulness, and hot tumors in the soul.

Now these principles take up all the language presented in our Greek. "*Let not sin reign in your mortal body.*" Here is an animal whose glory lay in a love now lost. Wrecks of it remain, but decaying hourly. He is damned if he cannot recover it. As, in a wild herd, the strong oxen trample the weak, so a thousand other affections eat out the heart of this one. We can supply what is needed in the parable. Ours is a "*mortal body*," dying in every sense, and sure to die physically whether we are redeemed or not. Paul points his finger at it as a seat of our "*desires.*" And having expounded how its "*desires*" become our sins by deadening and trampling better affections, he gives us this simple direction, "*Let not sin, therefore, reign in your mortal body* in an obedience to its desires," that is, this body's "*desires*" (αὐτοῦ). "**Nor through sin;**" (the "*dative of material:*" see a little further on, "**through God**" (τῷ θεῷ), "*sin*" being the efficient power in one case, and "*God*" in the other); "**give over your members as weapons of unrighteousness; but give yourselves over unto God as though alive from among the dead, and your members through God as weapons of righteousness.**"

These quite unnoticed expressions, giving over our members as weapons of unrighteousness "*through sin,*" and giving over our members as weapons of righteousness "*through God,*" are vastly explanatory of the whole system of the apostle. The very thing that gives us over is "*sin,*" and the very thing that gives us over savingly is "God." Each is the "*dative of material*" (τῇ ἁμαρτίᾳ and τῷ θεῷ). We encounter the exact counterpart in another epistle: "Mighty through God" (E. V., τῷ θεῷ). "The weapons of our warfare are not fleshly, but mighty through God" (2 Cor. 10 : 4). And while the other part of the present sentence has τῷ θεῷ in the more usual dative sense and is properly translated "*give over to God,*" it is sad that this part should be so translated. As the *power* in the Corinthians is nothing less than God, so the "*righteousness*" in the present verse, or the *giving over*, for that is itself the "*righteousness,*" is as much "*God*" within us as the other is "*sin*" within us, and the realizing of this is a great point in the whole epistle.*

---

* It is a dative without a preposition that is found in 1 Cor. 15 : 10 :— " By the grace of God (χάριτι) I am what I am."

"*Weapons,*" not "*instruments*" (E. V. and Re.). "*Weapons*" is the commoner meaning, and we retain it because there is a military cast which the apostle evidently intends. "*The wages of sin are death*" (6 : 23), that is, the "*rations*" or "*military pay.*" "*Sin*" fights desperately, and gets pay in "*death.*" And in another chapter Paul describes the conflict. "*I see another law in my members warring, etc.*" (7 : 23). The shame, therefore, that Paul cries out against in the Christian is that he should "*give over*" his "*weapons*" to the foe, instead of giving over himself to God, and, through that Great Friend, his "*members as weapons of righteousness.*"

Now follows another of those cavil-provoking sayings of the apostle :—"**For sin shall not have dominion over you, for ye are not under law but under grace.**"

15. What then? May we sin, because we are not under law, but under grace?

This cavil is strong simply by a mistake. It is the all-pervading blunder, which is ever crowding in, that hell is a place of pain, instead of a place of both sin and pain. It seems impossible to realize that the law is responsible for the continuance of sin an hour ; for, though we sinned, if the law denounced only pain, pain enough for that one sin would soon expiate it (Prov. 19 : 19 ; see Author's Com.), and life $\tau\hat{\varphi}\,\theta\epsilon\hat{\varphi}$, that is "*through God,*" would return at once. This epistle to the Romans is finely calculated to make us believe that sin is given up to sin (1 : 24, 26, 28), and that, hence, its strength is the law (1 Cor. 15 : 56), and that, if the law is satisfied (aorist), it must be choked back in its demand, for our abandonment for sin is the prolific source of the eternity of our pains and sinning. Satisfy the law, as Christ has done, and let a sinner comply with the conditions of that sacrifice, and Paul's speech is as simple as a child's. Sin is a vile deceiving of me, and an enormous curse ; but, as long as law rules, I will remain a sinner. I am **a slave**, as Paul calls me. But in this grand discussion of redemption, it is this very point that he attacks :—

"*Sin shall not have dominion over you, for ye are not under law but under grace.*" Had he said, "Pain shall not have dominion over you," the cavil might have had some sense. Deliver me from pain, and I may sin without it. But Paul not only connects sin with pain, and not only makes sin the darker element of perdition, and not only makes perdition eternal, both pain and sin, but he makes sin the precursor of our agonies. He does indeed make Eve's sin prelude our own, as the precursor of our sorrow, but he makes our own sin travel before our sufferings. He teaches that plainly :—"The sting of death is sin" (1 Cor. 15 : 56). And, therefore, personal righteousness is the boon of the apostle, and personal sinfulness is our grand perdition. It is easy, therefore, to expound him. "**May we sin because we are not under law?**" Why, horrid! Being "*under law*" means being under "*sin.*"

16. Know you not that to whatsoever ye give yourselves over to obey as slaves, slaves ye are to whatsoever ye obey, whether of sin unto death, or of obedience unto righteousness?

Being "not under law," cannot possibly show itself but in the relaxing of the law-hold by the diminishing of our sinfulness. To say, Let us sin "*because we are not under law,*" is to say, Let us weave straws in our hair because we are no longer insane. Nay, it is worse than that, for that might be a mere glad freak, but to **obey from the heart** (v. 17) the great precepts of the Redeemer, is the essential "**fruit**" (vs. 21, 22) of not being "*under the law,*" and as he cannot *obey from the heart*, who is seeking excuses not to obey at all, the apostle means his logic to be actually entire. We are "*under law,*" or we are not. If we are "*under law*" we will "*sin,*" for the law demands that "*sin*" shall be given up to "*sin.*" If we are "*not under law,*" the words have no meaning unless we have diminished sin, for the law does not ordain the lash, but the lash and sinfulness; and if sinfulness "*reigns,*" we are just mocking ourselves by the thought of our deliverance.

17. But thanks be to God that ye were slaves of sin—
That is, that that condition of things is past—
17—but obeyed from the heart the form of teaching to which ye were given over.
Men are not machines, or Paul would have said enough; but men are free agents. Men are not carried into sin, so that they are forced into sin, without their agency, but they die willingly ; that is, their death, which is their sinfulness, is a thing of choice. So of "*law ;*" when we are "*not under law,*" we are not raised like an idiot, or as we may hope an idiot may be, immediately back to life, but we must struggle for it. The power is τῷ θεῷ (vs. 10, 11), but it is not given *ex vi*, but in rousing our will. It is not ridiculous in the apostle to say, that, to a dead certainty, we once "*died to sin*" (v. 2) ; and yet to exhort us eagerly not to live in it (v. 12).

Moreover our death was imperfect. Our death will not be really perfect till the time Christ's was, viz., when He physically died. He had not "*died to sin*" (v. 10) till His temptations ceased, and we "*died to sin*" when we were converted, and have been dying ever since, and shall not be really dead till we rise in judgment. Hence Paul calls sin, "*sin unto death*" (v. 16), that is, the sinner's increase in sinfulness ; and "*obedience*" an "*obedience unto righteousness ;*" that is, an imperfect "*obedience*" which is leading gradually to perfect righteousness. Now he tells us that it is an obedience to a "**form of teaching,**" and we understand his language at once. It is not a perfect righteousness, but it is an "*obedience of faith*" (1 : 5 ; 16 : 26); that is, a compliance with those commands of the Redeemer which slowly lead us on to a perfect "*righteousness.*"

Hence now another gem of the epistle !

18. But having been made free from sin, ye were made slaves to righteousness 19. (Humanly speaking) on account of the weakness of your flesh.—

This is very graphic ! Paul is to end this passage by shouting out, " O, wretched man that I am ! Who shall deliver me out of the body of this death ?" (Re., 7 : 24). And if this sort of ruin survives even in the Christian, we can easily understand what is meant by being "**slaves to righteousness.**" We are "*not under law :*" that is certain : and we "*died to sin ;*" that, actually, and in an aorist past, occurred ; and "*sin shall not have dominion over us,*" for we were "**made free**" from the law of sin and death. But all these things have happened inchoately, as with every grace. And, therefore, Paul insists that we are "*slaves* **(speaking humanly),**" and that we must take up a daily cross, and welcome chastisement in our struggle with iniquity.

It is this complicated condition of our case that gives covert for cavil. If we "*died to sin*" outright, or if we were squarely out from "*under law,*" then "*may we sin ?*" (v. 15), or can "*we continue in sin ?*" (v. 1), would be preposterous ; and the argument against it, that the law's great curse was sin, and we are out from under it, and that we died the death in every respect of sin, would show slavery to sin in the very face of it to be impossible. But the misery is, we are sinning, and, what is worse, we are doing nothing but sin ; our being made righteous is a thing inchoate ; and, therefore, we have to dig down into the apostle's argumentation, and make all these reserves. "All that is born of God overcometh the world" (1 Jo. 5 : 4). "(We) cannot sin because (we are) born of God" (1 Jo. 4 : 9). We "*died to sin,*" and "*we are not under law.*" Nevertheless we are yet but "*slaves to righteousness,*" because of "*the weakness of (our) flesh.*" We have not "overcome the world ; " we have not "died to sin," and we are not out from under the law, in results inwardly achieved, except in that small beginning which we have of piety.

19.—For as ye gave over your members as slaves to uncleanness, and to opposition to law unto still greater opposition to law, so now give over your members as slaves to righteousness unto sanctification. 20. For when ye were slaves of sin ye were free to be righteous. 21. What fruit had ye then of those things of which ye are now ashamed? for the end of those things is death.

Here is a wonderful solution ! Scarce a clearer thing occurs in Scripture. The lost are sinners, and the saved are sinners. The lost are free, and the saved are free. They are "**free to be righteous**"—the lost and the saved. This is a most important dictum of the apostle. The angels are free to sin, and so is the Almighty. We ought to nurse this light, and blazon it abroad. We lost it in a mediæval age, and theology still looks askance at our full freedom. Unless a soul were "*free to be righteous*," it could not possibly be wicked. But now Paul, rising to the height of our need, tells us a certain something that solves all the difficulty. The wicked are free to sin, and they sin more and more, making themselves slaves to sin, so as to be nursed into greater and greater opposition to the law. So the righteous sin, being free to do it ; and they sin shamefully, and confuse us, in the way we mention, as to the eminent difference. But Paul states that difference, and states it on the other side. Men are "*free to be righteous.*" But alas! alas! they never use that freedom. This is the curse of the law. All are "*free to be righteous*," but "*death*," which the law brought, means a depravity of *will*. Men never *wish* to be righteous, and never will be, without the grace of the Almighty. And when Paul says, "*Ye are not under law, but under grace*" (v. 14), he means this very thing—that we got grace to have a better will. This is what is meant by being freed from sin. It means freed from an engrossing will to sin. And this is what is meant by being "*enslaved to righteousness*," not joyfully perfect in it, for that would not be "*humanly speaking*," nor would it be to be "*enslaved.*" But Paul states just the condition of the Christian ; free to sin, and shamefully given to sin ; "*free to be righteous*," and earnestly trying to be righteous, and succeeding this far, that while the ungodly sinner, equally free, could be asked "What fruit had ye" (by your liberty to be righteous)? What single result did it give you in all "*those things of which you are now ashamed*"? the Christian can triumph in the words that follow:

22. But now, having been made free from sin, but having been enslaved to God, ye have your fruit unto sanctification, but the end eternal life.

"**Having been made free from sin;**" but wretchedly little; just as we are sanctified but little (8 : 23), and cleansed but little (Is. 64 : 6), and quickened but in the very least degree (1 Cor. 3 : 1), and with faith but as a grain of mustard-seed, we are "**enslaved to God;**" alas! how hard the bondage sometimes (Matt. 10 : 38; 16 : 24; Rom. 7 : 24), but we "**have (our) fruit unto sanctification,**" the lost not using their liberty to be righteous, and therefore having no fruit at all (Ps. 1 : 4), but we having our fruit unto sanctification, and at last, when the work is completed, perfectness and "**eternal life.**"

"**For,**" says the apostle, presenting the whole at a glance—

23. For the wages of sin is death, but the grace of God is eternal life in Christ Jesus our Lord.

But now let us go back (vs. 18–23) and attend to some main particulars. "*Having been made free from sin*" (v. 18). The English cannot give directly the second aorist participle. Our versions often change it into what is more direct; as for example "*which was made*" (1 : 3, E. V.). Sometimes "*when*" is used (Acts 2 : 37), and we might say in the present instance "*when we were made free from sin.*" The simpler choice however is probably the best, not "*being made free from sin*" (E. V. and Re.), but, using such past as we have, "*having been made free.*" "*Ye were made slaves*" (aorist), and the thing was done at a certain time. And Paul immediately places that act in its proper relation. "*I say a human thing,*" or still more literally transmuted, "*I speak of what is human.*" Men have confounded this with Paul in other places,—"*I speak after the manner of men*" (E. V. & Re.; 1 Cor. 15 : 32; Gal. 3 : 15). This Greek is not that Greek at all. This Greek occurs but once. It means "*I describe what is distinctly a human condition.*" Nothing could be more express. A man is converted. At that aorist moment he is "*made free.*" Alas! what freeing! And at that same moment he is joined to another master. Alas! what a condition of obedience! And, therefore, Paul says, "*I speak of what is human,*" and calls it *a slavery to right-*

eousness, a very good word for such a service which is unwilling and half-hearted. He says, "*Ye were made slaves to righteousness on account of the weakness of your flesh;*" and, in the next chapter, facts come out in respect to the natural man (vs. 14-24) which show where a Christian begins; what he started out of in his original conversion; how the word *slavery* is good for the sinner as well as the saved, he being enslaved to sin (vs. 14, 23, 24) against many a better judgment; and how the Christian does not answer to this next chapter of the apostle, because he is not "*carnal, sold under sin,*" but how he does answer to it in his desperate fight; how he has to spur himself even into common duties; and how *being a slave* seeming to be too harsh a condition to so good a mistress, is too flattering a state for him, inasmuch as he is not even a patient *slave*, and performs in the very slenderest amount the duty that belongs to "*righteousness.*"

Nevertheless he tries; and this expounds the other passages. The sinner does not try. And, therefore, though he is "*free to be righteous*" (v. 20), (for if the apostle meant "*from righteousness*" (E. V.) he would have said so; and why did he leave ἀπό off in this critical region of his writing?), though he is "*free in regard of righteousness*" (Re.), yet he struggles fitfully at times, but never uses his liberty. He struggles sufficiently against sin to illustrate Paul where he declares that he is a *slave* to it; and yet he submits to sin sufficiently to increase its power, and to grow in "*opposition to* (the) *law* (of the Almighty)." "*For as ye gave over your members as slaves to uncleanness, and to opposition to law unto still greater opposition to law, so now.*" It is really hard to keep up with Paul in the way he packs his ideas. Not only is the Christian a *slave to righteousness*, sweet as that mistress is, but he has to be stirred up to induce him at all to submit to bondage. Indeed this is God's great method to coerce his "*slaves.*" Such is the curse of sin that, though its victim is free to be righteous, and though, what is more touching yet, he is a slave to uncleanness, and a thousand times struggles and resists his bondage, yet Paul can even taunt him with his utter want of will :—Where did you ever gain any thing against the enemy? "*What fruit did ye ever have of those things of which ye are now ashamed?*" But here, in the depths of his own forlorn bondage, the Christian gains something. He is but a "*slave to righteousness,*" and yet has the dim beginning of life, and, therefore, the faint upheaval of a better will. This is all that he has received of ransom, and all that he has yet achieved of his eternal living. This saves him. Paul calls it his "*fruit unto sanctification*" (v. 22), and expounds it carefully. The sinner, however unwillingly (see next chapter), gives over his members as slaves to uncleanness, with the result of constantly increasing uncleanness, and the saint, however churlishly, gives over his members as slaves to righteousness, with the result of constantly increasing righteousness, the indulgence in "*sin*" ending in "*death,*" and the struggle for "*righteousness*" ending in "*life in Christ Jesus our Lord.*" "*Sanctification*" (Re.), therefore, is the very hinge of the sentence. King James ought not to have said "*holiness*" (E. V.), and it is almost unpardonable in the nineteenth verse. Ἁγιασμός never means holiness,* but that rising out of sin which is the gift of the Redeemer. It is bad enough to say, "*Ye have your fruit unto holiness ;*" but it quite dislocates the thought in the verse I mention. There "*unto sanctification*" (Re.) balances the sentence *unto further lawlessness*. But "*righteousness unto holiness*" (E. V.) is miserable ; where is the difference ? As the slave of sin repines over it, but indulges it unto further wickedness, so the slave to righteousness writhes under it in horrid crucifixion and pain, nevertheless in churlish feebleness obeys, and by that feeble stirring of the Spirit gathers strength and passes

---

* It occurs but ten times in N. T. Greek. Five of those times (1 Cor. 1 : 30 ; 1 Thess. 4 : 3. 4 ; 2 Thess. 2 : 13 ; 1 Pet. 1 : 2) it is translated "*sanctification*" (E. V.), and "*sanctification*" (E. V.) nowhere else occurs. The other five times it is translated "*holiness*" (E. V.), and always unhappily (6 : 19, 22 ; 1 Thess. 4 : 7 ; 1 Tim. 2 : 15 ; Heb. 12 : 14), especially in Heb. 12 : 14, where it is much more appropriate to say, "sanctification, without which no man shall see the Lord."

through that great wonder-work of Calvary, his *"being made righteous,"* or his *" sanctification."*

CHAPTER VII.

1. Or are ye ignorant, brethren (for I speak to persons knowing law), that the law, rules its human subject as long as he lives.

The **"or"** (Re.), which our English Version treats as an interrogative, and therefore, determines to remove, is not only significant, but really has a very wide significance on the part of the apostle. It swings him back into the previous chapter. For closeness of reasoning he had taken one thing for granted, and now he resumes it, that very peculiar thing, that sin breeds sin, or, to express it in legal phrase, that **"the law,"** as its very chiefest threatening, gives us over to sin, or makes its *"wages death"* (see last verse); **"Or, are ye ignorant"** (Re.) he says **("for I speak to"** Romans, **"persons"** who of all others on the earth pride themselves in understanding **"law"**), **"that the law rules its human subject as long as he lives?"** This alternative chance, viz., that they did not know, warrants him in going back and speaking in more fulness. The like use of *"or"* occurs in the previous chapter (v. 3). " *The law rules its human subject as long as it lives,"* we were disposed to say. The Greek admits the *"it,"* and the after verses might seem to demand it. We have already seen, however, how Paul might not like to say that the law was dead. *"Do we then bring law to nothing?"* he had inquired (3 : 31), *"nay, but we establish law."* We will see how he manages this under the coming metaphor. Meanwhile *"its human subject,"* a rendering that may seem forlorn, is put instead of the racier Saxon, simply *"man"* (E. V. & Re.), to avoid excluding the *"woman,"* who is really the point of the figure, and to distinguish ἄνθρωπος (v. 1) from ἀνήρ (vs. 2, 3), ἄνθρωπος being not necessarily of any sex, and ἀνήρ representing the law, and being he as to whom the woman dying, *" has been brought to nothing as to the law "* of her husband.

2. For the woman who is under marriage to a man has been bound to the living man as law; but if the man die, she has been brought to nothing as to the law of the man.

It is impossible to translate very literally. Paul evidently wishes to mould the sentence and thereby to shape the metaphor for the service of his thought. That we died (6 : 2) the moment we were converted, means any thing rather than that the law died. In the sacrifice and cruel death the law triumphed, and through eternity one jot of it shall not pass. And yet the figure of the wife seemed to demand that the law should be the husband, and that to set the sinner free the law should die. The apostle, in order to avoid that, shapes the allegory. Instead of pointing to the husband's death, he speaks of the wife, and he robs us of English clearness by using a verb which is a favorite in his epistles. It literally means to *make a man idle*. It comes from the words *a* and *ἐργον*, which would signify *without work*. It is translated (E. V.) with vast variety (Lu. 13 : 7; Rom. 6 : 6; Eph. 2 : 15); often to *make void*, (Rom. 3 : 31), or to *destroy* (Rom. 6 : 6), or to *bring to naught* (1 Cor. 1 : 28), or to make of *none effect* (Rom. 3 : 3). It is translated just below, "*We are delivered from the law*" (E. V.). We might say, "*Made dead from the law of the man;*" but that would clash with the more literal expression (v. 4). Paul evidently would say, If the husband dies, the woman dies, that is, to all law to that husband, and, therefore, we write, "**brought to nothing,**" as the nearest English we can think of. Below we shall say, "*brought to nothing in respect to law, having died to that in which we were held*" (v. 6). It is the nearest to the Apostle's imagery. The law is infinitely far from dead, but we are dead to it. The husband was indeed dead, but Paul's illustration was, so was the wife. As to any claim of law, she was dead. And what a terrible claim the saint has died to if he repents, we read of further (vs. 8–10) in this same chapter.

3. Then, therefore, the man living, she shall be called an adulteress if she become another man's ; but, if the man die she is free from the law, so as that the same woman is no

adulteress though becoming another man's. **4. So likewise ye, my brethren, were made dead to the law by the body of Christ, that ye should belong to another, even to Him who was raised from among the dead, that we might bring forth fruit unto God.**

4. "So." It is that word καταργέω that has shaped the figure in the aim to convey the reasoning. The woman has been "*brought to naught.*" The whole system under which she lived has been broken up. So of the believer. The law is not dead, but gloriously triumphs. But he is dead. He has been **"made dead to the law."** And though it takes hold of him with vital warmth for the first time in his history, yet it is dead as to its claim. "The handwriting that was against him" has been taken out of the way; and that handwriting, strange to say, plunged him in sinfulness. Here now comes the strong part of the chapter. The splendor of being dead to law is that it ceases to make us sinful; and just how it does so Paul goes on to explain, with singular boldness of speech, and yet with singular guard upon so dangerous an argumentation.

5. "For when we were in the flesh." Now just there let us pause to link this sentence with the other. The other had the expression, **"body of Christ."** It is too obvious to be told that "*flesh*" in the present sentence, and "*body*" in the other, are not literally what they seem. "*Flesh*" in the writings of Paul includes a thousand tastes that are mental and refined, and sweeps in the whole man outside of the Spirit of God. The "*body of Christ*" means similarly. It is all of Him except His Godhead. It is all of Him, just as in the instance of His people, except that, in their case, we keep out of the word their enlightened spiritual part, and in His case, that same part as seat and throne of His absolute Kingship and Deity. When He says, " My flesh is meat indeed," He means infinitely far from the carbon and nitrogen of His frame, but His whole man's being as sacrificed for sin. Its very carnality, in a reverent sense, was the secret of His torment. When He said, " The Spirit truly is willing, but the flesh is weak," He indicated the office of the "*body*" in His torment. It was not the crude muscle; else He could have borne it. It was the whole weak man outside of the Spirit of His Godhead. We are saved by grace, and we are saved by God, and the God-facts in the case make Him our hope, and our sole dependence for our being made better. But we are saved by "*flesh.*" Without "*flesh*" we could have no redemption. All of Christ outside of His Spirit could be tempted, which God never could; and through temptation could be tortured; and through His torture could be a sacrifice; and through the sacrifice could assert a price in it as of God; all of which He could not do as God; and all of which explains the language of our text. We are " (sanctified) by His blood" (Heb. 13:12). It is in these lights that we are to " (discern) the Lord's body" (1 Cor. 11:29). His "flesh is meat indeed." And so in this present epistle, " *We are made dead to the law by the body of Christ.*"

"**Who was raised from among the dead.**" Paul keeps constantly in view that being "*dead to the law*" releases a man from sinfulness. We always are dreaming differently. The grief that fills our eye is guilt. The grief that fills Paul's eye is sin. This is a flaw among the Reformed. The great fact in this epistle is that to save us is to make us righteous, and to damn us is to leave us wicked; and, therefore, we mar the great word out of the Greek (*make righteous*), when we give it a forensic cast. Paul says "*dead to the law,*" and means by that chiefly "*dead*" to that claim which gives us over to wickedness. We see his intensity of thought by the immediate rebound: dead to law, that we may live (Gal. 2:19); dead to the old husband, that we may bring forth to another (v. 4); dead to sin, that we may live to God (6:11). And here he rivets the sentence by drawing Christ into the scene. He never sinned, but was tempted to. He never yielded, but died ten thousand deaths as against the " infirmities " that " compassed him about." And while, if you look at all the commentaries, they will tell you that this rising "*from among the dead*" was from the rock in the Garden, the whole passage shows that it means morally, not out of actual sin like us, but out of awful "*death*" (6 : 3), that horrible "*infirmity*" which His Godhead enabled Him to fight, till He was made " perfect by sufferings."

5. For when we were in the flesh the sufferings of the sins which were by the law were made active in our members to bring forth fruit unto death. 6. But now we have been brought to nothing as to the law, having died as to that in which we were held, that we might serve in newness of spirit, and not in oldness of letter.

This is to provoke the next cavil, and we see at a glance how strong it is. It says, almost in terms, that the law makes sins. And yet, like the sun, it only shines down. If a man sins, he is not stopped in his accursed being. He lives on. That is the first point. And how could it be otherwise? But if he continues to sin, will sin breed holiness? Would that agree with any other system? Nay, must not sin breed sin, and each act of trespass make a man worse? Does not that agree with all the analogies of nature? Then, in legal language, all that Paul has asserted is the result. Christ supervened upon a stem of wickedness to graft Himself upon the root. "**For when we were in the flesh;**" that is, when we had but a modicum of Spirit, answering to our common conscience, which even the devils have, and which is slowly wearing itself away—"**the sufferings of the sins**"—we have seen how Christ suffered. It is a fine stroke in Paul to talk of *sin's sufferings.*" Christ's agonies were His temptations into sin. But Paul speaks at the close of the chapter (vs. 14, 24) of the agonies of every man. But these verses he brings in first. " *The sufferings of the sins which were by the law.*" How natural the immediate challenge, "**Is the law sin?**" (v. 7). Paul, under that, is to bring out most startling verities (vs. 8–11). " *The sufferings of the sins which were by the law :*" " *Sins,*" therefore (past all duplicity of speech), to which Paul means to say that "*the law*" gave us over. "**Were made active in our members.**" As in many another phase of anthropology, the bearing of the law upon sin is in two particulars. We can illustrate it as in the work of Christ. Christ saves us in two particulars. He saves us in court by ransom. He saves us in our souls themselves by a blest enrighteousment. So, correspondingly, in respect to sin, it is incurable in two ways, though one is the consequence of the other. It is incurable in court, because the curse was "*death*," and it is incurable as a disease, in the way that we call helplessness. Now, the law, as the occasion of sin, is in like forms dual. (1) One of these forms he has considered; but now (2) Paul approaches the other (see below vs. 7, 8). The law occasions sin (1) by actually punishing with it as a curse. That Paul has never doubted. He has said boldly, " *The wages of sin is death.*" He is to declare to the Corinthians, " The strength of sin is the law." And he has pictured our death to the law as meaning that we are "*alive to God through Jesus Christ our Lord.*" Now he is provoking another challenge. "*Made active.*" This is a favorite passive (2 Cor. 4 : 12 ; Eph. 3 : 20 ; Col. 1 : 29). Our version loses its force in that respect. In that important clause, " Faith made active by love " (Gal. 5 : 6), blinking the passive ruins everything.

Let us pause a moment upon this. If I say, " worketh by love" (E. V., see also Re.), I afford a text which has been propping a dangerous error. But if I say, " made active by love," I put the love directly into the faith, and I bring out that which afforded the ancient definition that "*fides formata*" has its *differentia* in charity. It is the pest of Protestantism that faith should be thought saving if it be mere dependence ; and it has come to pervade our church, and to loosen society, and (what casts shame upon Christ) to illuminate our jails and our gibbets,—that a man can get to Heaven by understanding the gospel, that is by having cut from it (it may be on the night preceding his execution) all thought of the necessity of repentance, and that he be told, that if he will cling to Christ on a personal understanding of His sacrifice, he will certainly be admitted to paradise. The verb means " to *work*, to *do*, to *be active*, especially of mental activity. Aorist " (Liddell). The middle is not to be taken for granted ; and the passive can not mean to "*work.*" When Paul speaks of " comfort made active in enduring" (2 Cor. 1 : 6), he utters something much more clean-cut than "comfort that works in enduring." And so, "made active by love" puts the whole doctrine of faith into the exactest condition for the people. It must be a faith that has love in it, just as the atmosphere must have oxygen in it. And to put the faith first and love afterward, is to tempt the sinner to have the faith and never get the love, for as Jeremy Taylor urges, if we are justified by faith, and, once justified, must alway persevere, what is to keep the sinner from launching upon the Christ, and failing afterward in the imagined consequence? We are "*made righteous by faith*" (Gal. 2 : 16). It is "*reckoned (to us) as righteousness*" (4 : 5, 9). It is that "*from*" which the "*righteousness of God is manifested*" (1 : 17). That is, the excellence of God must be reflected in our souls (and what is that but love?) before it can be handed on in a living way "*from faith to faith*"; because "*the righteous man must live out of his faith*" (1 : 17): faith must be the dawning of his life. And what does all this mean but that faith must be moral in its visions; must in fact be a moral illumination, with a morally illuminated Christ; very graphically, therefore, must be "*made active by love*"; and very manifestly, therefore, does not belong to the felon, unless over night in his prison his "heart (has been) opened" (Acts. 16 : 14), he has "received the love of the truth" (2 Thess. 2 : 10), he has been regenerated in answer to prayer, and his whole moral being reached by being born again" (Jo. 3 : 3, E. V.) into a new sight of sin (Job. 42 : 6) and a moral view of the loveliness of his Redeemer? All this is meant by "made active by love."

We understand easily, therefore, the present expression, "*were made active in our members.*" "**To bring forth fruit unto death.**" "*Sins which were by the law,*" that is, to which "*the law*" gave us over, "*were made active in our members,*" and, as a consequence of every indulgence, made things worse —as Paul expresses it, fed "*death,*" that is, *bore fruit* to the increase of those shocking "*wages*" which Paul calls "*death.*" "**But now,**" having died with Christ, that is having death actually paid down and exhausted, which we, except in the God-man, could not have done, "**we are brought to nothing as to** (ἀπό) **the law, having died to that in which we were held.**" It was the husband that died, but the law was too vigorous to be subjected to such an emblem. Paul, therefore, remembers that the wife also was *emptied out* or *made idle from* the law of her husband; and this is the phase he would press. "*We are brought to nothing as to law*," that is, cursed with sin by it no longer. And the cause was in Christ, "*having died* (with Him) *to that in which we were held*"—that we might begin to cease from sin—that is, "*that we might serve in newness of spirit, and not in oldness of letter.*" Paul ends with this. And we see in what compact shape he wedges in at the last a new idea. Not only have we "*died to sin,*" but we have died to that form of the curse which gives us over to hypocritical sinning. Paul has discussed this in another chapter. "*Not one who is so in what is apparent, is a Jew, nor is that which is so in what is apparent in the flesh, circumcision*" (2:28). Paul leaves the subject so that our modern idolisms are equally put out of the way. "*One who is so in what is hidden is a Jew.*" He goes at once to the seat in moral affections; and then he uses an expression which applies to this day as well as to Paul's. "*Circumcision is of the heart; in spirit, not in letter.*" The true "*circumcision*" of the soul, that is, conversion, is to be complied with not simply in the "letter." " If ye be circumcised;" that is, if ye be only circumcised in the outward or literal way, "Christ shall profit you nothing." And so in our day, if a man only believes, that is, reads the "letter" of the truth and believes it, and rests his soul upon it; if that is all; if he really leans upon Christ and clings to Him, and his clinging is personal and singularly exclusive, so that he is trusting to nothing but a personal Redeemer, still, if all he has reached is the letter; if he understands soteriology perfectly; if his view is complete of a personal sacrifice, in all respects but "*what is hidden*" (2:29), still if he does not *know* Christ, I mean in His loveliness, and if he does not hate sin, except in its dangerousness, he is no believer. How absurd to get to

Heaven by mere believing things! The expert theorist and the sharp mind, best capable of understanding the "letter," would be most convertible, and the reality is often the other way. Faith may be dim in the "*letter*," if it be warm in the "*spirit*." And that now is the meaning of our text. The "*law*," if it withdraw its curse, delivers us over to a genuine conversion, which may be very weak, beginning only in a budding and imperfect faith, but it will be a genuine faith, possessed by the new-born Christian, and not by the idolatrous Israelite; and therefore answering to the language, "*that we may serve in newness of spirit, and not in oldness of letter.*"

7. **What shall we say then? Is the law sin? By no means. On the contrary, I had not known the sin but by law; for, indeed, I had not understood the desire except the law had said, Thou shalt not desire.**

Paul had pushed his idea to the very verge of a mistake, and now, to clear his reasoning, he states what that mistake would be. He has allowed it to escape him that "sins" are "by the law" (v. 5). And, hence, to shield that which may easily be turned astray, he writes the quick question, "**What shall we say then? Is the law sin?**" and then brings forward the second (2) of the two forms in which law becomes the "**start**" of iniquity (see also next verse). That form we must be very particular in describing. Not only does the law breed "*sin*" by inflicting it as a penalty (and by this we must be understood as meaning, abandoning the sinner to his sinfulness), but it breeds it in this way,—that "**I had not known the sin but by law,**" on an expounding of which depends this whole passage. It does not mean that unless Sinai had spoken, and that in the Jewish sense, we could not sin. That we have already denied (5:13). It does not mean that unless our parents had taught us, or the letter had in some way been read of moral commandments, we could not transgress, for that again would be extreme; all men have natural conscience (see 1: 20). But the key is this conscience itself. Without law there can be no transgression. This we must press *a l'outrance*. Some goodness is needed for any sin. And to hold so perilous a position, let me advance to the very edge. The devil cannot be impeached unless upon a basis of conscience. If he merely knows moral distinctions, as Paul would word it, "*in the letter*," that arch fiend may have traditions of sin, but cannot sin. He may hear that he is sinning, but that is not sufficient. He must feel sin ; that is, he must have wrecks of conscience ; and as conscience eternally decays, it keeps him at the top of the list as a never-ceasing transgressor. This is plainly Paul's doctrine (3 : 20 ; 4 : 15). And now he applies it in our texts. "*I had not known sin but by the law.*" That is, I could not possibly sin without a conscience. This conscience must have its knowledge too. "**I had not understood the desire, unless the law had said, Thou shalt not desire.**" A new-born infant has conscience, but what light can it show ? Some teaching comes with every condition. The whole multitude at the bar will hear one sentence, "Out of thine own mouth will I judge thee" (Lu. 19 : 22). And this teaches the second (2) form (see Com. v. 5), in which law begets iniquity.

We must notice, in passing, two varieties of speech. Paul says in the first clause, "*law*," and in the second clause, "*the law*," and we have already virtually explained it. "*I had not known the sin but by law ;*" that is by law œcumenical, that law which all men possess. Again, "*I had not understood the desire unless the law had said, Thou shalt not desire.*" Nor can we explain this quite as well as when we have considered another distinction. He says in the first clause "*known*," and in the second clause "*understood.*" We learn from Liddell that there is a real difference. Γινώσκω means to know a thing (direct), and οἶδα means to know (something) about a thing. Paul marks this difference. We know "*sin*" much more directly than we know that "*desire*" is "*sin.*" Indeed "*sin*" is "*sin*" *in esse*, but "*desire*" is "*sin*" only because it acts out or exercises its *want* of something better. To *understand about* desire is necessary, for some law must tell us "*Thou shalt not desire.*" And, therefore, it is wrong to vary the expression and say "*lust*" (E. V.), and particularly wrong to vary *that* subsequently, and say "*covet*" (E. V.). The wrong thing in the sinner is to want love. That Paul everywhere teaches (13 : 8, 10 ; 1 Cor. 13). Loves of other sorts, though they be of the most refined, are wicked, because they indulge and practically exercise this deficiency. The devil, who has practically some love left, or is unready at least for some measures of deficiency, "*knows*" what deficiency is, for he has to struggle and resist measures of it which are still enticing him. And he *understands* about "*desire*," for he knows that it is innocent in itself, and that in Gabriel or himself a "*desire*" of power is only circumstantially and consequentially a wickedness. It spoils things to say, "*Thou shalt not covet*," for both the Hebrew and the Greek (Ex. 20 : 17) have the same more innocent expression. The force of the passage is seen in this very innocence. Paul simply quotes the LXX, and implies that men would have been slow to *understand*, unless the decalogue had made them familiar with so simple and harmless an apparition.

8. But sin, taking a start through the commandment, achieved in me all desire ; for without law sin is dead.

Here it is again ! "**law**" instead of "*the law*" (E. V. & Re.). Paul's speech is the strictest possible. To say "*the law*," and to imagine the commandments given to Israel, is to wreck all law and all possible morality. Paul is trampling that very thing. Men sin back to Eden. But no law, no transgression. Therefore men had a law ; and that law in its root was conscience. Ten thousand Sinais could make no law without it. And this Paul is seizing upon. "**Sin, taking a start through the commandment.**" This word haunts all philosophies (ἀφορμήν, *a starting point :* it is not any common word, "*occasion*," E. V. & Re., as in Gen. 43 : 18). Men, worrying over the abstrusenesses of Ethics, like to say that benevolence starts us ; or, puzzled with psychology, admit that there occur deeper developments, but that sensation is the "*start*." Paul presses the idea that if there be no conscience, there can be no sin ; that sin, therefore, takes its "*start*" from conscience ; that conscience is the necessary and deepest inscription of "*law*"; that on a capacity that conscience gives, sin achieves the wickedness of its *desires ;* and that, come what will in the way of consequence, the very thing by which we know sin, viz., conscience, is necessary to its being committed ; for, boldest of all, unless a man have law, and that not in the letter only but in the spirit so far as concerns a common spirit or a moral sense, he cannot commit iniquity, or, as the apostle expresses it, **" sin is dead."**

9. **And I had been alive without the law at any time; but the commandment coming in, sin got its life and I died; 10. And the commandment which was to be unto life, was found for me in its very self to be unto death. 11. For sin, taking a start by the commandment, deceived me and by it slew me. 12. So that the law is holy and the commandment holy and just and good.**

Δέ may be translated **"and"** when it begins both of two adversative sentences. The "*but*" of verse eighth answers for verse ninth in their common contrariety to verse seventh. **"I had been alive without the law at any time."** Paul sweeps on to another ending. Here he has gathered back both influences of law. (1.) The law curses me with sinfulness. If there were no law, the curse would be remitted. Again, (2.) the law curses me with knowledge. If there were no law, I could not be a sinner. "*I had been alive without the law* at any time." The word is ποτέ, and means "*once*" (E. V. & Re.) only derivatively and with lesser claim. **"But the commandment coming in;"** that is, coming into the case ; "*the commandment coming in*" as a thing to be considered, **"sin got its life, and I died."** In the universe of God no man perishes without a conscience. **"The commandment which was to be unto life ;"** and by this is meant, that conscience is the very rudiment and root of life : **"Was found for me in its very self to be unto death. For sin, taking a start by the commandment"** (How could sin set out at all if I had no conscience ?), **"deceived me, and by it slew me "**(sin having this advantage, that if it enters but for once, then the law is on its side, and gives me over to sinfulness). And as law is the very expression of my conscience, and I could not sin without a conscience, and I could not be holy except in conscience, and the only possibilities of Heaven must be in the light to which the conscience will attain, I must end with the apostle's paradox, that it is by the commandment that (2) sin deceives me, and by the law that (1) it takes my spiritual life, but that, for all that, I must agree with the apostle, that conscience has no fault but that it is not strong enough, and that the law has no fault but that it has not hold enough upon my being, but that on the contrary, as Paul concludes it, **"The law is holy and the commandment holy and just and good."**

I approached this rendering with fear, because no one has been found to suggest it, why, I cannot imagine. Ποτέ certainly means "*at any time*" (Eph. 5 : 29 : see Robinson), and other renderings are open to doubt because of their endless variety. "*When the commandment came*" (E. V. & Re.) cannot mean upon Horeb, for that would imply that men were "*alive*" and spiritually safe and perfect in the earlier stages of the world. The flood then must have swept men for being innocent. But then, just as mad has been another reading. Watts has embalmed it for the use of the church.

"I was alive without the law,
  And thought my sins were dead.

" My hopes of Heaven were firm and bright,
  But, since the precept came,
  With a convincing power and light,
  I find how vile I am."

The idea is that we were alive in our own imagination. But the startling result would be that when we ceased to be alive, or when by the grace of the Almighty, we opened our eyes, we "*died.*" We turn the verse into utter absurdity. Dying does mean living, and that in the near text of the apostle (6 : 3, 4), but nothing of that sort just now. "*The commandment ordained to life, I found to be unto death*" (E. V.) ; and expository of this form of dying are some of the strongest texts in the Bible. "*Sin deceived me, and by it slew me*" (v. 11). It wrought "death in me by *that which is good*" (v. 13). And then, to sum up all, comes a sentence which should have corrected all our mistakes in respect to this important passage,—"*For we know that the*

CHAPTER VII.

law is spiritual, but I am fleshly, sold under sin" (v. 14). Paul, with very little preface, then leaps to the conclusion, "*so that*" (and his view is less than usually laid open), I, not having "*known sin but by the law,*" and the law furnishing only the starting point for transgression ; its seat being in the heart ; and its voice the very voice of the Almighty ; all worlds being happy only by this very law ; we might as well impute sin to God as to trace it to His seat in the conscience. Paul has glanced through these things enough to prompt us ; and, meaning to make his conclusion the occasion for another reply, he ends this one more suddenly :—"*So that the law is holy and the commandment holy and just and good.*"

13. Did then that which is good become death unto me? By no means; but that which is sin, with the result of its appearing sin, working out in me death through that which is good, with the result that that which is sin, through the commandment, should become exceeding sinful.

We cannot clarify the idea of Paul. His postulates are obvious. (1.) We would not remain sinners but for the law ; for "a wise son makes a glad father" (Prov. 15 : 20), and our great Father, in his love, would not have a bad son unless the very key stone of law were "*death*" as a punishment for transgression. And again, (2.) we could not remain sinners unless we knew the law. For unless conscience survived, in however failing a condition, even Lucifer could not trespass. "*The law is holy.*" But even the holiness of law is necessary to possibility in sin. To kill a man we must have a man to kill. And before I can cry out, "I have sinned against Heaven and in Thy sight," I must see the Heaven that I offend, and know the law that I have broken by my miserable iniquity.

The tallest sinners in the pit will be the intelligent possessors of the gospel.

14. For we know that the law is spiritual, but I am fleshly, sold under sin.

All the words for *being*, except the most earthy, are derived from *breathing*. It is so in the Hebrew. The word for life is *breath*. And then there are stages in the figure. Another word is seized upon for soul. But it is still *breath*. And then when a finer is needed, still another vocable meaning *breath* is used to signify spirit. The Latin falls into the same habit; and when we come to the Greek, ψυχή (*breath*), when worn out in its more general usage for the soul, needs some other expression, and falls upon another expression for *breath* (πνεῦμα), which means the moral soul, which is strengthened when we are converted, and which goes among all mankind by the name of conscience. Spirit, in the writings of Paul, usually means our conscience. It is opposed to the "*flesh*," which takes for its meaning all the rest of our nature. A man may be an exquisite gentleman, but the finest things in his desires are of the "*flesh*," except as they are of the Holy Spirit. When Paul says, "There is a psychical body and there is a spiritual body" (1 Cor. 15 : 44), his meaning is simple. He means to say that the soul will dominate the earthly sinner, and the spirit the heavenly saint. He means to say that the soul has our natural light, and the spirit our moral intelligence; and though he is far from making a duality of essence, any more than of the "old man" and the "new man," yet he carries it even to the body. We have a soul-body below, and a spirit-body (that is one harmonized to obey the conscience), which is to rise hereafter into the Kingdom of the Father.

The apostle here, therefore, is perfectly plain. "**The law is spiritual.**" What is that but meaning that the law is moral? And as the spirit is but the moral part of man, the law is solely meant for it. "**I am fleshly.**" Paul is evidently speaking of his lost condition. For though he says in another place, "Are ye not fleshly?" (1 Cor. 3 : 4), there it abundantly appears of the fleshly remains of our state by nature. Here it is all the other way. It may not be for a moment doubted that Paul may think of the dark remains of his original wickedness, and when he speaks of "*evil* (being) *present with* (him)" (v. 21), he may not put it away from his thought upon himself; but that Paul is describing the lost and not the saved, or, if one likes it better, describing the "old man" apart from the grace of salvation, the one clause, "**sold under sin**," triumphantly establishes. This one touch has split the passage for many an exegete. It has become a favorite resort to understand a sinner for eight verses (vs. 7-14), and a saint afterward. What a miserable recourse! Paul never wavers a moment. He has spoken of the "*sufferings of sins*" (v. 5). Now he is to unfold them. And leaving the adverse difficulties to the last, let us see how finely he depicts the impenitent transgressor.

15. For what I work out I do not know; for not what I wish do I practice, but what I hate that do I.

How could anything be more profound? What is sin? It is any emotion, innocent in itself, which is deficient in two higher affections. If I love my horse, and a sad neighbor needs my care, the care of my horse becomes my transgression. If I love all innocent pleasures, and am spurred by the thought of them to all my enterprise in life, my whole life becomes sin; as is the whole actual reality, if the whole pleasure of life is not crowned by a love to the Almighty. Sin is privative, therefore. How can I "**know**" privative deficiency? If I knew sin, I would be righteous; for the same light that reveals me Christ, reveals me wickedness. The Bible is full of that thought, and it is all summed up in the phrase, "This is life eternal,—to know Thee, the only true God" (Jo. 17 : 3).

But, then, these three verbs as to *doing* (E. V.) or *practicing* (Re.) are all different expressions. The first means to "**work out**," and is applied to "*death*" in this epistle (v. 13). The second means to "**practice**," and is said by Liddell to have to do with habit in sin. The third means to "**do**." Our version has erred in smothering the difference.

We need not be so profound, therefore, after this correction. "**What I work out I know not.**" How unspeakably true this must be. "Godly sorrow worketh repentance" (2 Cor. 7 : 10). "Tribulation worketh patience" (5 : 3). "Freed from sin, ye have your fruit unto holiness" (6 : 22). From the very nature of the change you "*know*" these things when they happen. But let the change be the other way, and it settles noiselessly. A man may see by his bloated cheeks that he is becoming a drunkard, but who, in gentler circles of iniquity, feels the "*death*" he is working out? (Job 36 : 13; Jer. 9 : 6). This is the very easiest doctrine. Men do not hate God, and they do not love sin, I mean in its strictness as moral delinquency. They do not hate mercy and glorious purity of heart, and the thing would be impossible; and we do harm when we say they do, for the Bible does not say so, and they themselves may justly deny it in their absolute consciousness. The Bible is altogether more prudent. "The fleshly mind is enmity to God" (8 : 7), but it gives a reason, and that reason is roundabout and indirect. "(Men) hate light, neither come to the light" (Jo. 3 : 20), but there is interposed at once derivative reasonings. A God infinitely perfect could no more be hated than a blue sky. And as to benevolence and nobility of act, how foolish that a man could hate them—except just in the sense of the apostle. "The fleshly mind is enmity to God, *because it is not subject to the law of God*" (8 : 7), and man "hates light, neither comes to the light," as Christ altogether explains when he adds the expression, "*lest his deeds should be reproved*" (Jo. 3 : 20). It is the consequences of sin that men are dreading when they hate Jehovah.

And as the Bible never says anything different from this, we may come boldly to the language of the apostle. "*What I work out I do not know.*" It would be awful to me to destroy the noblest part of my creation. *What I practice, therefore, I do not wish.* This is a common feeling with the impenitent. In fact it is universal. "**What I hate, that I am doing.**" The imperial character of conscience, which, even in the pit, beckons a soul back from further death, makes sin a torment even to the wicked ; and thoroughly realizes the next verse :—

16. But if I do that which I wish not, I consent unto the law that it is good.

Now, why had I not better bring on at once the twenty-second verse, "*I delight in the law of God after the inward man*"

(E.V.)? This has done all the mischief. Men, entering upon the study of the passage with the expression "*sold under sin*" (v. 14), have said at once, it is Paul as an impenitent. But coming to this, "*I delight in the law of God*," a whirlwind has sprung up. The attempts at harmony are curiosities for exegetes. The Greeks said it was a sinner. The moderns preponderate the other way. Some have split the passage as we have seen, and made Paul personate another in the midst of this most careful picture. And, therefore, with proper timidity in respect to the risk, we think the expression "*sold under sin*" is a harder statement to neutralize than the rest, and therefore we take that as our cue for the integrity of the whole design. But where really is the difficulty in the twenty-second verse? The "*inward man*" is not "*the new man*," on the contrary the "*inward man*" in certain cases is itself to be renewed (E. V.). In fact the only other text except one (Eph. 3 : 16) in which like Greek appears, is this : " Yet the inward man is renewed day by day." It means simply the conscience ; that part of a man that sends him to hell or to heaven. The Almighty asked, " Who hath put wisdom in the inward parts ?" (Job 38 : 36). There is in fact no word in the Bible that means the saved heart in contrast with the pneuma of the impenitent. The song says : " Their inward part is very wickedness" (Ps. 5 : 9) ; and, more to our purpose, " Thou desirest truth in the inward parts " (Ps. 51 : 6) ; the need of which another Psalm exemplifies, for it says, " They curse in their inward parts " (Ps. 62 : 4) ; and Jeremiah, looking to this cankered condition of the conscience, utters the covenant, " I will put my law in their inward parts, and write it in their hearts " (Jer. 31 : 33); so that there is no difficulty at all in this part of the sentence. But "*I delight*"—that is rather a strong experience ! For a thief, red with the blood of a murdered passenger, to depict his condition as one of " *delight in the law*" of the Almighty, would seem to turn all reason out of doors. But let us look at that expression. The Greek has already said, **" I consent to the law "** (v. 16'; that is "*I talk with* (or like) *the law*" (σύμφημι) ; and all those who split the passage into two will agree with me that that is telling of the impenitent. But how is this in essence but just the idea of the other, "*I delight in the law of God!*" if we go down to the naked vocable, "*I sympathize—I have a pleasure in common with the law*" of my Sovereign? The tallest fiend in the pit, and that is Satan, if he had done some act not so subverting in its results as to breed him pain, and yet so noble as to touch cords that hell's degrees of sins had not yet ruined, might answer to this very word, "*I have a pleasure with it*" (συνήδομαι). Hell will have such recoils through all eternity; or else its fires would cool, and they would begin to be unjust.

But if these principles remain, they are the man in his noblest part. The noblest part of the devil is his conscience. And in a certain distinguishable sense it is the imperial part. Could I stand up and say, would I be lost or saved? or, going further inward and looking at the whole body of my iniquity, would I be a bad man or a good? the devil himself impulsively might speak for righteousness. Paul's language, therefore, is not in the least too saintly. Let us look at it.

17. But now it is no more I that work it out, but the sin that dwells in me.

Who is this "*I?*" Our first impulse was to say, it is the conscience. In fact we prepared a page in which we insisted on conscience as the imperial part. As man was created for his conscience (πνεῦμα); as that is the beautiful machinery for which all else is but the case; as our Saviour could only have been dealing with this when he said to Martha, there is but one thing needful; and as this is what wakes up under conviction, and lacerates the sinner till he cries out, "*O wretched man that I am,*" we thought it no risk to say that this "*inward man*" was the "*I*" intended in the text. But the speedy uprooting of any such idea explains the embroilment that has characterized all the attempts upon the sense. We are close upon a passage which says: "**In me, that is in my flesh.**" God forbid that we should be confusing the Epistle by confounding the conscience with what is fleshly. But yet the "*I*" must be cousin-german to the flesh in some shape or other, for what does the apostle say? If "I live," it is "not I, but Christ" that "lives in me" (Gal. 2 : 20). It is plain, therefore, that it cannot be the pneuma or conscience part of a man, for what is the pneuma but Christ's part, and precisely that which does live when Christ comes to reign within us? We do not wonder that the controversies on this part of Paul would fill a volume. And when we come to a fresh attempt, we are pushed back again. We are ready to say, yes, but it must be the pneuma, for what other part of a man could "*delight in the law?*" What but the conscience could talk with or for the law (σύμφημι, v. 16)? And what but the conscience could answer to the picture, "*What I would, that do I not, but what I hate, that do I*" (E. V., v. 15)? Just as we are thinking of sitting down in despair, this idea flashes :—Why not make the "*I*" to be the impenitent sinner, just as he stands? How often are knots untied by tumbling back into just such literalness of meaning! Who can "*I*" more naturally be than "*I?*" Now who is "*I?*" Paul, soul and body, flesh and spirit, just as he stands, a ruined and ungodly sinner. This view rallies all the passages. "**It is no more I that work it out;**" for I desire life, and not death, and am hating the ruin of my spirit, and not nobility of character. And we would draw attention here to the introduction of the word "**mind**" (νοῦς), which noiselessly takes the place of the pneuma in the twenty-third verse. The "flesh" is the whole of a man outside of the spirit. But it includes his nicest reasoning gift. The "*flesh*" picks up facts from the "*spirit,*" and learns to estimate them. Being linked in ungodly men with the remainders of a conscience, it learns to set a value carnally upon a noble life, and to shudder, more sometimes than a Christian, at rank enormities. Look simply at these things. Conscience is not a stranger. It is one aspect of intelligence. It is a sight of holiness, just as the same mind has a sight of beauty. How natural that it should pervade all my thought, and that the verdict of what is right should characterize all my thinking.

And the universality of this "*mind*" (v. 23) appears in the very word "*sin.*" It means to miss the mark (ἁμαρτάνω). I have a mind to be happy, and I *miss it*. I would like to be noble, but this liking is not strong enough, because my conscience is decayed, and my flesh masters me, and I *miss* nobility of living. And this explains all the terms of the apostle. He tells me I am a slave :—"*The law is spiritual, but I am fleshly, sold under sin*" (v. 14). He tells me I am a dupe, and that explains my being a slave (v. 11). "Deceived me, and by it slew me" (v. 11). And away back of Paul for twenty centuries the Bible reeks with this same idea. The escaped freedman is one "Who does not lift up his soul unto vanity" (Ps. 24 : 4), that is, grasp a shadow when he is desiring happiness. "The heart is deceitful above all things," Jeremiah tells us (17 : 9); and that it is self-deceitfulness comes out in still bolder appeals. "My tongue deviseth evil," says the inspired Psalmist; and that it is evil to the sinner's self appears in the illustration, for he says it is "like a sharp razor working deceitfully" (52 : 2). And the same Psalmist challenges this duped enslavement where he exclaims, "How long will ye love lies?" or, in the words of our Version, "How long will ye love vanity, and seek after leasing" (Ps. 4 : 2)?

Let us understand the "*I*," therefore, as meaning the *man* in his impenitence, and then each verse will explain itself.

18. For I know that in me, that is, in my flesh, dwells no good thing, for to will is present with me, but to work out the good, not.

Here already we have a need of our definition. "**In me**" does not mean "**in my flesh,**" for we cannot harmonize the conscience without making the "*I*" include the conscience. But Paul has already said, "*I am fleshly*" (v. 14). How perfect then is his consistency ! He does not doubt that he has a conscience, but he is constantly representing it as over-ruled and dying ; and therefore he has a right to his expression : "*In me, that is, in my flesh.*" "*I*" being over-ruled by "*my flesh*" am predominantly "*fleshly*" (v. 18) ; and though my conscience animates my "*mind*" (v. 23), and fills it with better desires, yet it is deceived (v. 18) and enslaved (vs. 23, 24); for in "*my flesh*," the dominant part, "**dwells no good thing, for** (though) **to will is present with me,** (yet) **to work out the good, not.**" "*I find*" (εὑρίσκω, E. V.) seems to have little MS. authority. The Revisers and most moderns omit it. "*Good*," in the earlier part of the sentence, means *virtue*, perhaps from a root meaning to *admire*. "*Good*" in the latter part means *the beautiful*. In my flesh dwells no *virtue*, and, as that is my dominant part, my appreciation of *the beautiful* (morally), which is high, gets no opportunity of being trained or listened to.

19. For the good which I would, I do not; but the evil which I would not, that I practise.

If a man really wishes to do a thing, he has done it, I mean in the region of morals. For to love an act or to desire it, if it is an act that can be done, insures that it will be done, and is in itself the virtuous part of it; for as this same apostle has said, "love is the fulfilling of the law" (13 : 10). We must be careful, therefore, not to derange that first principle of morals. But to have our longings when the action is not just present, when it is in the future, when it is in the past, when it is in the distance, or when it is only in the fancy; above all, when it is by itself, and is not swept from us by the overruling desires of the flesh, is the idea in the mind of Paul. We would like to do the καλόν (*the beautiful*), but we do **not** like to enough, and sin is just the tyranny of a superior affection.

20. But if I do that I would not, it is no more I that work it out, but the sin that dwells in me.

To the onset of the question, now therefore, If the "**I**" be the man himself, and man is dominantly "*flesh*," and "*flesh*" by its innocent desires becomes guilty in its desires when they become exaggerated by a deficiency of better, how can Paul say that it is not "*I*" that work the wickedness? We can give now some easy replications. "**If I do that I would not.**" Paul's apparent paradox seems to justify itself by the will. Paul's idea seems to be that the weaker will may be more properly the man. For look at the attributes of it. In the first place it is the more *general* will. In the choice of the whole life together, who is there that would choose sin? In the second place, it is the *future* will. In all that broad expanse that reaches out in the eye of the present, all men are on the side of what is noble. Again it is the *happy* will. Paul speaks significantly of "*the sufferings of sin.*" Again, it is the *longing* and *aching* will. Men feel that they are delinquent, and yearn after what is high and noble. These are the ideas of Paul. The whole cast of the chapter goes to show that that side of a man that has on it the conscience, deserves to be called more truly the "*I,*" because that part stands to what it says, repents not of what it designs, and wills and hesitates now, even under the brow of sin, to confess the gyves that are fettering it away from its felicity.

21. I find, then, the law, that when I would do good, evil is present with me; 22. For I am pleased with the law of God after the inward man.

We discover by reading the commentaries that Protestants shrink from two things, first, from calling **"the law"** anything but the moral law, and, second, from imagining the conscience to have the same moral affection, and, when renewed, to be the same sanctified heart as belongs to the believer. The first of these mistakes has led to a peculiar pointing. Dr. Shedd translates the twenty-second verse with the comma after ποιεῖν. He puts "**good**" in apposition to "*the law.*" And he gets rid of "*the law*" as meaning anything else than the decalogue, by reading thus :—"*I find then that to me wishing to execute the law, which is good, evil is present.*" The only pay for such a forced adhesion would be that we could carry it out. But how about the twenty-third verse, and the "**law in the members,**" and "**the law of the mind,**" and "**the law of sin?**" It was a bold place to attempt such a gloss, for these three come immediately after. How about "*the law of the spirit of life, and the law of sin and of death?*" (8 : 2). It is plain that "*law*" may mean a *a state of facts*, or a *rule* or *order of realities*. "*The law*" of an earthquake is the way it ruptures the crust, or the direction in which it is seen to move. We might quote other passages (3 : 27). But when this adhesion to an exclusive sense attacks the second sentence of the two, it actually favors Pelagianism by the craze of the attack. Do listen to a commentator on this second verse (v. 22): "Conscience does not delight in holiness (συνήδομαι, v. 22); it only approves of it (σύμφημι, v. 16) . . . Such terms as θέλω and μισῶ are inapplicable to the conscience. Reason and conscience belong to the understanding, and not to the will ; they are cognitive, not voluntary ; perceptive, not affectionate ; legislative, not executive " (Shedd *in loco*). Let it be considered that this is not the definition of a word, but of the furniture of a lost man's nature, and that we are invited to believe that a man may have conscience, but no sense in the sense of any moral emotion. How completely this plays, by recoil, into the hands of the Pelagians ! If this be orthodoxy, men will say, it is utterly accursed. How can I know holiness without emotion ? At this late day such things just sacrifice the truth. The whole of law is wrapped up in two emotions. Our Saviour teaches it (Matt. 22 : 40). How can I know beauty without feeling it ? And how can conscience move an inch in what Dr. Shedd calls approving holiness, if holiness be an emotion of love, unless it have that emotion ? and if it have it in a decaying and dying form (as Satan has), that is all we need affirm to meet, in the orthodox sense of deficiency, the Pelagian view. A man is totally depraved when he has not enough conscience ; but a man is not depraved at all when he has no conscience. Total depravity does not consist in no moral emotion (least of all in the wrong sort, for there are not two sorts of morals), but it consists in a deficiency of it, and that deficiency must increase if we are not miraculously renewed. Renewal, therefore, must be of the conscience, or, as the Bible calls it, the regeneration of the heart. And sin's deficiency does not leave us without some love for virtue, but with too little ; and as sin itself is a loving too little (13 : 9, 10), this is our total depravity, for it affects every faculty, and every act and exercise that is possible to the heart.

"**The law**" (v. 21). That means the state of the reality. "*That with me wishing to do what is beautiful.*" The veriest sot has a conscience ; and that, by the very law of its nature, has the kingly office. Its voice, but for its deficiency, would be listened to ; and, in spite of its deficiency, I confess the splendor of loving, and the exalted excellence that resides in doing right. "**I am pleased with the law**" (συνήδομαι, v. 22). Paul has already said, "*I talk with the law*" (v. 16), that is, I *say the same thing*, or *assent to it*. And what does being "*pleased with*" it mean more? And as to the "**inward man**" we have treated that along with the whole sentence (see com. on v. 16). Paul prays that they might be "strengthened with might by the Spirit in the inner man" (Eph. 3 : 16). It was thus that they were to be sanctified. And of that design is the exact gospel. Every sinner has an "*inner man*," and that *inner man* is not the self-sufficient conscience of the Pelagian, which can remedy itself, but the fading conscience of the lost, the embers of which will endure eternally, but the light of which will continue to decrease, unless in this world brightened by the saving cross and by the saving power of the blessed Redeemer.

23. But I see another law in my members warring against the law of my mind, and bringing me into captivity in the law of the sin which is in my members.

Eagerness to comprehend all this under "**the law**" of the decalogue, if it were felt, might easily be indulged, for these *orders of the facts or laws of the reality* are all exacted by Sinai. "**The law in my members,**" or, as it is afterwards called, "**the law of the sin which is in my members,**" is really what was announced in Eden as its head anathema (Gen. 3 : 3), and "**the law of my mind,**" namely that some wrecked conscience shall be left, is an essential part of it. Just this conflict that is described will be the curse upon lost sinners through infinite ages.

"**Mind.**" A new term. Paul drops the expression pneuma ;

for though the lost have that (viz., conscience), yet they have more than that (see com. v. 17). Paul pictures the whole opposition to "*death ;*" and that opposition consists, not in the present emotion of conscience, but in that and all we have ever learned. The sinner *knows too much* to perish. And were it not for "*the law of sin in* (his) *members,*" he would break out. He is in "**captivity,**" therefore. He is in "*captivity* **in the law of sin.**" The preposition should be *in* (see MSS.). The sinner is "*deceived*" (v. 11); at least he feels so when finally awakened; and all through his history he carries with him a "*mind*" which would have led him aright, containing more than a "*heart*" (2 : 5), because including with the conscience awful convictions of the truth, and fearful terrors in respect to perishing.

24. O wretched man that I am! who shall deliver me from the body of this death?

Of course this is all consistent. A sinner a hundred times cries out against his bondage. He finds "*a law.*" And now the apostle hardens that into an actual "**body**" or organized system. Nay, not quite so abstract: his actual "*body*" organized to sin. This expression has been traveling toward us. "*The body of sin*" had to be "*destroyed*" (E. V.), so we read in the sixth chapter (v. 6). Latterly we have been hearing of sin in our members (7 : 23), that is, the seat of the "*desires of the flesh.*" And now we put it all together. There is an organized "**body of death;**" and it is too strong for a decaying conscience; and Paul, by crying out:

25. But thanks be to God through Jesus Christ our Lord.

finishes his picture; only making the "*death*" the darker by showing that there is no hope of deliverance save in "**Jesus Christ our Lord.**"

It is not very important to diagnose the next passage. It may be Paul proper, or it may be Paul in his natural state or "*old man,*" just as in all the rest of the passage. It makes little difference. He had uttered the wailing cry, "**Who shall de-**

liver me *from the body of this death?*" and then suffered the sky to open with the only possible deliverance. After that the ending may be in his own person—or not. It makes never the smallest difference. The expression "**I myself**" may mean that or not. The truth is the same in either case.

25. So then I myself, in the mind, serve a law of God, but, in the flesh, a law of sin.

The Christian does not climb higher than such a sentence; so that "**I myself,**" in this case, may mean a Christian. With Paul's "**mind**" he served "**a law of God,**" just as the sinner does, and that to the extent that he starts back from greater reaches of iniquity; with this difference, however, that if it be now at length the risen Paul (v. 25, *first clause*), he serves more, and is growing, rather than decaying, in his onward service. He is serving graciously in the one case, and feebly and decayingly in the other; whereas, on the reverse side, both serve a law of sin, protestingly and strugglingly on the part of Paul, and protestingly and strugglingly on the other part, but with struggles, on this latter part, less in strength, and without any looking to the grace of the Redeemer.

"*I*," therefore, is simply the impenitent man; and if it changes in this last verse, it is upon the indication of that "*I myself*," and it is in a branch of the statement following the outburst about Christ (v. 25), and equally true with either meaning.

"**In the mind**" and "**in the flesh**" are both datives without a preposition, and, therefore, indicate a closer connection with the *service* than either ἐν (in) or διά (by). The indication is that both "*the mind*" and "*the flesh*" constitute in their emotions and conditions their respective service. We do not deny that the dative sometimes means the instrument (Jo. 21 : 8; 1 Cor. 9 : 7), but it is usually in physical matters, and very rarely in those texts which are dealing with pictures of the mind.

CHAPTER VIII.

1. There is, therefore, now no condemnation for them who are in Christ Jesus. 2. For the law of the Spirit of the life in Christ Jesus freed me from the law of the sin and the death. 3. For (a thing which the law could not do in that it was weak through the flesh), God, sending His own Son in likeness of sinful flesh, and on account of sin, condemned the sin in the flesh, 4. With the result that the law's righteous-making be fulfilled in us, who walk not after flesh but after spirit.

Paul lays a foundation for a phrase, and then confidently uses it; or he uses a descriptive sentence in a thoroughly intelligible way, and then suddenly condenses it to avoid repeating his language. In fact in all Scripture, and in all secular speech, that course occurs; so that the word "faith," for example, means more than mere mental belief, and the word "clean" (Jo. 15 : 3) and the word "righteous" mean actually not "righteous," but only beginning to be less sinful. Books would choke our dwelling houses if we could not shorten them by certain catch words, so to speak, which do not at all describe the plenary thought which they are to convey. "**In Christ**" has been long ago prepared for by the expressions "*died with*" Him, "*crucified with Him,*" "*baptized into*" Him, and, above all, "*bred in with Him,*" so as to "*live with Him*" (6 : 3, 5, 6, 8), the meaning being that we so stand "*in Christ,*" that forensically we are bought off, and spiritually we are "*made righteous*" by Him through His redemption. There is a strong minority of MSS. which add, "*who walk not after the flesh but after the Spirit*" (E. V., v. 1); but, on the whole, it must be rejected. It is a perfect description of "**them who are in Christ.**" "**No condemnation.**" The expression is very strong, both from the word and its position in the sentence. "**For the law.**" Here comes again the language which turns us away from the law proper, or the decalogue, to the same word as meaning a state of the reality (see 7 : 21-25). And yet when we come to reflect, "**the law**" is lurking in the neighborhood after all, and we need not be surprised that it starts up again in the next sentence (v. 3). Every law, either of grace or wickedness, was writ on Horeb. And, therefore, when it says, "**The law of the Spirit of the life in Christ Jesus, freed me from the law of the sin and the death,**" it may indeed mean the order of the facts, or the rule of the reality, but what is that but the description of what was announced on Sinai? "*The law of sin and death*" was precisely that proclaimed in Eden, "In the day thou eatest thereof" (Gen. 2 : 17). And "*the law of the Spirit of the life*" is as forensic as the other. Both these laws must prevail, before Sinai, with all its thunderings, can be laid at rest. ("*The law of the Spirit of the life in Christ Jesus.*" First, it is "*in Christ.*" He alone won our deliverance. Second, it is a "*life in Christ.*" This is the form in which our deliverance is achieved. Third, it is a "*Spirit of life in Christ,*" or, in other words, a moral conscience revivified by the Holy Ghost : in other words our being "*made righteous*" is our great salvation. And, fourth, it is a "*law of the Spirit of the life;*" and that there can be such a "*law*" is itself a forensic reality, for it is a "*law,*" as the sentence proclaims, that *sets me free* from another "*law,*" viz., that dire rule that makes sinners sinners, that establishes me in sin, that makes sin an incurable disease, that makes it grow and reign, that makes this the great Sinai curse, and that embodies it all under that terrible name, "*the law of death.*" "**Freed me** "(aorist), that is, did it at a certain time : began to free me (for all these terms have the reserve of incipiency), "*from the law of the sin and the death* " at the time of my conversion.

3. "**For.**" This is for the forthcoming reason for the *freeing*, which the apostle has so definitely stated. "**A thing which the law could not do;**" literally "*the impossible thing* (τὸ ἀδύνατον) *of the law.*" In the next chapter the apostle speaks of "*the possible thing of God*" (τὸ δυνατὸν αὐτοῦ, v. 22). It is forlornly sad that this bearing of that sentence should have been lost. When both the versions (E. V. & Re.), and

all our commentators read, "*wishing to make His power known*," it is one of those numerous cases where the sense of the Spirit is just cut in two at the moment of completion. Paul is dealing with the thought that God does the best He can, in the sense which God Himself encourages in numerous passages (Is. 5 : 4 ; Lam. 3 : 33 ; 2 Pet. 3 : 9); and he suddenly brings out the expression, "*willing to make known what is possible for Him*," and the commentators ruin it by the sense, *wishing to show His power*. In the present case, nobody has mistaken the meaning,—"*the impossible of the law*." And Paul at once prompts us as to what it is :—" *The impossible of the law* " is the δικαίωμα (a "**making righteous**"). The δικαίωμα of the law is one of the most splendid things in the universe. It exists in the case of the Almighty. God is *made righteous*, or constituted holy, by his grand obedience to law. So are angels. So was Christ. So are other worlds, we have reason to be confident. The δικαίωμα of the law is the great "*righteous making*," and among boundless peoples. But, on earth, it fails. Why is that? Paul describes it by the language, *No righteous making by the works of the law* (Gal. 2 : 16), and his evident meaning is that works which the law can prompt are never by that prompting holy (see com. 3 : 20). And why? He answers in unnumbered fashions. Because we are dead (v. 6); because we are slaves (v. 21); because we are deceived (7 : 11); because we are cursed (Gal. 3 : 10); because "*the law of the Spirit of the life in Christ Jesus*" must make us free "*from the law of the sin and the death ;* " or, to take now the present picture, because "it" (the law) "**was weak through the flesh.**" It could make God righteous, because He is strong, or the angel Michael, or an unfallen planet, but "us" it cannot reach, because it "**was weak through the flesh.**" Paul had said this before, "*When we were yet weak, Christ died for the ungodly*" (5 : 6). Our conscience is too "*weak*" to resist our flesh, and it is growing weaker. This constitutes an incurable curse. The law cannot reach that ; and so Paul preludes what he is about to say :—" *What the law could not do*." "**God sending His own son.**" This does not prove that the "*Son*" was begotten before God's incarnation in Him, for other men were spoken of as "*sent.*" "There was a man sent from God whose name was John" (Jo. 1 : 6 ; see also Matt. 9 : 38 ; Lu. 11 : 49). "**In the likeness of sinful flesh.**" A Presbyterian rather surprises us by the following comments: "'Ἁμαρτίας, the genitive of quality, showing that the human nature spoken of is a sinful and corrupt human nature, if contemplated *in itself* and *apart from* the miraculous conception by the Holy Ghost. The qualifying epithet ἁμαρτίας describes human nature simply as it descends from Adam. As such it is a sinful nature. St. Paul is contemplating it from *this point of view* only, when he employs the epithet. It does not follow that when a portion of this sinful and corrupt human nature is *assumed* into union with the Eternal Logos [let us rather say with the One Jehovah.—M.] it is still sinful and corrupt. In and by the miraculous conception it is perfectly sanctified, so that though it is sinful flesh or corrupt human nature in Mary the mother, it is a 'holy thing' or perfect human nature in Jesus the child. Compare Lu. 1 : 35 ; 2 Cor. 5 : 21 ; Heb. 4 : 15 ; 10 : 5 ; 1 Pet. 2 : 22. . . . The Logos does not take into personal union with himself a human nature created *ex nihilo* for this particular purpose, and which, consequently, could not be a σὰρξ ἁμαρτίας, but he assumed into union with himself a human nature that descended by ordinary generation from Adam down to the Virgin Mary, and which in *this* connection and relation was *sinful flesh.* Before, however, it could be a constituent part of the God-man, it must be entirely purged from the effects of the Fall" (Shedd, Com. *in loco*). Take away the allusion to an "Eternal Logos," which John carefully aimed to correct (see "Is God a Trinity?" p. 89), and add the idea that Christ's intended *sacrifice* purged His humanity *ab ovo* perfectly and before sinning, just as it did that of any pre-Christian like Abraham imperfectly and after sinning, and we have in Dr. Shedd a singularly correct exposition. "*In the likeness.*" This word ὁμοίωμα occurs but six times in the Testament. On each of those six occasions it means, not simply *like*, but very closely and essentially *like*. Four of the cases are in Romans. "*In a likeness of an image of corruptible man*" (Rom. 1 : 23), means strangly and very ruinously *like*. "*In the likeness of Adam's transgression*" (Rom. 5 : 14), means very specifically *like* it. "*In the likeness of His death*" (6 : 5), means eminently *like*, yet with differences. "*In the likeness of men*" (Phil. 2 : 7), means to all intents and purposes a man, yet with differences, as for example that He did not sin, as for example that He had no father, and as for example that He was one with the Almighty. So, as Dr. Shedd has partially declared, " *God sending His own son in the likeness of sinful flesh*," sent Him *like* in most intimate particulars ; first, as of the race of Adam ; second, as under that curse ; third, as inheriting infirmity ; fourth, as horribly tempted ; fifth, as horribly tortured, His torture caused by His temptation ; sixth, as dying and rising ; and seventh, as being a man like us, in every sense not now hereinafter to be distinctly declared. For, first, He is unlike us in His Divinity. Specifically and actually and in eternal person He is what none of us is, God and man in two distinct natures and one person forever. And then He differs, second, in sinlessness. He was *like* " *sinful flesh*," but with that difference, for the reasons stated, that He was never "*sinful*." And then if we add all the primacy of His redemption, that He is the head and we are the members, that He is the God and we are His people, that He is the Shepherd and we are the flock, that we are the lost and He is the Redeemer, that He is of the first Adam, but nevertheless also the last Adam, and saved, we hope, Adam and millions afterward, we have reason to see amazing differences, and yet one vast likeness,—that He was born of sinful blood, and inherited curses from His kindred. "**And on account of sin.**" " *God, sending His own son in likeness of sinful flesh, and on account of sin*, **condemned sin in the flesh.**" It has been "*condemned*" and will be "*condemned*" whenever the lost sink into perdition. But the passage becomes expressive only when we finish it. "**With the result.**" See all that has been said of ἵνα in other passages (4 : 18 ; 6 : 1, 6 ; Gal. 5 : 17). It is nothing wonderful to *condemn sin*, but to *condemn sin* with certain *results*, that is the glory of the apostle. The law makes

God righteous, and Christ, and Gabriel, and glorious myriads of the unfallen, but it makes me miserable, and damns me, and follows me through the eternal age, but lo! wonder of the universe! Christ has altered all that, and by His very "*likeness to sinful flesh,*" and "*on account of sin,*" that He might abolish it, He has managed to condemn sin, which is all the law demands, and then to set loose the law itself that it may return to its universal work,—"*with the result* **that the law's righteous-making be fulfilled in us, who walk not after flesh but after spirit.**"

"*Righteous-making.*" There is no deference to the apostle in saying "*righteousness*" (E. V.). Why did not *he* say "*righteousness?*" Δικαίωμα has a distinct orthography, and it means the making of any thing or man *right* or *righteous*. Law is nothing to a cow or horse, but can become law only to a conscience. Nay, we can weave that sentence closer yet, and say that it requires conscience to make a law, or to give it any being, or impart to it any binding efficacy whatever. Law, in this grander sense, makes all the righteousness in the universe. But to make anybody righteous, he must have a conscience, and this only the Holy Spirit can supply. If the law ceases to have power to make any creature righteous, it is a sign the conscience has decayed. The law cannot cure that, only the Almighty. But "*what the law could not do in that it was weak through the flesh*" (that is the flesh running riot through feebleness of conscience), God did. He satisfied the law by another method of *condemning sin;* that the "*righteous-making*" power "*of the law*" might be restored, with the result indicated at the close, that we should "*walk not after flesh,*" which with an enfeebled conscience will always take the rein, but "*after spirit,*" viz., *after that quickened conscience, after that roused and animated sense* which Christ bought for us, and which is the gift of the Holy Ghost.

This now is the main stem of the reasoning. But we wish also to go back and take up other ideas, which Paul, in the exuberance of his thought, has made it carry with it. When Paul speaks of *condemning sin,* he means mainly condemning it by adequate punishment in the cross of the Redeemer. But, almost entangling the text, has come the thought, which some exegetes have made the only one, that Paul by the whole trend of his explication must mean *condemning* to its *overthrow*. When the damned criminal is tormented in the pit, sin is "*condemned*," because, as in the case of Christ, it is adequately punished; but, instead of being "*condemned*" by overthrow, it grows immortal. The question is, Did not Paul mean the very opposite of this in the language we are considering?

Let us go back to the beginning. The word "*condemnation*" (v. 1), is the pregnant word in all the passage. It is beyond doubt entirely forensic; but Paul has prepared us to be entirely intelligent about it by the close discussion in the previous chapters. It is entirely forensic; but the very nature of the verdict in this penal court is a verdict of abandonment to sin. There is no point stronger than this in the epistle to the Romans. It lies at the very foundation. Paul turns it over in every form of expression. He rarely speaks of torment; though, let it be understood, "*tribulation and anguish*" are a distinct threatening of the law. But even "*tribulation and anguish*," though they are bodily, and though they are mental, are themselves also in part put down as moral. And that grim monster, our physical dissolution, back in the very dawning of the world, was seized upon as the very darkest illustration of sin. God said, "In the day thou eatest thereof thou shalt die" (Gen. 2 : 17). Moses constantly repeats the picture; " Behold I have set before you this day life and death, blessing and cursing." Paul more than any one else adopts the same ancient illustration. "The wages of sin is death." And he puts it always in the most practical position. "*I had been alive without the law at any time.*" With Paul, therefore, the κατάκριμα ("*condemnation*") is not a thing that breeds torment, and, as an incidental thing, leaves us in our sins; but just the other way. The κατάκριμα in its very gist is wickedness. And Paul, in the previous passages, has detailed the only deliverance. The only deliverance from sinfulness is suffering, and such suffering as Christ could endure, imparting to it the innocence of His humanity and the price-speaking significance of His impersonate Godhead ; and when the deliverance comes, just as in the instance of the κατάκριμα, the redemption is entirely forensic, but in its main essence moral. Instead of delivering us from the curse, and then, as a consequence of that, making us holy, the δικαίωμα or "*righteous-making*" of the cross is the very gist of the gospel benefit. It mars the gospel to speak of the "imputation of righteousness." The imputation of suffering from so innocent a Prince as Christ is enough for our redemption, and then the imparting of righteousness is the very substance of the bestowment when we are to speak of our gracious pardon. There is indeed a surplus over in the shape of "*hope.*" Paul is about to say (v. 24), "We were *saved in the form of hope;*" and that thought is expressed by the word "*earnest*" (2 Cor. 1 : 22 ; 5 : 5.). When we are converted we have a "hope of righteousness which is by faith " (Gal. 5 : 5). But our great seedling blessing is our holiness ; and our great mother curse is our sin. And the κατάκριμα, which this chapter triumphs in, is not a forensic verdict chiefly of pain, but a forensic verdict chiefly of sin, and that we may make no mistake in this, all Paul's previous reasoning comes here into play.

For example the δικαίωμα is purchased. That is to say, the making of us righteous is the thing bought by the suffering of the Redeemer. In the second place the δικαίωμα must be by God. That is to say, He who created us must create us over again by the Holy Spirit. God, as He moves in creatures, is called the Spirit ("*breath,*" Heb. and Gr., Job 26 : 13), and, as He moves morally in creatures, is called the Holy Spirit. This, unlike the "holy arm " (Is. 51 : 9 ; 52 : 10), or the " holy name " (Deut. 28 : 58 ; Ps. 111 : 9), has been snatched by Platonic mutilators of the truth, and made to degrade our Christianity. This Holy Breath of our divine Regenerator meets a part of nature where He was always present, viz., our conscience, and it is by renewing that that a man is justified (made righteous).

We understand then at once the language that is to come so

prominently into play. The "*spirit*" is that part of a man that is tenanted by the Spirit of God, and the "*flesh*" is all the other part ; and now we need scarcely do more than repeat the different verses as they occur. "*The law of the Spirit of the life in Christ Jesus has made me free from the law of the sin and the death*" (v. 2). "*The law*" for good is just as much of Sinai as "*the law*" for evil ; for Christ has paid "*the law*" till it demands our sanctification. "*For what the law could not do in that it was weak through the flesh.*" This is transparently intelligible. He is about to say, "**So then they that are in the flesh cannot please God**" (v. 7), and, one sentence previously, "**For the mind of the flesh is death**" (v. 6), and the reason is obvious :—If Christ has bought us, and we are to be saved by the Spirit, and we quench the Spirit, of course we "*cannot please God,*" and originally without any Christ at all, being left entirely to the "*flesh,*" the law would be impotent except to curse. But ("*a thing which the law could not do in that it was weak through the flesh*), God, *sending His own son in the likeness of sinful flesh, and for sin, condemned sin in the flesh*" (v. 3). The verb is in the aorist. We do not like to press such points. But the word *condemn* is never elsewhere applied to "*sin,*" and never anywhere in any such case as this given in an aorist meaning. It will be innocent certainly at least to use it as an illustration. Condemnation is never finished in an everlasting Tophet. We are "*condemned*" and we are "*condemned.*" Christ finished transgression and made an end of sin (Dan. 9 : 24), and, therefore, in Him transgression *was punished* in an aorist sense. "*With the result that the righteous-making of the law*" (the "*righteous-making*" in every sense, that is, the *right-making* of the act and the "*righteous-making*" of the subjects of it ', "*might be fulfilled in us ;*" and then, as a matter of course, comes this description, "*who walk not after flesh, but after spirit.*"

This damned state of being in the "*flesh*" Paul characterizes thus as being a "*walk*" or voluntary trespass, but he goes deeper in the verse that follows, and makes it a matter of our **"thinking."**

5. For they that are after flesh do think the things of the flesh, but they that are after spirit, the things of the spirit.

The question that agitated theology some decades ago, whether all sin consisted in moral exercises, is completely ploughed under in these chapters of Paul. Sinfulness is a deficiency of love. Love is in two separate senses. A man is a sinner who does not love God sufficiently in one sense, and his neighbor sufficiently in another. And the Bible measures out to us with exactness the bounds of this sufficiency (Matt. 22 : 37, 39.). What did the old theologian mean ? If he meant that sinfulness was an exercise, the very idea was absurd. If he meant, however, that a sinful state, like a sinful act, might be punished, again there is a tinge of foolishness, for we have seen, and most abundantly from Paul, that sinfulness is itself a punishment. Let not men sit loose to the idea of torment, for we believe in it as an eternal penalty ; but sin is the great mother curse, and so far as sin means sinfulness it is itself the higher penalty of the violated law. If, however, sin means acts, of course they are moral exercises. But the question really goes deeper. The puzzle that agitates men's minds is precisely that with which the apostle grapples. If the question mean, is there anything sinful in the mind except moral exercises, we would answer yes and no. Sinfulness is a deficiency. If a deficiency is a " *thing* " we would answer, Yes. But Paul goes so far in asserting the mere privativeness of transgression that he says, " *What I do I know not*" (7 : 15). We cannot see a nothingness. We can see with the eyes of "*flesh*," that is, the joys and tastes of our unsaved nature. And we can see with the eyes of conscience, a thing that confuses our ideas, for there is a spiritual sight left in God's part of our decaying humanity. But our *deficiency*, who can see that ? Paul, therefore, solves the riddle when he declares that our "*flesh*" is the seat of our iniquity. Conscience being altogether too weak, is trodden upon and smothered by other desires. And those desires which in heaven would be our glory, on earth are our sins, because they "*exercise*," so to speak, our deficiencies of "*spirit*," and are those desperate lusts which violate our remaining virtue.

Now, as the being of the mind shows itself only in its daily exercises, the mind is destroying itself thought by thought. Every act sinks it, and, what Isaiah says under a beautiful image, "We all do fade as a leaf" (Is. 64 : 6), Solomon grapples more boldly, for he says "emotion" (and the word covers everything, aroused *feeling* of any kind), "kills the foolish man" (Job 5 : 2).

6. For the thinking of the flesh is death, but the thinking of the spirit is life.

Paul's picture is now complete. Let us bring up the other part of it. "**For they that are after flesh do think the things of the flesh.**" This is the very nature of the curse. When once the conscience is weakened, what then? The "*flesh*" being stronger than the "*spirit*," will of course do most of the "**thinking**," and if each *thought* kills, there is evolved just what the Bible describes, viz., a sinking and a dying condition of the sinner. Our being, so far as we see it, floats in a perpetual current. That current soils or clears itself. Each good thought clears it. Each bad thought fouls it. Now, as "*they that are after flesh do think the things of the flesh*, the thinking of the flesh is death;" and as "**they that are after Spirit**" do think "**the things of the Spirit, the thinking of the Spirit is life.**" This is saying all the truth; for to say with Christ, "My meat is to do the will of Him that sent me" (Jo. 4 : 34), or to say with Paul, "Herein do I exercise myself" (Acts 24 : 16), does not go a stone's throw further; for the virtue of an act is in the thought (14 : 14), and the value of an "exercise" does not consist in the agitation of a nerve, or the practice of a muscle, but consists in the "*thought*" that rules and prompts it. So that if the "*thought*" of the flesh is of "*the things of the flesh, the thinking of the flesh is death*," while "*the thinking of the Spirit*," which must be the special gift of a redemption, "*is life*."

6. —— (and peace, 7. Because the thinking of the flesh is enmity in respect to God, for it is not subject to the

law of God, for neither can it be; 8. But they that are in flesh cannot please God).

It will be seen that we draw a line around these sentences by way of parenthesis. Paul keeps close in all his epistle to ideas that are subjective; at the same time he would tremble if he forgot anything forensic. He pauses, therefore, to keep up a continual balance. Having plunged more deeply than usual into philosophic reasoning, and shown by the very nature of the soul that evil "*thought*" blackens and deadens and will damn the sinner, he takes in by a sort of eddy of his rhetoric the fact that nature is but the order of the Most High. Sin breeds sin by a curse, and the curse is but the creature of "**the law.**" If "*the thinking of the Spirit is life,*" therefore, by an order equally lawful, Paul takes occasion to throw in the idea that it is also "**peace**"; and then, by a neatly carved parenthesis, he gives the obvious reasons, "**Because the thinking of the flesh**" (and how well he may say this is evident, because "*the thinking of the flesh*" constitutes all possible transgression)—"*Because the thinking of the flesh* **is enmity in respect to God:**" See remarks on this under a previous passage (7: 22): "**For it is not subject to the law of God.**" Of course not: for if holiness consists in love, or, if you please, in "*thought,*" how can love spring in that which by its very nature as defined, has the "desires" of other things. "*It is not subject to the law of God*, **for neither can it be.**" And then the residue thoroughly defends our reasoning. It is unfortunate to say, "*enmity against God*" (E. V. & Re.), for the preposition is εἰς not κατά, and the enmity is both ways, of us *against God*, and of God *against us*. 'Εἰς expresses that; and therefore, we have said, "*in respect to*" the Almighty. Paul's only comment on the "*enmity*" will not suit "*against*" (E. V. & Re.); for it is this:—"**But they that are in flesh cannot please God.**"

The phenomenon next to be considered is that a little particle εἴπερ, which no commentator seems to have considered, gives a fresh turn, and imparts a new significance, where progress in the discussion seemed rather to fail. It would naturally strike the apostle that there were no people "*in

Spirit"; and that being "*in flesh*" was so universal in our humanity, that "*thinking the things of the flesh*" would more exercise the saints than what pious exercise they had in the "*things of the Spirit.*" Paul, therefore, having laid down the fundamentals in the case, and committed himself to the fact that "*the thinking of the flesh is death,*" shapes the teaching to the case of the believer. He says boldly, "**Ye are not in flesh, but in Spirit,**" and then, to make true so impossible an idea, he has the same reserve that our Saviour needed when He said, "Now ye are clean through the word that I have spoken unto you." The apostles were anything but clean. When Paul, therefore, says, "Wherefore holy brethren, partakers of the heavenly calling" (Heb. 3 : 1), he drops the sense to the proper state of the reality, just as we shall see he does in the present instance :—

9. But ye are not in flesh, but in Spirit, if even a Spirit of God dwell in you.

It would have been strangely confusing if Paul had not said this. He of all men needed some such "**if even.**" He had looked Corinth boldly in the face, and said to its saved saints in the broadest language, " Ye are yet fleshly" (1 Cor. 3 : 3) ; and then would make them confess it ; " For while one saith I am of Paul, and another, I am of Apollos, are ye not fleshly ?" To take for granted, therefore, that all saints thought "*the thinking*" of the Spirit, and to sweep them into all the blessings of the Kingdom without a word of explanation, were not like Paul, and, therefore, just such a turn in the passage should be looked for as we are about to unearth. Paul, to arrange it, brings in a new word (οἰκεῖ). He is willing to admit their saintship, if the Holy Ghost in His saving efficacy "**dwell in**" them at all. Their infirm beginnings in the Spirit account for their delinquency. And, therefore, he is ready to pronounce upon them at once : "*Ye are not in flesh but in Spirit ;*" and to do it upon this new departure, "**If even a Spirit of God dwell in you ;**"

9.— But if any man have not a Spirit of Christ he is none of His.

Paul has thus brought all down to the gracious level of the Gospel.

"*If even.*" This word (εἴπερ) occurs six times in the whole New Testament. The lexicons agree that it means "*if even*" sometimes, and that is enough for our translation; but it really looks as if the whole six cases had a touch of the same significance. They are all of Paul except one, and that one is perhaps more distinctly interesting than most of Paul's cases. It is in the language of Peter (1 Pet. 2: 3). He is commanding, "As new-born babes, desire the sincere milk of the word that ye may grow thereby" (E. V.), and then adds, what in the ordinary translation seems superfluous, "If so be ye have tasted that the Lord is gracious" (E. V.). Winer goes so far as to say that 1 Pet. 2 : 3 seems to be of a rhetorical nature ! (Win. Gram. §. 53, 8). And yet what really does it mean unless we give to εἴπερ its peculiar significance ? If you have even "*tasted*" that the Lord is gracious, then, under the instinct of that taste, "*grow*," nursing your desire for the sincere milk of the word. Paul says, "*If even* there are those called Gods, as there are Gods many and Lords many" (and anything else in those days was a very improbable claim), yet "to us there is but one God, etc., etc." (1 Cor. 8: 5). And in arguing for the resurrection he says, If the more universal thing does not happen, or, expressing it in his own language, "*If even* dead men are not raised, then is Christ not risen" (1 Cor. 15 : 15). "*If* we *even* suffer with Him" is one of the other cases, and we shall meet it presently (v. 17); and the only remaining one is 2 Thess. 1 : 6.

"**Dwell.**" The meaning of the apostle seems to be, Reign in us and fill us with His fruits, He certainly does not, but "*if* (He) *even dwell in*" us, or, to express it in a kindred English, if He make even an imperfect *lodgment* in our nature, then we may be said to be "*in Spirit;*" and here Paul takes his stand. We must have this, or not Christ in any fashion ; or, abiding by our text, "**If any man have not a Spirit of Christ, he is none of His.**"

"*A Spirit.*" A little further on we have, "*a spirit of bond-*

age," and a little further still, "*a spirit of adoption*" (v. 15). We are debating whether "*spirit*" without a capital would not answer better, as "*spirit*" in man and in God border so closely together (1 : 4 ; 8 : 9 ; Gal. 5 : 17) ; but all is so of the Holy Spirit* that it may do no harm always to be marking our debt to God for our sanctification, though the anarthrous condition of the πνεῦμα should certainly be noticed.

A third person of a Trinity, and a procession of this third personage from the first and the second, and long controversies and wars that established this, make "*filioque*" a word that will one day be a shame in the church. That Paul should have doubled on his idea, and said "*a Spirit of Christ*," is ruined by those ancient rationalisms. Nothing in Germany is more cold than this. The "*Spirit*" is God, or as Paul afterwards expressed it, "Now the Lord is that Spirit" (2 Cor. 3 : 17). The "*Spirit of Christ*" is that of which Gabriel spoke, which overshadowed his mother (Lu. 1 : 35). It is God Himself without whom Christ was a "worm" (Is. 41:14 ; Ps. 22: 6). And recognizing God as immediately in Christ, and, in fact, immediately Christ, and immediately in us, though in our case only *lodging* imperfectly within us, is the only way to hold up naturally before us our baptism into the Redeemer.

10. But if Christ be in you, the body is dead because of sin, but the spirit is life because of righteousness.

"**Christ in you.**" The chapter began with just the opposite arrangement of the language, for it spoke of those "in Christ" (v. 1). Paul seems to have employed all his terse expressions mainly in this epistle. It is fortunate that in each case he thoroughly explains. Before he ventured upon the expression, those "*in Christ*," he explained thoroughly our

---

* Spirit is the God-part of man. Even if it stands with a small s it is conscience ; and conscience is God in the human soul. When our spirit is warmed by God's Spirit, "God is in (us) of a truth" (1 Cor. 14 : 25). And our Saviour takes care to say this. He says, "Spirit is God." "The hour cometh and now is when the true worshipers shall worship the Father in Spirit and in truth. Spirit is God, and they that worship Him, must worship Him in Spirit and in truth" (Jo. 4 : 23. 24).

being "*baptized into His death,*" and our being "*planted together*" (E. V.), or, more strictly to give the Greek, our being "*bred in with Him in the likeness of His resurrection.*" He does not forget the same necessary prelude here. He speaks of the Spirit in us (v. 9); calls it "*a Spirit of God,*" and then, as given to the Redeemer, "*a Spirit of Christ*" (v. 9); and then, as won by His death, and actually embraced by His divine nature given to His people, speaks of it as "*Christ in you.*" Our blessed Redeemer is in us, not when His flesh is, in the shape of a transubstantiated wafer, nor when He Himself is, by a foolish notion of the omnipresence of the Man, but when the God is present, that is when Christ's Godhead is working within us, to subdue our sins, and to "**deaden the deeds of the body**" (v. 13). "*But if Christ be in you,* **the body is dead because of sin.**" Pitiful views of Christ as a Pagan Second Person, and pitiful views of the Spirit as the Platonic Third Person, and pitiful views of "**righteousness**" as being an affair of court, are very apt to breed a miserable letting down of all the great principles of the inspired oracles. What is the death of "*the body!*" And moreover "*the body*" is not "*dead;*" it is the last thing to die in this splendid history of our being. Moreover it is the yoking of the mule with the horse to talk of "*the body* (being) *dead because of sin,*" and "*the spirit life because of righteousness.*" This very linking should keep us straight in these particulars. To say

11. But if the Spirit of Him who raised Jesus from among the dead dwell in you, He who raised Christ Jesus from among the dead shall quicken your mortal bodies also through His Spirit dwelling in you,

and then to translate the whole as though it were of a rising out of Joseph's tomb, is to forget, first of all, that all rise, saint no more certainly than sinner; to forget, again, that Paul is in the midst of a great forthright line of spiritual argumentation, and to forget, thirdly, that mere body-raising is not the great work of "*a Spirit of Christ,*" and the raising itself, whether of His body or ours, is but a slender part of the fact of our redemption. We would have less to say in the way of complaint if

Paul had not been so careful. He has given us no end of light upon these physical illustrations. "*Flesh*" has become almost technical. And to give more body to it, that is to give it more the look of a strong and well centered organization, Paul calls "*the flesh*" "*the body*" (6 : 6 ; 7 : 24 ; Col. 2: 11), meaning infinitely far from our mere organized clay, but all our most refined tastes and all our most elevated worldliness which is not patterned after the Spirit of the Almighty. It is a great luxury to bring all these lights together, and to show by unbounded evidence the spiritual sense of "*the body*."

If Christ be said to be "*in the likeness of the flesh of sin*" (v. 3), that being understood to mean in the likeness of our whole nature, what madness to look back upon "*the body of sin*" (6 : 6), or in fact upon any of that whole context, and imagine that "*the body*" and "*the flesh*" ought not to have corresponding interpretations. But if "*the body of sin* (being) *destroyed*" (E. V.) means, as Paul expounds it, "*that we henceforth should no more serve sin*," how unwarrantable, when we come upon the expression again, to say that "*the body* (being) *dead because of sin*" means that our clay is dead ; when, in the first place, our clay is not "*dead ;*" when, in the second place, our "*flesh*" in Paul's sense of the word "*is dead ;*" when, in the third place, it is dead *quoad* "the flesh" even in the Christian ; when, in the fourth place, it is balanced against so high an idea as that the spirit is life, and when, in the fifth place, "*the body*" as not "*the flesh*" in the Paulinian or higher sense, would drop the thought quite out of the line of argument ; for "*the body* (being) *dead because of sin*," if counted as our fleshly nature, and "*the spirit* (being) *life because of righteousness*," if counted as our new man, fit exactly, and are all that can redeem the passage from creating a break in the chain of reasoning.

This view will strengthen as we proceed.

"**But if the Spirit of Him who raised Jesus from among the dead.**" There are certain passages of the Scripture with which the current theology never grapples. Why is Christ called "The first begotten from among the dead ?" He was not the first to rise. Why is He called "the first fruits of them that slept?" Why, in this passage, is He said to be "raised *from among* the dead?" No commentator ever notices this. And yet there is a method in the speech which long ago should have claimed a signification. On the base of the body no meaning can be shown. Christ was raised long after the Shunamite's son, and months after Lazarus. But if we hold it as meaning that Christ was cursed (Gal. 3 : 13) ; that He was a child of Adam ; that He was tainted by Adam's blood *in posse*, and unless kept off by God through covenanted grace, *in esse*, as an heir with all the children of Adam ; that He was, therefore, "infirm" (Heb. 5 : 2), and temptible (Heb. 2 : 18), and θανατωθείς according to another apostle, that is, given over to "*death*" as far as "*the flesh*" is concerned, and " quickened (only) by the Spirit" (1 Pet. 3 : 18); then all this lies under sun-light. He was "*raised from among the dead*" in the most intelligible sense. Men dead in sin lay all around Him. He was " the first begotten from among the dead;" not in time, for Enoch rose out of sin before Him ; but in the order of nature. He had to be arranged for first, that any might be begotten afterward. And this language He thoroughly approves ; for what sentence could be more humiliating than this : "Who in the days of His flesh, when He had offered up prayers and supplications with strong crying and tears unto Him that was able to save Him from DEATH, and was heard in that He feared " (Heb. 5 : 7)?

"**Body**" therefore means the "old man " with all his organized tastes and powers. When, therefore, Paul says that "*Christ*" may be "*in*" us, and nevertheless our "*body* (be) *dead because of sin*," he means that we have an "old man" that would take possession of us again if the Spirit left us. The Peter with his "I go a fishing" would never come back to Christ if left to his "*dead body*." Paul had remembered this when he said, "*Ye are not in the flesh but in the Spirit*," yet had put it on the lowest ground, "*If even a Spirit of God have got so much as a lodgment in you*" (v. 9). The whole organized "*flesh*" remains, and he calls it a "*body*." He calls it in this passage, "*the dead body;*" in the sixth chapter, "*the body of sin*" (6 : 6); soon after, "*the body of this death*" (7 : 24); then presently he is to speak of "*deadening the practices of the body*"; and afterward of "**the redemption of our body,**" which we are yet to explain ; and then, in Colossians, of "*putting off the body of the sins of the flesh ;*" and finally of *quickening our* "*mortal bodies.*" These are all of this same apostle ; and he must be a stiff exegete who refuses to say, that Paul illustrates by "*the body*" the sum total of our carnal nature. "**Because of sin.**" That is the very essence of *death*. "**Because of righteousness.**" That is the very essence of "**life.**" It is indeed a very meagre "*righteousness*," and a very struggling and incipient "*life.*" But such is the very idea of Paul. The "new man" has a powerful ally. If He *gets a lodgment* (οἰκει), we must treat Him shamefully, or He will grow. "*If the Spirit of Him who raised Jesus from among the dead* (οἰκει) **dwell in you, He who raised Christ Jesus from among the dead,**" and did it perfectly, so as to "*quicken* (His) *mortal body,*" that is, give life to His "*flesh,*" though it would have been by nature "*dead,*" will "*also quicken*" yours, though not perfectly as with Him, but partially, by the *lodgment* of the Spirit, who begins at once the conflict for us.

The phrase "**mortal body**" is singularly well chosen. As it is to be inclusive of Christ, νεκρόν, or "*dead,*" would not answer. His σῶμα or *fleshly nature* was never "*dead,*" but horribly "*mortal.*" It was chased by death, that is, pressed awfully by sin, as the very essence of His sacrifice. "*He who raised Him from among the dead,*" that is, away from falling into sin, and not only kept Him sinless, but lifted Him at last from anything "*mortal,*" and by that is meant from being tempted to transgress, will also lift us up (for thus far we have little else than what Paul is yet to call a "hope of righteousness" Gal. 5 : 5), and will raise up even our "*flesh*" (and by that is meant, will make righteous our whole man); or, in the metaphor of Paul, "**will quicken** (our) **mortal bodies also by His Spirit that dwells in us.**" Thus, according to Paul, we have "the old man" and "the new man." The "new man" is nothing more than a better conscience; renovated indeed by the Holy Spirit, as is made possible by redemption. That spirit "*is life because of righteousness*" (v. 10). "*Righteousness*" is the attribute of the conscience, and nothing gives it but the Holy Ghost ! The "old man" is our "*body of death*"; and we long to be rid of it. Yet it has all our peerless treasures of a natural kind. This splendid creature, with its taste and intellect, life eats in upon till it is more and more appropriated by the Redeemer. Paul duplicates his picture a little afterward; for what he calls here life, quickening at last even our dead nature, or, the whole of our "old man," that is, in present tropical description, our "*mortal body*," he serves up over yonder (v. 24) as the subject of our "*hope*." He says "*We were saved in the shape of hope*," because "*hope*" was among our chief treasures when we were first converted. Redemption is mainly hoped for; for the largest fruitage of redemption is yet to be. For "*if we hope for that we see not, then do we with patience wait for it.*" And, gathering all his "*hope*" into one expression, he uses over again that figure of the "*body*," for he says, "*And not only they*" (that is the suffering "*creatures*"), "but ourselves also, who have the first fruits of the Spirit" (that is who have a Spirit merely *lodged* within us as a base from which to fight for us), "*even* we ourselves groan within ourselves, waiting for adoption, to wit, the redemption of our body" (vs. 23, 24).

"*The body*," therefore, is the whole man, outside of grace, and the apostle hopes that in "*the day of redemption*" (Eph. 4: 30), that is, the day *par excellence* entitled to the name, our "*dead body*" will be "*raised*," that is our "old man" will be filled with the blessings of "*redemption.*"

If this be so, we ought to be allies of this struggling grace. Paul returns to the idea of our share in the work :—

12. Then, therefore, brethren, we are debtors, not to the flesh to live after flesh.

The battle is not so far fought that we can win if we desert.

13. For if ye live after flesh, ye will die; but if in Spirit ye deaden the practices of the body, ye shall live.

If I live, it is not I that live, Paul would say, but Christ that liveth in me (Gal. 2 : 20). The raising of our dead nature is not only by Christ, but it is a miracle ; and Paul would have us to believe that it is the most God-like act that God had ever committed. Indeed he sheds a kindred light upon it as in the present passage. He would have us " Know what is the exceeding greatness of His power to us-ward who believe," and then brings in immediately the case of Christ ;—" Which He wrought in Christ ; " and then falls upon the same idea of Christ's being raised up from among the spiritually dead and from fleshly ruin. To suppose he meant His clay would be singularly weak. His grave speech betokens what Christ calls "sanctification" (Jo. 10 : 36), "which He wrought in Christ when He *raised Him from among the dead*, and set Him at His own right hand in heavenly things" (Eph. 1 : 19, 20).

And yet, for all that this is so the work of the Almighty, Paul treats it as though it were our own. He warns as if it were wholly ours. "**If ye live after flesh, ye shall die.**" Christ Himself was warned in a similar manner ;—" If Thou wilt walk in My ways and if Thou wilt keep My charge, then Thou shalt also judge My house, and shalt also keep My courts, and I will give Thee companions among them that walk with Thee " (Zech. 3 : 7). This mingling of God's will with man's will is quite intelligible ; for it is on man's will that God's will must operate ; and it is by such words as those of Paul that God, here called "*the Spirit*," operates upon man in the work of redemption. "**If in Spirit ye deaden the practices of the body, ye shall live.**" Mortal could give glory to his Maker no more enthusiastically than Paul, and yet he says, "I keep under my body, and bring it into subjection, lest, having preached to others, I myself should be a castaway " (1 Cor. 9 : 27).

"**In Spirit.**" It must be in the region of a renovated conscience. Nay, it must be as conscience itself (*dative*) that the *deadening* work must go on. The inward man, being renewed, makes the outward man perish. "**Deaden ;**" θανατόω. We must *give up* these " practices " *to die*. This Greek never means to *kill* (E. V., 2 Cor. 6 : 9), and it never means to "*put to death*" (E. V., Matt. 10 : 21). It means to *deliver over to die*, or *to make a dead man of a person*, forensically or from the certainty of his dying. An observance of this would have saved a very important passage. Peter does not say, " Being put to death in the flesh, but quickened by the Spirit " (E. V., 1 Pet. 3 : 18), but he says, " Made a dead man of as to the flesh, but made alive by the Spirit,"—language which perfectly describes our exalted Head. To make all this certain, let us examine the Bible. θανατόω occurs eleven times in the New Testament writings. When Paul says, " For thy sake are we killed all the day long " (E. V. & Re., Rom. 8 : 36), this Irish-English reveals the mistranslation. He uses the word in two other cases, one, " Ye were made dead " (7 : 4), which we have already considered ; and the other, "chastened and not killed " (E. V. & Re., 2 Cor. 6 : 9), obviously meaning, " chastened but not delivered over to death." The six other cases are found in the Gospels, and are applied to Christ and His persecuted people. The chief priests took counsel together "to hand Him over to death " (Matt. 26 : 59 ; 17 : 1 ; Mar. 14 : 55), for, "to put Him to death " (E. V. & Re.) was distinctly forbidden. And then " some of (the disciples) should they cause to be put to death " (E. V. & Re., Luke 21 : 16). "And the children shall rise up against their parents, and cause them to be put to death " (Matt. 10 : 21; Mar. 13 : 12). We are so particular about this word because we shall meet it in other cases. We give over the "*flesh*" to die when we yield to the Spirit. "**The practices of the body**" is another demonstration that it is not the clay Paul is speaking of either in the case of Christ or His people.

14. For as many as are led by a Spirit of God, they are sons of God.

The word θανατόω seemed to require some such comfort as this. If we can only "*deaden*" our "*flesh*," or, using another metaphor, crucify it (Gal. 5 : 24), and hang it up to die, where is our safety ? We have none actually, Paul would say.

And yet we are not all adrift. The forces of nature are stronger than the forces of grace, at least so far as this, that the thinking of the flesh exceeds the thinking of the Spirit (Phil. 2 : 21). Faith, which is another term of the apostle, Christ said was as a grain of mustard seed. To look on at the fight, tacticians would predict our overthrow. But Paul introduces an element of sonship. Love is weak in the believer, but it is strong in the Almighty. And though the threat, *"If ye live after flesh ye shall die,"* would seem to have been fulfilled already, yet the mere *lodgment* (οἴκησις, v. 11) of the Spirit has vast weight. We must utterly quench Him, or He will continue to help. And this Paul assures us of under the image of a son.

15. For ye did not receive a spirit of bondage again to fear, but ye received a spirit of adoption wherein we cry Abba, Father.

We have no saintship at all unless we are converted. But conversion is so miserable a thing, and we begin so low down that we would still be without hope, unless we saw breaking in upon our conscience these evidences of affection.

16. The Spirit itself bears witness with our spirit that we are children of God.

Christ particularly tells us that " He (the Spirit) shall not speak of Himself," and that unnoticed sentence means that the Spirit does not tell us anything ; that is, that God does not make fresh communications when He converts a heart. Christ tells us, " What He shall hear, that shall He speak ;" and that most reasonable sentence frowns upon all sights and voices and actual words in the heart of a sinner. Where God enters a soul " What He hears," that is (in that quaint language) what He finds there of previous intelligence, He warms into life. God, in this work, chooses to call Himself a *Holy Breath*, and what He imparts is really only holiness ; that is He warms into life our already possessed truth and gospel. God's **" Spirit "** and "**our Spirit**" is our conscience (Jo. 4 : 24; * 1 Cor. 14 : 25; see also Gal. 2 : 20). And His "*Spirit*" witnesses with "*our spirit* **that we are children of God,**" not by telling us, Thou art my begotten son, but by mending our conscience, and making us feel that some power is at work in our behalf. "**Ye did not receive a spirit of bondage again to fear,**" though that even was the Spirit of the Almighty, and its desperate struggles were His preliminary work (7 : 23, 24), but ye see work achieved and "*flesh*" conquered. Your consciousness reveals the change. It may be very weak, and you may lose it (Matt. 13 : 21), for it is but a "taste" of God's graciousness ; but still He will hold you fast, and He will save you, unless you trample Him, and this holding fast, though you sin, convinces you of His kind heart, and is really that " **Spirit of adoption wherein we cry Abba, Father.**"

17. **But if children, also heirs, heirs of God, but joint heirs with Christ, if we even suffer with Him, that we may also be glorified together.**

Jesus Christ is a man with the one personal Jehovah incarnated in Him. That word incarnated means not, wildly, that God became man transmutedly and in a downright way, but, taking that word *incarnated* or *infleshed* in its more Pauline meaning, that the Holy God became personally one with the σάρξ ("*flesh*"), technically so called, of the blessed Redeemer. If the Redeemer was "born of the flesh," and, according to His own doctrine, " That which is born of the flesh is flesh " (Jo. 3 : 6), then being "born of the Spirit" in His case was what there was in being born of God. It was not a common influx of the Spirit, but an impersonate condition of the Godhead. The Spirit was given to Him (Jo. 3 : 34) without measure. God Himself was begotten within Him. And as this was Christ's only birth, and He was generate, instead of being

---

* The Greek here should not be reversed. Middleton himself covers the case with his exceptions (see also Jelf, Gram., §. 460, 2). They that worship must worship in spirit. And to enforce that, John seats God in our conscience just as we have claimed. "Spirit is God" (see com. 1 : 9, also 1 Tim. 6 : 5).

regenerate, of God, the great fruit was holiness. God's great wealth is holiness. Of course it is man's great gift. And as sinfulness is that bottomless pit (Mar. 3 : 29, Re.), in which we sink forever unless delivered, we can understand the words of the apostle, "*For as many as are led by a Spirit of God they are sons of God ;* **but if children, also heirs,**" heirs of the greatest thing that God can possess; children through the very loins of God; heirs through the very birth of Christ ; lost, without His Godhead, and saved by that Godhead's fruit ; nothing, without the gift of holiness, but, with that gift, "**heirs of God, but joint heirs with Christ;**" for Christ Himself is nothing without His Godhead. Isaiah, on any other base than that, almost ridicules Him; calls Him a "worm" (Is. 41 : 14); speaks of Him as "an abomination" (Is. 41 : 24) ; calls "His sword dust" and calls "His bow stubble" (Is. 41 : 2); says He conquered by ways His feet had never actually travelled (Is. 41 : 3) ; and He Himself says, "(I) can do nothing of (myself)" (Jo. 5 : 19); and is predicted of in this strange soliloquy : "I am a worm and no man, a reproach of men and despised of the people" (Ps. 22 : 6). But, with the Spirit, and that in a method of oneness never before known, "the Lord (who) is that Spirit" (2 Cor. 3 : 17) bestows upon Him the thing which is that which is most glorious in Himself. He makes Him righteous. Through him He makes others righteous. And who then can fail of the sense, "*If children, also heirs, heirs of God, but joint heirs with Christ,* **if we even suffer with Him, that we may also be glorified together ?**"

Christ, as a man, though a worm, helped Himself, just as we all must do, though saved by the Spirit. His self-help came with the result of suffering, just as it must come to all of us ; for we are told by the apostle, "We must through much tribulation enter into the kingdom of heaven" (Acts 14: 22). This needs to be very plain. Christ's sufferings were "unto blood, striving against sin" (Heb. 12 : 4). This was His sacrifice. He endured a thousand deaths conquering temptation ; and as He won the victory, His sufferings turned out all innocent, and

He was able to hand them over as a sacrifice for His people. But Paul says, we have sufferings also. He speaks of "filling up that which is behind of the afflictions of Christ" (Col. 1 : 24); and in the present passage he expounds that perfectly. Christ's forensic object was to atone for men. Christ's personal object was to "learn obedience" (Heb. 5 : 8). He never sinned; but He was horridly tempted. His object was to get rid of temptation. This is turned over in the Scriptures in many clarifying lights. He was sanctified (Jo. 10 : 36). He was made righteous (1 Tim. 3 : 16). He was redeemed (Heb. 9 : 12). He was saved (Zech. 9 : 9, see Heb.). As the form in which He was to be glorified, it pleased God "to make the captain of our salvation perfect through suffering" (Heb. 2 : 10). He was "made perfect" (Heb. 5 : 9); not that He was ever sinful, but that that could not be considered the highest shape of obtainable perfection which had to writhe in anguish through a ceaseless fight with iniquity. Now our sentence may be made plain. We have not to redeem anybody, and we are anything else than sinless. But on this very account Paul puts in that word εἴπερ. It is one of the six cases in the whole New Testament (see comment v. 9). For the very reason that we are so awfully carnal (1 Cor. 3 : 3, 4), and sin so much (Ec. 7 : 20), and that it is so hard to show as to "*the thinking of the flesh* (v. 6) just where and in what degree the saint differs from the world, Paul turns again to that little particle. For just as it had been said, "If ye have even so much (εἴπερ) as *tasted* that the Lord is gracious" (1 Pet. 2 : 3); and as Paul had said, "*If even* (εἴπερ) *a Spirit of God* (οἰκει) *has a lodgment in you*" (v. 9), so now he says, not if ye be perfect, or not even if ye be prevailingly spiritual, but "*if we even* (εἴπερ) *suffer with Him,*" that is, if the Spirit has a lodgment in us, and we enter into that desperate fight that He waged with His temptations.

Do notice one thing :—That fight always conquers. " Resist the devil, and he will flee from you." That sinner who, as with the Trojan horse, has the Spirit within his citadel, no matter in how miserable a corner he keeps it, yet if he will not thwart it, but will begin to "*suffer with Christ*," and take up His cross and resist, may dismiss fear. "Hoc signo vices" is written on his sky. And however desperate the fight, like his blessed Redeemer, he will be "*made perfect.*"

18. For I reckon that the sufferings of the present time are not worthy to be compared with the glory that shall be manifested to us-ward.

This is self-evident, and needs no comment. If Christ could "see of the travail of His soul and be satisfied," assuredly we can. "**Compared**" need hardly have been put in italics (E. V.); for though ἀξία means only "**worthy,**" yet the preposition implies the contrast.

19. For the eager looking of the creation expects the manifesting of the sons of God.

The language means "**looking**" with head intent. Κτίσις has had almost every exposition. It cannot mean "the creature"—"the old man," for it is set in opposition not to "the new man," but to the saints. It cannot mean sinners, for it says they shall be "**made free**" (v. 21). It cannot mean the material world, for it is too serious for that; nor can it mean the whole world, for that would include the saints. It cannot mean the whole universe, for that is not made subject to vanity. It seems most consistently to mean the whole world outside of its people. That would not imply that the animals that have ever lived are to be "*made free*" and glorified. It might be true, though we know nothing in that direction. If the chalk cliffs are to be restored to life, they would require half a planet for room to live in. We know literally nothing. All that it is necessary to suppose is, that this whole globe, which, long before man, by its spectacles of death seemed to be a token of his coming, will be renewed when he is renewed; that the old star will break out in new forms of life; that the golden age will at last be realized; that the fountain of perpetual youth, which we expect for ourselves, may be realized for brutes; that "we, according to His promise, look for a new heaven and a new earth;" and that while, with us, our great heirship with Christ will be, that therein shall dwell righteousness (2 Pet. 3 : 13), the whole "*creation*" shall have something to expect in "**the manifesting of the sons of God.**"

20. For the creation was made subject to vanity, not willingly, but on His account who subjected it, 21. With a ground for hope that the creation itself also shall be set free from the bondage of corruption into the liberty of the glory of the children of God.

"**Not willingly.**" How does this agree with the argument that an appetite for a thing is a pledge of its acquisition? Does a brute acquire immortality? "**But on His account.**" On account of God. For the sake of carrying out His grand administrations. Whether it be God, or whether it be Christ, is not a question : God is in Christ. Our great triumph is that Jesus Christ is God. He is the first born. All things else were begotten in Him. "Along with Him were all things created (Col. 1 : 16, διά of accompaniment); not along with Him in time, for He was not born till long afterward ; but along with Him in the bundle of the decree. He was to be far above principality and power, and, therefore, the universal whole was schemed to suit Him. He was the central Personage ages before Him. To express it differently, in the order of plan " He was before all things " (Col. 1 : 17 ; see also Jo. 1 : 30 ; Rev. 13 : 8). " All things stood together in Him " (ib.). In fact, He is more than God, for He is the plenary God and that Sacrificial Man that is necessary to the world's redemption.

22. For we know that the whole creation groans and has birth-pangs together until now.

This ought to soften us toward brutes, for it is our fault, not theirs, that they have a life of suffering. If it is a new fauna that is to be blest, the old can have no compensation.

23. But not only so, but even ourselves also, who have the first fruits of the Spirit, even we ourselves groan within ourselves, waiting for adoption, to wit, the redemption of our body.

"**Not only so.**" Not only is the earth, which has been cursed by man, to be renovated, and that on the judgment day, "*the day of the manifestation of the sons of God*" (v. 19), but the earthy part of these "*sons*" is to be renovated also. Only the wicked are to perish. In this world adoption is a *quasi* and singular thing. And, therefore, the Bible uses the words over again for the great hereafter. "Brethren, now are ye the sons of God" (1 Jo. 3 : 2); and yet listen to Paul when he speaks of "**waiting for adoption.**" "Now ye are clean," says Christ, but the very speaker had ages to pass before He could "present (them) without spot or wrinkle" (Eph. 5. 27). So of all our joyful adjectives. We are "redeemed" (1 Pet. 1 : 18), but it may take thousands of years to speed on the real "day of redemption" (Eph. 4 : 30). This habit of the Bible is almost universal. We are "righteous" (Lu. 1 : 6), and undoubtedly that means a brightening of our conscience; but so far is it from a deserving of the name, that Paul does not hesitate to throw us all back in strictness of speech and to say, "We, through the Spirit, wait for the hope of righteousness by faith" (Gal. 5 : 5).

And so in the present passage. First of all, we have but "**the first fruits of the Spirit.**" Paul has been full of those expressions. We are "sealed" by the Spirit (Eph. 1 : 13). We have "the earnest of our inheritance" (Eph. 1 : 14). He treats the case hypothetically by the use of that little particle (εἴπερ). "*If the Spirit have even a lodgment in you*" (Rom. 8 : 9). And Peter takes up the case with even more emphasis, for he calls us "new-born babes;" he recommends to us "milk" and not strong meat; and he brings in that word εἴπερ as we have seen, and he describes all that a Christian reaches in this world by the expression, "If ye have even *tasted* that the Lord is gracious" (1 Pet. 2 : 3).

This makes all our passage easy. "*Ourselves also who have the first fruits of the Spirit,*" and who have, therefore, a huge "**body**" of "*flesh*," that has in it our noblest faculties, yearning like the solid earth for some relief, "**groan within ourselves,** *waiting for adoption,*" that is for sure-enough "*adop-*

tion," that which might look worth while in a divine *"son;"* to wit (and this is the great pregnant portion of the passage), to wit, the enrighteousment of our whole selves; to wit, the filling with the Spirit of all our fleshly tastes; to wit, our having a "spirit-body" where now we have a "soul-body;" to wit (1 Cor. 15 : 44), our appetites being attuned to a Godly centre of our life; to wit, our conscience being made perfect; to wit, our "old man" being destroyed in that which gives it its name, and having "**redemption**" in its splendid powers, our "whole **body** being full of light" (Matt. 6 : 22).

Some would put in the word *"full"* before the word "*adoption,"* and their reason is that we are adopted already (v. 15), and their justification is that though adoption is the common word, yet "*waiting*" has more in it than mere expectancy—that it means *waiting long* or "*waiting*" the time *out* to the very end. That would justify *"full"* if it were necessary, or if it agreed with the usage of Paul. But he employs this same word to express waiting "for the Saviour" (Phil. 3 : 20), or waiting for His coming (1 Cor. 1 : 7); he speaks of those who look for Him (Heb. 9 : 28), which advent of Christ is not partial now and *"full"* hereafter; and moreover, as we have abundantly seen, "*adoption*" and "righteousness" and "life" and "cleansing" and "redemption" are all spoken of in this double way, as though they all belonged to us now, and as though they all came to us fresh in the day of Jesus.

24. For we were saved in the shape of hope—

This is one of those "*material datives*" which imply the constitutive substance of the thing talked of. "By faith Abel offered unto God a more acceptable sacrifice than Cain" (Heb. 11 : 4). His faith was the essence of the sacrifice (see Com. on 6 : 10, 11). "**We were saved.**" Notice the aorist. At a certain date in the past, salvation accrued to us, but, in signal features, it was "**in the shape of hope.**"

24.—But hope seen is not hope; for what he sees, who hopes for?

It is not God Almighty that we shall "**see,**" or heaven in any material existence other than this planet. We know not where heaven will be with any certainty. And when we point upward we are only gesticulating. For upward does not mean the same thing two hours together, or in a winter or a summer orbit of our planet. Perhaps children should not as much imagine a heaven " up in the sky." Gabriel does not see God. He sees Him morally, and that is the meaning of our text. When the Spirit only *lodges* with us ; when we are only *sealed* by the Holy Ghost ; when we have the *earnest* and the ἀρχή (Heb. 6 : 1), and the "*first fruits*" only of eternal life ; when we have only so much as *tasted* that the Lord is gracious, then "*we are saved* (only) *in the shape of hope ;*" but when righteousness bursts forth ; when the whole body of sin is redeemed ; when God "*appears*" as John calls it, and we become like Him, because in John's ethical account of it we see Him as He is, then all this text is made clear. "**Hope that is seen, is not hope.**" Our poor little piety that sees very little, is the seed of "*hope.*" "**What he sees, who hopes for?**" If we saw God in His purity, we would be past "*hope.*" Gabriel has no other heaven but that. The " faith (that) is sweetly lost in sight," is that which David longed for :—" One thing have I desired of the Lord, that will I seek after, that I may dwell in the house of the Lord all the days of my life, to behold the beauty of the Lord and to enquire in His temple " (Ps. 27 : 4). Heaven will bring to us parts and powers and passions that will be very noble, and physical ease that will be very sweet, but it will bring to us no sight of God except Christ, and no vision of the " Invisible King " (1 Tim. 1 : 17) except that sight of His holiness which will make us like Him, and which we are to begin now to seek after with all our hearts.

25. **But if we hope for what we see not, we wait with patience.**

We are to cultivate the right sort of "*hope.*" We are to " look for and haste unto the coming of the day of God " (2 Pet. 3 : 12) ; not by the knife of the suicide, but by visions of the King. And we are to have long endurance in our gaze ;

for "*hope*" is a principle of courage ; and "**if we hope for what we see not, we wait with patience.**"

26. And likewise also the Spirit takes hold along with our weakness, for what we pray for we know not as we ought ; but the Spirit itself makes intercession for us, with unutterable groanings.

"**Likewise.**" That is, in the same line of eagerness and hope. "**The Spirit also.**" Not simply the original Spirit which the lost have, and even the devil. And not even the Christian's Spirit, that is, original conscience sanctified by a spirit of grace. For this much of God's Holy Spirit is not enough, but must have an ally outside **taking hold along with** the grace already possessed. But the Spirit here implied is the whole glorious God, who must do much more for us, or we shall yet be lost. The advance of this sentence is that the last spoke of *waiting*, this speaks of pushing, and, above all, by that splendid engine of advance, the exercise of **prayer.**

The obstacle to our advance is "**our weakness.**" That simply means the "*weakness*" of our conscience. It exists in hell. The fiends are so *weak* that they never can be saved. The world was equally *weak*, " For when we were yet *weak*, Christ died for us " (Rom. 5 : 6). We are still "*weak*" since the death of our Redeemer ; "*for what the law could not do in that it was weak through the flesh*," Christ has done by His divine efficiency, and now (wonder of all) we are still *weak*, and this brings us to the meaning of our sentence.

And why should we start at this ? Christ was *weak*. Under the cover of the English version it is half concealed from us that He was compassed about with "*weakness*" (Heb. 5 : 2). And it was "*weakness*" of conscience. The conscience He would have derived from Mary would have been too *weak* to hold Him up from sin, but the Spirit *took hold along with His weakness ;* that is His glorious Godhead added to His conscience enough conscience more, barely to cope with His temptations to sin.

We see then what "*our weakness*" is. It is not a weakness of fiends, for we are men. It is not a weakness of man unvisited, for we have Christ. It is not a weakness of the enemies of Christ, for we are His friends. And yet, alas! it is not the weakness of Christ, for He was held up against all iniquity by the Spirit, while we have but tasted of His grace, and are too weak not to be always sinning.

This "*weakness*" Paul presents in the same magnificent way in which he presented "*righteousness*" (1 : 17). It is a want of knowledge. Just as "*righteousness*" is begotten in the soul by having "*the righteousness of God revealed,*" so sin is begotten in the soul by having "*the righteousness of God*" hidden. Paul has just been saying that "*if we hope for that we see not, then do we with patience wait for it*" (E. V., v. 26). What troubles the saint is darkness. And, therefore, in that enginery of prayer he is ever ready to cry, "We cannot order our speech by reason of darkness" (Job 37 : 19). Light, therefore, is the great cynosure of prayer. And the difficulty of prayer is that I do not "**know**" the great thing I want to ask for. If I *knew* light it would be mine already. And, therefore, Paul, who has gone into the same reasonings about sin, and said, "What I do, I know not" (7 : 15), gives prayer the same magnificent description. The only thing worth praying for is holiness; and the difficulty of asking for it is that we do not know it. If we knew it, we need not ask. But God, who knows it perfectly, gets into our hearts, and, as a Spirit, makes intercession within us, not telling us anything, that is, not adding to our gospel facts, but warming what we have into life, making our thoughts, so far as they are **utterable**, no different from before, but rousing them into "**unutterable**" sighings, and as we ask for knowledge, giving it to us, making us know that we have the petitions that we desire of Him, and, whereas in "*our weakness*" as believers we "**know not as we ought**" the gift we ask, showing it to us, though it be "*unutterable,*" as the very way of giving it.

"*As we ought*" belongs to *knowing*, not to *praying*. We do know holiness. Even Satan knows it in the measure of his conscience. But we do not know it "as (καθὸ—in the measure that) *we ought*."

The Spirit *interceding*, that is, *taking hold along* with what conscience we have, enlarges the circle of our *prayer*, and instigates it to further knowledge.

27. And He who searches the heart, knows what is the thinking of the Spirit, because it makes intercession for the saints through God.

This for man is not without its comfort. It is a simple intimation. If it is God that prays, remember that it is God that answers. "**He who searches the heart knows what is the thinking of the Spirit.**" Surely; for it is Himself. "**Because it makes intercession for saints,**" not in words, nor in thoughts, nor in utterances distinguishable from the conscience—not in syllabled speech, like that of Balaam, not in things "*unutterable*" (v. 26) because not understood—but by "the exceeding greatness of His power" (Eph. 1 : 19) in quickening the conscience, and giving it, warmer and clearer, the moral sense that is possessed even by the wicked. We call "*the Spirit*" "**it**" because the Scripture calls it so (Jo. 14 : 17 ; see the Greek). In this particular text it makes the rhetoric better. The Spirit is really God (2 Cor. 3 : 17). The Spirit in unnumbered cases is really man (Jo. 13 : 21 ; 1 Cor. 14 : 15). It is subject to the same laws as other language. And we may say "*it*" (E. V. & Re.), or we may say "*He*" (E. V. & Re.), without endangering His proper Deity.

The italics in the sentence (E. V. & Re.) are more than usually unfortunate. Κατὰ θεὸν takes in no more "*will*" (E. V. & Re.) than any other attribute. Power and love and wisdom are just as operative. God as a totality is concerned in prayer ; and "**through God**" (see 1 Pet. 4 : 6) gives us to understand that as Christ was David's seed "*through flesh*" (1 : 3) and God's seed "*through Spirit*" (1 : 4), so prayer is made genuine "*through God,*" and is blessedly answered because God is in it. "*For saints*" means literally "*for holy people.*" This is for the same convenience of brevity as the words "*righteous*" or "**those who love God**" (v. 28). Who loves God? These words are all on a level, and refer to that slender beginning of holiness which comes from a mere *lodgment* of the Spirit (v. 9), and answers to that expression of a more recent text which speaks of "*the first fruits*" (v. 23) of that power in sinners.

28. And we know that with those who love God He works as to all things for good; with those who are the called according to a purpose.

The best MSS. put in the word " *God*" (ὁ θεὸς) after " **works with,**" so that the text would read, " God **works together as to all things for good, with them that love God.**" If we could adopt that Greek, there would be no doubt about the meaning. But while the MSS. which give it are the best (A B ℵ), those which do not give it are the most (C D F K L). We care very little, however, about the text ; for the repetition of the word " *God*" would mar the rhetoric of the sentence, and that " *God*" is meant as the nominative of "*works* " is proved in two particulars :—first, that such respectable MSS. thought so, and, second, from the whole cast of the sense. Paul is stating the astonishing nearness of the Almighty. He is about to sum it up presently by the outcry, " **If God be for us, who can be against us ?** " (v. 31). He had stated it strongly before by saying that *Christ was in us* (v. 10). And, reasoning forward from that, he has said that God is so within that He actually prays in the heart of the believer (v. 26); so "*makes intercession* " within, that He actually knows the prayers because they are His own (v. 27); creating a philosophical provocation to say, Yes, and He not only prays in our spirits, but He actually does everything else in the believer. He does not commit his sins, but as Paul most dexterously phrases His influence, "**We know,**" that is, it is a corollary of our being heirs with Christ, "*that as to all things He works for good with them that love God.*" That preposition συν ("*with*") reigns in this chapter. We are "*heirs with Christ* " (συγκληρονόμοι, v. 17). "*We suffer with Him,*" and "*are glorified together*" (still συν, v. 17). Presently we are to hear that we are to be "*conformed to the image of His son*" (E. V., συμμόρφοι, v. 29). Paul tells us that we are "quickened together with Christ " (E. V., συζωοποιέω,

Eph. 2 : 5 ; Cor. 2 : 13), referring to His rising as we rise out of the grave of spiritual ruin. And now we are told that "*as to all things God works with*" the believer (συνεργεῖ) even more than He prays with him (vs. 26, 27); for in prayer He chiefly elevates his conscience, but in more secular "*things,*" He shapes and guides him "*for good.*"

No sweeter text has been found in the Bible than the old (E. V.); no truer; or more legitimately used, if it were the sense! But, in the first place, "*all things* [do not] *work*" (E. V.). It is an imperfect rhetoric. And, in the second place, God does "*work,*" and in a most glorious sense, "*along with*" (συν) each fact as to the believer.

"**Called.**" This word occurs eleven times in the New Testament Greek : twice with Christ, and each time unfavorably, "For many are called, but few chosen" (Matt. 20 : 16 ; 22 : 14). The nine other cases are all favorable. Seven of them are with Paul, and one each with Jude and John. The meaning must be settled by the context. Here it is κατὰ πρόθεσιν. When a man lights a candle, he does it for "**a purpose**" (Matt. 5 : 15). When a man cuts a stone, he does it for a building (1 Pet. 2 : 5). When God is working with a believer as to all things, He has a use for him. "That in me first," Paul says, "Christ might show forth all long suffering" (1 Tim. 1 : 16). We are "*called,*" therefore, "**according to**" a *scheme* (πρόθεσιν).

29. For whom He did foreknow, them He also planned out beforehand in conformity with the image of His Son, that He might be a first-born among many brethren.

This text is strangely dexterous. The word "**image**" is a gem. When I was '**planned,**" Christ was "*planned*" also. And it will be remarked that this very word ὁρίζω is used first for Paul and second for Christ, in this very epistle. Paul is said, first of all, to be "*set apart*" unto the Gospel (ἀφωρισμένος, 1 : 1), and then Christ, in the fourth verse, to be "*determined upon as God's Son*" (ὁρισθέντος), the Greek being absolutely the same except in respect of prepositions (1 : 1, 4).

Christ, therefore, having been "*planned*" from everlasting, was the most illustrious personage with the Almighty ; in fact, He was an intended Self* in a coming incarnation. Hosts of Scriptures come up into the idea. The plan of Him centred all other plans. The thought is constantly repeated. He was the Alpha (Rev. 1 : 8). Cheops was hoary with age when He came into the manger, but not a stone of it was laid without a reference to Him. "With Him were all things created" (Col. 1 : 16), the meaning of which is explained by διά (see com. 1: 11, 12). That is, the whole plan of the universe was built upon Him. To redeem men He was "slain from the foundation of the world," that is κατὰ πρόθεσιν; and when it was determined that we should be "*called*," it had to be "**in conformity with the image of** (that) **Son**," He Himself existing at that time only as an "*image ;*" but an "*image*" so strangely grand, that that "*image*" must be formed as necessary to any other ; an "*image*" so distinct, that it had a glory with the Father "before the world was" (Jo. 17 : 5, see Augustine *in loc.*); and an "*image*" so prefigurative of the possibilities of redemption, that, unless He was, we could not be, so that He was, in the most vital sense, "**the first born among**" us, and "*the first born of the whole creation*" (Col. 1 : 15).

Now, this gets along, as Augustine beautifully pictures it to us, without remembering that He was the Almighty. But when we remember that He was God incarnate, the "*image*" even of His flesh becomes radiant with its large intentions. All power was to be given to Him (Matt. 28 : 18). He was to be head over all things for us (Eph. 1: 22). He was to sit at

---

* Moses said, Who shall I say sent me? and God said, "I WILL BE WHAT I WILL BE." Say unto the children of Israel, "I WILL BE hath sent me unto you" (Ex. 3: 14). This is the literal Hebrew. Jehovah (Ex. 6: 3) is but the third person singular instead of the first, and ought long ago to have been recognized as "HE WILL BE ;" Messianic in the very name, as predictive of the incarnation of the Most High. It was the "*image*" of this Jehovah as one day constituted God and man, that we were "*to be conformed to;*" not as "only-begotten" (Jo. 3 : 16), God and man, but in a subordinate sense one with Him, "**that He might be a first-born among many brethren.**"

the right hand of God, even as to His human nature the Chief Executive (Mark 14 : 62); and we are *"planned"* in conformity with Him so vitally, that the *"image"* of Christ had to be formed in Heaven before we could be dreamed of as ransomed, and before the possibilities of new-born saints could be conceived even in the Almighty's wisdom.

It will be seen, therefore, that this is not a separate brochure upon the decrees, but a natural sequence to previous ideas. Paul has put us very close to our Creator. God breathes for us our prayers, and *"works with us as to all things for good."* With such intimacy there must be overshadowing designs. Paul says we are ourselves designs. The whole universe once stood as an *"image."* We were *images*. Every one of those *images* has been distinctly realized. But among those *images* one was the core of the creation. To that *"image"* all others had to be conformed. And not one of us could be thought of except *"in conformity with"* Him without whom life from death would be a simple mockery.

The expression, **" Whom He did foreknow,"** is not a difficult one. The *foreknowledge* of a Creator agrees with His *predestination*, and yet the *predestination* of a Creator is not in contempt of His *foreknowledge*. God cannot do everything. Before He can predestine He has to look ahead as much as any creature. In other words, there is only one plan possible for the Almighty. Among all the creative myriads there is but one whole that is the wisest and the best. Our Creator has struck for that. He has strangely little license, this God of ours ; and has been walled in unchangeably since the depths of the everlasting. He has every license, and does what He will in the eternal ages. But what He wills to do is as fixed as fate, for there is but one wisest thing for the All Wise, and He was wise from everlasting. *"Whom He did foreknow,"* therefore, is I myself, if I belong to Christ, for I am the only possible man to stand in my lot and do my service. God glanced down the age and saw all this before He *"planned* (me) *out."* Moreover His foreknowledge is distinguishable from His decree in another eminent light. I am not all He would have liked me to be. The Deity that could say, "Oh that thou hadst known" (Lu. 19 : 42); or the Deity that could say, "How often would I have gathered" (Lu. 13 : 34); or the unforced artificer who could nevertheless declare, "What could have been done more?" (Is. 5 : 4); the God who could weep over Jerusalem, or of whom it could be said, He "will have all men to be saved" (1 Tim. 2: 4), needs His *foreknowledge* in its glance to see if the way be clear for mercy; for while "it is the glory of Gods to cover over a thing, it is the honor of Kings to search out a matter" (Prov. 25 : 2). The "*image*"-making had to be carried so far that Christ himself was an "*image.*" The whole κτίσις had to be an "*image*" that could agree together; and, though Christ was the Head, He himself had to be looked at in *foreknowledge*, before He could be shaped into a decree, which is the idea seized upon by Peter—"who verily was *foreknown* (προεγνωσμένου) before the foundation of the world" (1 Pet. 1 : 20), a fact that must occur in God before the "*Image*" could be framed "*in conformity with*" which saved souls could be predestined also.

30. **But whom He planned out beforehand, them He also called, and whom He called, them He also made righteous, but whom He made righteous, them He also made glorious.**

"**Called**" is no longer the participle (v. 28), but the main body of the verb. We have looked in vain in the New Testament for any other sense than *effectually* "*called.*" "**Made righteous**" would then mean *sanctified*. Paul says : " But ye are washed, but ye are justified, but ye are sanctified " (E. V., 1 Cor. 6 : 11). There it is exceedingly awkward to imagine anything else but that all the terms mean sanctification. Paul, a tasteful rhetorician, if that were not the case, would have thrust a forensic term between two that are subjective. But, alas for the skill of the apostle! in the present text it would be worse. If *make righteous* means to hand over to us the righteousness of Christ, then Paul would speak of *calling* first, and that afterward. How is that for a theology? If the sentence read, "Whom He did predestinate, them He also justified;

and whom **He** justified, them He also called ; and whom He called, them He also sanctified (for surely there should be some place for that) ; and whom He sanctified, them He also glorified," the argument might be the other way. But with no place for sanctification at all, unless making righteous means making holy ; and with calling put first ; and with justification put after calling, it is as if a sentence read this way : " Whom He called, them He also redeemed." It is these " Horæ Paulinæ" intimations that form *obiter* most powerful arguments. "*Foreknew,*" first ; "*planned,*" second ; "*called,*" third ; "*made righteous,*" fourth (a process not like calling, sudden, but lasting to the end of life) ; and then "**made glorious**" in an eternal heaven ; that boxes the compass of our experience ; but would leave a terrible chasm if " *made righteous* " did not answer to our subjective change.

31. What shall we then say to these things? If God be for us, who is against us?

We have remarked upon this already (vs. 9–11). He who lives in us (Gal. 2 : 20) ; He who is so morally ours that He moves within us what we propose and feel (Phil. 2 : 13) ; He who prays when we pray (vs. 26, 27), and actually " *works with those who love Him as to all things for good* " (v. 28) ; and, now, to take up the last texts, who schemed our "*image* " when He schemed the " *image of His Son,*" and schemed ours " *in conformity with* " His (v. 29), hardly need add a feature to the words of the apostle. We are God's men, " *known* " and "*planned*" and " *called* " and " *sanctified* " and "*glorified.*" No higher unity of interest can easily be conceived. And Paul may well exclaim, "**What shall we then say to these things?**" and add as the sum of our escape, "**If God be for us, who is against us ?**"

" *Can be* " (E. V.) undoubtedly mars the sense. It is like "*bountifully* " (E. V.) put into one of the Psalms. David cries, " Return unto thy rest, O my soul, for Jehovah has been dealing for thee ! " (Ps. 116 : 7). What does "*bountifully* " add to a sense like that ? Paul asks, "*Who is against us ?* " and it is amazing how deep the question ! The "*called*" has no enemies except his own wicked heart : and the apostle goes on to say that. Not ἀρχαί, not δυνάμεις. Satan himself is a friend to the believer ; for Paul has explained it, " *God works together as to all things for good with them that love Him* " (v. 28).

32. Here is something stronger too, as expressed by the word γε (indeed). Not only have we the assertions of the Almighty, but what might we augur ourselves ?—

3 2. He indeed who spared not His own Son, but delivered Him over for us all, how shall He not with Him freely give us all things?

Before, we had the make-up of the "*image*," and the inference ran that as the "*image*" of Christ was of one *foreknown* and *predetermined* as a great Deliverer, so His people must be "*planned out*" (v. 29) " *in conformity with* " that great design. But here he plunges farther down. What could God be thinking of in ransom, unless His will was to give us the largest grace ? "**He who spared not His own Son, but delivered Him over for us all, how shall He not with Him freely give us all things?**"

33. And mark you, says Paul, He can carry out His designs. It may be different for other worlds, but here He is " *in the way of judgment* " (Is. 26 : 8). For once He can be " *righteous, and yet make righteous* " (3 : 26). He can lift the curse of sinfulness. What devil (*i. e.* accuser) can be "*against us* " (v. 31) ?

33. Who shall lay anything to the charge of God's elect? God, who makes righteous? 34. Who is he who condemns? Christ Jesus who died? but rather who was raised from among the dead; who is at the right hand of God; who also makes intercession for us?

The interrogatory form of the thirty-fifth verse leads us to choose the same for all these other verses. Why not ?

And now the advantage of the simple Greek of the thirty-first verse more specifically appears. " *Who can be against us?* " (E. V.) would be very expressive, but " *who is against us* " is much more so. Paul has brought the Christian into the most intimate relations with the Almighty. He *lodges* in him (v. 9).

Paul has uttered that strange speech that when we pray, God prays. He "*makes intercesssion (within) us*" (v. 26). He has enlarged that idea. And on the memory that if He prays in us He doubtless does everything else that is excellent, he makes out of it a general proposition that " *He works with* (us) *as to all things for good*" (v. 28). And then the transition is easy, that we are "*planned out*" eternally in conformity with an original plan made for our Redeemer (v. 29). It is on the back of this that he asks, "*Who is against us?*" Our present sentences take that interrogatory to pieces. "**Who,**" for example, "**shall lay anything to the charge of God's elect?**" Why, only God could do it, and He is the very person who is busy in these intimate relations. He "*planned* (us) *out*" (v. 29), and He is busy **making** us **righteous** "*in conformity with*" our Surety. "**Who is he who condemns?**" Why, it only could be that Surety Himself. Could it be "**Christ who died,**" while He is positively busy for our salvation! Paul goes over the points of His redemption. He "*died;*" nay "**rather was raised from among the dead.**" Had He "*died*" in that awful shape in which temptation threatened (Heb. 5 : 7), what a final catastrophe! "**but**" He was enabled to resist temptation, and by the might of His Godhead was "*raised from among the* (spiritually) *dead*" (6 : 4). Under stern agonies He fought and conquered, and Paul goes on with his list, "**He is at the right hand of God;**" and in this place of Chief Executive "*who is against us*" if He is "*for us?*" He is not only God's "*hand,*" betokening the instrument of His general power, but He is God's "*right hand*" for His noblest administration. The Psalmist calls him so.* And, therefore, the transition is easy that He who in so many things **is interceding for us,** cannot, in the nature of the case, be the one to *condemn us.*

"**Also.**" The Spirit intercedes (v. 27) and Christ intercedes, and in different fashions. The Spirit, that is the Most High

---

* ' That thy beloved ones may be delivered save thy Right Hand and answer me" (Ps. 60 : 5). The introduction of "*with*" (E. V.) in italics ruins everything.

God, intercedes unutterably, that is by warming our conscience, and raising our desire when we pray. And Christ intercedes doubly ; first, by being that Most High God who is the Spirit, and, second, by His sacrificial work, which only could have been performed by our weak humanity.

It is in these sentences that the fact appears that the use of this whole passage to prove the doctrine of "*perseverance*" is utterly unwarrantable. The persons spoken of are " *God's elect.*" The doctrine of "*election*" itself has been used as a proof of "*perseverance.*" This is a strange fact in the history of the church. And yet what a miscalculation of the very meaning of "*perseverance!*" The doctrine of "*perseverance*" is, that a *converted* man will persevere. What has that to do with *election?* Our Saviour says that " he that endureth to the end the same shall be saved" (Matt. 10 : 22). Now *election* provides for this, for God foreknows and plans beforehand all necessary conditions. But conversion ! Who shall tell by any such passage as this where that is to end ? The real meaning of the apostle closes with the thirty-first verse :—"*If God be for us.*" But God may cease to "*be for us*" if we quench Him or grieve Him away (1 Thess. 5: 19 ; Eph. 4 : 30). The persons spoken of are " *God's elect*" (v. 33). They are sinners whom He sees all the way out into His Kingdom. And He is not speaking of sin, and its power again to destroy the sinner, but He is speaking of grace, and how invulnerable while it is kept in the heart. " If a man abide not in me he is cast forth as a branch" (Jo. 15 : 6). He is not speaking of sin, but of all other things that could be thought of against us.

35. Who shall separate us from the love of Christ—
that is from Christ's love to us, as appears from the thirty-seventh verse? Our love to Christ, however, is so interwoven in it that we need not be very particular.

35.—Shall tribulation, or anguish, or persecution, or famine, or nakedness, or peril, or sword?

This is a corollary of the twenty-eighth verse, which says that " He works together as to all things for good with them that love God." We must cease to love Him, or else these are our blessings. Why, they are sent for His very "**sake!**"

36. As it has been written:
For Thy sake are we given over to death all the day;
We are reckoned as sheep for slaughter.

The "*image*" (v. 29) in which we originally stood, offered itself to God shaded with all this "**anguish.**"

37. On the contrary, in all these things we are more than conquerors through Him who loved us.

"*Shall tribulation separate us?*" "**On the contrary** (ἀλλά), etc., etc.**" "In all these things."** How well that echoes the sentence (v. 28) "*as to all things for good!*" "**We are more than conquerors.**" To survive pain would be blessed. To get some advantage out of pain would be a success. To get all advantage and no mischief would be a victory. But to get just what we require, and to find in it God Himself working with us in our miseries for our supremest good, that is what Paul means when he speaks of our being "*more than conquerors* **through Him who loved us.**"

38. For I am persuaded that neither death, nor life, nor angels, nor principalities, nor things present, nor things to come, nor powers, 39. Nor height, nor depth, nor any other creation, shall be able to separate us from the love of God which is in Christ Jesus our Lord.

"**Death.**" That is the horror of the thirty-eighth verse. "**Angels**" and "**principalities**" could awaken no dissent. But Paul never hesitates about that word "*death.*" It is with him the ideal of spiritual ruin. Now if God be in us, "**height**" and "**depth**" and "**things present**" and "**things to come**" and "**powers**" can work in us no spiritual terror, but "*death*" in the terrible meaning of the apostle, how can that not separate between us and the Almighty? It can. But mark the language of the text. Can it "**separate us from the love of God which is in Christ Jesus our Lord.**" Let us take the idea to pieces. Can future "*death?*" No; for we can never fall into it while "*love*" continues. Can past "*death?*" No;

for it is out of that that "*love*" delivers us. Can present "*death?*" No; not while we "*love*" God. Paul has fenced his texts with great conditions. God's working "*as to all things for good*" is only "*with them that love*" Him. And this pæan over **"life"** and "*death*" is only possible if love continues; that is, if the Spirit of God, who never wilfully deserts, is not quenched (1 Thess. 5 : 19) or trampled on (Heb. 10: 29) by our own apostasy.

The only thing that can ruin us is ourselves; and Paul makes his list supereminently complete, for, after exhausting all the possibilities of earth, he throws in any other possibility of being,—"*Nor height, nor depth*, **nor any other creation."** That is, God can make nothing that will destroy His love, unless we have "counted the blood of the covenant wherewith we were sanctified an unholy thing, and have done despite unto the Spirit of grace" (Heb. 10 : 29).

CHAPTER IX.

1. I speak truth in Christ; I lie not; my consciousness bearing me witness in a Holy Spirit, 2. That I have great grief and continual sorrow in my heart.

Israel, by the effect of all this reasoning, is thrown entirely out of i.s most steadfast confidences, and given over, like any other false race, to perish. Paul has distinctly enounced "*Circumcision availeth nothing*" (Gal. 5 : 6); and, building upon conditions open to everyone, he has realized for the Jew that, instead of being saved by Abraham, Abraham himself was saved like any heathen (4 : 10). Paul chooses his speech, therefore, under the impulse of the profoundest pity, and yet with the knowledge that the Jew thought him a traitor, and, after his scourgings (2 Cor. 11 : 25) and stonings (Acts 14 : 19), would count him entirely incapable of love to his race. **"I speak truth in Christ."** What he says in the third verse is so extreme that the declaration, **"I lie not,"** which might seem unworthy of so great an apostle, appears the least that he could say. Jews were hungering for his blood. The man who had entered into their supremest service, sat with Gamaliel, steeped himself in the religious passions of his people, gloried in the law, and persecuted believers to the very death, was now claiming, in the awful rebound of his martyrdoms, to have a love and to exercise a desire which almost takes our breath by its half profane intenseness :—

3. **For I could wish that myself were accursed from Christ for my brethren, my kinsmen according to the flesh;**

There is no art of Greek criticism that can turn this aside from what it most naturally would be made to mean. When, therefore, Paul cries out, "*I speak truth in Christ,*" strengthening his word as a man by that higher holiness which he has been explaining as coming from the Redeemer, and when he speaks of his **"consciousness bearing witness"** with him **"in a Holy Spirit,"** it is not at all unimaginable that Paul had felt the necessity both in himself and among the Israelites of going down to the very inwardness of his thought before he trusted himself to such a sentence. There is a supreme shrewdness too. He is about to deal them more stunning blows. What could conciliate them more than this stern sentence, if they could only believe it?

Now what did it really mean? Certainly not that he actually wished to be accursed from Christ. And this touches the core of the difficulty. We have in another part of the Bible perhaps a stronger expression. Paul's speech is **"I could wish,"** and King James is right in giving that sense to the imperfect. But an earlier saint manifests no such reservation. With a mother's fondness Moses throws himself upon his knees and cries out, " This people have sinned a great sin." It is the same thing over again of a great saint warmed by Christ Himself into a miraculous affection. The Law-giver does not say, "*I could wish,*" but he comes out boldly with the cry, " If now thou wilt forgive their sin—but if not, blot me, I pray thee, out of thy book " (Ex. 32 : 32). The solution, therefore, is easy. It cannot be a mad speech, or two great oracles would not have made it. It cannot be an unmeasured speech ; for, though it is poured out generously by one, it is limited in the way we see by the words of the other. When such a man as Moses prays, he reserves the possibility of the thing by force of his submission to his Master. But Paul distinctly questioned the possibility. "*I could wish.*" As most commentators insist, he meant something by the choice of a tense. What could he mean? He meant gloriously this :— that the pain and torment he could bear, and the damnation of hope, and eternal loss. That same, Moses had meant. Like the shadow of a ship upon the sea, he meant this shadow of his dying Master. Rather than my whole race should die, let me die. And he meant literally and theologically thus: Let me be eternally cursed as far as I innocently dare, rather than eternal infamy for all my people.

"*My consciousness*" (v. 1). The word in the Greek grew to mean "*conscience*" (E. V. & Re.), but had not entirely ripened that way in the days of the apostle. "Spirit" ($\pi\nu\epsilon\tilde{\upsilon}\mu\alpha$) meant more squarely our moral sense (Jo. 4 : 23, 24 ; Eph. 4 : 23.) When Paul cried "1 have lived in all good conscience" (E. V. & Re., Acts 23 : 1), he would have cut his tongue out rather than mean it in our modern way. Peter calls "baptism" (that is, his figure there for conversion) not an entire washing, but an incipient one, or, as he graphically expresses it, "the inquiry of a good consciousness after God" (1 Pet. 3 : 21). In fact this text of Paul (v. 1) sheds light upon the whole use of the language. "*My consciousness bearing me witness ;*" that is, my inward knowledge of my own heart, and that in its condition as enlightened "*by a Holy Spirit.*" And that explains Peter's sense that "baptism" (used here, as circumcision is, Rom. 2 : 29, for a whole spiritual change) is not total cleansing, or "the washing away of the filth of the flesh," but only an incipient one, or, as we have just been saying, "the inquiry of a good consciousness ;" that is, differently stated, a sincere inquiry of the converted man "after God."

Some passages come very near our meaning of "*conscience*" (13 : 5; 1 Tim. 4 : 2) ; but in almost all there lingers the idea of mere sincerity (2 Cor. 1 : 12 ; see com. 2 : 15 ; 9 : 1).

"*For I could wish.*" This is a proper force of the imperfect; and, as it has been intimated, since there is, therefore, an actual expression of reserve, what more easy than to allow that to be the possibility of its being innocent? "*According to the flesh;*" in contrast with a higher kinsmanship, which Christ greatly celebrates (Matt. 12 : 48, 49), and which Paul would have distinguished as kinsmanship *according to the Spirit.*

Even if this sentence could be plausibly diverted, it would come bustling back. Its simple meaning would have the superior claim. "*Anathema*" is too strong a word not to mean damnation. And the reserve of the imperfect is sufficient to shield Paul from having wished to be an eternal sinner.

4. Who are Israelites; whose is the adoption, and the glory, and the covenants, and the giving of the law, and the worship, and the promises; 5. Whose are the fathers, and of whom is Christ as to the flesh, He being over all God blessed for ever. Amen.

It is the habit of the inspired writers to have no expletives in any sentence. When Matthew says, "The book of the generation of Jesus Christ, the son of David, the son of Abraham," he has a use for each expression. And in this list of Paul there is not a syllable that he does not intend as explaining his broken-heartedness in respect to his people. "**Who are Israelites.**" The very name of their ancestor, "A prince of God" (*Israel*, Gen. 32 : 28), made Paul sad. "**Whose is the adoption.**" There is a lower and higher "*adoption.*" There is a lower and higher covenant (Heb. 8 : 8). More striking still, there is a lower and higher *calling* (see 8 : 23, 30). It is the habit of Holy Writ to strike a thought at a lower and higher plane. Just below we understand that "**they are not all Israel that are of Israel**" (v. 6). We have already seen that with certain worshipers "*their circumcision has become uncircumcision*" (2 : 25). And within the limits of two chapters here, "*adoption,*" which is first saving (8 : 14, 17), sinks to the level of the present verse. "Israel is my son" (Gen. 4 : 22) the Almighty says to Pharaoh. To Paul's people, therefore, belonged "*the adoption,*" and Paul yearned after them in all these traditional and vivid lights. And yet at the very moment, Paul is building that most elaborate speech by which they are to be shown as utterly apostate. "**And the glory.**" Though we write Ichabod, like the wife of Phinehas. "**And the covenants;**" and these are all the solemn pledges of God to Israel. "**And the giving of the law.**" Than which naught could be more special. "**And the worship.**" It was all at Jerusalem. "**And the promises; whose are the fathers.**" This would touch a Jew, for Abraham was the very God of their mythology. "**And of whom is Christ,**" though he adds "**as to the flesh,**" for Tamar and Bathsheba and that bad Manasseh were the ancestors of Christ; and yet he brightens his enthusiasm by the gleam that this ill descended Redeemer was nevertheless a great tie to Israel, because, though coming of their blood, He was nevertheless "**over all, God blessed for ever.**"

This last expression, like the words "*I could wish myself accursed from Christ*" (v. 3), has been labored at with all sorts of adverse suggestion. But it always returns with a heavier demand, to its more rightful interpretation. It may be the strongest text of its teaching. But there must be some strongest text. We cannot be *sure* that the sentence may not break off at πάντων (all), and the rest be a doxology, "*God be blessed forever*" (Ewald, Fritzsche, Erasmus). But who can ever settle it? How can we be sure that this is not a subterfuge? And, as the vast majority of the church believe that Christ is really God, how can we ever forfeit our linguistic claims, or be dreamed of as turning away from the more simple exposition?

Such are the deep utterings of Paul, explaining his passion for the Jew people.

6. But not so at all because the word of God has fallen to the ground; for they are not all Israel who are of Israel. 7. Neither because they are Abraham's seed are they all children; but in Isaac shall thy seed be called.

"**Not so.**" There is more in this than has usually been translated. The word is οἷον, *so much*, or *so great*. This neuter form is nowhere else in the Testament. Paul has uttered an astounding declaration. He now adds to it. He says, I did not speak of being accursed from Christ because my people have been wronged. Adopted and raised and singled out as they have been, it is not that they have been cruelly defrauded that awakes my interest ; or, expressing it all in his Greek, I make not such a speech (οἶον) as this "**because the word of God has fallen to the ground.**" For he goes on to show that, in the original planning out, nothing was meant to occur but what had occurred. The illustrative and spectacular language that had been used they had abused into an error. "*Circumcision*" had been spoken of as purity, and Abraham had been spoken of as though he could breed pious people. "**They are not all Israel who are of Israel.**" They had had evidence that this " Prince of God " was a wrong dependence. So of Abraham's "**promises.**" God had indeed said, "I will establish my covenant (with) thy seed after thee for an everlasting covenant " (Gen. 17 : 7), but alas ! what a crazy promise if anything like a carnal "*seed*" were dreamed of or intended. Abraham was to stand as the father of the faithful, not from begetting all that believed, and not from begetting no one else, but as Jabal was father of Nomads from leading the way in that race of herd-people. That reserves were meant was found in the very family of Abraham; for "**neither because they are Abraham's seed are they all children; but in Isaac shall thy seed be called.**"

8. That is, the children of the flesh, those same are not children of God; but the children of the promise are reckoned as a seed. 9. For this is the word of promise, According to this time will I come, and Sarah shall have a son.

It was obvious from all that transpired that God intended great favor for the Israelitish people. But it would have been absurd in a hierarchy planned for righteousness, to give race-promises by birth, so that circumcision and a proper genealogy from their chief should make safe passage into an eternal Kingdom.

The rule of exceptions, or, rather, the fact of a spiritual intention in the promises is apparent further :—

10. But not only so, but Rebecca also, having had commerce with but one, even with our father Isaac, 11. (For there being none born as yet, or any to do good or evil that the purpose of God according to an election might rest, it was not of works but of Him who calls), 12. It was said to her that the older should serve the younger; 13. Just as it has been written, Jacob I loved, but Esau I hated.

"**Not only so, but Rebecca.**" Here was a different case. Before there were two wives, and Ishmael was the son of a bond-woman. But here there was a legitimate wife, and the children were from "**one.**" And not only so, but they were twin children, and Esau was the first-born. So intricate a passage could hardly be made more simple. In Paul's time, two tests were appointed by the Rabbis for a man's redemption:—first, Is he a Jew? and, second, Is he circumcised? (see Schöttgen & Eisenmenger). Paul has been disposing of the one, and is finishing it in these very verses; but in the very bosom of his speech he puts a parenthesis, which, in the most curt and yet most thorough fashion, replies to the other. He has been showing that God's promise to "*Abraham*," and then to "*Sarah*," and then to "*Isaac*," and then to "*Jacob*," was not squarely what they had conceived; for the very Scriptures of the times revealed a reservation. They were not to Abraham, but only to Isaac. They were not to Isaac, but only to Jacob; so that in the patriarchal history, "*The children of the flesh, those same are not children of God.*" But Paul, dealing gently, and advancing gradually, comes toward the close of the chapter, to still stronger quotations. Let it be observed, he takes all from their own Scriptures. Not only was Ishmael turned against, though the seed of Abraham; and Esau cursed, though born of Isaac, but an entire surrender is made of any difference. "*I will call them my people which were not my people*" (v. 25, fr. Hosea 2 : 23); and "*though Israel be as the sand*," only "*a remnant shall be saved*" (v. 27, fr. Is. 10: 22, 23). From the very law they worshiped in their churches, Paul, therefore, takes the proof that their superstitious trust to their being Jews could not even have been relied upon by the ancient patriarchs. Packed-in, then, in this solid argument comes the parenthesis which has been hardly noticed. It is complete in itself. His main point was to show that some men, not Jews, had been prophesied of as saved, and some men who were Jews had undoubtedly perished. Here comes in the other point. They must not only be Jews, but they must also be circumcised. And yet Paul says, That cannot be a proper reasoning in the case, for God declared that certain things should be, irrespective of any fact of circumcision. "**For there being none born as yet, nor any to do good or evil that the purpose of God according to an election should have whereon to rest, it was not of works but of Him who calls.**"

"**None born.**" The word "*children*" (E. V. & Re.) is not in the Greek. "**To do good.**" This is the aorist participle. "**Rest.**" Literally "**that the purpose of God according to an election might rest.**" But for the sake of the English we vary it a little; "**should have whereon to rest.**" "**It was not.**" This seems to be the inspired apodosis. And yet it has been never noticed. It demonstrates itself to be, both by its sense and grammar. "*It was not* **of works.**" This whole arrangement was designed, and was irrespective of any question whether the man would get himself circumcised or no. It was the great scheme "**of Him who calls,**" and not of the existing Esau. And, if it will be noticed, the parenthesis is the only part that deals with any ritualistic idea. Throw its contents away and all the rest is but a train of genealogic evidences.

"**It was said to her.**" This looks back for its connection to the tenth verse. "**Jacob have I loved.**" This word is often used in Hebrew for the *effects of love*. Solomon uses it that way. "He that getteth wisdom loveth his own soul" (Prov. 19 : 8). It is the same with hatred. God did not *love Jacob* in any usual way before he was born; neither did He **hate Esau.** All our usual speech is modified by the peculiarities of the believer. When we are called "*holy*" we have seen the strain upon the language (com. 2 : 6). When Jacob was born he was a sinner. When he was born again he was a desperately mean man. When any of us are converted, if God hates sin, it must be in a modified method that He can be thought of as loving anybody. Nor is this essentially difficult. Love of benevolence and love of complacency are the only moral loves ; and, therefore, there is vast imprudency of speech in characterizing "electing love " as though it belonged to either of these simple feelings. It is a pregnancy, meant to express a volume : and corresponds graphically with other sayings of the East. Wisdom cries, "All they that hate me, love death" (Prov. 8 : 36). She says, " I love them that love me" (v. 17); though how can wisdom love when it is a mere abstraction ? And so of the corresponding phrase,—" He that spareth his rod hateth his son " (Prov. 13 : 24); or, more striking still, "Whoso is partner with a thief hateth his own soul" (Prov. 29 : 24). " Electing *love*," therefore, is nothing but a pregnant word, including pure benevolence, including anticipated esteem as far as the objects of it shall be worthy of any, but including, above all, that effect, as though of "*love*," which results from the discovered possibility (see v. 22) of a soul's redemption.

14. What shall we say then ? Is there unrighteousness with God ? By no means; 15. For He says to Moses, I will have mercy on whomsoever I can have mercy, and I will have compassion on whomsoever I can have compassion.

The true philosophy of God includes the doctrine of His entire sovereignty. The sovereignty of God, which even infidels are inclining to under the modern naturalisms, has been frightfully marred by two additions, which men, otherwise good, have rashly made to it. One is, that God is sovereign over the actions of my mind, which He undoubtedly must be to be any God whatever, and *shapes the choices of His sovereignty for the display of His perfections ;* a gospel that is simply horrible. Hell must measure its depth of mischief. Atheists have attacked it with zeal, and then pretended that they were attacking Christianity. It has not a lineament of what is Christian. We are indeed taught that God does everything for display (Ps. 8 : 1 ; 29 : 9), but always as a gracious instrument. We are taught that this display is vital for our good (Ps. 63 : 2). We are taught, therefore, that it is an intermediate end (Eph. 3 : 10 ; Rom. 9 : 17). But that God damns a creature for display, and that such is His final, and therefore only, and, in itself, all-sufficient and absolutely positive and necessary end, must sink any conceivable system. And, sadly enough, the same men who teach this wickedness, teach another, namely, that this self-adulating conduct of the universe is sovereign in the sense of naked, stark and absolute pleasure of the governing will.

When we take the word "good pleasure," and put the word "mere" to it (West. Sh. Cat., Qu. 20), forgetting εὐδοκία, which it is meant to translate, and forgetting "good," which might be a reminder of the truth, we form habits of theology which God's character will not bear. "*The righteousness of God*" is the very thing revealed in the Gospel (Rom. 1 : 17). In the very heart of our religion, viz., Christ ; and in the very object of Christ, viz., the salvation of the sinner ; and in the very secret of salvation, viz., the will of the Almighty, to plant a motive like display, and then to forget even that, in a stark supremacy and such do-as-you-please vital sovereignty of work, is really to throw away the beauty that converts, and to put in its place a horror which repels the perishing.

Now the resting place of this mistake has been this ninth chapter of our English. Here are three verses. They stand apart, and undoubtedly they teach, if left to King James, this naked sovereignty of Heaven. Once more scholars have looked in upon them and left them the same (Re.). They must be very clear Greek, so any one would think. Moreover they are very different Greek ; so that if one were differently read, the others would still stand separate. Let me mention them together :—"**I will have mercy on whom I** (will) **have mercy, and I will have compassion on whom I** (will) **have compassion**" (v. 15). "*So then it is not of him that willeth,* *nor of him that runneth, but of God that showeth mercy"* (v. 16). *"Therefore hath He mercy on whom He will have mercy, and whom He will He hardeneth"* (v. 18).

Famous texts! We open a Calvinistic creed, and there they are as a matter of course. Under the head of Predestination no sentences have been used so much. In long ages of agitation we have looked to them for the harsh and the bitter. What a sadness if it has been all a mistake! And yet close criticism will find that such has been the fact. The first sentence is from the Old Testament (Ex. 33:19). Moses, after infinite condescensions, cries out, "I beseech thee show me thy glory." God answers him. He translates what He will do into these two promises, "I will make all my goodness to pass before thee," and, as though it were the same thing, "I will proclaim (my) name, etc."—; and then, with the *vav* of material fulfilment, he utters our text. I appeal to any fair mind whether it is morally possible that God meant that all His "*goodness*" was exhibited to Moses, and all His great "*name*" proclaimed, by telling him He would do as He pleased! What is conspicuous is the solitariness of the averment. There is nothing more. Man has grandly prayed, and God has gloriously answered. And now, that all the consummation is in this wilful speech,—I will do as I please! is of all hermeneutical dreams the most flatly scandalous. "*Parturiunt montes, nascetur ridiculus mus.*" And though we do not pretend to shape Scripture, yet reason can cry a determined halt, and say, The text, "This is my body," or the text, "Wash away thy sins," or the text, "I give unto thee the keys," or if there be any other conundrum in the Book, it shall be looked hard into for its sense, before we rest for a moment upon an absurd or wicked interpretation.

Doing this service for Exodus we find that the established significance has been an almost wilful presumption.

Let it be understood that there is no subjunctive in Hebrew. The sense of contingency is supplied by the future. "Can the rush grow up without mire?" (Job 8:11); that is simply the future. Our translators say "can," there; why not, therefore, in the infinitely weightier passage? Elisha says to the woman, "Sojourn wheresoever thou canst sojourn" (E. V., 2 Kings 8 : 1). This is precisely parallel. Why do the translators understand the subjunctive, and yet fatally forget it where it would have expounded and glorified the Almighty?

In a context where He was about to say, "Only my back parts can be seen," meaning the results of my administrations, why did not the translators seize so important an assurance to our faith (especially as they seized the far less important instances), and when God had said " I will make all my goodness pass before thee," see how splendidly He was fulfilling that speech when He said "*I will be gracious to whomsoever I* CAN *be gracious, and will show mercy on whom I* CAN *show mercy?*"

Taking refuge in the Greek, and saying, It is the Greek that is inspired (quoted as it is, and adopted now by the apostle), and insisting that the Greek (ὅς ἄν with the subjunctive) must mean the future, will not answer at all. Ἄν really belongs to ὅς, not to the subjunctive (Meyer, Alford, see Jelf, Gram. § 829 : 1). The subjunctive always expresses contingency. We confess that in most instances the contingency is not *potential*. But that is as it happens. The contingency is explained by the subject matter. When the Septuagint says, "Will a flag grow without mire?" (Job 8 : 11), or when the New Testament says, πῶς φύγητε (Matt. 23 : 33), our translators do not hesitate a moment :—"Can a flag grow without mire?" (E. V.) or, " How can ye escape the damnation of hell?" (E. V.).

The reader must always judge the sense. " Bake that which ye will bake, and seethe that ye will seethe "(ὅσα ἐὰν, LXX., Ex. 16 : 23). Here we would never say "*can*," for they *could* stuff all into the fire at a stroke. But the contingency in an instant emerges as one of convenience. Then when David says, "Seeing I go whither I may" (E. V., 2 Sam. 15 : 20), and when Elisha says, " Sojourn wherever thou canst sojourn " (E. V., 2 Ki. 8 : 1), the turn of the sense, though the future is the same, infallibly marks out the subjunctive differences.

For how else can we arrive at any meaning on the part of

the apostle? Dr. Hodge, upon the harshest ground of arbitrariness, says that Paul is simply stating what God claims; because we cannot go back of that. He does as He pleases, and simply is saying so. But in that we forget that Paul has volunteered an explanation. To say that he is shifting the responsibility to the Old Testament Scriptures is absurd, for it is an Old Testament Scripture that is in question (v. 13). It would be defending one speech of God by obtruding a worse. That is what tempts the infidel. Therefore Alford holds that what Paul is meaning, is, that what influences God, is actual mercy. "When I show mercy I show mercy." But that is hardly sufficient; for the difficulty does not lie in the region of mercy, but in the region of wrath. Give Paul the sense of those indifferent passages about "the flag" and "'the rush," and the text becomes of the first class. The chapter sweetens in a moment. Sovereignty remains just as total; and I believe it to be absolute. But it is not a do-as-you-please sovereignty. Paul brings Moses into a line with Christ. Just as the prophet said, "What could have been done more for my vineyard that I have not done in it?" or as Jeremiah, " He doth not afflict willingly;" or Christ, "How often would I have gathered;" or Paul, "Who will have all men to be saved;" or Ezekiel, "Have I any pleasure at all in the death of him that dieth?" so there can be no ripple of doubt that Paul's great answer was meant to be that God had said to Moses that He would have compassion on all He could, and save all that He was able.

To the objection that this denies God's omnipotence, we oppose, first, His own texts above given; but then further, we interpose a proper account of God's omnipotence. He could make all the sea-corals archangels, or, taken by themselves, He could make the chalk cliffs of England redolent of their ancient life, and then make each insect which made them, a planet covered with inhabitants. But query, Is it irreverent to say that He *could not do this* in the broadest, widest and most intelligible sense ? God has a mighty whole for His work; and it is perfectly consistent to imagine that He cannot remove even a grasshopper from our planet, athwart or aside of His whole design.

16. But let us move on to the next difficulty. "*So then it is not of him that willeth, nor of him that runneth, but of God that showeth mercy*" (E. V. & Re). This is the translation of everybody. And yet it is a wonder. The first syllable should have bred a pause. What a departure from all the thinking of the Bible to say that mercy "is not of him that willeth!" What, in all strictness, is it of, according to the rules of the gospel, except specifically this very thing? If a man *wills*, he is saved. As a man *wills*, be it to him. To bring the impenitent to *will* is the whole burden of gospel preaching. A man will not *will* without the Spirit; but that is not the idea. That is taught in another sentence where John says, "Which were born not of the will of the flesh" (Jo. 1 : 13). We may search in vain for a sentence which makes light of the human *will* as not the *sine qua non* of the soul's redemption.

But what then does the sentence mean? Lay it down smoothly in the Greek, and look at it! Remember Hebraistic habits of speech that love to place substantives last (Prov. 16 : 2 ; 21 : 2 ; 22 : 11 ; 27 : 9, see Com.). And, lest some men object the repeating of the article, remember Jelf's rule that in certain strong cases the article must be repeated (Jelf, Gram. § 459, 9). Therefore it will be seen to be remarkable that a certain sense which we now subjoin, has not been earlier the reading of the passage.

16. Then therefore it is not of the willing, nor of the running, but of the mercy showing God.

That meaning is entirely complete. With Paul's quotation that Heaven does all it can; and with the implication that, in announcing this, God fulfilled all that He had declared and made all His goodness pass before His servant, comes the simple corollary that then "**it is not of the willing nor of the**" *eagerly hastening God* that damnation comes, but of one whose great aim is "**mercy.**" It is not justice that is crushed by a theology like this, but justice that is ennobled. Just as the sun produces tempests as well as summer radiance, so God does but shine when He curses, and shine too in mercy and compassion, though, as the fruit of His mercy, in the shape of a needful rectitude, some men are the victims of His wrath, and suffer endlessly where He cannot save.

17. For, notice further; the word γάρ in the seventeenth verse has not its simplest sense, but rather an explanatory one (see com. 4 : 3 ; Matt. 1 : 18), as though the apostle said, It is on this wise, or in necessary agreement with this, that the Almighty says, etc.

17. So that it is on this wise that the Scripture says to Pharaoh,—For this very purpose did I raise thee up, that I might exhibit in thee My power, and that My name might be fully manifested in all the earth.

God's glory is His final end (see remarks v. 15), but it is glory in the old Hebrew sense. The word כָּבוֹד (*glory*) means *weight*. It came to mean *excellence*. As a little child would say, God's final end is to do right, which agrees with His highest glory in the sense of excellency. But when it comes to display, that appears at once subordinate. And here we see expounded the subordinate uses of display. They are immensely great. Paul recurs to them again in the twenty-second verse. And here in the seventeenth they are the methods of God's mercy. I did not damn Pharaoh at my will, but necessarily, and in pursuit of an eternal plan. And though in that plan only God's back parts could be revealed (Ex. 33 : 23), yet that Great Sovereign condescends to tell His servant that one thing he must accept; for that that one thing is the essence of His "goodness;" that by telling it to Moses He did thereby "proclaim (His) name;" that that one thing answered to his prayer that He would show him His glory; and that that one thing was, that He "*would have mercy on all on whom He could have mercy;*" and that that bent and purpose of compassion must be recollected as the proper gloss of the severest expressions of the sovereignty of Heaven.

18. I confess, however, that I feel weak when, after batter-

ing down two walls, which every commentator has helped in building, I come to another, and the inexpugnableness of this triple defence appears in the fact that they are all built of different material. How unlikely it seems to be that there should be three texts, all looking one way, all built of different Greek, each studied separately and pronounced upon alike by every interpreter of Scripture ; and that a student who avows that he hates their doctrine, should be right in teaching that all the expositors are wrong ; that all the passages fall into *his* view ; that the three texts are of the mildest, instead of the bitterest, in the word of God ; and that what intervenes to shew this, is different in every text, so that when one wall is broken down, it requires a different sap and mine in the least degree to affect the other ! Who would believe this ? And yet we could believe almost anything rather than the text, *"Therefore hath He mercy on whom He will have mercy, and whom He will He hardeneth"* (E. V., see also Re.). We are not conscious of being warped by reason. Something in the Greek has arrested us in every instance. But if we tried hard to escape King James, we could not feel very guilty, when Paul is deliberately asking, *"Is there unrighteousness with God?"* and puts us off with the reply (E. V.) that He does as He pleases ; that He hardens whom He will ; and that the result is simply of His pleasure ; that *" it is not of him that willeth,"* but, in the most starkly naked sense, of God where He chooses to damn.

Let it be distinctly understood, God's perfect sovereignty we earnestly declare. The very dust that floats by this pen was decreed eternally. The lightest act, like the laugh of the fair girl who by her speech at Nahor was to become the ancestress of the Redeemer (Gen. 24 : 14, 18, 19), is walled in like adamant. There can be no doubt of that. But that it is done for display, I mean chiefly ; or done at will, I mean simply at will, is abhorrent to all our feeling ; and that is a high act of piety that mellows this chapter of Paul, and lifts it out of that chamber of despair where it has so long brutalized the worshipers of Jesus.

But now let us approach the sentence. The chief priests and

scholars in Jerusalem, when they passed by, mocked Christ,—
"Let Him deliver Him now, if He will have Him" (E. V.,
Matt. 27 : 43). The sentence is εἰ θέλει αὐτόν. It is not classic
Greek, but it is precisely similar to the words of our passage.
The Septuagint says, "Sacrifice and offering thou didst not
will" (οὐκ ἠθέλησας, Ps. 40 : 6). And Paul, still more leaning to
Hebraistic use, throws away classic principle altogether; for
he actually talks of *willing in humility* (Col. 2 : 18), as though
the words were בְּחֵפֶץ, and as though there were no fealty that
he owed to the strict original. Now consider this license of
Paul, and our sentence is expounded at once. We are to take
note of a μέν (not expressed), and of the δέ,—"*on the one hand*"
and "*on the other hand*," and, in ways more certain than in
the other instances, this Scriptural thought emerges :—God
wishes the salvation of all, I mean in a certain and well understood sense of revelation (Lu. 19 : 42 ; Lu. 13 : 34), but He
ordains only the salvation of some. For reasons that are good
and noble—"**One man whom He has a desire after He
shows mercy to, and another man whom He has a desire
after He hardens.**" As though he would say, "God would
have all men to be saved, and to come to the knowledge of the
truth" (1 Tim. 2 : 4): but while "it is the glory of Gods to
cover over a thing," it is "the glory of Kings to search a thing
out" (Prov. 25 : 2). God cannot explain His administration ;
on the contrary, "the heaven for height and the earth for
depth, and the heart of Kings is unsearchable" (ib. v. 3); but
He condescends to assure the Lawgiver that He hath mercy
on whom He can, and Paul translates that as meaning—

18. **Then, therefore, one man whom He has a desire
after He shows mercy to, and another man whom He has
a desire after, He hardens.**

19–21. Translators still continue to do injustice to the
apostle. Μενοῦνγε ("*rather*") in the twentieth verse, Ἢ ("*or*")
in the twenty-first verse, Εἰ δέ ("*but if*") in the twenty-second
verse, and above all τὸ δυνατὸν ("*what is possible*" for Him), and
κατηρτισμένα ("*who have been fitting themselves*"), are all trampled
out. They are the very life of the passage. Paul does not

mean to adopt the doctrine that "**the potter has right over the clay.**" It would be an infamous idea. But his meaning is, Say that, "**rather**" than say the other thing. Μενοῦνγε, which occurs but four times in the Bible, is the very cream of the sentence. The objector, after such careful apologies for God as God had resorted to, comes after Him again, and Paul, rebuking this ἀνταποκρινόμενον, this desperate *answerer back*, uses this word μενοῦνγε. "*Rather*" than answer that way, answer this way. That "*the potter has right over the clay*," Paul does not dream, to wit, in the sense of creating a victim to suffer. Nothing could be more atrocious. If God has any moralities at all, they would cry out against such an exercise of power. The quiet expression "**but if**" in the twenty-second verse, shows that Paul is returning there to his actual argumentation. But here he is merely flirting the caviller :—"*Rather*" than say one mad thing, say the other, which might be distorted out of an ancient prophet (Jer. 18 : 6), and might seem to have as much a shadow-like capacity of reason :—

19. **Thou wilt say, therefore, unto me, Why does He yet find fault? for who has resisted His will? 20. Say rather, O man, 'Who art thou who answerest back over and again to the Almighty? Shall the thing formed say to Him who formed it, why hast thou made me thus?' 21. Or, 'Has not the potter right over the clay to make of the same lump one vessel to honor and another to dishonor?'**

Μενοῦνγε does not mean "*Nay but*" (E. V. & Re.) ; ἀνταποκρινόμενος does not mean simply who *replies* (E. V. & Re.) ; ἤ does not mean starkly nothing, so that we have a right to omit it altogether (E. V.), and εἰ δὲ does not mean "*what if*" (E. V. & Re.) ; so that if we insist that these particles, which are great lights in this connection, shall be treated as though meant by the apostle, we shall almost force the expositor to come into our better meaning.

22. **But if God, wishing to explain the wrath, and to make what is possible for Him known, endured with much long suffering vessels of wrath who had been fitting themselves for destruction ;**

It will be seen, therefore, that four things in this sentence seem to fix its meaning; first, the "*But if,*" seeming to imply that the apostle is returning to more deliberate considerations; second, the word "**explain**," which means *inwardly to explain*, or to *go to the bottom* of a thing. The expression is not "*His wrath*" (E. V. & Re.), but "**the wrath;**" and "*wrath*" in so merciful a Jehovah requires just such an explanation to be given by His dealings. Third, "**what is possible.**" It was a shame to translate this "*His power*" (E. V. & Re.). It is the same root that is translated, "*What the law could not do*" (8 : 3). And, fourth, "**fitting themselves.**" Now put all these together. The sense of *the middle* separates the lost from the saved. The lost "*had been fitting themselves*" (see admissions of Dr. Hodge). The saved "**He had before prepared unto glory**" (see next verse). "*What is possible for Him*" agrees perfectly with the fifteenth verse,—"*I will have mercy on whomsoever I can have mercy.*" And the specific purpose of *display* does not exhibit itself as the final end, but in agreement with the seventeenth verse, as the merciful means by which "*the righteousness of God is revealed from faith to faith*" (1 : 17), and by which God does what He can to "**explain**" what "*is possible for Him,*" to the creature.

"**Vessels:**" to keep in view the illustration of "*the potter.*" "*Who had been fitting themselves:*" to keep at a proper distance the illustration of "*the potter.*" No one can exaggerate the sovereignty of the "King;" but He dooms the lost and He lifts the saint by an entirely different responsibility. He damns the one from the very beginning, but because he *will* "*fit himself*" for his fate, and He lifts the other without any such prevision. He does not pretend that we will understand it. But He does tell us in this gentlest chapter of His word, that He will save all He can, and that He will "*explain*" as far as He is able "*what is possible*" for His grace, and what must be true of "*the wrath*" that blazes forth in so patient an administration.

23. **And that He might make known the riches of His glory upon vessels of mercy whom He before prepared unto glory,**

Let us recur to the points made. First, the King is unsearchable (Ex. 33 : 22). Second, He announced to Moses that He would save all He could. Third, the abandonment of any, as signified in such a passage as "*Jacob have I loved, and Esau have I hated*" is necessitated firstly and most of all by each man's wickedness, but, as concerns selections among the wicked to be subjects of mercy, is a deep mystery. Paul says there are reasons for it, for he gives the reasons for his own deliverance (1 Tim. 1 : 13, 16), but those reasons are far away out of our sight. But, fourthly, the reasons have to do with the uses of the gospel—I mean this, in part. The object of the gospel is to convert the sinner. The characterization of the gospel is that "*it is the power of God*" (Rom. 1 16). The operation of this "*power*" is in its revealing "*the righteousness of God*" (ib.), and the exhibition of this righteousness is largely in the treatment of sinners. That He may "*explain* (His) *wrath*" He punishes the lost (Of course He must do it justly) ; "**and that He might make known the riches of His glory,**" He saves a remnant. Fifthly, the implication is that His conduct is so wise that it is "*what is possible for Him*" as a King (v. 22). And, sixthly, after celebrating this as "*His glory*," and these very mysteries of His grace as "*the riches of His glory*," and holding out the joy that we were pre-determined to enjoy this "**glory**" ourselves, He lights down upon what is a habit of the apostle, viz., Scripture for it all. This Queen of the Epistles might be called, " Mysteries of Christ Proved out of the Writings of the Older Dispensation ; " for the lost *apodosis*, which has so troubled commentators, is really the apostle putting his pen upon this very point :—

24, 25. He says, as also in Hosea, of us whom He has also called, not of the Jews only but also of the Gentiles,
    I will call them My people who were not My people,
    And her beloved, who was not beloved ;
26. And it shall be in the place where it was said to them,
    Ye are not My people,
    There they shall be called sons of a living God.

It is thus that we solve many difficulties. First, the apodosis. The apodosis that we find is perfectly grammatical. If God, wishing to do a certain thing, bore, &c. &c., and, with the further design to accomplish still another thing ; (He avowed it long before, for) He says (as also with special application in Hosea), I will call them my people, &c., &c. Why this has not always been the apodosis, we cannot imagine. It explains the interpolation of καὶ ("**also**") ; "**whom He has also called.**" It is the echo of the word προητοίμασεν ("*whom He before prepared,*" v. 23), "*whom He has also called.*" And then again "**also in Hosea**" —one of those delicate touches in the apostle to save him a whole narration. For now, let us mention a second difficulty. A second difficulty was that Hosea is speaking of the Israelites. Paul does not stay to notice that, but boldly says "**Not of the Jews only, but also of the Gentiles.**" He plainly asserts that God has said it in ten thousand other ways besides Hosea. But he claims "**also**" Hosea. And he claims him on the hardest point, not only that Israel might be cast off, but, what was more startling to a Jew, that Israel was never fairly on ; that they were "*not all Israel that were of Israel*" (v. 6.) ; that they might easily credit the calling of the Gentiles when they themselves were *quoad hoc* Gentiles. And then the particle δὲ pushes that extreme by another quotation :—

27. On the other hand Isaiah cries out concerning Israel—

As though the apostle had said, Although the quotation before this might be supposed to apply to all men, and fairly to teach that we are "**not beloved**" till "**beloved**" through the blessed Redeemer, "**on the other hand**" Isaiah says what is specifically "**concerning Israel.**" It is mad to start at God's sovereignty or arrogate the election of Heaven, when the Jews never became His people themselves except outwardly, according to Hosea, and "*on the other hand,*" and in a way confined to Israel, Isaiah had **cried out** that the mass would never be a "*people*,"—that the multitude of them would all be curst ; for, as he expresses it :—

27. Though the number of the sons of Israel be as the sand of the sea, it is the remnant that shall be saved ; 28.

For it is a word which He finishes and cuts short that the Lord executes upon the earth.

Mistake is at best vague and clashing. The people could hardly have supposed that all Israel would be saved. For the prophets were full of denunciations. Yet they did teach that no circumcised Hebrew could perish (see com. 9 : 10). Infidelity is a slimy bog that obstructs rather than confronts the Gospel. The Sadducees hardly believed that there was no form of immortality (Acts 23 : 8). And yet our Saviour, against them, and Paul, against the Rabbinical extravagance about the Jew, go down to the very depth, and answer once for all, and out of their own acknowledged authority of Scripture.

He goes back further too in the prophet :—

29. And as Isaiah had said before,—

Unless the Lord of Hosts had left us a seed,
We should have become as Sodom, and should have been made like unto Gomorrha.

"Said before." Isaiah spanned sixty-two years (Is. 1 : 1). It was like quoting a prophet for each reign, "Uzziah, Jotham, Ahaz and Hezekiah, kings of Judah." Quoting this special language was referring to something a quarter of a century older than what went just before. And as the later Scripture was a prophecy (v. 27), and the earlier Scripture was a history (v. 29), the προείρηκεν ("*said before*") was graphic. Paul would overwhelm them with the argument that Israel always was and always would be cursed, and only blessed by the same law as the accursed heathen.

30. What shall we say then?

Paul is going to end with what Solomon would call "the conclusion of the whole matter" (Ec. 12 : 13). Godward he has brought out the fact that the discrepancies of fate are determined upon (1), not for divine display, and (2), not for "*mere* good pleasure," but for εὐδοκία, or God's "thinking fit," under necessary rules of administration. And now, manward, he centres all upon "**faith**" (v. 30). It was not "blood" (Jo. 1 : 13) ; and it was not rite (Gal. 5 : 6) ; and it was not "*works*," done by the letter under the mere instructions "*of the law*" (Gal. 2 : 16), but it was just the one solitary thing of obedience to the rule of faith in the Redeemer.

These are his sentences :—" **What shall we say then?** "

30.—**That Gentiles, not pressing after a righteousness, had put their hands on a righteousness, but it was the righteousness of faith; 31. But that Israel, pressing after a law of righteousness, came not the earlier to any law; 32. Why? Because, not out of faith but as it were out of works, they stumbled at the stone of stumbling; 33. As it has been written,**

> **Behold I lay in Zion a stone of stumbling and an entrapping rock;**
> **And he who believes on It shall not be made ashamed.**

30. "**Not pressing after a righteousness.**" Paul does not mean that the nations had no idea of virtue; but that the Jews had no other idea; that their very chief was a Lawgiver. He means to remind them that their rule was a theocracy; that their very *raison d'être* was, to be pure and holy. He calls to remembrance their sacred books, which were stuffed full of moral commandments. He remembers their sacrifices, which were meant to teach them "**righteousness.**" He only means to say that the heathen led common lives, with only common chances to know the Almighty, but that the Jews' very business was to be *righteous*. He was about to tell them (10 : 2) that they had "*a zeal for God,*" and actually wanted to keep the law, but that for one sole defect they were cursed (v. 32). The "**Gentiles,** *not pressing after a righteousness,* κατέλαβεν, *had gripped down* upon **a righteousness, but it was the righteousness of faith. But Israel,**" who had a vast system of ordinances to assist this very exercise of dependence, had nursed the ordinances and lost the faith. "**Pressing after a law of righteousness,**" they followed it even in the minutest details (Jo. 5 : 10) with a "*zeal*"(v. 2) totally different from any of the Gentiles. And yet Gentiles were saved, and they not! Why? Because Gentiles, like Abel, accepted Christ, and they, like Cain, had another offering.

All these words are expressive. 30. "**Put their hands upon;**" that actual gripe and seizure which consists in "*faith.*" "**A** *righteousness ;* " for it was not *the* perfect righteousness, "**but**" only that dawning one which rises in the sinner. 31. "*Pressing after* **a law** *of righteousness.*" Notice the guard put. Israel really did not *press* "*after righteousness ;* " and, therefore, they did not even attain the "**law.**" * They followed the law slavishly, that is, the shell or letter of the law. But as "*the righteousness of the law* " (8 : 4) is the sole kind of righteousness, they did not attain that. They simply kept the letter with bad hearts and dark consciences, or, as Paul describes it, "*a zeal for God, but not according to knowledge*" (10 : 2). "**Came not the earlier.**" φθάνω means more than "*arrive at*" (Re.). It means to *come the first*. "We which are alive and remain unto the coming of the Lord, shall not prevent (or come before, φθάσωμεν) them that are asleep" (1 Thess. 4 : 15). It helps us to mingle better the Jew and the barbarian. Both shall come (some of them), but neither earlier or with fixed permission above the other. "**Why? Because not out of faith, but, as it were, out of works.**" "*Works*" will save any body. "Repent and be converted that your sins may be blotted out" (Acts 3 : 19). What Paul means are "*works of the law*" (9 : 32). That, it is to be noticed, is the more full expression. A man is never saved by works which the law leads him to by merely thundering at him. He is never saved by mere preaching, that is to say, by *direction* † or eloquent appeal. Salvation must be "*by faith ;* " which, in simpler language, means turning to God in recognition of His grace, and seeking, through Him, a change of nature.

"**Stumbling.**" Isaiah connects the idea of a *trap* (Is. 8 : 14). A trap, first (1), deceives ; second (2), attracts, and,

---

* "*Righteousness*" (E. V.) is not repeated under the best authorities (see Re.).

† *Law* (Heb.) is from the verb to *cast*, and is derived from the idea of *throwing up* the hand to point out the way, that is, to *direct*. "*Works of the law*" were works induced by mere *direction*, works that could not be saving, because they required additionally the gift of the Holy Spirit.

third (3), ruins. Paul adds this idea to the thought of his Redeemer. "To the Greeks (He was) foolishness" (1 Cor. 1 : 23). They looked into His claims, and found them stupid. But "to the Jews (He was) a stumbling-block" (ib.). The Jews, of all other men, were prepared for the Redeemer. This was (2) the Messianic *bait*. They were hurrying on after Christ by the instigation of all their prophecies. This gave them the bitter fall when they stumbled against Him. For (1) they were *deceived*. They needed just such "**a stone,**" but the builders rejected it. They did not dream that this was their Messiah. While the Greeks were cool, the Jews were in a fury against their Redeemer. In their zeal for Christ they stumbled against Him; and (3) the horrid ruin of their crime was incident to those three facts : first, their aroused excitement about a King ; second, their utter ignorance of the Man ; and, third, the crime that all this begat. No wonder that Paul's feelings were aroused ; first, in profound pity for the Jew ; and, second, that this most improbable Prince, the "gin and the snare" (Is. 8 : 14) of Israel, might be found out in time as one by **believing in whom men might** "**not be made ashamed.**"

CHAPTER X.

1. Brethren, my heart's approval indeed, and prayer to God for them, is in the direction of salvation.

We must notice carefully this word εὐδοκία. It is not *"desire"* (E. V. & Re.). Paul says, "I obtained mercy because I did it ignorantly" (1 Tim. 1 : 13). He makes a still stronger statement, "I verily thought I ought to do many things against the name of Jesus of Nazareth" (Acts 26 : 9). The slightest generosity would lead him to think of that in respect to his people. "**My heart's approval,**" Paul would very naturally say, lies "**in the direction of** (the Jews') **salvation.**"

Notice the μέν which, as translated "**indeed,**" comes in well even in English idiom.

2. For I bear them witness that they have a zeal for God, but not according to knowledge.

What frightful sacrifices these Hebrews made (1 Macc. 2 : 32, etc.; 2 Macc. 15 : 1, etc.) !

3. For not knowing God's righteousness, and seeking to establish their own, they have not submitted themselves to the righteousness of God.

Paul did not mean that he *approved* of their salvation if God did not save them, but that his hopes lay "*in the direction*" of God's doing it. They had been so miserably deceived ! But now, he pictures just the common lack by which all perish. They had not **"knowledge."** The word is a very strong one (ἐπίγνωσις).

And this word ἐπίγνωσις means that inner moral knowledge (1 : 28 ; Heb. 10 : 26) so often characterized as of the "*truth*" (Ps. 51 : 6 ; 61 : 7 ; 119 : 142), so often called "*light*" (2 Cor. 4 : 6), which is really tantamount to "*love*" (1 Jo. 3 : 2), and which is the all-including exercise of a renovated conscience. What they needed for "*zeal*" was that it should be out of a converted heart (Acts 26 : 18). And to this agrees the further expression. Paul had said that the Gospel was "*the power of God*" (1 : 16). And he had explained that the reason it was "*the power*" was that therein, as its great object, "*the righteousness of God* (was) *revealed*" (1 : 17). That revelation is nothing more than this same causing to *know* of which this passage speaks. Paul had been showing that we could not be caused to *know* by the law ; in other words, we cannot be *taught* to be morally enlightened. Moreover we cannot teach *ourselves*. A man cannot enlighten his own conscience and heart. Therefore, a man cannot be justified by the works of the law, that is, *made righteous* in this impossible way, by the law instilling works, or creating good and illuminated actions.

4. For Christ is the end of the law for righteousness to everyone that believes.

A fine exposition of this is in the next verse :—

5. For Moses writes that the man who has done the righteousness which is from the law shall live therein.

It is not necessary that he should do it perfectly. He is not speaking of the hard demands that were made of the first Adam. When Moses said, "Behold, I have set before thee this day life and good, and death and evil" (Deut. 30 : 15), he does not mean that "life" lay only with the perfect. He meant just what Christ meant,—that if they would listen to these moral sayings of His and do them (Matt. 7 : 24), they would be choosing "life." This is meant by "*the righteousness from the law*" (see also 2 : 26 ; 8 : 4), which is just as true a righteousness, if it were attained, as "*the righteousness of God.*" But Moses knew, and Paul knew infinitely better than Moses, that commanding people to be righteous, and causing people to be righteous were entirely different things. Moses was correct in promising life to the keepers of commandments, and, therefore, "*the righteousness from the law*" is all they wanted. But keeping the commandments still remained as the condition, and their keeping the commandments was a thing absurd. Keeping the commandments involved "*knowledge,*" and moral "*knowledge*" was the light of God, and this grand requisite is the want of the sinner, and thoroughly explains all the language of the apostle. "**For they, not knowing God's righteousness**" (v. 3). Of course, that was their very difficulty. They could not open their own conscience. God, as the sole *Model*, was revealed to them in great mercies, and they could not see Him. "**And seeking to establish their own**" (v. 3), that is, to get good and holy by taking up the outward commandments. "**They have not submitted themselves to the righteousness of God**" (v. 3). That is (1), they have departed from the Model, resting satisfied with a righteousness of forms, and, furthermore (2), departed from the commandment. Thundered out from Sinai was the command to believe. The law recognized no other method of being reformed. "**Christ was the end of the law**"—blazoned in a thousand sacrifices. The chief occupation on Horeb was to see that He was prefigured. There was no way of obeying without Him ; and, therefore, as the only "*end*" of the commandment, He was the only means of "*knowledge,*" and thence of "*faith,*" and thence of "*works,*" for anyone who desired a recovery of "*righteousness.*"

To put it all plainly, "*Christ* (was) *the end of the law*" in two particulars. First, that a return to the law was described as repentance, and there was no repentance for the devils, but only for the beneficiaries of Christ; and, second, that Christ Himself was a part of the law, and that the chief weeks on Sinai were spent in describing Christ, and in binding upon the people that which He Himself afterward called the chief occasion of sin (Jo. 15 : 24), and the chief subject of the "work" (Jo. 6 : 29), and will (Jo. 7 : 17), and way (Jo. 10 : 6 ; Acts 18 : 26) of the Most High ; that is, to take Him up and believe on Him as the only cleansing.

The righteousness of God as meaning *imputed obedience*, and our *own righteousness* as meaning one which *we seek to establish* as satisfying the law, are the doctrines of our day ; yet nevertheless are mere Lutheranisms. It is anomalous that things absent from fifteen centuries, should become so fixed in the last three. These are in no respect useful. Christ can become all our hope in the way the fathers described Him. He died for us. All that I need is pardon. Secure to me a continued pardon, and make it triumphant and complete in the day of judgment, and all my curses must be removed, and my chief curse is my iniquity. It impairs grace to dream that that is not sufficient. In fact tell plainly where it is not sufficient ! If I am sinful, and therefore guilty, and therefore given over to sin ; and then, if I am ransomed, and, therefore pardoned, and so completely pardoned at the last that I am entirely sanctified, where do I need the righteousness of another ? It does not detract from Christ's work, it adds to it, to make "the one sacrifice perfect forever them that are sanctified." And there are evidences in this very chapter that forensic "*righteousness*" is not conceived of. "**For Moses writes that the man who has done the righteouness which is from the law shall live therein.**" This would not be true if "*righteousness*" must be imputed. But take it as we have explained, that the condition of salvation is "*righteous-*

ness ; " that that "*righteousness*" must be in the sinner ; that that " *righteousness* " begins not perfect ; nevertheless, even in its dawning shape, that Moses and all the prophets have declared that we will " *live thereby ;* " that this " *righteousness* " is nothing more than the washing (1 Cor. 6 : 11), and the cleansing (2 Cor. 7 : 1 ; 1 Jo. 1 : 9), and the repentance (Acts 20 : 21), and the conversion (Acts 3 : 19), and the turning from sin (Ez. 33 : 11) of all the preachers of the Word, and we have just what Paul describes, a thing not reached through being commanded, but reached through being instilled. " *The righteousness from the law,*" and with no other prompting, would save a man if he possessed it, but who is going to possess it ? The command of it merely genders to bondage ;

6. But the righteousness which is from faith speaks on this wise,—Say not in thy heart, who shall ascend into heaven ? (that is to bring Christ down) ; 7. Or who shall descend into the abyss ? (that is to bring Christ up from among the dead) ; 8. But what says it ? The word is nigh thee in thy mouth and in thy heart (that is the word of faith which we preach), 9. That if thou wilt confess with thy mouth Jesus as Lord, and believe in thy heart that God raised Him from among the dead, thou shalt be saved. 10. For with the heart belief is had unto righteousness, but with the mouth confession is made unto salvation. 11. For the Scripture says, Whosoever believes on Him shall not be made ashamed.

Paul's view and the Jewish view of salvation by "**righteousness**" (v. 5) are here discriminated. They are discriminated in three particulars. Paul's speech would become confused if we did not recognize the fertility of his figure. (1) "**Say not in thy heart, who shall ascend into heaven ?**" This is an echo of a Proverb, "Who hath ascended up into heaven or descended ? " (Prov. 30: 4; see Author's Com.). The words are Messianic. Paul has the idea of Solomon. Somebody has had to do great things. His first point, therefore, against Israel is, that they are taking on themselves far too much the work of the Almighty. "*Righteousness*" (v. 5) would have been nothing without an atonement ; and to bring Christ down, as God and Man, and to raise Christ up "by exceeding greatness of power" (Eph. 1 : 19) "**from among the dead**" of our fallen race, had to be done, but what had the Jews to do with it? Then the first intimation of Paul was that the Jews took too much upon them of the great first agencies necessary to their salvation. It was as easy to raise Christ up as it was to raise them up, and as a work of supernatural power they had nothing to contribute. "**Faith,**" therefore, placed this matter in a right light. (2) Faith, secondly, placed all matters in a right light. There was no requisite but faith. This point is often harped upon in Scripture. The burden of its appeal is, "Thou art careful and troubled about many things." Christ said, If any man say, Lo here is Christ, or, Lo there, go not after him. "Why as though living in the world are you subject to ordinances?" (Col. 2 : 20). This Paul everywhere presses. (1) The first point therefore, was, that great things had to be done, but they were not the persons to do them. (2) The second point was that but one thing has to be done, so far as is in the scope of the sinner's responsibility. And now again (3) a third point was, That that one thing is "**faith.**" "*Say not in thy heart,*" who shall do things utterly beyond human accountability, but do one little, infirm, reasonable thing to bring near you the help of the Redeemer. Paul knew perfectly well that they could not do even that one. But there is the point where God chooses to begin with His people. "**Whosoever** shall call upon the name of the Lord shall be saved" (v. 13). In the more simple human sense, that we can do ; but in the more important and divine sense we will not even do that. Paul begins there as the low down region where God chooses to move upon His people. "*Say not in thy heart*" who will do this or that thing, either (2) wholly indifferent, or (1) divine and impossible, but (3) do this thing, go humbly to God under the direction of me His servant, and God will listen, and bless your humblest petition for help.

"*Faith*" becomes saving "*faith*" where the feeblest "*call*" of the terrified and convicted sinner becomes the feeblest trust of the penitent and loving child of God. True faith has this moral *differentia*. There is much in Scripture to establish that. Christ, when decrying "Christ here" or "Christ there," says, "The Kingdom of God is within you." We are not to seek it in ordinances, but earnestly in moral light. And what He distinctly means is fixed by a simile. As the lightning shines all over Heaven (Matt. 24 : 27), so "*righteousness*" is no wretched act, like circumcision, but an illumination everywhere within the heart, and Paul tells just where it begins, viz., in a "*call*" upon God, whatever you choose to name it, in the way of seeking or dependence. Paul, in fact, has returned to the simple idea, that if a man wishes to be saved, circumcision is nothing (1 Cor. 7 : 19), just as baptism is nothing, but he must find out that he is a sinner, and then seek **"the righteousness which is from faith;"** the meaning of which now is very conspicuous. It is not "*the righteousness which is from law;*" for though that is as good as any other, it cannot be engendered. The law cannot move us to a genuine righteousness. To bestow that is a miracle. It must be the gift of the Almighty. And, therefore, it must be a "*righteousness* (or moral cleansing) *from faith.*" It is the acknowledgment of God wherein God chooses that it shall begin. Faith, when righteous, is itself its beginning. That moral "lightning" which shines from one part of a man's conscious sky to another begins in "*faith;*" the common "*faith*" of the law changing under its own prayer into the moral and saving "*faith*" of the regenerating Gospel.

Let us clear up now some notable expressions.

"*Law*" (v. 5); *any law*. There is no article. The Buddhist law, where it embraces morality, would save a man if he were actually turned to it. But what is to turn him to it? Turning or converting a man is the very acme of the Gospel. Christ becomes the only accomplishment for the law; for Moses says that a man who has obeyed "*law*" shall live therein, and no man will obey law except by the help of Christ, and, what is more specific still, without acknowledging Him.

This acknowledgment may be very obscure. But even Socrates, if we are to suspect that he may have been saved, or Cornelius, or, going back to a much obscurer time, Abraham, or, choosing still more strikingly, Lot, must have had some Gospel; that is, they must have recognized their own sinfulness, and must have looked upon God as in some way an adorable Redeemer.

"*Therein*" (v. 5); that is, the man who does righteousness shall live not *by* but "*in*" his righteousness. His righteousness shall be his life (Prov. 19 : 23 ; see Com. on Prov. *in loc.*).

"*The righteousness which is from faith.*" The righteousness *is* faith. Faith as effused with love is the dawning righteousness, and is in fact of the nature of the only righteousness that even God can manifest. There is but one lightning that flashes over the heavens. And we remember that Abraham's faith, whose only imperfection was its sinfulness, was hailed as a first fruits, and was reckoned as far as it went as a righteousness (Jas. 2 : 23). Abraham, made perfect in Heaven, will have lost his sins, but will have no other righteousness than faith gloriously made perfect in its moral vision. There is no morality in God except the morality of an omniscient ἐπίγνωσις, discernment of virtue (Hab. 1 : 13 ; Jas. 1 : 17).

"*From faith.*" Why does it not say "*in faith*"? Because though righteousness consists in faith, it is also "*from faith,*" just as one stage of holiness is produced by another. Righteousness is not from law; because law cannot command righteousness so as to induce it. There are, therefore, no "*works of law*" (Gal. 2 : 16), that is, works produced by law without a divine interference; but there is a righteousness from faith, not simply because faith is righteousness, but because God has interfered already. (1) Faith is His handiwork. Moreover (2) it is the point where He commands approach; and (3) where He begins to bless the returning sinner.

"**To bring Christ down.**" Men can have nothing to do with God's incarnation. "**Nor to bring Christ up.**" These must be wrought without us,—not only our own cleansing, but the resurrection of Christ from the death of His dead mother. The Jews took too much upon them of their own salvation.

"**But what saith it?**" The real arena of work, now that all is finished, is in the acquiescence of the conscience. We are to obey Christ. And for this, which must be childlike, "**the word is nigh us**" (v. 8). I do not mean that we can do this without God. But here it is that we must expect God. The tree cannot grow of itself, but it cannot grow at all at its trunk. It must gather at its roots, and at its outmost foliage. And there it cannot grow of itself. It spreads itself to the actinic ray, and it drinks by its rootlets in the earth. It could not live without nature; but here is where it is to expect nature. It is not to go up to Heaven, but it is to drink just where God bids it. And our tree-life reads thus:—"**The word is nigh thee.**" That is, the truth that God uses to bless, is close, like the carbon of the air. And there is present the actinic ray; that is, God is always striving to bless (Gen. 6 : 3 ; Job 7 : 18). "**That if thou wilt confess with thy mouth that Jesus is Lord.**" Infinitely far from meaning, If thou wilt just say so. But if, in Oriental phrase (Matt. 12 : 34), out of the abundance of the heart thou, a morally changed man, hast thy conscience opened to the Lord Jesus ; as Paul expressed it, If thou wilt " believe in the Lord " (Acts 16 : 31); and, if, repeating that idea, thou shalt "**believe in thy heart that God raised Him from among the dead, thou shalt be saved.**" * Here is no talisman for a superstitious conversion, but here is the lowly door where men are to enter into the Kingdom. We are to learn that we are sinners ; and, with the word in our mouth that gives direction for our salvation, we are to seek God just there : "**For with the heart belief is had unto righteousness, but with the mouth**"—Notice the "*but*" (*δὲ*). Faith must necessarily be of "*the heart ;*"

---

* We will not repeat the interpretation. See 6 : 4 ; 8 : 34. The great chrism of Christ which made Him *Christos*, was not resurrection from the grave, but that **raising from among the dead**, wrought by the Godhead that was incarnate, which, with sighs and tears and wrestlings, separated Him from among sinners, and made the child of a dead woman escape her sinfulness, and slowly rise from among the dead, even in the respect of "infirmity" and being "tempted," by a gradual probation (see again Heb. 5 : 7, 8 ; 2 : 10).

for as *moral* faith it amounts to righteousness; but it must not stop. It will show itself in the hands, or, to invoke the Oriental simile (Heb. 13 : 5 ; 1 Jo. 4 : 2, 3), it will spring to the lips. It will pervade our whole nature. See how far Paul has traveled from the idea that descent or circumcision can be the question of pardon.

12. He is ready now for another step. Men are all alike:—

12. For there is no difference of Jew or Greek, for the same Lord of all is rich unto all who call upon Him; 13. For whosoever shall call upon the name of the Lord shall be saved.

"Call." This is just such another word as "*confess*" (v. 9); only it is still more superficial. Dreadful snares have been spread in the church like those in Israel. "This is my covenant," God told the people,—"Every male child shall be circumcised" (Gen. 17 : 10). Men have played wild with the text, just as Roman Catholics have with "This is my body" (Matt. 26 : 26). The deadliest snare of all is in this word "*call.*" Men are not to be pardoned by simply crying out to God; any more than they are to be saved by the water of baptism. On the contrary, God warns against such idea (Matt. 7 : 21). But it is appalling how many are waiting for just that. When men are launched from a gibbet exultant from an over-night forgiveness after a mere terrified "*call,*" they owe their delusion to an abuse of just such texts. We are to "look and live." But it is a "look" very different from that of thousands in our communions, and involves a moral beholding of Christ. It is a "(receiving of) the love of the truth" (2 Thess. 2 : 10). This very passage (v. 10), tells us that it is "*with the heart belief is had unto righteousness.*" And though we may go to Christ in terror, we must go at last in love, for it is only when the "*call*" is touched with what is moral that it has fastened upon Christ, and borne away from Him an actual salvation.

Paul's emphasis, however, is upon the word "**all**" ($\pi\tilde{\alpha}\varsigma$, vs. 11, 13). His use for the text is to mingle Jew and Gentile (v. 12). And now he takes another step :—

14. How then can they call on Him in whom they have not believed?—

His argument is, If all who "**call**" are to be saved, those who are expected to "*call*" must be preached to. He wishes to defend his ministry to the Gentiles. That is his specific object; and, mark you, he has been appealing (vs. 11, 13) to their own Scriptures. If in your own Scriptures it is said that "**all**" (πᾶς) *who call on the name of the Lord shall be saved* " (v. 11), and that "**all**" (πᾶς) who believe "*shall not be made ashamed,*" why do you object to me for ministering to the Gentiles? For "**how can they call on Him in whom they have not believed?**

14—But how can they believe in Him of whom they have not heard? and how can they hear without a preacher? 15. And how can they preach except they be sent? as it is written, How beautiful are the feet of them who preach the gospel of good things!

We cannot tell how many heathen have been saved. We do not know whether Cornelius (Acts 10 : 1, etc.) had ever heard of Christ. If He had, would it not have been mentioned (Acts 10 : 35)? Abraham and Job and even Peter (Acts 1 : 6) cannot have known as we do of a Redeemer. It is to the point to say that this passage teaches nothing on the question. Paul had said, All that believe on Christ (v. 11), and all that call upon His name (v. 14), shall be saved; and all churches agree that everything about Christ is a powerful engine of salvation. But Paul does not speak to the other point. He only argues, If the Holy Ghost has taken the pains to tell us that the revelation of Christ may be the salvation of any, why do you object to me for saying that preaching Him may be of the Holy Ghost? If all who call upon Him will be saved, why not all hear of Him? for "**how can they believe on Him of whom they have not heard? and how can they hear without a preacher? and how can they preach except they be sent?**" And how welcome to the Divine Mind must this work anywhere be; for "**it is written, How beautiful are the feet**" (that is, how noble is the activity, 2 Sam. 22: 34) "**of them**" ("that preach the gospel of peace," E. V., said to be spurious, see Re.) **"who preach the gospel of good things"** (Is. 52: 7).

16. But they did not all obey the gospel—

Compactly put in is the idea that they were alike in another particular :—All to be preached to, but few reached and rescued.

16.—For Isaiah says :—

Quoting their own Scriptures,—

16.—Lord, who has believed what we had for them to hear ?

Paul, showing the same peculiarity of proving everything by their Hebraistic writings, goes on sententiously to other points. If Isaiah cries out so passionately, "**Lord, who has believed our** ἀκοῇ"—"*our hearing*" or, as we have been free to translate, "**what we had for them to hear**," then we have inspired warrant for two other things, first, that "**belief**" was to have come "**from hearing**," and, second, that "**the hearing**," in this case, was "**by a word of Christ.**" This was well argued enough, for the chapter which that verse begins was the celebrated chapter of the eunuch which he was reading sitting in his chariot, and which helped so very much to supply the faith which Philip recognized when he undertook to baptize him. The next verse includes these two points :—

17. Therefore the belief comes of hearing, but the hearing by a word of Christ.

We easily finish the chapter. Paul makes out four lesser points :—First, everybody did hear, and it was Jew and Gentile alike. Second, the Jews knew the fact ; for, recollect, in saying these things, he is solely proving them out of their own Scriptures. Thirdly, they had been uttered by their own prophets more boldly than had been done by Paul. And, fourth, the Israelites themselves had been prominent above the the rest in the bitterness with which they had repelled the gospel. These four points are a sufficient account of the four next quotations, and their intention by the apostle.

18. But I say, did they not hear? Rather
   Their sound went out into all the earth,
   And their words unto the ends of the world.
19. But I say, Did not Israel know? First Moses says:
   I will provoke you to jealousy by that which is no nation;
   By a foolish nation will I anger you.
20. But Isaiah is very bold and says:—
   I was found of them that sought me not;
   I was made manifest to them who asked not after me.
21. But to Israel he says:—All day long did I spread forth my hands to a disobedient and gainsaying people.

It will be seen how all these authorities illustrate Paul's text, "*For there is no difference between Jew and Greek*" (v. 12), and how he has already guarded the twentieth verse, "**I was found of them that sought me not;**" for this, nakedly uttered, would be a dreadful presentation of the Gospel. But he had already said that there was "*no difference between Jew and Greek, for the same Lord over all* (was) *rich unto all that call upon Him*" (v. 12). This *seeking*, or *prayer*, or *coming to God*, or *calling upon His name*, or *asking after Him*, as we may choose to give it a designation, was just the thing that distinguished men where Jewish blood did nothing. Paul would hardly deny that. And therefore the expression, "**I was found of them that sought me not**" (v. 20) is unbearably mistaken, unless we go to another verse. Paul had said "*that the Gentiles, not pressing after righteousness*, (had) *put their hands upon righteousness*" (9 : 30). And we explain that in the light of both passages. The Jews for centuries had pretended to be "*pressing after*" God. The rest had done nothing of the kind. And, therefore, in the immediate neighborhood of each other we have texts which will explain their mutual meaning. "*I was found of them that sought me not*" is in the spirit of the expression, "Oh that men would shut the doors; neither let them kindle fire on my altar for nought" (Mal. 1 : 10). Such *seeking* as the Jews had done was an abhorrence; and the Gentiles, freshly awakened, would *seek* differently from many of the Jews, in that humble and honest sense which would obtain salvation.

CHAPTER XI.

1. I say then, Did God cast off His people? By no means; for I also am an Israelite, of the seed of Abraham, of the tribe of Benjamin.

We must not relax for a moment the vigilant idea that Paul is arguing from Scripture, and not from reason. The Hebrew writings are the gist of the epistle. He remembers just at this pose of his argument how the Hebrews will say, You are contradicting the very promise that made us a nation. This promise is given in many forms (2 Chr. 20 : 7 ; Is. 41 : 10 ;) but with his usual terseness of appeal Paul chooses one of them. Samuel had said, " The Lord will not forsake His people " (1 Sam. 12 : 22) ; and Paul defends himself, actually using the same word, ἀπώθω (to *reject*), and defends himself boldly, broadly making the appeal, **" Has God cast off His people ? "** and answers that appeal out of their own Scriptures, and in three particulars. (1) First, God had not "*cast off His people*" in the sense that none of them could be saved ; at least it was not for him to think so, for he was of that "*people* "* and he was claiming to be both a saint and an apostle. It raises a smile, however, to see the covert logic that is included under this starting out of the reply. What did they care for Paul ? Not the Gentiles, to be sure, but the Jews, for whom these sentences were given ! The very point that he had to establish was that he was a saint and an apostle. It spreads a broad humor over his speech when we remember how he shuts them in by a sharp dialectic. Either he was a saint, and then his first point is gained, that " *God has* (not) *cast off His people* " in such a sense that all of them must perish, or else he was not a saint, and the more execrable his apostate character, the more thoroughly was it true that " *God* (had) *cast off His peo-*

---

* He was not only "**an Israelite,**" but born so ; and not only "of **Abraham's seed,**" but, what was further significant, he was "**of the tribe of Benjamin,**" a house that was the least contaminated by dispersion and exile.

ple" in the exact sense that he taught, viz., that some of them were not "*elect*" (v. 5), and that only the remnant were of the seed of Israel (v. 7).

(2) The second point was bolder yet. "*God* (had not) *cast off His people*" in any sense which was not originally intended :—

2. God has not cast off His people whom He foreknew;—

And he quotes for this far back in the time of Elijah—"in Elijah" as the saying is ; that is, in the speeches and the annals of that greatest Old Testament seer. Do not impeach me of wrong when I teach that a great number of Jews will perish ; and do not say that "*God has cast off His people*" in a sense in which He promised not to (1 Sam. 12: 22), and in a sense in which He defined a "*people*" in His mind as a "**people whom He foreknew;**" for as far back as the time of Elijah He contemplated utter losses from among the Jews. "Or;" this is the way he begins his statement. "*God has not cast away His people*" whom He ever intended or marked to be His people ; "*or*," is it that you are thoughtless of the facts ?—

2.—Or, know you not what the Scripture says in Elias, how he talks with God against Israel, 3. Lord, they have killed thy prophets, they have digged down thine altars, and I only am left, and they seek my life. 4. But what says the oracle unto Him? I have left unto myself seven thousand men who have not bowed the knee to Baal. 5. So, therefore, also at the present time there are those left according to an election of grace.

"**Talks with God.**" "*Intercession*" (E. V.) is too strong a word. Elijah would not pray against his people. (See ἐντυγχάνω, Xen. Mem. 3, 2, 1). Χρηματισμός is not an "*answer of God*" (E. V. & Re.) ; and though it may be resolved into that, yet why not say literally an "**oracle**"? "**Left**" (vs. 4, 5). It is well to connect by the same English, words from the same root (λείπω). Where the argument is documentary, it brightens the connecting link. "**To Baal.**" *Baal* has the article, and the article is feminine ; but that does not warrant us in translating "*to the image of Baal*" (E. V.). For though εἰκών ("*image*") is feminine, so is Baal sometimes (1 Sam. 7 : 4 ; Hos. 2 : 8 ; Zeph. 1 : 4). Besides, if it meant "*the image of Baal*"(E. V.), it would be more likely to stand τῇ τοῦ Βάαλ, as Baal has always the article (see Alford).

In all the reasoning of the apostle he has not lost sight of the idea of "**grace.**" He has stripped it of its wantonness He has written that exquisite chapter, the ninth, so gentle, and so much abused. He has caused God's goodness to pass before us by uttering that marked text "*I will have mercy on whomsoever I can have mercy.*" He has spoken of foreknowledge, and said "*whom He did foreknow, them He also planned out beforehand*" (8 : 29). And yet neither by the restriction of what he calls "*that which is possible for God*" (9 : 22), nor by the marking out by foreknowledge of what will suit as an "**election**" among the people, has he robbed God of "*grace.*" He has looked at the whole manward, and said, This and that and a thousand other things are not saving, but man determines the question of salvation by the instrument of "*faith*" (Heb. 11 : 6). And yet, confused as these considerations might come to be, he keeps a clear thread of understanding held fast among them all. "*Faith*" does not interfere with "*grace,*" for "*faith*" itself is a gift of the Redeemer. Moreover "*faith*" is a recognition of "*grace.*" *Foreknowledge* (8 : 29) does not interfere with "*grace,*" for foreknowledge is the mere omniscience of the Almighty, determining, in His eternal purpose, its gracious objects. All these things make "*grace*" more complete. And, therefore, with its entire voluntariness, and its entire goodness, and its entire wisdom built upon the largest preconception of the result, Paul makes a parenthesis not quite in the forthright line of the other reasoning. He is led off into it by that word "*grace.*" (1) "*God has not cast away His people,*" for He has not cast away me. Moreover (2), He "*has not cast away His people,*" in any sense, whom He "*foreknew,*" and for this Paul had called into the account abundance of their writings. He is to present (3) a third point (v. 11); but before he reaches it he goes off upon a side consideration.

6. But if it be of grace, then it is no more of works; otherwise grace is no more grace.

The whole system of the Jews is toppled over by this assertion. Paul's bitterness against "*works*" expends itself usually in two directions; first, upon that whole system of "*works*" which could be brought about in a man by the mere *direction* of the law; and, second, that maze of ceremonies which had grown to be a trust. Paul is not so often as we think alluding to the *merit* of works, or a trust to any *perfect* righteousness which could satisfy the law, but he is denying certain *sources* of holiness. Good works cannot spring up by the mere teaching of the law (2 Cor. 3 : 6); nor could good works be engendered by the mere emblems of the gospel (Gal. 5 : 6). "**If it be of grace.**" That is "*if it be grace.*" It is the *material dative.* "*By*" (E. V. & Re.) is just the furthest word possible. "**Then it is no more of works.**" "It is no more *out of* works." The word is ἐκ. If faith in the soul is even itself a "*grace*," then "*it is no more from works.*" That is, to state it in its simplest sense, "*works*" in the soul are themselves a "*grace*," and, therefore, must be engendered graciously; all that Paul would deny is that, first, the decalogue, and, second, and least, the ceremonies of the Jews, could *teach* a man "*faith*," instead of his resorting for it directly and at once to the "*grace*" of the Divine Redeemer.

The parenthesis would be too heavy if the remainder of the verse (E. V.; see the MSS.) were allowed, but all seem satisfied that that is spurious.

Paul goes on then to the very harshest quotations. It is natural that he should do so. He would not choose such language if it were his own, but he is assailing them out of their own Scriptures. What he is laboring to beat down is the idea that God has not cast away His people in a sense of giving over to death millions of Israelitish worshipers. In the quotations, dreadful things appeared: first, that men were damned who were seeking not to be; second, that in this process of damnation God actually "**hardened**" their hearts; third, that He did this by giving them "**a spirit of slumber;**"

and, fourth, and worst of all, that saints, delivered by what Paul calls "*grace*," are to rejoice, or, what seems to be the meaning, are to exult and to imprecate curses, and that in the most unfeeling and bitter form.

Here, of course, is a passage where the cause for calling it up, and the responsibility for defending it, are quite different things. Paul is talking of a people who were already beginning their schemes to destroy him. His strong point was their own law. He could only tenderly appeal where they held divine truth, taught from childhood, and sounding in set sentences of speech in their synagogues and on every Sabbath. Provoke them as he might, he never could provoke them as against their law. When, therefore, the time had come when such a thing as a lost Jew must be acknowledged, and that not simply by a Gentile, but the rather and as a far more important thing, under the teaching of an inspired apostle, by the true Israelite, and even by the lost Jew himself, it was a thing to be supposed that he would pick out strong verses; and if their bitterness was to be explained, he would leave that to the skill of their scribes, only pressing the fixed and the inevitable in his quotation :—

7. What then? That which Israel seeks for, that he obtained not; but the election obtained it, and the rest were hardened. 8. Even as it is written, God has given unto them a spirit of slumber, eyes not to see, and ears not to hear unto this day. 9. And David says,—

Let their table become a snare and a chase,
And a stumbling-block and a punishment unto them;
10. Let their eyes be darkened that they may not see,
And bow down their back always.

Comment, however, may follow the more immediate polemic. The ruder the assault upon their prejudices, the better. And as missiles are sometimes left rough, in order that they may tear the wound, so Paul counts it sufficient to quote their own books, and leave the terrible sentences to go in unexplained. And yet he himself, and especially in that ninth chapter, has given the means of explanation. (1) God has indeed refused what His people deliberately sought after; but Paul has already shown, that, in the first place, the object that they sought was wrong, viz., "*a law of righteousness*" (9 : 30), rather than righteousness itself ; and, second, that the method was mistaken; they sought it not by faith (9: 32). (2) In regard to "*an election*," and in regard to "*an election*" which seemed to have the hard character of an arbitrary choice (9 : 15, 22), Paul has smoothed that entirely. He has represented it, and that in a very intelligent manner, as guided by foreknowledge. "*Whom He did foreknow them He also planned beforehand*"(8: 29); and then, to show exactly how that foreknowledge operated, he has left us to see that it did not interfere with His sovereignty, but that it guided it, and the *vis a tergo* in all kingship being His love, it led Him into those mysterious depths (8: 38, 39) which could not be revealed to men (Ex. 33: 23), but in respect to which He had long ago given assurance to Moses that He would foreknow as men and elect as saints and convert as sinners the last man of the race that was possible in His eternal Kingdom. This was a large excuse. But to the Corinthians he had gone further. He had explained (3) what was meant by *hardening* the heart (2 Cor. 4: 4). James had already said (1: 13), "Let no man say when he is tempted, I am tempted of God." And Paul, in this text for the Corinthians, speaks plainer, and shows that this blinding of the sinner is altogether privative. It is not-doing, rather than doing. "In whom the God of this world" (and it is a thousand pities that this has been considered not God but the Devil)—" In whom the God of this world," that is, the Supreme, if we may follow Calvin, "hath blinded the minds of them which believe not, εἰσ τὸ μὴ αὐγάσαι, "so that there do not shine to them the light of the Gospel of the glory of Christ, who is the image of God." It would be a hard thing that God could not direct His own activities. And when He condescends to tell us that He does the best He can, and does not "*plan out*" a people till He "foreknows" the consequences (8: 29), the rhetoric after that is of little moment. If an inspired poem calls hopeless impenitence, pouring upon a people a spirit of slumber (Is. 29: 10), the harshness makes little difference after Paul has distinctly uttered those generous sentences. And so of the last point (vs. 9, 10) :— (4) Men would upset the Bible on the ground of the imprecatory Psalms (Ps. 109: 7–15, 17–20). In fact, to our surprise, Barnes, who is sober in many things, is guilty of this:— " It is not at all improbable that many of those imprecations were wrong. David was not a perfect man ; and the Spirit of inspiration is not responsible for his imperfections " (Com. Rom. *in loc.*) ! Better certainly than giving up the Bible to men's own judgment (for if David in devotional Scripture is not to be trusted, then Paul ! then anybody ! Where is the ποῦ στῶ in any of the revelation ?), is it to remember that the imperative in the East is an emphatic prediction. When I say, even in our own land, " There, now, you just go to the dogs ! " I do not mean to command, but to predict —and to deter. Christ was not urging Judas when He said, " What thou doest do quickly." And when Isaiah says, " Make the heart of this people fat " (Is. 6 : 10), he was by no means instructing in a principle of the pastoral care; but He was putting, in the acutest form, the prediction of their wickedness. This Psalm is Messianic. It is quoted from (Jo. 2: 17 ; 15: 25), and in the most express way as to the vinegar for drink (Matt. 27: 34, 48). It is utterly absurd that Christ, who was dying for the wicked, could be uttering in importunate prayer maledictions against them.

Paul, therefore, may be understood in his *purpose* (which is to show that a Jew may be miserably " cast off "), without, as the first thing, being challenged for a meaning : for not only has he taken these bitternesses from the Jews, but he himself has gone the farthest in explaining generously their hard ideas.

11. Paul comes now to his third position. He has said (1) that Jews were not "*cast off*" in the sense that none were saved. He has shown (2) that the Jews were not "*cast off*" in the sense that any perished who were " children of the promise " (9: 8). And now his position is to be (3) that the Jews were not " *cast off* " in the sense that any were, except

for a necessary purpose of God, or to bring about important consequences in the history of His Kingdom.

To develope this point he asks the categorical question :—

11. I say then, Did they stumble that they might fall?—

The evident drift of this inquiry is, Does the fall of anybody, and particularly of a Jew, take place for the fall's sake? or out of the resentment of God? or, as we are too apt to imagine, out of His "*mere* good pleasure"? Paul replies at once:—

11.—By no means; but that by their fault salvation might be to the Gentiles to provoke them to jealousy.

This chapter has seemed puerile. That one man's "**fault**" could be the "**salvation**" of another, and, above all, that a man's own sin could save him, as, for example, his being **provoked to jealousy,** seemed impossible; and we confess to a great deal of study before we could be tempted to treat the passage. We come to these results:—First (1), that Paul does not mean to teach that **he provoked the Jews to jealousy "in order to save some of them"** (v. 14). On the contrary, this was a part of the apostle's argument. The Jews were furious. They were hunting him in all parts of the earth. And well they might. He had stood by them in trampling the faith, and had incontinently turned traitor. Doubtless they attributed to him the lowest principle. Now, to handle such a case demanded unspeakable carefulness. We have seen how he pleaded against them their chiefest idol; I mean "*the law,*" which the Jew was always worshiping. Quoting from that is the strength of our epistle. It is an unnoticed cleverness in Paul how he turns against them their own furious feeling. He does not conceive it broadly, or flash it on them in an ungoverned sense; but he unearths it out of their own Law-giver. Who notices the sentence "*I will provoke you to jealousy by them that are no people*" (10 : 19 ; Deut. 32 : 21)? Paul's recurrence to that very word παραζηλόω, is, very much like all his other sentences, an appeal to their cherished writings. If he were not persecuted, he would not be a prophet. And, therefore, he returns to the expression. In the present text, it does not mean that their fault was the heathen man's salvation, in such a sense as that, by a sort of ricochet, in saving him it might save them also ; but simply that it was fulfilling their Scripture. We cannot see that it was a wholesome thought that provoking a man to jealousy would save him. But we do see that rousing the Jew to the discovery that his very fury was predicted, and that, as is expressed again just below, Paul might by his ministry to the Greeks provoke him, as the prophets had foretold, and also save him (v. 14), would be consistent teaching, and strictly in the vein of all Paul's Old Testament appeals.

But then on the other hand (2), one man's fall being another man's recovery, if not too broadly stated, holds out a thought easily discernible in many Scriptures. Every man's fate is to minister to the gospel. If he lives, he will bless ; if he dies, he will not curse (Lu. 19 : 24). Solomon has this thing in wonderful cleverness of speech. He calls the saved man the rich ; and he calls the lost man the poor. And he does this in many unnoticed and gospel asseverations (Prov. 28 : 8, 11 ; 29 : 16, see Com.). " The rich and the poor meet together," he says, the idea being that they are necessary in the developments of heaven. And he adds, confirming his profound idea, "the Lord is the Maker of them all " (Prov. 22 : 2).

Now in this epistle to the Romans it is not hard to illustrate these important considerations. Paul says, " *For this very purpose* (viz., one of " *mercy*," v. 16), *have I raised thee up, that I might show in thee my power* " (v. 17). The old prophets spoke of giving " men for them " (Is. 43 : 4). And Paul says, " But if God, willing to explain the wrath, &c., &c.," (9 : 22). Temperately, and in carefully expressed ways, we are to learn from the passage that the damnation of Israel, like every other historical event, would be overruled for good, and that the contumely of the Jews would not interrupt, but further, the breaking down of walls, and the broader dissemination of Messiah's mysteries.

"**But**" (δέ) is the next word in the Greek. Paul is expecting to explain, not only that they did not stumble for the very sake of the fall, but as Jews nationally they had not stumbled that they should fall at all. They had lapsed, or been guilty of a "*fault*," but their purpose as a people had all to be fulfilled. We must understand, as incident to the whole, that "*glory, honor and peace* (was to be) *to the Jew first*" (Rom. 2 : 10). The gospel was to begin at Jerusalem (Lu. 24 : 47). Judaism was not to lose by its harsh tutelage; but for generations to come was to furnish root and branch in the great "**olive tree.**" And if its casting away was to be helpful to the Greek, more abundantly, by every principle of light, its return would be, whenever in any age or place it discerned the gospel. This is what Paul is busy upon in the verse that follows:—

12. But if their fault be wealth for a world, and their loss wealth for Gentiles, how much more their fulness!

13. "**But**" is the opening word. Paul seems to remember that he is speaking not to the Jews, but rather in the great Western Capital to a Gentile mass. He ventures the same ideas therefore in an adjusted method:—

13. But I am speaking to you Gentiles. On the one hand, therefore, to the degree that I am an apostle of Gentiles I honor my ministry. 14. If in any way I provoke to jealousy my own flesh, and save some of them.

Such influences were honorable in themselves. The **provoking** was prophesied of (see 10 : 19), and the **saving** had already begun, and one, as we have seen, is not to be connected too closely with the other. "**I honor my ministry**" because or "**for**"—

15. For, if the casting away of them be a reconciling of a world, what shall the receiving be but a life from among the dead?

The rescue should be rejoiced in as for itself.

16. "**On the other hand**" we should suspect as much from all the array of the history. Israel had always been a holy nation to God. God had always converted all the true Israel. Paul had put his hand upon the key when he had asserted

that there was much advantage in being a Jew, and explained it by the one speech that "*the oracles were believed*" (3 : 2). That was the acme of their blessing. Not that they were converted as a race ; but that they were converted as a race more than any other. And that this work would go on. "*On the other hand ;*" (δέ) responding to the μέν of the thirteenth. "*On the one hand*" Paul's ministry was honorable as diverted from his race, and "*on the other*" it was hopeful as to that race itself, because now and for some time after, there was every sign in that race itself of eminent blessing, because,—

16. On the other hand if the first fruits be holy, then also the lump; and if the root be holy, then also the branches.

This seems to be a profound acknowledgment that holiness in one age of a land is to bless it and not curse it in another. Holiness never curses. So the idea of a first fruits was, that they were an earnest (Eph. 1 : 14). Breaking off of the lump (Num. 15 : 20, 21) meant that of the rest there should be a blessing. Such was the inspired metaphor. And the Jews responded to it in their present condition. They still had advantages (3 : 1, 2). Having furnished all converts in the past, they furnished most in the present. And Paul, from the general principles of grace, would argue, not that all Jews would be saved, for Judaism in a very serious respect had been "**broken off;**" not either, as some believe, that all will be who are living at the last day ; but that many might hope to be. Paul speaks in this sort of fashion :—"What knowest thou, O wife, whether thou shalt save thy husband" (1 Cor. 7 : 16)? And, again, of the progeny of such a marriage, "Now are (your children) holy" (v. 14) ; by which he does not mean that the children would be saved (any more than he intends here that all the Jews would be converted), but simply that they were likely to be saved, and "holy," therefore, in this promise. If the Jews had furnished an ἀπαρχή to God, *quoad hoc* that was a fine chance for more ; and **if the root (was) holy,**" no matter how far back the piety, so might "**the branches**" be, and so would they be likely to be, as of an ἀρραβών of grace, however hid and trampled by abounding wickedness.

This is turned over differently in his address to the Gentiles. "**If they** (the Jews) **abide not in unbelief, they shall be grafted in**" (v. 23). But that is a most important "*if;*" and it seems not much helped by the γάρ that follows :—("**For) God is able to graft them in again.**" But let us translate the eight verses :—

17. **But if some of the branches were broken off, and thou, being a wild olive, wast grafted in among them, and becamest partaker of the root of the fatness of the olive,** 18. **Boast not against the branches; but whether thou boast, it is not thou the root bearest, but the root thee.** 19. **Thou wilt say then, Branches were broken off that I might be grafted in.** 20. **Good; by unbelief they were broken off, and thou standest by faith. Be not high-minded, but fear.** 21. **For if God spared not the natural branches, neither will He spare thee.** 22. **Behold, therefore, goodness and severity in God ; upon them that fell, severity, but upon thee, God's goodness, if thou remainest in the goodness; otherwise then thou also shalt be cut off.** 23. **But they also, if they remain not in unbelief, shall be grafted in ; for God is able to graft them in again.** 24. **For if thou wert cut out of the olive, wild by nature, and wast grafted, against nature, into a good olive tree, how much rather shall they who are natural be grafted into their own olive tree.**

17. "**The olive.**" This is Paul's only mention of "*the olive*" as an emblem of the church. But Zechariah (Zech. 4: 12), and John (Rev. 11 : 4), the former long before, and the latter long after, have quite established the metaphor. "**Grafted.**" There is no *grafting* in a way like this. *Grafting* is from a good tree set upon a bad. Paul reverses the figure ; some say from a habit in the East. But if wild branches were set upon a decayed stock, and both were freshened (see Hodge), that still would not be the gospel. Christ is anything but decayed. Besides, we doubt the result. And it would be what Paul disowns. The branch would be bearing the root, and not the root the branch (v. 18). The main

feature of a graft is, that, "**broken off**" from one tree, it will grow upon another. The Gentile "*broken off*" from his own people, is to grow upon the Jews, that is upon that Great Jew. There had "**come out of Zion the Deliverer**" (v. 26). A Great Jew had become church,—Head and members (Eph. 1 : 23). And natural Jews had been "*broken off*," that *inward* Jews (2 : 29) might be "*grafted in.*" Paul builds a challenge to universal humanity. 18. "**Thou bearest not the root.**" There is an ellipsis in the passage. "**If thou boast,**" remember— or "**if thou boast,**" alas for you ! "*Thou bearest not the root, but the root thee.*" 20. "**Good :**" a very strong Greek expression (καλῶς) "*beautiful ;* " or, as we would say, "*exactly !* " This Paul applies to their conceit,—"**The branches were broken off that I might be grafted in.**" "*Exactly so,*" says the apostle. But the whole difference is made by "**faith,**" and that is a loving recognition of the grace of the Sanctified. 21. "**For if God spared not the natural branches**" (κατὰ φύσιν). This word φύσις is chameleon-like. Men are said to be "*Jews by nature*" (Gal. 2 : 15), which means, as here, "*natural branches*," which have actually to be "*broken off*,"—so naturally do they come under the grace of God. Men are said to be dead "by nature" (Eph. 2 : 3), which means, much more emphatically, by birth and reality lost. Men are said to "*do by nature the things contained in the law*" (2 : 14), which is heaven-wide again. Men "*by nature*" (v. 21) do no such thing. "*By nature*," though it is the same word φύσις, means in that second chapter "*by natural evidences*," or "*under the teaching of natural facts*" (Rom. 1 : 20). We must be on our guard, therefore, about φύσις wherever we see it. 22. "**Otherwise.**" Ἐπεί does not mean "*otherwise.*" "*Otherwise*" is the proper word to supply, but it is another case of ellipsis. "**Then**" is the sense of ἐπεί. And with "*otherwise*" supplied we arrive at the legitimate sense. "*Otherwise* (then) grace is no more grace" (Rom. 11 : 6). "Otherwise (then) it is of no strength at all" (Heb. 9 : 17) ; and so in the present passage, "**otherwise, then, thou also shalt be cut off.**" 23. "**For God is able ;**" δυνατός, the word previously noticed (9 : 22). There is nothing that forbids Him. It will be consistent and actually the fact that many shall be saved.

25. This consistency which man could not certainly determine, namely that God could still save Jews, and not let them be absolutely cursed, Paul wraps up under the name of a "**mystery,**" which is an old name for anything that required a special revelation. It could not be known beforehand that "**blindness** (only) **in part** (would happen) **unto Israel, while the fulness of the Gentiles was being gathered in.**" Paul approaches this with one of his set phrases of appeal :—"**I do not wish you not to know.**"

25. For I do not wish you, brethren, not to know this mystery, lest your thoughtfulness be confined to yourselves, that blindness in part has happened to Israel while the fulness of the Gentiles be entering in.

What is the real fact about the gospel? There is no arrest, as far as is doctrinally revealed, of the full gospel to both Jews and Gentiles (1: 16). There is no cessation of grace (10: 11, 13). There is no advantage to the Jew except that many believed (3: 2). And there is no supplanting by the Greek, except that Jew and Gentile were alike brought into the Kingdom (10: 12). We utterly deny a prospective in-sweeping of the Israelites. And if any one begs us for an immediate reason, we answer, Because Christ puts us on our immediate guard lest the Judgment surprise us at any moment. How can that be true, and all these other things? We believe there is no prophecy in the New Testament Scriptures. And if anyone is shocked at this, we beg him to begin back at the original idea. If any moment may usher the Redeemer in the clouds (Matt. 24: 44; Lu. 12: 40; 21: 34, 35), and the dead, small and great, may be judged, what mockery to stuff the time with events. We believe there is no Millennium. We believe there is no personal reign. We believe there is no solidarity for the Jew, or geographic trifling about the rocks of Palestine. And we beg any one who testifies his disgust, simply to answer one question,—How can I be listening for the trumpet (1 Cor. 15: 52), or waiting for my Lord in "the air"

(1 Thess. 4: 18), or supposing in my short life that the dead may be raised (1 Thess. 4: 17), when there are shoals of unfinished events, and the "*seals*" and the "*viols*" and millennial splendor of the church and the restoration of the tribes and the terracing of Palestine, are all to be interpolated before my rising? If I had to be hanged, and it might be instantly, and the knock at my cell be at any moment, it would have a queer influence to know that a new jail had to be built, and no end of events happen before I or anyone else could ascend the scaffold. We believe all these unveilings are pictorial gospels, and, as in this very passage that we treat, there is some Greek that turns aside the superstition that has been imagined.

"**Confined to yourselves.**" There is a difficulty about the MSS. The majority read παρά (E. V.). The weightier read ἐν (Re.), and are adopted by later scholars. The expression φρόνιμοι ἐν or φρόνιμοι παρά is exceedingly important in another passage (12: 16). We do not think the meaning "*wise in your own conceits*" (E. V. & Re.) brings out the mind that was intended. The word παρά means *before*, as *before* a judge (see Jelf). The meaning of the apostle seems to be that we are not to be **thoughtful** *nobis judicibus*. And as making ourselves the judge is very apt to make the award *for ourselves*, this seems to be the main idea of the reasoning. Don't imagine the Jew to be given up, lest ye be thoughtful only for yourselves. Solomon says, "Be not wise by thine own eyes" (Prov. 3 : 7 ; LXX. παρὰ σεαυτῷ), that is, by looking at things through your own vision. And when we come to the important passage (12: 16), we shall find that this understanding is vital. Paul will be giving a recipe for rejoicing with them that do rejoice, and weeping with those that weep; and he will end causally in this, "Be not thoughtful for (παρά) yourselves."
"**Blindness in part.**" That is, the Jews, like everyone else, are some of them saved and some of them lost. "**While.**" Not "*until*" (E. V. & Re.). Here is where the "*Restoration*" idea is imagined. "Ἄχρις οὗ may mean "*while*" (Heb. 3: 13; 2 Macc. 14: 10). So may the aorist subjunctive, εἰσέλθῃ, have the

bearing imputed to it (Jelf, §. 401, 3, Obs. 1). "**And so all Israel shall be saved.**" Jews are to be gathered "*while*" Gentiles are being gathered; and so "*all Israel*," not in the " Restoration " sense, but in the widest sense (Jo. 10: 16), Jews and Gentiles, are to be converted and gathered in. " *The children of the flesh, those same are not children of God* "(9: 8). " They are not all Israel that are of Israel "(9: 6). " He is not a Jew who is one outwardly" (2: 28). And, therefore, Paul has given us abundant scope to look for such passages as this. "*All Israel*" (will have been) *saved*" when Jews have been going in "*while*" Gentiles were going in, and all Jews "*inwardly*" (2: 29), whether Greeks or Israelites, shall have accepted each his place in the everlasting Kingdom.

26. And so all Israel shall be saved"—

Now there is a further logic in the clause that follows. Paul had said that God never "*foreknew*" any other Israel than the men who were converted. He draws in now the further thought that the very "**covenant**" of God was expressed and intended only "**when** (he took) **away their sins**":—

26.—As it has been written:—
  There will come out of Zion the Deliverer;
  He will turn away ungodlinesses from Jacob.
27. And this covenant with them on my part
  Is when I take away their sins.

Paul quotes pregnantly; sometimes from three or four passages digested into one. He has in this quotation three or four points to fix. First, that salvation comes out of Zion. There were in the Old Testament Scriptures two beautiful figures—one Moriah, the other Zion. These landmarks are kept well apart in Scripture. Moriah was the temple site, and the temple was for the exhibition of the Almighty. David memorably expresses it when he says, " In His temple every whit of it (marg.) uttereth glory" (Ps. 29: 9). The Jew, when he wanted to inquire, inquired in the temple (Ps. 27: 4). Zion was a very different metaphor. Zion was the seat of kingship. Moreover, it was the seat of kingship that was granted to

Jerusalem. When the King came in person, He began at Jerusalem (Lu. 24: 47). When the apostles began to minister, it was "*to the Jew first*" (Acts 3: 26). And there was great wisdom in this. Paul, when he inquired for synagogues (Acts 13: 5; 14: 1), knew where were the great key-points. And this eminent beginning was often prophesied. " The Lord bless thee out of Zion " (Ps. 134 : 3). " The Lord shall send the rod of thy strength out of Zion " (110 : 2). These were all sources for the inspired quotation. The song exclaims, " Oh that salvation were come out of Zion " (Ps. 14 : 7). And Paul, as the first thing, was quick in the concession that the Jews began the light, and sent it prosperously out of their Holy Hill. But, secondly, the very object of the light was to turn them from their transgressions. They were no favorites of the Prince, but enemies. This was wonderfully marked in all the prophetic passages. " The Redeemer (should) come to Zion," but how? not to the Jews as Jews, but distinctly as is summarized in Paul's quotation, " To them that turn from transgression in Jacob " (Is. 59 : 20). And, third, the very term of the "**covenant,**" and that anciently delivered, was that it was only a "*covenant*" with the actual subjects of its blessings. " This is the covenant that I will make with the house of Israel,—I will put my law in their inward parts " (Jer. 31 : 33). Recollect ; this was their own Old Testament script. And it agreed with all the rest of his positions. " *God* (had) *not cast away His people whom He foreknew* " (11 : 2) ; and Paul, obscurely somewhat. because he is brief, takes in all these bearings under that word " when " (v. 27). " **And this covenant with them on my part is when I take away their sins."**

28. According to the gospel, indeed, they are enemies for your sakes ; but according to the election they are beloved for the fathers' sake.

We are shown the folly of " electing love " as conceived of as a distinct affection. There are but two loves, *benevolence* and *esteem ;* I mean but two sorts, outside of family affection ; and what a fine support to this idea that we find God in this particular sentence loving and hating the same people. We have already explained (9 : 13) that this rhetoric of inspired men is a terse way of expressing a mere likeness to love, in the matter of its consequence. " All they that hate me love death " (Prov. 8: 36). "**According to the gospel,**" that is, the great announced facts of the heavenly message, "**they are enemies for your sake.**" That is, they will perish, like their fathers, if they do not believe ; and perish in certain discoverable senses for the sake of you Gentiles ; that is, in opening your way ; just as all the buried talents are given to all the improved talents (Matt. 25 : 28) in ten thousand senses in nature and in grace. "**But according to the election,**" that is, for the very purpose for which they were originally chosen, and with the same results as have always happened, the Jew will gain by his original calling as a people. They had furnished the very Christ of prophecy, and the very saints for all the apostleships.

29. For the gifts and calling of God are without repentance ;

And if they did not continue to be first, it must be, like death in the Wilderness (Josh. 5 : 4), in strange contrast with their triumphs at Migdol.

30. For as you once did not believe God, but now have obtained mercy, these being unbelieving, 31. So also now these have been unbelieving, that with your obtaining mercy they also might obtain mercy.

" *Through* " (E. V.) and " *by* " (Re.) are unnecessarily strong in both these verses, for there is no ἐκ or διά, and the nouns are in the dative. The dative often implies the mere condition of the circumstances (see Goodwin). That is enough. We, therefore, employ the participle. "**These being unbelieving.**" We might exaggerate beyond the sense the idea of the sin of the Jews as promoting grace for the Gentiles.

32. For God has shut up all in unbelief that He might have mercy upon all.

So Paul finishes this catholic argument. "**All**" is a very favorite word with him. We are *all* sinners (3 : 23), and *all* punishable for sin (2 : 9), and *all* people that may believe (1 : 16); we are *all* equal under the law (2: 11), and *all* open to the gospel (10 : 12, 13). We are *all* certain to reject it (1 Cor. 2 : 14). We are *all* instructed by the law (2: 14), and *all* incapable of being saved by it (Gal. 2: 21). We must *all* be saved by works (2 : 13), but we must *all* be led to do them by grace (8 : 7 ; 10 : 4), and not by the mere commandment (3 : 20 ; 8 : 3). " Works of the law " in the sense of what the law could stir us up to do, no one will perform (3 : 19), and therefore by the law, left nakedly to itself, is only " the knowledge of sin " (3 : 20). *All* Israel will be saved in the sense that God ever intended Israel (11 : 26). *All* else will perish (11 : 7). *All* will perish from unbelief (9 : 32) ; and *all* not directly but by His **" knowledge "** (v. 33) beforehand **" God has shut up in unbelief;"** so that *all* who are saved are objects of His regenerating **" mercy."**

33. O the depth of the riches both of the wisdom and knowledge of God! how unsearchable are His judgments, and His ways past finding out! 34. For who has known the mind of the Lord? or who has been His counselor? 35. Or who has first given to Him and will have it returned to him again? 36. For out of Him and by means of Him and with respect to Him are all things. To Him be the glory forever. Amen.

CHAPTER XII.

1. I beseech you, therefore, brethren, by the mercy of God—

I am careful of this collocation. I wish to bring out all the beauties of the passage. If I had translated certain verses (see chap. 9) as they have always been translated, no wonder that this appeal should go on escaping us. What have we been taught to believe ? Why, that God does as He pleases ; not in the sense of a *wise* pleasure, or, if we might properly understand it, of the *good* pleasure of Heaven, but in a sense that has utterly destroyed Paul's beautiful argument. Paul had summoned one of the spectacles of the gray past (Ex. 33 : 18-23). No one was more familiar with the deep things of the Almighty. Doubtless he understood those pictures of Solomon, " It is the glory of Gods to cover over a thing, but the glory of Kings to search a thing out "(Prov. 25 : 2). This passage of our epistle is cousin-german to the words that follow : " The heavens as to height, and the earth as to depth, and the heart of Kings there is no searching " (Prov. 25 : 3). Now, remembering that God was exhibiting this same truth in dramatic scenery, hiding the Law-giver in a rock and printing on him the symbol that only God's " back parts " could be revealed, it seems a distressing failure that the whole point of this should be lost by our ruinous English. God had said, " Only a whisper can be heard of (me) " (Job. 26 : 14). Solomon had said, God would like to save everybody. It is the glory of God to cover things, but of God as King to search them out. Paul breaks out in the words we have rendered, **" O the depth of the riches both of the wisdom and knowledge of God! How unsearchable are His judgments,"** covering over sorrow with the black pall that Solomon threw over the King. What a shame it is that when God gave the Lawgiver the only possible light, and Solomon repeated it, and Paul quoted it as his text, we should have so lucklessly quenched it all. God is absolutely mysterious ; but what matters that, if He saves all He can ? Paul had multiplied this in splendid verses. God cannot explain, but He can assert. And He has said " *I will have mercy on whomsoever I can have mercy.*" And Paul elaborates it, that Providence is an abyss, but that this light plays over it. He is doing all that is "*possible for Him* " (9 : 22). What could He do more than He is striving to accomplish ? (Is. 5 : 4). It is not of the willing but of the mercy showing God (9 : 16). And Paul sums up with another glorious assumption ;—" *One man whom He has a desire after He shows mercy to, and another man whom He has a desire after He hardens* "(9 : 18), leaving us to the sad conclusion that the same merciful sun needfully produces calm and tempest.

1. "**I beseech you, therefore, by the mercies of God.**" With the comments we have given this is a glorious appeal. Why quarrel with so kind a King? "**How unsearchable are His judgments!**" And yet, under that black night, He lets this flash out to us,—I am doing the best I can. " The heart of Kings is unsearchable," but down in its hid depths this I will reveal, that even in such a thing as eternal death, it is all that can be arranged : I am "not willing that any should perish; " and, still, eternal sorrow is as necessary as the very substance of my being.

These things in God are also the great things in man. Benevolence and love of holiness, which are the philosophical translations of love to man and love to God, are what the Proverb calls "chains about our neck" (Prov. 1: 9). Heaven would be impossible without this chamber of man's best being. And as to the Almighty, these same two commandments supply His life. They give Him a reason to be. He would not create without them. They supply His name, "God is love." They supply a heaven to us ; for we shall rejoice at the memory of His holiness. They supply a heaven to Him. For God could not be happy, any more than His creation, unless He had Himself to think of, and Himself in that noblest part, His boundless affection for all His creatures.

Now Paul puts his finger upon the noblest incentive to good works when he writes that appeal, "*By the mercies of God.*" Here is a King under enormous difficulties, with a boundless administration, over unending Kingdoms of life and light. There are puzzles in such an administration that no archangel could fathom. We might know that there would be. God confesses them. He admits that there must be "exceeding greatness of power," even in our poor world, to save us who believe. Out of the darkness of such a system He cannot explain, but He can protest. And He places before our minds for worship that sweetest of all conceptions, a God that has done the best for everything since the world was made; a God that would be broken-hearted if He had not; a God propped up by the expression "What could have been done more for my vineyard that I have not done in it?" infinite in possession, if not now, hereafter, and infinite in work, if not here, in the ages future, and yet, more than any mother, pitying the lost, and yearning over him as though there were none but he, and doing everything on earth He can to save from perishing the poorest and meanest of the sinful. Paul's appeal, therefore, is based upon the body of his epistle;—"*I beseech you, therefore, brethren, by the mercies of God.*"—

1.—That ye present your bodies a living sacrifice, holy, acceptable to God, which is your reasonable service.

Christ was obedient in His death. We must be obedient in our life. "**Reasonable.**" The reasons we have been giving. "If God so loved us, we ought also to love one another" (1 Jo. 4: 11).

2. And be not conformed to this world, but be ye transformed in the renewing of the mind, that you may approve what is the will of God, good and acceptable and perfect.

"**World;**" (αἰών), literally meaning *age*. There may be a thought of that; for the "*world*" is better than its people. But αἰών and κόσμος can hardly make out the distinction, for they are occurring similarly. Love not the κόσμος, John says (1 Jo. 2: 15); so that we must give up the formal distinction. "**Renewing;**" a *material dative*. "**Be ye transformed,**" not "**by the renewing**" (E. V. & Re.), but, as though it were *beth essentiæ*, "*Be ye transformed*" in that shape, so that it shall consist "*in the renewing of the mind.*" "**Approve.**" Not "*prove*" (E. V. & Re.). "*Approve*" is nearer to the sense. The greatest change upon our planet is that by which men learn to "*approve*" God (Job 42: 6).

3. For I say, by the grace given unto me, to every one that is among you, that he think not of himself more highly than he ought to think, but that he think so as to think soberly, according as God has distributed to each a measure of faith.

Paul gives himself as a clinic. Intending to refer everything to "**grace**," he gives himself as an example; for he implies that it is "**by the grace given unto** (him)" that he is led to instruct. Because, as one must be "*transformed in the renewing of the mind*" before one could "*approve*" either God or man, so now all thought or act is to have its "**measure**" in the amount of "**faith.**" "**Of himself**" is not in the Greek, but ὑπερφρονεῖν means to be *high-minded* (see the Lexicons). Paul intends to forbid estimating anything above the measure of its piety. We are all members of Christ, and are to estimate our doings only as they flow from Him.

4. For as we have many members in one body, but all the members have not the same office, 5. So we who are many are one body in Christ, but, as regards each, members one of another 6. But having gifts differing according to the grace which is given to us, whether prophecy, according to the proportion of faith, 7. Or service, in the service, or the teacher, in the teaching, 8. Or the exhorter, in the exhortation, the giver, in simplicity, the ruler, in diligence, the mercy-shewer, in cheerfulness.

Such is the Greek; and the mass of italics (E. V.) continued in the Revision, are quite without warrant. And, at any rate, where is the great point in saying, "*Or ministry, let us wait on our ministering*"? The apostle is showing that we must estimate ourselves "*according to the grace given.*" He teaches that we are not to boast in being members of Christ, but to ask, What sort of members? He sees that the members of the mystical church have very different office; and claims that each particular office be measured by its "*grace*"; "**prophecy, by its faith; service** (by its) **service; the teacher** by his actual **teaching; the giver,** by a sweet **simplicity; the ruler, by diligence; the mercy-shewer, by cheerfulness.**" Through this hard-pan measuring, which is up from the bottom and down to a basis in the actual grace, Paul illustrates our thinking soberly, and rates successful service "*as God has given to everyone the measure of faith*" (v. 3).

9. Let love be without hypocrisy.

CHAPTER XII.

Notice the grammar of the apostle. Just below (v. 15) it will be exceedingly important. Participles should have their proper sense ; for that will give us long sentences of an explanatory kind, instead of our chopping up the chapter into short imperatives.

9.—Abhorring that which is evil ; cleaving to that which is good ; 10. In love of the brethren being tenderly affectionate to each other ; in honor preferring one another ; 11. Not slow in diligence ; fervent in the spirit ; serving the Lord ; 12. Rejoicing in hope ; patient in tribulation ; urgent in prayer ; 13. Participating in the necessities of the saints ; hunting up ways to be kind to strangers ; 14. Bless them that persecute you ; bless and curse not.

"**Abhorring.**" The "evil" meant is the only positively abhorrent "*evil.*" The word "**tenderly affectionate**" (φιλόστοργοι) means, usually, affection of near kindred. Paul is well sustained by his Master, " For whosoever shall do the will of my Father, the same is my mother and sister and brother" (Matt. 12 : 50). "*Business*" (E. V.) is quite too free in the eleventh verse. The word is σπουδή, and there can be no objection to what is literal, viz. *haste*, "**diligence.**" Important MSS. have καιρῷ (" *time* "), which would make quite a different meaning. But "**serving the Lord**" (κυριῷ) has the precedence of claim ; and the usual objection that it would break what is special into a clause that is too general, will not hold. In the heat of work to remember that it is for God, is quite as special as the heat or the work, and quite as needful a waking up as any point of what might seem more special duty. 12. "**Urgent**" (προσκαρτεροῦντες) means *pressing well on.* We leave our prayers too often like eggs in the sand. We are to expect, and insist, and inquire, and repeat, and in fact *claim*, when we present a petition. Jacob was προσκαρτερῶν when he became a Prince in Israel. 13. "*Communicating to*" (E. V. & Re.) is classic and common, but no more correct than "**participating in**" (see Rom. 15 : 27), and not so expressive. "**Hunting**" is more than " *ready to be kind,*" because it is a *pursuing after* occasions for it, as in the chase. It is more than for hospitality's sake in its modern sense (E. V. & Re.), for it is for φιλοξενίαν, or *love* of the *stranger*. "*Hospitality*" (*hospes*) once meant that. 14. "**Bless, &c.**" Paul, usually, keeps the difficult duty to the last.

15. But now a still more necessary parsing! To give his meaning Paul takes us out of this catena of participles, and shapes an infinitive. There is created a most interesting passage. Men have swept it into the round of mere imperatives (E. V. & Re.). But why? It would not be normal. Here is a most careful writer. He carries the logic of precision to what is high-strained and artificial (Gal. 3: 16). Where could be the motive for the infinitive (καίρειν), especially if all these participles were to be taken in an imperative sense? Paul would be wearied out with a broken rhetoric; and with inevitable disgust, would recoil from such an infinitive with a jussive purpose. In fact there is no such infinitive. Καίρειν, in its use as a salutation, is altogether another thing. It is a declared and understood ellipsis. We may supply λέγω. Moderns say, "*Send greeting*," till they get tired of so much formal speech, and say simply " Greeting! " No one pretends that that gives it as a participle, and with a new efficiency. Nor can we quote Phil. 3: 16. On the contrary, that is weightily the other way. Our versions read, " Let us walk by the same rule; let us mind the same thing " (E. V. & Re.). The Revision omits the half, but *quoad* the point at issue they agree perfectly. Yet when we look at the sense, both versions are misleading. Paul is imagining two degrees of knowledge, a knowledge not yet reached, and one already imparted. He says, " As far as we be perfect let us think thus; and if in anything ye think otherwise, God will reveal even this unto you. Nevertheless whereto we have already attained, in order to walk orderly (*infinitive*) by the same rule, in order to think (*infinitive*) the same, be ye followers, brethren, of me, &c." (Phil. 3: 16, 17). Nothing could be more convincing, or could be more evincive of the purpose of the apostle. And precisely similar is his rhetoric in the present instance. He does not *wish* to command *rejoicing*, and therefore, he does not use, but scrupulously avoids, the practical impera-

ative. And he does not command, because there is a habit of holy writ which he scrupulously follows. God does indeed command us to do abstract things. He commands us to love (Matt. 22 : 37), and commands us to hate (Ps. 97 : 10), and commands us to rejoice (Phil. 4 : 4), and commands us to believe (Jo. 14 : 1); just as the ill gotten imp in the fable commands the poor man to break his faggot, without instructing him to take it apart. But God, when He comes down to practical detail, commands the more voluntary things, which lead by promise to those less under the compass of the will. For example, He commands us to repent ; but, instead of teaching us to stand up upon the floor and by a sudden spiritual wrench to enact repentance, God unravels to us the means. He tells us the great method of repentance; viz. to beg God for it. He tells us the great act of repentance, namely, to look for it to Christ. He takes to pieces the more abstract whole, and tells us to pray and to work for our soul's entire surrender unto God. And now exactly so the apostle. The infinitive was never more prescriptively in place. He does not mean, " *Rejoice with them that do rejoice* " (E. V. & Re.) ; because he is going to give directions how to do it. He does not send a man among the mourners, and say, Now "**weep:**" or among the dancers, a poor forlorn wretch, and say, Now "**rejoice ;**" but he gives the man the recipe for attaining to that which, at the start, would be impossible :—

15. In order to rejoice with them that do rejoice, and to weep with them that weep, 16. Thinking the same things for each other, not thinking high things, but being carried along by lowly things, be not thoughtful just for yourselves.

This is a Kohinoor. I don't send you to a spiritual feast-making, and command you on the spot to " *rejoice ;* " nor do I admit you to a deadly Baca, and cry out to you at once to " *weep ;* " but I give you directions for those stages of approach which fit you for the act when you arrive. **Thought** is altogether voluntary. Accustom yourself to think for other people. When you make a bargain, *think* for the other side. In scheming for your life, scheme for your clan or for your race, which is perishing. Like the very fowls on your place call up the whole brood when you find anything good. That plainly is Paul's device. **"In order to rejoice with"** other people, learn the art of thinking for them when you are thinking for yourself. And hence the Great Apostle arranges other participles with even deeper knowledge and profounder principle as among men. 16. **"Not thinking high things."** Multitudes think grand things for others; but, first, they must do grand things for themselves. Fortune first! and while that is making, they are dogs! Scholars, when they have learned, merchants, when they are rich, the Congressman, when in the Senate, or the miser, when he is dead, are all going to will great things. The apostle forbids it. **"In order to rejoice with them that do rejoice, and to weep with them that weep, thinking the same things for each other** (that is, the same for others that you do for yourself), **not thinking high things, but being carried along** (This is very expressive. Taking things as they come. Not what your heart findeth to do; not what your wit findeth to do; but "what your hand findeth to do," as Solomon says), **carried along by lowly things;"**—and then follows the imperative, **"be not thoughtful just for yourselves."**

Compare now any of our English. *"Be not wise in your own conceits"* (E. V. & Re.). What is that to the purpose? *"Be of the same mind one toward another"* (E. V. & Re.). When? and how? *"Condescend, etc."* (E. V.). Why say, *"to men,"* and thus alter the gender in the compass of a verse? The Revisers correct that much. How sad that the way toward a more thorough revision should again be sealed up, and that Paul's sweetest conceptions, like those in the ninth chapter, should fall again asleep, without any possibility of their charm being laid bare for another century.

We have already noticed the being "wise in (our) own conceit." Chapter eleventh (v. 25) is where it translates (LXX.) being "wise by (our) own eyes" (Prov. 26: 12). The preposition is παρά, and means *before*, as *before* a judge (see Jelf).

"*Thoughtful before* (ourselves)" means too exclusively *thoughtful by our own eyes*, that is, in ways as we look at it. "*Be not thoughtful just for yourselves.*" That is, give not yourselves up to those views of things which your selfish eyes will take, instructed by a lapsed conscience, and looking too closely at your own.

The apostle moves on now to another exordium, with its prepositive participles:—

17. Rendering to no man evil for evil; giving thought beforehand that honorable things as from you shall fall under the view of all men; 18. If possible, as to what is of your part, living peaceably with all men; 19. Not avenging yourselves, beloved; on the contrary, give place to wrath; for it is written, Vengeance is mine; I will repay, says the Lord.

17. "**Rendering:**" ἀποδιδόντες (see 2: 6). It need not mean *recompensing* (E. V.). He, Christ, did not *give again* (E. V.), or *give back* (Re.) the book to "the servant" (Lu. 4: 20), for probably "the servant" had not given it to Him. "**Things honorable**" (Re.); the same as "*things honest*" (E. V.) in the time of King James. The word has changed. Hence an eager idea of Paul has to a large extent gone for nothing. He wishes Christians, not only to be correct, but noble. They are to *adorn* the doctrine of God their Saviour (Tit. 2: 10). The obsolescence has spoiled other sentences. Peter says, "Having your conversation honest among the Gentiles" (1 Pet. 2: 12); and Paul,—urging it frequently:—"Providing (or thinking out beforehand) honest things" (2 Cor. 8: 21); then changing to σεμνά (venerable), "whatsoever things are honest" (Phil. 4: 8); or, changing again to εὐσχημόνως (*handsomely*), "Let us walk honestly" (13: 13). It is a pity under this ancient English to cloak all these fine texts, and especially that sentence of our Saviour "Let your light so shine before men that they may see your good works" (E. V. The word is καλά, *beautiful*. It may not be too late to change this in many parts of the Bible); "that they may see your handsome acts, and glorify your Father which is in Heaven" (Matt. 5: 16). "**As**

to **what is on your side."** You cannot regulate the other party. The Revisers still say, "*as much as lieth in you*" (E. V.). We wonder at that, for it is a tautology. Paul had already said, "**If** (it be) **possible.**" 19. "**Not avenging yourselves, beloved.**" One of the forlornest mistakes in any doctrinal ethics has grown up under this passage. It has been imagined that God may *avenge*, but not we. There has eventuated, therefore, the idea of a Vindicatory Justice, which is a primordial attribute of the Almighty. How sad the consequence! The Aztec, blackening his God, and smearing His semblance on the earth with the filth of his sacrifices, is not so blasphemous as the Christian, when, with his enlightened creed, he attributes revenge to the Most High. The difficulty is not hard to deal with. There are but two virtues. The Bible is constantly ready for that (Matt. 22: 40); and speaking of one of them it says, " Which thing is true in Him and in you " (1 Jo. 2: 8). There are but two things, accordingly, that are right either in God or man. Unless **"vengeance,"** therefore, is a primordial trait in man, it cannot possibly be in the instance of the Almighty. God and man are alike in the originals of virtue. And if the two sole righteousnesses are love to the welfare of others, and love to God, or, in God's instance, love to that which makes Him loveable, viz., the principle of holiness, where can there be anything primordial outside?

To understand our passage, accordingly, we must distinguish. "*Vengeance*" has two meanings. It is like the word *machinations*, which may begin as of what is innocent, but may end as of what is bad and bitter. "*Vengeance*" has a noble meaning (*vindicare*), and, what is more to our point, ἐκδικέω, which is what we are directly to account for, means to *set right* or to *arrange justly*. "*Vengeance*" in its bad sense we are not to consider. Or rather, as "*vengeance*" in its bad sense is a perversion of the other, Paul, in this whole passage, is giving directions about ἐκδίκησις as a dangerous and difficult work on the part of men.

In the first place, there is to be weeded out of it everything like revenge:—

20. On the contrary, if thine enemy hunger, feed him; if he thirst, give him drink—

We can illustrate revenge here with absolute clearness.

Man has but two duties, (1) to love the welfare of his fellows, and (2) to love the principle of holiness. Now, as resentment can flow from neither, resentment is positively forbidden: and as these two duties have no exceptions whatever, it follows that benevolence must go right on, oblivious of human injuries. To say, Undoubtedly, except with the Almighty, is horrible! There is but one virtuousness. And God Himself has taught us that there is but one; for He says, enjoining benevolence, "That ye may be the children of your Father which is in heaven; for He makes His sun to shine on the evil and on the good, and sends rain upon the just and upon the unjust" (Matt. 5: 45).

Now a second point will bring out all the meaning of the passage. Ἐκδίκησις, which excludes all idea of resentment, is the necessary upholding and enforcing of eternal law. It is really the fruit of the two great emotions of righteousness, and not itself a co-ordinate desire. Paul's sentiment is, that we are to leave it to the administration of Heaven. "*Avenging (ourselves)*" has two difficulties; first, it favors resentment; and, second, it traverses in many cases God's forms of established vindication (see next chapter). "**On the contrary** (ἀλλά), **give place to wrath.**" We are to notice at last a real imperative leaning back upon its host of participles. Paul is willing to imagine that there will needs be anger, for he has said so in the epistle to the Ephesians (4: 26),—" Be ye angry and sin not." But he commands us carefully to "*give place to*" it, and means that we are to stand still, and let the wrath hurtle by. "*Give place to*" God's anger some have preferred to say (Alford, *in loc.*); and thereby a very innocent interpretation has arisen. "*Give place to*" the enemy's anger some have imagined (Ewald). It makes little difference. But the recurrence of the word ὀργή in the next chapter (v. 5); and the caution that they "must needs be subject, not for *the anger only*," but "for *conscience sake*," and the objection that the one meaning is a little too fierce, and the other a little too yielding, carries us back to the first explication :—"*Not avenging yourselves, beloved ; on the contrary, give place to (your own) wrath ;*" and he means by that, Neglect it, and let it storm on ; "**for it is written, Vengeance is mine ; I will repay, says the Lord.**" Not that we ourselves are not sometimes to "*repay*," but that we are to do it as God does it, without the wickedness of revenge, and, moreover, as God orders it, which we are about to explain in another chapter (13).

20. Before we reach that, however, we have an interesting disclosure. Paul had quoted from the Proverbs. The ideas are very simple. We are to have nothing to do with resentment, but are to love our enemies, and are not to punish except as an ordinance of the Most High (see next chapter). But while the thought is plain enough, the Scriptural authority is very remarkable. Solomon had simply said, " If he who hates thee hunger, give him food to eat ; if he thirst, give him water to drink ; for, shovelling live coals thyself upon his head, Jehovah shall punish thee also " (Prov. 25 : 21, 22). The Seventy altered this. It is singular that Paul should have copied their alteration ; and most singular of all, that this copying on the part of Paul should have regulated our translators (E. V., Prov.), and that they should have copied the Septuagint for the Old Testament instead of the original Hebrew. Quoting from the Septuagint is not an uncommon inspiration (11 : 26, 27 ; 1 Pet. 4 : 18) ; and where the Greek was proverbial, it might be useful in its effect. In this passage, however, Solomon has the best sense. "(*Heaping*) *coals of fire*" (E. V.) has always been an ungainly figure ; and the fierceness of that imagery everywhere else being found to apply to punishment (Ps. 120 : 40 ; 140 : 10), it ought in our English Old Testament to be kept to that sense, and we hope will be found in that way in the coming Revision.*

For divine reasons no doubt, Paul, however, stands as he has been written (E. V. & Re.).

---

* We since see that it is not.

20.—For so doing thou shalt heap coals of fire upon his head.

And this cast of the Greek makes necessary a little more careful exposition. Do not you punish, but leave it to the Most High. If you keep sedulously away from being resentful, God is the avenger of all such, and pours the coals of vindication upon the real offender. Let not that be what you pray for, but take courage from the fact. In one catholic sentence afterward (v. 21), he gathers up a single maxim. Let evil never assert the mastery. When provoked, let not that drive you to the additional mischief of malignity. And inasmuch as "(*giving*) *place to wrath*" is a noble exercise, count that your wealth. The sentence is to be universal. "*Overcome evil with good*" (E. V.) is too much the old thought that we are to love our enemies. And "*Be not overcome of evil*" (E. V.) looks too much in that connection like mere meekness: whereas it is a direction of the apostle under all calamity. Don't succumb to calamity, but conquer it. Don't conquer it by curing it and trampling it under foot, but by placing it under tribute. And don't levy upon it a mere transitory gain, but a thorough transformation into blessing. Notice all the particles:—

21. Be not defeated under the evil; but defeat the evil in the good.

CHAPTER XIII.

1. Let every soul be arranged under authorities that hold the higher place—

Here begins the denouement of the true ἐκδίκησις. We are never to punish out of resentment; and as the motive is, to be useful, Paul brings us to the salutary idea of not taking the law into our own hands. The translation should be precise; for it avoids that horrible night-mare of "the divine right of kings." If he proceeded to say, "*Let every soul be subject to the higher powers*" (E. V. & Re.), it would drive us to the necessity of qualifying and claiming the reserve, viz., "in case an execrable sovereign cannot be thrown off." But by the Greek as it is, we are carried to the exact wisdom in the matter. Paul is giving the very kernel of the idea of government. We are not to avenge *ourselves*, which would turn the earth into a Bedlam, but we are to let anger sweep on by employing the avengement of Heaven, and by doing that, not simply in waiting for a vindicating stroke, but by **arranging** "**authorities**" which can hold of the Almighty.

1.—For there is no authority except under God; but those that exist have been arranged under God.

"*Ordained*" (E. V. & Re.) is too strong a word, and "*of*" (E. V. & Re.) is not the connecting particle. Nero was "*ordained*" of God; and so was Christ "*ordained*" to be crucified; but God's grandest saint would have been grander if he could have hurled Nero to the ground. Paul did not mean "*ordained*." But, in a way that we can hardly improve by comment, he meant just what he has written. Men are not to be avenged piece-meal, but are to be "**arranged**" into governments. And then the theory is to be, that each is to be avenged by men above him, and by an "*arranged*" authority.

2. So that he who arranges himself against the authority, is set against the arrangement of God; but they so set shall receive to themselves condemnation.

3. And yet, for the first time, if we attend now to the exact expression, we encounter a sentence which needs must have a limit:—

3. For governors are not a terror to the good work, but to the evil.

That, alas! is far from being true! So that the earlier part of the passage must now be called in, and must apply a necessary reserve. Men must arrange governments. Paul is urging that there be no taint of resentment, and no adversity to enemies except the needful ἐκδίκησις. He insists that we leave that to Heaven, and, where man must interfere, to authorized government. He accents that by the expression, "**every soul.**" Not a mortal must escape. There must be "*authority*" with an Argus eye. Paul has a right to be understood as making men responsible for the choice of that "*authority.*" And when it has been so chosen as to make it reverential to suppose that it is "**under God,**" or when, as the best that can be had, it holds the place that can be held by no other, men must submit.

3.—But dost thou wish not to have terror of the authority? Do that which is good, and thou shalt have praise of the same; 4. For it is a servant of God to thee for good. But if thou doest the evil, have the terror, for it bears not the sword in vain. For it is a servant of God, an avenger, in matters of anger, upon him who does the evil.

4. Paul means by "**anger**" (v. 4) *our* "anger"; to which we were to "*give place*" (12: 19). We are to "*arrange*" to have it satisfied in a governmental way.

5. Wherefore this arrangement under others is necessary, not for the wrath's sake only, but also for the conscience sake.

We have almost a completed picture. (1) No "*wrath*" in the shape of any resentment (vs. 17–20). (2) No wrath sporadically indulged *ipso judice*, each man for himself. (3) No wrath, ordinarily speaking, except under the arrangements of government. (4) No "*wrath*" under government, however prudently "*arranged*," out of "**wrath**" itself "**only,**" however innocent, but "**also**" and chiefly out of "**conscience**" toward God.

6. Paul deftly supplies, *obiter*, a thought on the vexed question of "**tribute**" (Matt. 22: 17). Men are to pay it to the Almighty:—

6. For for this cause ye pay tribute also; for they are executors of God's service, pressing earnestly forward as to this very thing.

7. Like the treatise on *revenge* (12: 17, etc.), and the treatise on *government* (13: 1, etc.), both of which are first-class, we are

to have from this verse to the tenth, a still more profound account of the whole nature of morality:—

7. Give to all what is owing; tribute to whom tribute; custom to whom custom; fear to whom fear; honor to whom honor. 8. Owe nothing to anybody save love to one another; for he who loves the other has fulfilled the law.

"Owing." We render this with a part of the verb to "*owe*" to keep up the connection. If we say "*due*" (E. V. & Re.), we are in danger of hiding it (see next verse). The apostle has already represented that in paying tribute to man we are really paying tribute to the Almighty (v. 6). He now goes deeper, and makes clear the very germ of ethical obligation. He says, **"Give to all what is owing,"** numbering a whole list of claims: and then winds up with the doctrine that we are not to "*owe*" anything (alas! alas! for the silliness that would make this mean that men are not to "*owe*" debts!). It is the force of the Eastern imperative. It means that we *do* not "*owe*" anything. It is a grand affirmation of morals that a man cannot "*owe*" anything but **"love"** the one **"to another."** The Greek μηδέν forbids ὀφείλετε to be read as an indicative; but an imperative is the strongest sort of an indicative. When the text says, "Make the heart of this people fat" (Is. 6: 10), as English it is infamous, but as Hebrew it is a tenfold indicative. Paul simply means, You *do not* "*owe*" anybody anything but love. And the belief that the capital of the world must lie dead, and no man must borrow it, and so "*owe*" anything to anybody; that a child must "*owe*" nothing to his father, or an apprentice to his master, or a State to its inhabitants, is silly beyond imagination. We smirch the Bible by such things. Paul immediately explains:—

9. For this, Thou shalt not commit adultery, Thou shalt not kill, Thou shalt not steal, Thou shalt not covet, and if there be any other commandment, it is summed up in this word, namely, Thou shalt love thy neighbor as thyself.

To give his reasons, let us regard the clear sweep of the

passage. It is not the whole law (but, really, if a man keeps one table, he will keep the other), but it is the whole essence of mutual obligation. Other Scriptures have repeated it (1 Cor. 13: 1, etc.; Col. 3: 14). Truth and honor and chastity, and respect for friends, and regard for enemies, intolerance for sin, and tolerance under wrong and harm, are summarily comprehended in this, as Christ long ago said (Matt. 22: 40), "**Thou shalt love thy neighbor as thyself.**"

But Paul digs down deeper, for he gives this philosophic reason:—

10. Love works no ill to the neighbor; therefore love is a fulfilling of law.

Nor can we parry this. It will not do to say, One excellent trait may *imply* the others, but need not claim that it *includes* them; a saint utterly honest will be utterly chaste; and Paul may be right in saying that a man who loves cannot lie, and that a man who has benevolent affection will not be a ruiner of families or a public scandal. The case must be stronger; not what love *implies*, but what it *includes*. Paul means to say, that duty is made up of love; not solely that love and sin are inconsistent with each other, but that sin is just that thing, a simply not-loving, and that the second table of our duties, as he intimates here (v. 9) and elsewhere (Gal. 5: 14), is "**summed up**" as one, by benevolent regard.

11. And this, knowing the occasion, that now it is high time for you to awake out of sleep; for now is our salvation nearer than when we believed.

"**And this;**" referring to all the summing up of their duty (Chaps. 12, 13). "**High time**" (E. V. & Re.); simply ὥρα, *the hour*. "**To awake.**" Paul calls life "**night**" (v. 12), and impeaches men of a mad tendency to "**sleep.**" "**Salvation.**" This is an old habit of the Bible, to call conversion "*salvation*" (10: 10), but to baptize with the name afresh when we are thoroughly converted on the day of judgment. We were "redeemed" nineteen centuries ago (1 Pet. 1: 18); we were "redeemed" again a few years ago when we were brought into the Kingdom (Col. 1: 14); but we are "redeemed," by a third use of the word, at that unknown date which we are to esteem above all others as "the day of redemption" (Eph. 4: 30).

12. The night has gone forward, but the day has drawn near—

The expressions are moderate. It does not say "*far spent*" (E. V. & Re.), for that might leave out the young. It does not say, "*The day is at hand*" (E. V. & Re.). Paul draws attention to the fact that "**the night**" is flying by, and "**the day**" nearer. It is well to notice the language; there has been an obstinate opinion that Paul thought that the day of the Lord was at hand. Such misconceivings of the fact destroy the idea of inspiration. Moreover Paul corrected this very conceit (2 Thess. 2 : 2). Paul's eschatology was certainly very simple :—First, that the *parousia* was the Judgment (1 Thess. 4 : 15); second, that men were not alive between death and the Judgment Day (1 Cor. 15 : 17–19, 32, 54; Heb. 11 : 39, 40); third, that all that was awful was delayed when we left the world, by a dreamless slumber (Heb. 9 : 27); and yet, fourthly, that death and judgment come together; that is, that they come together in the dead man's consciousness; the interval between being lost as being only a dreamless nothingness.

To build, therefore, upon the Greek a mistake in Paul as to one thing, is simply to imagine the possibilities of misapprehension anywhere; and to build, upon anything in Paul, a millennial idea, and, above all, a pre-millennial advent, is to make light of Scripture generally; for the Scriptures are everywhere warning us of the suddenness of the coming Judge (Matt. 24 : 36–44, 50, 51), and this would be putting between, no end of intervening history (see com. 11 : 25).

"**The night has gone forward, but the day has drawn near.**" That suits no other idea than that of this passing life. "*The night has gone forward;*" that is "*the night*" of the earthly trial of the clouded and darkened believer. "*The day has drawn near;*" that is "*the day*" of dying, when, like a telegram under the sea, heaven will seem to come at once.

CHAPTER XIII.

"*It is high time to awake*," because "*salvation*," for the first time worthy of the name, will break upon us instantly, as far as we shall consciously know, and that bright hour comes each instant nearer since the day that we believed.

A noble book might be written on the one subject of spiritual "**light.**" Solomon calls it "*wisdom*" (Prov. 1 : 2). Our Saviour often speaks of it as "*knowledge*" (Jo. 17 : 3). It is often called "*understanding*" (Prov. 16 : 16 ; Is. 6 : 10). It is really nothing more than *conscience*. When a man's conscience is enlightened, which is the only change at the moment of the new-birth, that is really the new born condition of holiness, or piety, or godliness, or righteousness, or moral appreciation and benevolent regard, just whatever we choose to call it. "*Love*" (2 Thess. 2 : 10), in the sense of esteem, is but the enlightened discernment of the sweetness of the truth, or, if we would speak less abstractly, of the sweetness of the moral object which the man is looking at. Grace, after that, is a progress. Give a man light, and the love, of the First Table, is not even a sequence. It is the appreciative regard itself. Faith is the same thing, with certain elements of confidence turned upon a revealed Helper. Repentance is the same light, turned upon sin, instead of upon holiness. Nothing is more needed just at present than to simplify piety by calling it "*light.*" The sinner passes from "*darkness*" to "*light*" (Acts 26 : 18); and to say, No, light follows afterward ; or, A man must have faith first, and that will bring moral appreciation, is the curse of the Reformed. Conversion is "*light*" in answer to prayer, and that, in its very dawn, is a moral "*light.*" That explains its being the fruit of a regenerating work. To say, as our Protestants do, Faith first, and moral illumination afterward, is to turn it all backward. Regeneration, as all Protestants agree, is a moral metamorphosis of the lost. Regeneration, as is equally agreed, brings forth faith. Faith then, it can only be madly added, must prelude and effect a moral change. And yet this is the vagary of the creeds ! And it is the bane of orthodoxy. The ample doctrine of the word is that what a man must first aim after is "*light.*" He must get it at the cross of the Redeemer. The influx of "*light*" *is* regeneration, and realizes every grace. The sun shines upon the earth, and breeds all daylight colors. And so "the light of the knowledge of the glory of God" shines upon work, and breeds diligence ; shines upon sin, and comes up repentance ; shines upon the lost, and takes the form of compassion ; shines upon God, and in the very vision of Him is the very substance of our love ; shines upon Christ, and draws to it all the elements of confidence ; so that there is truer speech in saying that faith is the effect of holiness, than that holiness is the effect of faith, though both are mistaken rhetoric. Long before a man has any holiness, he has a certain sort of faith, and there is really the secret of the error. The faith that my mother taught me has brought me to the mercy-seat, and, in that far off unsaving way, is saving ; but what all Protestants call "*saving faith*" is nothing of the kind. It is the in-breaking of the actual "*light ;*" and that "*light*" is not only moral, as one incident of its sort, but it is in a grand sense morality itself. It is the waking of the moral sense that constitutes regeneration, and is the saving change in the faith of the redeemed.

12.—Let us, therefore, put off the works of darkness,—

Notice the language. It is the *genitive of material.* The very " **works** " are " **darkness.**"* Just as all virtues trace to " *light,*" because, as these texts inform us, they really are "*love*" (13 : 10), so all wickedness consists in darkness. If all trespass is by a deficiency of "*love*" (13 : 9; 1 Cor. 13), and all love is but an excellence of vision (1 Jo. 3 : 2), all

---

* *Works* convey different notions, according to our mood. "*Works*" morally, or as deserving of reward, are love. It is the love in them that makes them moral, or the want of love that makes them wicked. And in this view "*works of darkness*" are darkness as the only thing productive of guilt. But "*works*" physical, or the mechanic performances of the sinner, viewed externally, are the *fruit* of "*darkness,*" here the genitive being the genitive of efficiency and not of material, just as we say "*works of the law,*" meaning such works as the law by promises or threat (without the Spirit) might occasion or engender (see com. 3 : 20).

sin is "*darkness*," and those become most singularly intended texts which speak of the " power of darkness " (Col. 1 : 13), and which speak of chained spirits, not incarcerated by walls, but " under darkness "(Jude 6), and, in another place, as having " chains of darkness " (2 Pet. 2 : 4), showing that eternal confinement in the Pit is effectuated by being blind (Is. 42 : 7), that being the head condition of a state of wickedness.

Now Paul condenses another thought into the remaining syllables (v. 12); **"Let us, therefore, put off the works of darkness;"** and we might naturally suppose he would add, **"Let us put on the** (works) **of light."** But that does not suit him. In the epistle to the Ephesians he enlarges the oncoming idea. He imagines the Christian in battle. He says, " We wrestle not against flesh and blood " (Eph. 6: 12). What would make pretty poor "*works*," he sees will make very tolerable **"weapons."** And therefore he enlarges in the Ephesians what he merely glances at here, "*Let us put off the works of darkness,*"—

12.—And let us put on the weapons of light.

As though he had said, "*Works,*" of course; but they look to me much more like **" weapons."** When I have called grace by its very highest name, and gone back to the very **"light"** of God for its origin and character, it seems almost a burlesque upon the word to say *works of light*. But what are too mean for the name, in half-hearted believers in the cross, make dangerous weapons. Satan flies at "*the light*" that is in the meanest Christian. At any rate, these are our meagre "*weapons*." And Paul, in his speech to Ephesus, makes the most of them. He says, " Having done all (we are to) stand." And he catalogues our "armor" in a way to bring out masterfully that they are "*weapons of light.*" In the first place, we have "the girdle of truth;" that means inner "truth," the appreciated realities that are moral (Eph. 4: 24; " holiness of truth," E. V., marg.); that "truth" which God is said to be (1 Jo. 5: 6); and it is properly a " girdle," because it holds all the rest, and binds them all together when they hang upon the wall. Next we have the "breast-plate," which is a man's personal "righteousness," which, though a rent and cut corselet, is nevertheless the best he has, and, strange enough, grows sounder and stronger as he fights in it. Next, we have the sandals, which, to take the Greek literally, are "the readiness of the peaceful gospel." "Over all" (επί), or, if we yield to a new reading (ἐν), "along with all," that is, to cover all our own infirmities, "taking the shield of faith ;" and then, as the emblem of "hope" (1 Thess. 5 : 8), "the helmet," and then, as the instrument of grace, "the word." It is interesting to see how all are "*weapons of light,*" and how "the whole armor" is gauged by "*the light*" that grows in the believer. They all hang upon "the girdle of truth" (Matt. 22: 40).

13. Let us walk nobly as though by day ;—

Two of Paul's recent ideas (12: 17; 13: 12) are here wedded into one. Not only are we to **"walk nobly,"** in contrast with that mere *honestness* (E. V. & Re.) which the Revisers ought certainly to have weeded out, but we are to think of it as the creature of "*the light.*" What cannot the lost be if "*the day*" breaks? And those night-birds, where will they be when "*the light*" arises? **"Let us walk handsomely** (εὐσχημόνως) **as though by day,"—**

13.—Not in revelling and drunkenness, not in chambering and wantonness, not in strife and envying. 14. But put ye on the Lord Jesus Christ, and for desires of the flesh make ye no provision.

"Put ye on." The idea of armor comes back, but it is now broadened. Things are "*put on*" for either of four purposes, to cover our nakedness, or to warm our bodies, or to defend our lives, or to ornament our persons. Accordingly, "*Put ye on* **the Lord Jesus Christ."** To hide our nakedness we must have His pardons. To warm our dead life we must have His Spirit. To fight our fight we must have Him in us and by us. And to "*walk handsomely as though by day*" we must "*put* (Him) *on*" as our whole model and strength. For if we live, no such living as that is by anything that we can live, but by Christ that liveth in us. And the life that we now live in the flesh, must be by faith in the Son of God, who loved us and gave Himself for us (Gal. 2: 20). Then follows the close. If we are to live handsomely, we are to put Christ before us in many ways. "**Make no provision.**" This is like many Scriptures. "God sent me not to baptize" (1 Cor. 1: 17); that is, not by contrast or in any conceivable comparison. "Take no thought for your life" (Matt. 6: 25); that is, by contrast, or as a first consideration. "Ye had not had sin" (Jo. 15: 22); that is, no sin worthy, after that, of any but half regard. In the present instance, the intention is more direct. "*Make no provision.*" On the contrary, cast your life in an entirely different way. He is a happy mortal who no longer says, I will "*make*" this or that "*provision*" for my daily necessities; but, From this time forward I positively refuse. Hereafter, I work for God. And as I cannot bless Him in any immediate way, my trade is,—to be useful. Hereby I drive from me every different act or care. And as, to serve my Maker, I must serve His creatures, and as, to serve His creatures, I must maintain myself, and as, to maintain myself, I must pursue my business, I will throw all into that shape, anticipating my heavenly life, where I shall serve perpetually my fellows, and find thereby the highest welfare to my being.

Πρόνοιαν "**for desires of the flesh,**" seems a better arrangement of the Greek than πρόνοιαν "*for the flesh*" (*gen.*), *in respect to* (εἰς) *desires.*" But the difference hardly matters.

"*Desires.*" Desires that are altogether innocent may become desires altogether guilty when they are the only desires we have; because they are the exercises of the human soul that act out and, each time, increase our *want* of better affections. "*Flesh ;*" all of a man that is not spiritual. The whole of a creature outside of his conscience is "*the flesh*" in the meaning of the apostle. "He that sows to his flesh," constitutional and unliable to blame as "*the flesh*" may be, of these constitutional tastes "reaps corruption :" not that they themselves may be corrupt, but sowing to them betokens the guilt implied in the want of the *pneuma* or moral "*desires.*" This closes a lengthened exhortation beginning with the twelfth chapter.

CHAPTER XIV.

The twelfth chapter declared that a man must "*think soberly*" (v. 3) ; that, as far as he allowed himself to judge of his ministry, he must make an estimate of it "*according to* (its) *proportion of faith.*" "*Faith,*" too, must be judged by its "*service*" (v. 7). And "*service,*" in a most interesting way, is accounted that which can be accredited only as it *serves*. Teaching can be of faith only as it teaches, and exhortation only as it exhorts. Giving must be weighed only by its simplicity ; ruling, by its diligence ; the mercy-shewer, by his cheerfulness. So Paul starts his consideration of character. He spends two chapters upon "*faith*," ennobling it as *handsome*" in behavior (v. 17), and limiting it down to an affection of the heart (13 : 8). He begins now another *fasciculus* with the word "**but.**" Do all these things to strengthen your own "*faith*," but, all the more, be tolerant and kind to those who are "**weak**" believers :—

1. But him who is weak in the faith accept, nor that, either, to become judges of his opinions.

Notice the strange cunning of the apostolic procedure. He is willing to suppose everything. His argument is painstakingly *ad hominem*. He arrays himself on the side of the less scrupulous (v. 2), and is willing to suppose that the scruples he is to consider sprang from **weakness of faith.** Or he will yield to the theory that it is "*weak*" in another sense, viz., ignorant, or simply silly. He pitches his recourse high up in the region of the gospel. His first consideration is that man must "**accept,**" because "**God has accepted.**" The presupposition is that the man has "*faith ;*" now if it be the silliest sort of "*faith,*" so that it boggles about "**herbs**" and slain meat, no matter ; if the man has "*faith,*" it is a sign that he has been with the Redeemer.

2. One man has faith to eat everything. Another, a weak one, eats herbs.

CHAPTER XIV.

Paul decides that he is not only to be "*accepted,*" but accepted not for the purpose of criticising his opinions (v. 1).

3. Let not him who eats despise him who does not eat; and, on the other hand, let not him who does not eat judge him who eats, for God has accepted him.

"*Received*" (E. V. & Re.) is not quite cordial enough. The word is προσλαμβάνω, literally to *take close to* one (*accipio, to "accept"*). Let it be noticed that "*doubtful disputations*" (v. 1, E. V. & Re.) are quite wide of the mark of διακρίσεις διαλογισμῶν.

Paul proceeds now with a number of considerations which we will mention in their order. First :—

4. Who art thou who judgest another man's servant?—

Paul would be far from the thought that we are not to **judge.** On the contrary, he would agree with John that for certain διαλογισμοί we were to wash our hands of a man. Mere tolerance is one of the last ideas of the Bible. "He that abideth not in the doctrine of Christ, receive him not into your house, neither bid him God-speed" (2 Jo. 9, 10). But Paul is tired of scruples. What he wants is the eternal distinction between what is first and what is second. He has already described "*faith,*" and shown that it is to be the element in all our measurements. "*In preaching*" it is to be the element "*in* (our) *preaching*" (12 : 6). We are not to ask what mistakes he made, or what want of Demosthenean power, but what "*faith*" had he. And that is to be asked in all our services. And so when he comes down to the "*weak,*" it is not the question how "*weak,*" or what mistakes does he make in minor principles or acts, but we are to accredit the great liberty of thought, and leave his blunders to the care of the Almighty.

4.—To his own master he stands or falls;—

And yet Paul does not even leave him to his Master. He follows him further. Granting the great principle of "*faith,*" his blunders are not to ruin him. "**The Lord is able to make him stand;**" and "*able,*" not simply in the commoner sense, but in the sense of a previous passage (9 : 22), that is, in consistency with the whole gospel (16 : 25). The poorest simpleton, if he have "*faith*," must be "*accepted*" by the church, "*for God has accepted him*. "Who art thou that judgest another man's servant?" Not only to his own master does he stand or fall,

4.—But he shall be made to stand ; for the Lord is able to make him stand.

As a second consideration, along with another picture, Paul brings out the principle that though a man may be excused for the weakness of his opinions, yet that he should have a care in forming his opinions, and that this care should be commensurate with his devotion to God. .

5. One man esteems one day above another; another esteems every day alike. Let every man be fully persuaded in his own mind.

Thirdly, opinions thus formed, though wrong, evince a better spirit than mere correctness of opinion. This is a prime part of the apostle's reasoning :—

6. He who regards the day regards it to the Lord ;—

Suppose a man were singularly apt in forming his opinions ; or suppose a man were singularly true in carrying them out, which would be the higher character? This is a fine stroke. See how piously the man acts even in his delusion :—

6.—And he that eats, eats to the Lord, for he gives God thanks; and he that eats not, to the Lord he eats not, and gives God thanks.

Paul would plainly imply that it is better to be an earnest worshiper even under some secondary mistake, than at all in the least degree less earnest in a perfect ritual.

7. For he goes on to say, and this is a fourth point, "No one lives to himself." Not only is it a high excellence in a man to be devoted even under some mistakes, but Paul brings it into view that it is the whole of piety. Forming a shrewd opinion is wise, but carrying it out is heavenly:—

7. For no man lives to himself, and no man dies to himself. 8. For whether we live, we live unto the Lord,

and whether we die, we die unto the Lord; whether we live, therefore, or die, we are the Lord's.

Abraham knew little of Christ, but Abraham was earnest. Peter had grossly wrong opinions (Matt. 16: 23), and about much more serious matters than eating herbs. Exquisite Christians are lunatics about half the faith.

But Paul, with wonderful condensation, brings out a fifth point. Not only is living to God the great end of the believer, and, therefore, of unspeakable importance above the secondary half of his creed, but to help him to do so was the great end of the Redeemer.

9. For to this very end Christ died and lived, that He might become Lord of both dead and living.

10. Sixth, Paul shames the Christian, because he himself is to be the victim of the most scathing judgment.

10. But thou, why dost thou judge thy brother? Or especially thou, why dost thou despise thy brother? For we are all to stand before the judgment seat of Christ. 11. For it is written:

    As I live, says the Lord, to me every knee shall bow,
    And every tongue shall confess to God.

Why judge a "brother" about trifles, when we ourselves are to be humiliated at the last about much graver wickednesses?

12. So then, each one of us is to give account of himself to God.

This grandest apostle is the albatross of the Scripture dialectic. His wing is ceaseless. We dash without a break into his seventh appeal. Beware of your own personal act! Eating and drinking is a trifle, but violating conscience is a terrible iniquity. Mark how he builds deep and solid. "**I know and am persuaded.**" Eating may be in doubt, but the fact I now mention is beyond a cavil. "*I know and am persuaded,*" and, therefore, I of all others might cheer you on in laughing at these simpleton believers. It may be foolish to scruple, but it is infinitely more foolish not to hesitate. "*I know and am per-*

suaded that there is nothing unclean of itself, but (and here is a principle that sweeps over six verses, 13–18) to him who thinks anything unclean, to him it is unclean." Paul seizes deftly all the threads of thought. Not only are you tempting another, but you are sinning awfully yourself:—

13. Let us, therefore, no more judge each other, but do ye judge this rather, not to place a stumbling block or a trap in a brother's way. 14. I know and am persuaded in the Lord Jesus that there is nothing unclean of itself; but to him who thinks anything unclean, to him it is unclean. 15. For if thy brother is grieved on account of meat, thou walkest no longer lovingly.

Paul is edging up closer. Thus far, he has been talking of *judging*. Now he is plunging deeper in his reasoning. Conscience is so much nobler than meats that he is about to enjoin upon the "strong" that they actually "*bear the infirmities of the weak*" (15: 1). See how he advances his redoubts:—

16.—Destroy not him with thy meat for whom Christ died.

He is actually meddling with *my* meat!

"**Become Lord**" (v. 9). This corresponds with the eighth verse, where Paul gives it as the great end of life to be "**the Lord's.**" Of course Christ's great end (man-ward) is to make us "*the Lord's*" (v. 9). If, as the conceded point, He has made the "*weak brother*" His, then "**Destroy not him with thy meat for whom Christ died.**"

Having such weak people in charge, it is strangely necessary that we do not injure them. Meats are unimportant, but a wounded conscience is a terrible mishap. "**Let us, therefore, no longer judge each other, but judge ye this rather, not to place a stumbling block or a trap in a brother's way**" (v. 13).

"*I know and am persuaded*" (v. 14). See how much stronger this makes it! Paul settles the question, for he adds, "**in the Lord Jesus.**" And yet, though he *knows* that the doubters are all wrong, and knows that they will wickedly resist this appeal to inspiration, yet he takes the extreme ground that *we* *are to go over to them!* The passage is a very striking one ; but before we inspect it all, let us complete with care some other expositions.

"**Unclean**" (v. 14, E. V. & Re.), because *common* (which is the real word) meant that in the Jewish habit of speech (Acts 10: 28).

"**Lovingly.**" The terms are precise. They mean "*according to love.*" Paul aims to be exhaustive. He has said in one chapter that we "*owe*" nothing but "*love*" (13: 8). Meat is a trifle. "Neither if we eat are we the better ; neither if we eat not are we the worse" (1 Cor. 8: 8). It may cause us great personal inconvenience to do without a dish. Moreover the troublesome saint is confessedly silly, and Paul, "*knows*" it that way, and knows it by inspiration, or, in other words, "*in the Lord Jesus* ;" and yet as a splendid decision, which has lived all these centuries in the church, the weak are to govern the strong, and that for grand considerations, which are the genuine out-beaming of the Gospel.

Paul takes the ground that we are to be governed by "*love*" (13: 9). The very world, we everywhere find, was begotten by "*love*" (Prov. 8: 22-30). We have no obligation to men but the obligation of "*love*" (13: 8, 10). We have a lot of weak communicants. Their comfortable conscience is more important than our eating meat. To seduce them against their principle may "*destroy*" them forever. That is all of it. And there emerges Paul's verdict to Corinth, which has been so often quoted, " If meat make my brother to offend, I will eat no flesh while the world standeth " (1 Cor. 8: 13).

We need hardly explain the sentence "**for whom Christ died**" (v. 15). If "*Christ died*" for a man, surely we can go without meat for him ; particularly if there be the slenderest danger that we tempt and "**destroy**" him.

16. Paul advances now to the eighth consideration. If a man is a Christian, "**the good**" in him is exceedingly precious. He may be a very "*weak*" Christian, yet if his weakness consists in scruples, and his scruples are felt and pressed out

of love to the Master, we are to be careful! Bringing out into bold relief his weaknesses will hide his better qualities, and, in fact, show scruples in *us;* for it will show that we are not moved by the grander traits, but stick, ourselves, in the small particulars. This is plainly the apostle's meaning:—

16. Let not your good, therefore, be evil spoken of.

"**Your good.**" Paul had been using before the second person singular. He now changes to the plural. "*Your good*" is now the good of the whole body. Do not speak evil of the "*weak*," for they are part of you; and don't reflect upon yourselves; for "**men**" (v. 18) will side with the "*weak*," and "**approve**" the man who longs to do his duty, above the man who laughs at him for scruples about food or holidays.

"*Accept*" him, the word had been (v. 1), and there had immediately been imposed the caution, "*not with criticisms of his opinions*" (v. 1). If he is a Christian (and do not "*accept*" him unless he is), then he loves Christ, and what is butcher's meat in contrast with affection? That is the point which the next sentence presses:—

17. For the kingdom of God is not meat and drink, but righteousness and peace and joy in a Holy Spirit.

18. The very scruples of a man may be warmed by these principles of life; and if they are, "**men**" will show respect— to say nothing of the Almighty. In fact, this is everything that can deserve respect. The only question is, Is he a possessor of even the feeblest affection?

18. For he that in this serves Christ, is acceptable to God and approved of men.

We were strongly tempted to the idea that ὑμῶν (v. 16) might be connected with βλασφημείσθω, and might be one of those rare cases of a causal genitive (see Goodwin, Gram.); bringing out the meaning, "*Let not the good*" (viz., of these weak-minded believers) *be evil spoken of by you.*" But though poetry is full of such causal constructions, prose is not; and though Paul in any one of these aphoristic sentences may be quoting poetry, yet we could rarely know it ; and unquestionably the other connection of the pronoun is the more usual, and has the higher right.

"**In this**" (v. 18) is the more authoritative reading, and is a neuter expression, including the whole state of spirit (v. 17). "**Holy Spirit**" (v. 17) is without the article, and to translate it so should offend no creed, for all translators sometimes translate that way, we mean when the article is missing (Matt. 22: 43, E. V., see Re.; Acts 19: 2, E. V., see Re.; see also Revisers in 1 Cor. 2: 12, and Rev. 11: 11), and do not consider themselves as thereby altering the fact that when it is not missing, it may express directly a living "Deity" (Acts 13: 2; 2 Cor. 3: 17). "**The Kingdom of God**" (v. 17) is undoubtedly all the universe. Our bodies belong to it ; but in the way of eminence only our intelligent being. But the apostle goes a vast deal further, and borrowing his idea from the Redeemer, means " The Kingdom of God (that) is within you " (Lu. 17: 21). He gives to it, in the way of supreme honor, our moral part. God wields immense potency in rolling the stars, but Paul ascribes higher power to His moral Kingdom. Conscience is its centre. And to restore a conscience, is a higher act than to upbuild matter to its very rim. " What the exceeding greatness of His power?" is the problem which is to task eternity ; and Paul turns its grandest edge and compass to the thought that it is a " power to us-ward who believe " (Eph. 1: 19).

19. Paul's ninth consideration is, that picking at these lesser points destroys the whole enterprise of salvation:—

19. Let us, therefore, press forward toward the things of peace and of edification each for the other.

"**Press forward.**" The verb is a strong one. "**Each for the other.**" This belongs both to the "**peace**" and to the "**edification.**" " *Things whereby we may edify one another* " (E. V. & Re.) is a translation that does not recognize this. The "*peace*" like the *edifying* must be pressed-after, "**each for the other.**" I must have "*peace*" with him, and I must see to it that he has "*peace*" with me.

20. For meat throw not down the work of God.—

"Throw not down," as opposed to *edifying* (v. 19). The Greek is καταλύω, not ἀπόλλυε (v. 15, "*destroy*," E. V.). And so, very naturally, the apostle adds:—

20.—All things may indeed be clean, but it is an evil thing for a man to eat so as to occasion stumbling.

"*Peace*" and *upbuilding* (v. 19) are higher things than eating "meat." The "*meat*" may be innocent, but not the act of eating it. It cannot be my *duty* to eat meat, in the sense in which it may be my duty to remove a stumbling block. "**For meat throw not down the work of God. All things may indeed be clean, but it is an evil thing for a man to eat so as to occasion stumbling.**"

21. And then the obverse idea!—

21. It is a noble thing not to eat flesh or to drink wine or to do anything whereby thy brother stumbles.

"*Or is offended or is made weak*" (E. V.) has the authority against it (see MSS.), but it is by no means certain that it is not a true reading.

22. It is like Paul to keep his strongest considerations to the last. Like Christ, if that story is true of Him (see the MSS.), calling upon certain accusers to throw the first stone if they are innocent (Jo. 8: 7), he quietly raises the question, as his tenth point, whether these "*strong*" believers (!) have not peculiarities of faith which they themselves are not following. His mode of intimating this is of the most delicate possible. "**Happy is the man!**" He is a creature of rare felicity who does not often believe one thing and do another.

22. The faith which thou holdest, hold in accordance with thy self before God.

That is, Thou scornest this stickling in meat, and "**holdest**" a "**faith**" proudly above this mob of weak believers. But have a care! Thine own very "**self;**" how does it hold in all its deep convictions in the respect of this alleged believing? Art thou always doing that which thine innermost "*self*" believes that thou oughtest to do, and that, ἐνώπιον τοῦ θεοῦ, *in God's sight,* or, what is an equivalent expression, "**before God**" (Lu. 1 : 6, 15) ?

I trow not :—

22.—Happy is he who judges not himself in that which he approves.

23. All unconscientiousness Paul says "**is sin.**" All men he seems to suspect are unconscientious. He evidently implies that it should make us modest in judging. "**But**" (δέ); and this word answers to Paul's *doubting* over what he *holds ;* not only are convictions to be hearkened to, "*but*" doubts are supreme in their place :—

23. But he that doubts is condemned if he eat, because it is not of faith ; and whatsoever is not of faith is sin.

"**The faith which** (ἥν) **thou holdest**" (v. 22). This reading has all the authority. But whether it has or not ; or whether we read interrogatively (E. V.), or in any of the different ways, makes not the smallest difference. It is well to say "*holdest*" (ἔχεις), and not "*hast*" (E. V. & Re.), for "*holdest*" is more artificial than "*hast,*" and answers better to the idea of seeming or supposing oneself to *hold.* "**In accordance with thyself.**" This is the proper force of κατά. " The Gospel *according to John,*" means the gospel " *in accordance with*" his remembrances of it. " *According to himself*" or " *according to itself*" in the Bible is translated very wrongfully "*alone*" or " *by himself,*" and we hide thereby most important significance. Even Paul (though the other is admissible) might have been better said to dwell " *according to himself*" when the others went to jail (Acts 28 : 16), rather than "*by himself*" (E. V. & Re.), καθ ἑαυτὸν meaning " *to himself*" or " *at his own will*" or " *disposal,*" the limitation being that it was " with a soldier that kept him." This criticism, however, becomes imminent when the apostle James is looked into. When he says, " Is dead according to its very self " (2 : 17), it is ruin to translate him, " Is dead being alone " (E. V.). The Revisers also damage him by saying (and this with unspeakably less warrant) "is dead in itself" (Re.). The book is *afterward* to say, "And not by faith *only*" (μόνον, v. 24). The apostle is attempting to argue (what is the very strongest of all asseverations), that faith, being the most pregnant of all gifts, and being, according to that other apostle, the very "substance of things hoped for" (Heb. 11 : 1); that is, in its needful *differentia*, if it be saving, being the very light of holiness itself, is "*dead*" if it is not holy. And whether ours be saving faith or common, its dicta in either case rebuke a counterfeit, so that in either case, "if it have not works it is dead according to its very self" (Jas. 2 : 17 ; see Excursus *ad fin.*).

The bearing is evident. Paul insists that our faith, if we pretend it, shall be "*in accordance with*" ourselves. We shall not believe one way, and behave another. Nay, that our outgiving shall fit the body of *ourselves*. And he makes it all more solemn when he says ἐνώπιον τοῦ θεοῦ, that is, when he lets in upon the question of our obedience, the fact that we are under the eye of the Almighty.

CHAPTER XV.

Eleventh:—

1. But we who are able, are bound to bear the weaknesses of those who are unable, and not to please ourselves.

"**But**" is the appropriate particle. You have scruples of your own, but in this question of meat, you are "**able**" to act with freedom. Your brother is "**unable.**" The point is well taken. We lose it entirely if we translate "*strong*" and "*weak*" (E. V. & Re.). The elenchtic triumph depends upon the idea of δύναμαι. You may have your own weaknesses and scruples, "*but*," in this matter, you are "*able*" to make a concession, and your weak brother is "*unable.*" That makes all the difference. The same adjectives have been noticed elsewhere. We hear of "*what the law could not do*" (8: 3, ἀδύνατον), because it was morally "*unable.*" We hear of what God *could do* (9: 22) for the obverse reason. Paul had pressed the idea that what a man thought, he must follow (14: 14); now, if the sticklers at Rome thought that they must live upon herbs, so it must be. And he brings out the splendid law that we must sacrifice ourselves to the advantage of others. They were "*unable*" to eat certain things and be innocent, we are perfectly "*able*" not to eat without moral surrender. It is on this high ground that we are to expound the apostle : and we arrive at the sense by noticing these fresh words which are introduced into the passage. "**We who are able;**" that is, whose consciences are perfectly uninvolved. "**Are bound;**" the word is stronger than "*ought!*" (E. V. & Re.), and binds absolute duty. "**To bear;**" that is, to *lift up* or *carry*. "*We who are able,*" and have no conscientious obligation to live upon meat, ought to shoulder the burdens of those who are "*unable*" to touch it, even though the burden be a **weakness** (ἀσθένημα); the apostle returns to the original expression (14: 1). And we are to bear each other's "**weaknesses**" on a principle which the apostle follows in the second verse, and which he immediately robs of all possibility of extravagance.

2. Paul would be far from saying that we are "**not to please ourselves.**" If a man should wear a cut-off coat, or keep his hat on before a king, Paul would be the last man to do the same, simply to "**please his neighbor.**" Paul speaks sententiously, but with wonderful precision he strikes the idea again, and this time makes it complete:—

2. Let each one of us please his neighbor for that which is good to edifying.

A man boggles at meat. Merely to "*please*" him I am not to eat herbs. But the passage puts a whole case together. First, the meat is innocent (14: 14); second, the man does not think so (ib.); third, he is "*unable*" to touch it (ib. and v. 23); fourth, we are "*able*" not to touch it, and be absolutely guiltless (v. 1); fifth, simply to please him I would make no such submission. But Paul makes out the entire case. If I can innocently "*please*" him, and thereby do him "**good,**" and thence, not as an occasional, but, as Paul beautifully implies, an invariable consequence, **edify** and make him better, then I am "*bound*" for the sacrifice. We are left to settle the question of detail. A man may rebel against any particular demand. But Paul leaves us upon the high ground of "*good.*" Once settle that the sacrifice of flesh will *edify* my neighbor, and the point is gained. "*It is noble neither to eat flesh or to drink wine, or to do anything whereby thy brother stumbles*" (14 : 21).

3. Our translators were wrong in saying "*even Christ*" (E. V.) ; and expositors have fallen into the snare, and made Paul emphasize self-sacrifice by saying, "*Even Christ*" submitted to it! What would Christ *be* without such sacrifices? The Revisers are aware of the mistake, and say, "*For Christ also.*" This might seem near enough. But the expression is καὶ γὰρ, and the usage of Paul makes that merely significant of an additional argument (2 Cor. 3 : 10 ; 13 : 4 ; Phil. 2 : 27 ; 1 Thess. 3 : 4). The meaning is not "*Christ also,*" but "*for also,*" the καί simply informing us that now we are to have an additional confirmation. Not only does it stand to reason that to do a neighbor "*good*" is better than to eat meat (1 Cor. 8 : 13), but, says Paul, there comes in still another reason. There is the example of "*Christ.*"

3. For, furthermore, Christ pleased not Himself; but, as it is written, The reproaches of them who reproach Thee fell on me.

We are not to rest contented with this bare text from the sixty-ninth Psalm, for Paul has a way of quoting a text as a sort of taste and indication of all its context (4 : 18 ; 7 : 7). Perhaps this is a reason why we should welcome πάντα, if it only had a little better authority, in the text that follows. We must exclude it, but we will show it in its place in brackets :—

4. For whatsoever things were written aforetime were (all) written for our learning,—

The "*all,*" even in this single lyric, would include very remarkable things. If Paul meant to refer to the whole Psalm, as we think he did, it shows the instance of instances of the keenest self-inflicted sorrow. It is a Psalm which has helped that hybrid notion of what it is to be Messianic, which has imagined that one of the songs of David may speak of himself in one part of it, and of Christ in another. No sentence could have suggested this except only the fifth verse. The first verse, " Save me, O God ; for the waters are come in unto my soul ; " and the ninth, " For the zeal of thine house hath eaten me up ;" and the twenty-first, about the " gall," and " vinegar," could hardly be denied as Messianic utterances. But one wonderful sentence has ruined everything :— " O God, thou knowest my foolishness, and my sins are not hid from thee " (v. 5). That confession of sin has backed men squarely out from even a dream that the whole Psalm belongs to the Redeemer. But instead of disturbing anything, it is really the crown text of the Psalm. How often a verse is trampled and kept in a condition of waste by a single misprision in the rendering ! The Psalmist is really reaching the very conception of the apostle. Our whole distress comes from a linguistic neglect. There has been the neglect of a particle (ל). Let me translate all as it stands :—" Oh God, thou knowest as to (ל) my sin (foolishness E. V.)," that is, that I have none. The unriddling of all comes immediately : " For for thy sake I have borne reproach " (v. 7); what has distressed us as a confession, is positively a splendid innocence. It is hard that that grand *lâmedh* (ל) should have been thus for centuries overlooked. The English version has disposed of the other clause ; for it has corrected it in the margin. " O God thou knowest as to my sin, and my guiltinesses " (vicarious or inherited) " are not hid from thee." Let not my shame shame others (v. 6) ; " because, for thy sake I have borne reproach " (v. 7). And then instantly the quotation of Paul, " For the zeal of thine house has eaten me up, and **the reproaches of them that reproached thee have fallen upon me."**

Paul has so much in his sentences that it is hard to notice everything. But we must not miss the fact that he does not say "*for his good to edifying*" (E. V., v. 2), but "*for good.*" We soon return upon the idea that pleasing one's neighbor does as much good to one's self as to the neighbor whose scruples we would spare. Paul does not forget this. He quotes our glorious Example, and then implies that tolerating others is most of all effective in "*edifying*" ourselves. "*For whatsoever things were written aforetime were written for our learning,*"—·

4.—That we through the patience and through the encouragement of the Scriptures might have the hope.

Nor is it at all to be forgotten that "**the patience**" and "**the encouragement**" and, even, "**the hope,**" so marked with the definite article, are all in "**Scripture.**" "**Through the patience and through the encouragement of the Scriptures might have the hope**" (of the Scriptures). Paul pursues his listeners with their own writings. And intending to press upon the Jews their national "*edification*" in the acknowledgment of the Gentiles, he steals up to it by gentle conciliation, always pushing forward into the front the words of their own law which they idolatrously reverenced.

5. But may the God of the patience and of the encouragement give unto you to think the same thing as among one another, in agreement with Christ Jesus.

Here is the connection with what is behind (v. 4). If we want "*the hope*" revealed in "*the Scriptures*," we must have "*the patience and the encouragement that is in the Scriptures.*" We are taught these by the example of Christ. Nevertheless they must be **given** to us by "**God.**" And we must not be deaf to the eloquence with which Paul doubles upon his idea. Not only is the God he appeals to, "**the God of the patience and of the encouragement,**" who must needfully "**give**" them to us, but he entreats further. He overtures the saints to agree better than they did, and especially on the point he is about to broach to them (v. 8). He wishes them "**to think** (more) **the same thing among (themselves),**" as he beautifully expresses it "**in agreement with Christ Jesus.**" If they really cared, they could get to that state in essential matters. And we are to notice in the next verse that this would really be to "**glorify God.**" Each syllable tells. If "**the glory of God**" (v.

7), (and by that we are to mean moral "*glory*," 6 : 4 ; 2 Cor. 3 : 18 ; 2 Pet. 1 : 3), shines out in the example of Christ, and we cry to God to be affiliated to that example, then each filament of these texts becomes distinct ;—May the God of the patience and the encouragement give unto you to think the same thing as among one another, in agreement with Christ Jesus :—

6. That with like mind, in one mouth,—

(And let it be understood, this is "**like**" to Christ and "**in one mouth**" with Christ as well as with His people ; for so the close suggests to us : for we thereby shine out with the same "**glory**" that He does ; for mark exactly the expressions :—"**that with like mind, in one mouth,**"—)

6.—Ye may glorify the God and Father of our Lord Jesus Christ.

"**Encouragement**" (vs. 4, 5). This is a most unmanageable Greek. Probably every expositor has tussled with the task of some one English to translate it. It really means to *call to one's side*. It means, therefore, to *advocate* (1 Jo. 1 : 1), because our defender calls us to his side. It might mean to *fight for* us. It certainly means to *call on* (Matt. 26 : 53). It means to *exhort* (Acts 15 : 32), and to *entreat* (Matt. 18 : 32), and to *console* (2 Cor. 1 : 6), and to *encourage* (see Robinson and Liddell), because all these words have a covert thought of calling in, or summoning the person near. We have often looked narrowly at the word *help*, as for example in the text " I shall give you another helper" (Jo. 14 : 16) ; but like a brook with the banks thrown down, it would flow at once over too wide a surface. We have to leave it to its fate of being *par excellence* the much translated New Testament expression. But here undoubtedly it ties itself to the expression of "*edifying*." "*Edifying*" is no random or on-a-sudden "*good*" (v. 2). It requires "*patience*," and "*patience*" is hopeless without παράκλησις. Military men might call it " *aid and comfort*." Paul tracks it to " *the Scriptures* " (v. 4), and teaches that " *the hope* " there taught is not to be had without these other things.

He tracks them above all to God (v. 5). He tracks them as having been given to Christ (v. 6). And he begs that "*the God of the patience and the encouragement may give* them also to us, or, as a means to that end, may grant that, being of "*like mind*" with one another, and with His Son, we "*may glorify the God and Father*" of our blessed Redeemer. These are very pregnant sentences.

7. And he brings the whole series now to bear on the great Gentile prejudice (Eph. 2 : 14). "**Wherefore accept each other;**" and that will include of course the Jew *accepting* the Gentile. "**Meats**" (Heb. 9 : 10; 13 : 9) were, after all, a part of the great quarrel. The Jews, instead of being the "*strong*," were, strangely enough, the "*weak*" (14 : 1), and Paul bowed to them unduly, when not under inspiration (Acts 16 : 3; 21 : 23, 24), in many a point of unfounded stickling for their symbols:—

7. Wherefore accept each other, as Christ also accepted you, to the glory of God.

The points are brought together. "**Accept.**" *Take close* to each other (Philem. 17), so the word means, in the most affectionate inter-communion. "**As Chrst also accepted us.**" What an irony! "*Accept*" a meat eater, or, to build it a little bigger, a man outside of Abraham, because Christ accepted us, and we, disgusting and abominable transgressors! "*Accept* **each other.**" Let it be mutual. The Gentile must "*accept*" the Jew. And now he sums up on that idea of "**glory.**" As it is "**the glory of God**" that is shining out in these condescensions of our Sacrifice, so let it shine out in us, "*as Christ also accepted us to the glory of God.*"

8. "**For I say.**" Paul now is to introduce his ultimate point in the great international quarrel among believers :—

8. For I say that Christ became a servant of circumcision in the behoof of God's truthfulness, to confirm the promises of the fathers, 9. But that the Gentiles, in the behoof of mercy, might glorify God ;—

A various reading in the seventh verse as between "*accepted you*" and "*accepted us*" is somewhat important. "*Received us*" (E. V.) would have nothing specific; but "*received you*" (Re.), which has the overwhelming right, applies to the Gentiles, to whom, in the majority, Paul was evidently writing. As Christ has overlooked all narrowness of race, and "*accepted you*," so do you "*accept each other.*" You the majority, and you the minority, "*accept*" alike; "*for*"—and now he brings forward an argument (v. 8), "**Christ**" was undoubtedly "**a servant of circumcision.**" He was circumcised Himself, and, through His mother, was a devotee of Israelitish ordinances (Lu. 2 : 22 ; "*their*" not "*her*"). Moreover, He was "*a servant of*" the *circumcised.* He rarely abandoned Palestine. His chief centre was Jerusalem. And it was not all trial of the Syrophenician when He said, "It is not meet to take the children's bread, and to cast it unto dogs" (Matt. 15 : 27). The Jews were evidently building upon this, and it is a brief theory of such conduct in our Lord that is now coming forward as a shelter for the heathen.

Paul admits a *servantship* of Christ to "*circumcision*," and then, in two irrefragable ways, first, by the intention of all this, and, second, by their own positive Scriptures, shows that Christ was to flow over from the Jew, and by the very force of its Jewish beginning make His ministry bless both them and the nations.

"*For I say*" (This is the way Paul often gathers himself up, Gal. 3 : 17; 5 : 16; Eph. 4 : 17). "*I say*" Christ did really "*accept you*" and all nations ; for though He was "*a servant of* "*circumcision*," yet it was (1) to fulfil prophecy ; and as prophecy is not made simply to be fulfilled, it was (2) to secure certain advantages, for the sake of which the things predicted were ordered to come to pass. In the first place, therefore, it was "**in the behoof of God's truthfulness**" to accomplish the fulfilment of "**the promises of the fathers, but,**" "in the second place, "**in the behoof of** (God's) **mercy, that the Gentiles might glorify God;**" all of which he props by ample quotations :—

9.—As it is written,—
  For this cause I will confess thee among the Gentiles,
  And sing unto thy name.
10. And again it says,—
  Rejoice ye Gentiles, with His people.
11. And again,—
  Praise the Lord all ye Gentiles,
  And let all the peoples bless Him.
12. And again Isaiah says,—
  There shall be the root of Jesse,
  And He that arises to rule over the Gentiles;
  On Him shall the Gentiles hope.

Put all this together.

Christ was beyond doubt "*a servant of circumcision*" (v. 8) : confined Himself to Palestine ; conformed Himself to hereditary ordinance ; consigned Himself to Israelitish following ; conceived Himself as brought into being for these two results, —first, that the prophecies might be fulfilled which made His whole kingdom to be started among the Jews (Is. 2 : 3), and, second, that by their vigorous beginning it might be set up the more vigorously among themselves and among other nations: all this, made clear by a certain remorseless logic, namely, that their own Scriptures teemed with it ; that the whole outcome of it was their own ; that words of which they made idols expressed it perfectly ; for it was this form of annihilating appeal with which the apostle annulled their prejudice all through this sharpest and grandest of the inspired epistles.

"**Of the fathers**" (v. 8). Such is the Greek ; and "*to the fathers*" (E. V. & Re.), for which the Revisionists supply "*given*" and our old English version supplies "*made*," are not so correct. Paul could easily have said that. "*The promises of the fathers*" is the more comprehensive expression, for it brings upon the horizon others' good, as well as for the Jews. It was flattering to the Jew, for it made those demi-gods of Israel depositaries for the whole world, as well as for the oaths and pledges which were only for their people.

13. He follows with a benediction, in which we are to be wide awake for particles, as indeed we ought to be in all Scripture. "**But**" is not to be changed into "*now*" (E. V. & Re.). Paul has been arguing of great national prophecies. He turns to immediate prayers. And then afterward to their own witness of the Spirit (v. 14). And, following that, to "*promises*" to him (v. 15), and evidences to be derived from his own mission to the Gentiles (v. 16). All these he starts upon with "**but**" (δέ). We must not omit it. "*But* **God.**" For however much we may look to promises as old as Abraham, what the present may do for us is not to be overlooked. God **filling a man with all joy** is a better evidence in kind than law or prophet. Have these other evidences, "**but**"— There is the force of the particle. "*The God of hope*" (E. V. & Re.). This would be well enough in almost any other sentence. But here he has been talking of "**the hope**" (v. 4; see 8: 24). Moreover, the word has just been written, "*On Him shall the Gentiles hope*" (v. 12). The omissions will most uncomfortably appear if we throw together the whole genuine translation :—

13. But may the God of the hope fill you with all joy and peace in believing, that ye may abound in the hope through power of a Holy Spirit.

14. "**But.**" The apostle strikes again with evidences that are personal and still more close. "**I myself am persuaded.**" And lest they should ask him, How? he appeals in the next verse to "**the grace given to** (him)." And lest they should laugh at the conceit, he appeals in the next verse to "**signs and wonders,**" which, of course, were a firm base for all that he could claim :—

14. But I have become persuaded, my brethren, even I myself in your behalf, that even ye yourselves are full of goodness, filled with all the knowledge, able even to instruct one another.

This is all reduction on the part of the apostle of argument and proof down to their own time. The prophets prophesied of us, he had said (vs. 9-12), "*but*" then also I am a prophet. This may be a very wild and a very bold claim (τολμηρός), "*but*" there are the miracles (v. 19). And, claiming to be a prophet, I return with that prophetic insight back to you, and declare that **"you yourselves"** (v. 14) are evidences, **"full of goodness, filled with all the knowledge, able even to instruct one another;"** and, therefore, needing not to look to the prophets to know that Gentiles *may* be saved (vs. 9-12), but being evidences yourselves of the mercy of God to Gentile nations.

15. "**But.**" These particles move swiftly forward. This is the third "*but.*" The prophecies favor the Gentiles (vs. 9-12), "*but*" (1) may God settle the fact by actually blessing you, and by *filling you with all joy and peace in believing* " (v. 13). Not only so, "*but* (2) *I have become persuaded* that He *has* blessed you, and that you are "*full of goodness,*" having become evidences against the Jewish narrownesses yourselves. These evidences might be doubted, "*but*" (3)—Now we will add all the remainder of the testimony :—

15. But I have written the more boldly in some measure, as one admonishing you, on the ground of the grace given to me of God, 16. That I might be a public officer of Christ Jesus in respect to the Gentiles, serving in priestly form the Gospel of God, that the presenting of the Gentiles in sacrifice may be acceptable, being sanctified through a Holy Spirit.

It will be noticed that Paul has two ends, which indeed may be concentred into one ; first, that the Gentiles might be accepted as legitimate saints, and, second, that he himself might be listened to as their legitimate apostle. His strongest argument is in the nineteenth verse :—

17. I have therefore a ground of boasting in Christ Jesus in things pertaining to God.

His strongest argument is two things,—miracle and Gentile conversions. Perhaps we had better say one thing, for the "**power of signs**" and "**the power**" of the new birth, what are they but the same ghostly attestation ?—

CHAPTER XV.

18. For I will not dare to say anything of those things which Christ has not wrought by me in order to Gentile obedience in word and deed, 19. In power of signs and wonders, in power of a Holy Spirit, so that from Jerusalem and round about unto Illyricum I have thoroughly fulfilled the Gospel of Christ,

"**In some measure**" (v. 15). "**I have written the more boldly in some measure.**" This modest disclaimer of pretending to too much, must be traced to what has gone before. From eaters of meat Paul had risen to the Gentiles, absorbing the petty difficulty about flesh into the grander feud between the "Greeks" and the Israelitish people. He had appealed again to their law, and showed that it accepted the heathen. And then, as we have just been seeing, he breaks off from that, and comes to the very evidence at our doors. For heathen men *had* been accepted. "*Ye yourselves are full of goodness*" (v. 14). Now it is after this appeal to their own exhibited acceptance that he uses this expression of reserve;—"*I have written the more boldly in some measure.*" The prophets have heralded the Gentiles; but then also I am a prophet. And ye have heralded yourselves. But then I bear witness to that fact "*the more boldly in some measure,*" because, not only do ye exhibit it yourselves, but I, who am a "discerner of spirits" (1 Cor. 12 : 10) announce it as an inspired verity. And I attest my right to boldness, because "**from Jerusalem round about unto Illyricum, in power of signs**" I have built the base of these divine annunciations.

"**Public officer of Christ**" (v. 16, λειτουργός, from λαός, *people*); not merely "*minister*" (E. V. & Re.). "**Serving in priestly form;**" not merely "*ministering*" (E. V. & Re.). "**Presenting of the Gentiles in sacrifice;**" the whole a consistent allegory. Paul stands up to the altar λειτουργός, a servant of the people ; "*serving in priestly form ;*" offering up "*the Gentiles in sacrifice ;*" and claiming now as the point of his speech that they are "a sacrifice acceptable, well pleasing to God through Jesus Christ."

20. But counting it mine honor thus to preach not where

Christ has been named, lest I be building on another man's foundation; 21. But in the manner written :—

> They to whom no announcement of Him came, shall see;
> And they who did not hear shall understand.

"In the manner written" (v. 21). This corresponds to "thus" in the twentieth verse. "Not to preach" in that way, but this way (καθώς). Merely "*strived*" (E. V.), or "*making it my aim*" (Re., v. 20) is too general. We are to "*adorn*" the doctrine of Christ. And Paul makes it his καλόν or noble work (Rom. 12 : 17), to play the apostle, and pioneer the way for the after labors of the Kingdom.

22. "**Wherefore;**" not only because I preferred pioneer work, but because, at an earlier day, when such work might be done at Rome, I was so engrossed; "**I have been hindered by many things.**" We have no right to say "*many times*" (E. V., *marg.* & Re.), or "*much*" (E. V.), for the simple reason that such readings can never prevail. As long as τὰ πολλὰ is a great deal more catholic, and cannot possibly be forbid of its meaning as a general neuter, the form "*many things*," so long as it makes excellent sense, will always return :—

22. **Wherefore also I have been hindered by many things from coming to you.**

23. "**But now.**" Meyer's idea that the "*wherefore*" (v. 22) cannot refer to his pioneer preferences, or Rome would be no "**place**" for him ever, forgets two announcements of the apostle, first, that chances for such work were giving out where he was, and, second, that he was to *pass through* Rome on a still grander and wider enterprise of pioneer endeavor :—

23. **But now, having no more place in these parts, but having a strong desire these many years to come to you, 24. Whensoever I take my journey into Spain I hope on that account in my journey through to see you, and to be brought on my way thitherward by you, when first in some measure I have been satisfied with your company.**

24. "*I will come to you*" (E. V.) is undoubtedly an interpo-

lation. The uniform verdict is that we are to throw that phrase out, and that we are to consider the sentence as broken at the end of the verse (see Re.), then that it is to be resumed with an awkward "*I say*" (Re.), so as to start again in the twenty-fifth verse. We have had scores of such expedients in the Bible (2 : 20, 21 ; 5 : 12 ; 16 : 27) ; and we do not remember one that was really necessary. The Greek at fault is γάρ in the twenty-fourth verse. Some men would manage by casting that out. But while the authority for casting out the other is absolutely complete (A B C D F ℵ), the authority in the instance of γάρ must be reckoned nothing (F). We have to accommodate ourselves to its being kept, and beyond all doubt there are instances, though exceedingly rare (Matt. 1 : 18 ; Rom. 9 : 17*), where γάρ, in its illative effect, retires from its more usual position. We have given it its required force by the expression **"on that account."** And if this exception to the general idiom is allowed, all lies smooth, and both phenomena are explained ; first, the spurious copying in of "*I will come to you*" (E. V.), or, second, the equally unauthenticated plan of rejecting γάρ in order to accomplish the same purpose of a continuous reading of the sentence.

Whether Paul ever went to Spain is, of course, the old controversy. If he was imprisoned twice, he may have done so, but even then it is unsettled. If he was imprisoned once (I mean at Rome), we hardly can suppose he did go ; and, in either case, the plan of the journey must have been different from any which he here contemplates. Among the notabilia of exegetes a larger room ought to be allowed for those things which it is practically certain we never will be able even to conjecture.

---

* This unnoticed bearing of γάρ becomes strangely telling in Rom. 9 : 17. "So then it is with this *animus*," that is, in the light of the previous passage (v. 16), "that the Scripture says to Pharaoh, For this very cause have I raised thee up, that I might show in thee my power, and that my name might be declared throughout all the earth."

25. But now I go to Jerusalem to minister to the saints. This is not exactly a high ideal of "**Jerusalem**" believers. Why were they "**poor?**" And, with the habits engendered by the gospel, why were they "*poor*" so long? A famine had accounted for it (Acts 11 : 28, 29), and they had had bitter persecutions (1 Cor. 7 : 26). But the famine was twenty years before, and the persecutions were scarcely general—except perhaps in cutting off the humbler classes from the opportunity of labor. Jerusalem was the metropolis of the Jews. All society was builded upon the continuance of their faith. The threats of a new religion would seem traitorous. Few nobles would embrace it. Few of the middle class, unless roused by a very miracle of grace. And masses of common people would be the "**saints;**" impostors in many an imaginable case (Phil. 3 : 18) : "*poor*," because they had never been rich; and slow to be moved, in their accustomed poverty, to the higher and nobler purposes of a diligent religion.

Besides, they had "had all things in common" (Acts 4 : 32). This would be poison to a modern religionist. Luke merely records it. He nowhere says it had the divine approbation. We believe much in scripture is merely stated without comment (Judges 7 : 16 ; Jo. 21 : 3). To our modern thought the sinking of estates and the feeding of the lazy by the diligent, would be enough to blight business, and bring the provinces to be appealed to for a century of years. Those Ananias scenes were probably a mistake ; and if the apostles do not say so, it is like Paul's circumcising Timothy (Acts 16 : 3), a thing of which we have a right to judge, and in respect to which we are not in the least instructed by the actual narrative.

26. For Macedonia and Achaia have thought it well to make some contribution to the poor among the saints at Jerusalem ; 27. For they thought it well, and are really debtors of those people.

The Jews, as some one has remarked, had been "the librarians of the Christian world." They had borne the bondage of the faith (Acts 15 : 10), and had been rewarded for it by manifold conversions (3 : 2). Their nation had contributed Christ (9 : 5) and perhaps Paul was gently hinting that they had contributed *him ;* and that Gentiles had flocked into the church through the direct instrumentality of his own apostleship.

27.—For if the Gentiles have partaken of the spiritual things of those people, they are bound also publicly to serve them in fleshly matters.

Simply *"to minister"* (E. V. & Re.) is not far from the truth ; but why not preserve the Greek ? The individual Gentile could not pay back the individual Jew, but he could λειτουργῆσαι, that is, literally, *work for the people* (λαός). He could give back in a **public** way **"fleshly"** things (*"carnal,"* E. V. & Re., has slided from its sense) in return for **" the spiritual things "** which Christ and His Israelitish *"saints"* had been the means of for the heathen.

28. Having, therefore, completed this, and sealed this fruit to them, I will come on by you into Spain. 29. But I know that, coming to you, I will be coming in a fulness of Christ's blessing.

" And sealed this fruit to them." This is one of those fine passages that Paul's terseness causes to be lost. No commentator gets it ! The *" fruit "* here spoken of is not for the Jews, but for the Gentiles. What a noble division for a sermon ! In the first place, *"the fruit"* of alms-giving is not for the receiver but for the giver. In the second place, Paul had raised that *"fruit"* for Macedonia, and in the third place, he had **" sealed** (it) **to them."** *" The fruit"* of their alms-deed would be for their eternal well being. It seems sad that such a sentence should be secreted for hundreds of years.

But, now, the reasons for this lying in secret ! Good scholars will smile at us, and at our newly suggested signification. And they will say, The sense is impossible. And it will be all the more easy to see it if it be so, or, whether that verdict can be maintained, because the reasons for the whole are built upon a single pronoun. If we examine the passage we will find αὐτός, in its different shapes, four times ; twice as αὐτῶν (v. 27), and twice as αὐτοῖς (vs. 27, 28). It will be impossible to imagine, it will be said, that three of these pronouns (v. 27) refer to one class or body of men and one (v. 28) to the other.

It would seem hard to go back to the "vulgarity" (Godet) of imagining Paul, in this solemn epistle, to have narrated that the money sent by him had been *sealed up!* and, in fact, almost impossible, after the nobler and grander significance; but what are we to do? There have been immense strugglings about the sense, and that is a suspicious indication; but look at the Greek! Men will laugh at the intimation that Paul could suddenly have changed in the use of the pronoun αὐτός. But let us look at that. Is Greek any different from English? Look at the English. "*It hath pleased them verily, and their debtors they are. For if the Gentiles have been made partakers of their spiritual things, their duty is also to minister to them in carnal things*" (v. 27). Is there any fixity of the pronoun there? Besides, who gave us such certainty in the Greek? The grammars talk very differently (Winer, § 22 : 4, b). And so does the Bible. In Mark we read, "They bring unto Him (αὐτῷ, Christ) a blind man, and exhort Him (αὐτόν, Christ) that He should touch him (αὐτοῦ, the man)." What says the pronoun here? See also Mark 9 : 27, 28. And again, in John 11 : 37, with the pronoun οὗτος. "Could not οὗτος, which opened the eyes of the blind, have caused that even οὗτος should not have died?" If any one greatly prefers, he might consider the closing αὐτοῖς to belong to all the parties in the case, and suppose that "*fruit*" to both was "*sealed*," that is, made permanent, by both giving and being grateful.

29. "**But.**" Paul's plan seems but little for Rome, as he confesses that he is but taking them in his route. "*But*," he says, "**I know**" that, notwithstanding this, though my longer errand is "**to Spain,**" yet "**to you I will be coming in a fulness of Christ's blessing.**" Δέ is rarely to be lost, and translating it "*and*" (v. 29, E. V. & Re.), or "*now*" (v. 30, E. V. & Re.), is usually a measure that has in the end to be given up.

30. For look at its next occurrence. It is not, "*Now I*

beseech you, brethren" (E. V. & Re.), but the same disjunctive particle (δέ). Paul has been saying, My aim is "*Spain,*" *but* in my mere passage through I shall bring "*to you*" serious blessing. Then he inserts another δέ. "**But,**" though I expect to bless you, I do humbly entreat you to bless me.

The cause was reasonable. He never came to Rome, at least upon his own plan of travel. He was going to Jerusalem ; and, as he afterward found out (Acts 21 : 11), " not knowing what would befall (him) there " (Acts 20 : 22). The particles, therefore, are exactly in place. When he came to Rome he would bless *them* (and he did, though in very different circumstances, Acts 28 : 31).

"**But,**" now, for himself :—

30. But I exhort you, brethren, by our Lord Jesus Christ, and by the love of the Spirit, that ye strive together with me in prayers to God for me, 31. That I may be delivered from the unbelievers in Judea, and that my ministration, which is for Jerusalem, may be made acceptable to the saints, 32. So that, coming to you in joy by the will of God, I may together with you find rest.

30. Do not the Revisionists carry too far the right to use the pronoun by mere force of the article, as in this instance of ταῖς before προσευχαῖς ? King James, with no such claim, inserts it in italics. But a closer reading of the passage would not want it at all, and would reject it altogether. The prayers were not to be all theirs, but they were to unite with *him* "**in prayers**" to the Almighty. 31. "**Be made.**" Paul had reason to fear (Gal. 2 : 2, 9) that Jerusalem church people might find it not altogether "**acceptable**" to have him as the alms-bestower from among the churches of the heathen. Ἐλθών and ἔλθω are indifferent readings in the thirty-second verse. Neither authority nor sense gives us much to choose in our selection between them.

33. "**But**" (and here again, see Rom. 15 : 5, the apostle gives up his own will in respect to the particular way in which "**God**" shall bless) :—

33. But the God of peace be with you all. Amen.

We must not too perseveringly roughen our translation by insisting upon the article ; but undoubtedly there is purpose in the expression, "**the God of the peace.**" The correspondence is exact with the fifth verse. Paul had been laboring there to tell them how "*the hope of the Scriptures* might be bred by "*the patience and the encouragement of* (them)." He finishes all thoroughly, and then indulges himself in the appeal, "*May the God of the patience and the hope*" do all directly ! His course is the same in this passage. He has ventured to be specific with the Almighty, and to suggest to the people what he meant to do for them (v. 29), and what he begged that they might pray for for him, along with his own prayers for his deliverance in Jewry. God blessed neither. And yet He blessed both. For He answered these specific "*prayers*" in "*the fulness of the blessing*," which Paul asked in his more general petition. "**But**," as though he had said, "*God*" may choose other ways to bless ; "*May the God of the peace*,"—that is, of this whole peaceful "**rest**" (v. 32) that I am aiming to enjoy with you in my journey, "**be with you all**," though I never make the journey, and though He realize "*the peace*" (as indeed He did) in other and still more glorious administrations.

CHAPTER XVI.

1. But I commend unto you Phœbe, our sister, who is a deaconess of the church which is in Cenchreæ,

"**But.**" There are readings which omit this, but the preponderance is in its favor. I beg the other things (15 : 30), but "**Phœbe**" I directly send to you. "**A deaconess.**" Not διακόνισσα. That was a coined word, not used till afterward. Διάκονος might be feminine. "**Cenchreæ**" was one of the ports of Corinth. That there was an office of "*deaconess*" the following are the proof passages (16 : 1; 1 Tim. 5 : 9).

2. That ye may receive her in the Lord in a way worthy of the saints,

CHAPTER XVI. 377

The question, Which this means,—" **worthy of**" them who "**receive,**" or " *worthy of* " her who is to be received, need give no difficulty. The worthiness of the manner of the act is traceable to the saintship of both parties.

2.—And that ye provide her in whatever matter she may have need of you; because also she herself has been a patroness of many, and of me myself.

Not simply a "*succorer*" (E. V. & Re.), but a woman of position, who could *stand before* one (προστάτις, feminine of προστάτης), and open the way. It will be observed that Paul puts this woman first. There is no reason to doubt that she was the carrier of his epistle (see closing inscription), and may very well have been sent by Paul to conciliate the Roman churches, herself " *a deaconess* " in another communion.

3. Greet Prisca and Aquila, my fellow laborers, in Christ Jesus,

"**Prisca**" is the original name. Priscilla is a term of endearment (*dimin.*, Acts 18 : 2). The wife stands first, perhaps as the more prominent and active worker.

4. Who for my soul's sake bowed their own neck; to whom not only I give thanks, but also all the churches or the Gentiles. 5. And greet also the church which is at their house.

We have not the smallest clue to what the apostle means by this **bowing of the neck**. No incident explains it. We are left sheerly to the language. The mere probabilities of the language seem to intimate a moral **bowing** rather than one upon a scaffold. In the first place, ψυχή, in the wide majority of cases, means "**soul.**" In the second place, *putting down* the "**neck**" (for that is the distinct Greek), means generally humiliation (Gen. 49 : 8 ; Mi. 2 : 3). In Eastern war the victor set his foot upon the neck (Jos. 10 : 24). In the third place, the word is " *neck*," not " *necks* " (E. V. & Re.), which points again to other than a literal exposure to beheading. In the fourth place, the word is not *lay down* (E. V. & Re.), but *put down* or *bow*. That counts somewhat. And, in the fifth place, some great act of humiliation, or modest retirement from the front, on the part of these fellow crafts-people of Paul, would be more likely to be alluded to without separate detail, than the more stirring feat of risking their lives in his succor.

Some ingenious commentator suggests that this **"church (in the) house"** may have owed its location (see also Acts 18: 3 ; 1 Cor. 16 : 19) to certain weaving lofts that were necessary in the tent-making of Prisca.

5.—Salute Epænetus, my well-beloved, who is a first fruits of Asia unto Christ.

While the reading " *Achaia* " (E. V.) was preferred, difficulty was made because this honor was assigned to Stephanas in another passage (1 Cor. 16 : 15). But a solution which Meyer calls a "make-shift" (*in loc.*) is hardly so bad as that, viz., to insist that the appellation might be for both, as there is no presence of the definite article.

6. Greet Mary, who toiled in many things for your behalf. 7. Greet Andronicus and Junias, my kinspeople and fellow prisoners, who are of note among the apostles, and who were in Christ before me.

'Ιουνίαν may be either **"Junias"** or " *Junia* " (Re., *marg.*). We never can tell. If it was a man, it agrees a little better with the association, viz., **"among the apostles;"** but if it is a woman, and she is in association with her husband, it agrees sufficiently well with that, and with other habits of the passage.

8. Greet Amplias, my beloved in the Lord. 9. Greet Urbanus, our fellow-worker in Christ, and Stachys, my beloved. 10. Greet Appelles, the approved in Christ. Greet certain among the household of Aristobulus.

10. Not "*them which are of* " (E. V. & Re.). There is a care about that. Not all this man's **"household,"** but **"certain."** The difference is made by ἐκ τῶν (see v. 11).

11. Greet Herodion, my kinsman.

Paul seems to have had a powerful family* (v. 7 ; Acts 23 :

---

* Some think the word should be translated "*fellow countrymen*" (Godet).

16). Had it been otherwise, he hardly would have been taught by Gamaliel (Acts 22 : 3 ; see also Acts 22 : 25-29).

11.—Greet such of the house of Narcissus as are in the Lord.

See com., verse 10.

12. Greet Tryphæna and Tryphosa, toilers in the Lord. Greet the beloved Persis, who toiled in many ways in the Lord.

These (τὰς and ἥτις) are, of course, all women.

13. Greet Rufus, the chosen one in the Lord, and her who is both his mother and mine.

It is not an obscure conjecture, but a lively probability, that this "**Rufus**" was the child of the cross-bearer, Simon (Matt. 27 : 32), and that the "**mother**" was the wife of this African, and herself a negress. If Simon was converted by his adventure, and his conversion saved his wife, and his wife trained her children, and her children became distinguished in the church, and she herself most active and tender in her piety, how interesting does that scene among the soldiers immediately make itself. And yet these *ifs*, which, stated as we have done, seem almost ridiculous, are bound by the strongest links when we connect them by the name of "*Rufus.*" It is not at all likely that there were two Rufuses in the church, and that both of them were only once mentioned, and that each of them was so distinguished as to be named familiarly and lifted up above other believers. But unless there were, this Rufus, who here receives the salutation, was the child of the negro Simon ("the father of Rufus," Mar. 15 : 21), and the child of a woman so tenderly devout, that Paul stands ready to call her "**his mother and mine.**"

This much is scarcely conjecture ; but the filling out of the picture is strangely attractive. Was Simon converted at Golgotha ? or did the soldiers mark some expression of compassion, and make fun of him, or else punish him, by laying on the cross ? Did Simon convert his wife, or was there in that African home a most motherly saint, who led Simon to the cross, and reared Rufus and Alexander to be her eminent children? We cannot tell. But it would be folly to pass this sentence without the thought, that here, thirty years farther on, the scene at the cross might be bringing the ripe fruits of a glorious and divinely recorded influence of a wonderful devotion.

14. Greet Asyncritus, Phlegon, Hermes, Patrobas, Hermas, and the brethren that are with them.

These may or may not be names since traditional in the earliest writings.

15. Greet Philologus and Julia, Nereus and his sister and Olympas, and all the saints that are with them.

There seems no familiar name here.

16. Greet one another in a holy kiss.—

A command, like washing the saints feet (1 Tim. 5 : 10), or taking off our shoes for reverence (Mar. 1 : 7), or anointing guests with oil (Lu. 7 : 46), scarcely meant to be for all time, but illustrative, and in that day a suitable means of expressing good will and customary consideration for our brethren.

16.—All the churches of Christ greet you.

17. **"But."** Turning from what is affectionate and good, Paul brings before them the possibilities of discord and evil :—

17. But I exhort you, brethren, to have a view to those who create the divisions and the occasions of stumbling, contrary to the lessons ye have learned, and do ye turn away from them.

"**Lessons**" is better than "*teaching*" (Re., *marg.*) in the mere matter of English; for we cannot say, "**Ye have learned** *teaching.*" And it is better than "*doctrine*" (E. V. & Re.) in the matter of the sense; for the διδαχήν was practical as well as theoretical, and "*doctrine*" has too circumscribed and uncomprehensive a sense.

18. For such persons are not serving our Lord Christ, but their own belly;

It is not necessary to take "**their own belly**" literally, or to imagine, with Meyer, a tendency in "**such persons**" to an Epicurean taste, but to understand it, as in the Epistle to the Philippians, of intense selfishness. When Paul says, "Whose God is their belly" (Phil. 3 : 19), we are not at all sure it might not comprehend an ascetic Pharisee, or a miser, too deadly selfish to worship his "*belly*" sufficiently, if we were to speak in a literal sense.

18.—And by the good and fair talk deceive the hearts of the innocent.

"*Simple*" (E. V.) is not so good as "innocent" (Re.), because it does not provide that a man, anything but "*simple*," may be **deceived** because of his *innocence*.

19. For your obedience has come abroad to all men.—

Therefore you may belong to this very company of guileless ones.

19.—I rejoice over you, therefore. But I would have you wise as to that which is good, but as to the evil not mingling with it.

"*Simple*" (E. V.) in the eighteenth verse is from the Greek ἄκακος, which simply means *not evil*. And though the Revisers improve the translation by the word "*innocent*" (Re.), yet it is easy to see that guilelessness and a certain sort of simplicity is at the bottom of the text. But to repeat the translation "*simple*" (E. V.) in the verse that follows after, and for the Revisers to say "*simple*" also, is hard to understand. The word is ἀκέραιος. It means *unmixed*, or *not mixed with*. It never means "*simple*," in the *artless* or *guileless* or *easily deceived* sense, in any classic sentence. And Paul would be utterly at variance if he told of a deep snare for the "*simple*" in one text, and then urged those endangered by it to be "*simple concerning evil*" (E. V. & Re.) in another. The word should be better translated than it is in other passages. We are to be as "wise as serpents, and unmixed or uncontaminated as doves" (Matt. 10 : 16) ; that is, we should have the cunning of the serpents, but stay out from among them. "That ye may be blameless and uncontaminated* (that is, *not mixing with them*), in the midst of a crooked and perverse nation, among whom ye shine as lights in the world " (Phil. 2 : 15).

20. But the God of peace shall bruise Satan under your feet shortly.

We have not in the English three features of what Paul had in the Greek :—first, the article before εἰρήνης, which might recall to a Greek mind "**the peace**" which Paul had been striving for in all his recent directions. His *greetings* had been redolent of it (vs. 3-16); and so are now these stern warnings against discord. We will not introduce the article; but the Greeks had the advantage of us. Second, the article before "*Satanas*," and, third, the meaning of Satanas, which lay naked to a Grecian's eye. The language of the Greek reveals more Paul's purpose in the uttering of such a prophecy. It all fits up closer by the help of what is noticed at a glance! I send you fervent greetings. But to make it possible to love and to greet and to help each other, flee discord. Keep utterly *unmixed* with agents and agencies of quarrel. Watch against being cheated of religious peace. And "*the God of the peace shall bruise the Adversary* (who is at the bottom of these attempts) *under your feet* ἐν τάχει, *quickly ;*" and then follows the usual benediction :—

20.—The grace of our Lord Jesus Christ be with you.

We have not entered into the ideas which would suppose that these two last chapters were fragmentary, and were not all sent together through Phœbe, or through any other person, to any of the Romans, or to any other of the churches. The reasons for such suppositions are, that all these fragments, as some are disposed to name them, are in no instance all of them in any one known manuscript. That is a strong consideration. But our interest in the whole thought is lessened by the fact that it makes not the smallest difference. How

---

* This is the only other New Testament case.

these sentences were fixed, or whether all were sent to everybody, and whether some of these closing matters, possibly whole salutations, were not meant for different cities, are questions hardly worth answering. Or, to speak with more perfect verity, they hardly concern a doctrinal student of the Word, however much they may interest explorers into the text.

If Phœbe went around with different endings, and appended this or appended that at a personal discretion, what bearing could it have? It might seem that something of the kind might be discreet. Or if even some fragments are false, it might seem sad to add to our uncertainties, but how could we help it? and they are really so few, that the Word of God would remain singularly well kept, after all the turmoil of intervening generations.

We sacrifice nothing, therefore, if we treat Paul's Greek as though an unseparated monograph. If there be anything spurious, let it be shown, like any other false reading in the Bible. If there be anything kept in Phœbe's hands, and added for particular believers, so much the better. It was part of Paul's inspiration, under the hand of God. If there was anything for other people whose names were on distant lists (as some conjecture about Aquila, Prisca, Epænetus, etc.,), what matter? It has been a blunder of the church; but how strange that so little of the sort has tinged the inspired light of this wonderful epistle!

21. After greeting, in the way that we have seen, certain selected Romans, he sends greeting generally from those about him.

21. Timothy, my fellow-worker, greets you; and Lucius and Jason and Sosipater, my kinspeople. 22. I Tertius, who wrote the epistle, greet you in the Lord.

22. Doubtless Paul's amanuensis. 21. Why Timothy is so much out of our notice, and who Lucius and Jason were (v. 21), we never shall be able to make certain.

23. Gaius, mine host, and of the whole church, greets

you. Erastus, the treasurer of the city, greets you, and Quartus, the brother.

24. The weight of MS. authority is on the whole against the twenty-fourth verse* (see Revision).

25. But to Him who is able to establish you according to my gospel and the preaching of Jesus Christ, according to the revelation of a mystery kept silent through times eternal; 26. But now made manifest, and by prophetic writings made known according to an arrangement of the eternal God, to all the nations unto an obedience of faith ; 27. To an only wise God, be that through Jesus Christ to which there shall be glory forever. Amen.

25. "But;" as something stronger and warmer than all our salutations to each other. "To Him who is able." This is more than mere ability or power (see 9 : 22 ; 15 : 1). It is a power to do a thing, and yet be consistent with what is eternally wise. "According to my Gospel." That creates the eternal consistency, and makes God "*able*" (3 : 26). "Establish;" see remarks upon this, 1 : 11. "Mystery." What could be more profound than the plan of pardon? "Kept silent,"—before and after the creation ; before, as a secret of a decree back in the everlasting, and after (v. 26), till a "revelation" was made, "and" (τέ) that "by prophetic writings, according to an arrangement of the eternal God." "Unto an obedience of faith." "*Obedience*" (which when we look at its very nature, love, is all that is moral in the world) is of the very nature of faith, and marks this, which occurs twice in the New Testament, as a very vital expression (see "*obedience of faith*," 1 : 5). 27. "Only wise," as He only can be who possesses foreknowledge and power. All else is venture. "To which." This is the only possible reading that gives syntax to the sentence. We will not go over the controversies. The puzzle springs from ᾧ, which cannot be gotten rid of. Our Bibles reject it, but out of a sheer desperation—which sanctions everything; but which must recoil; for few questioned

---

* 24. "The grace of our Lord Jesus Christ *be* with you all. Amen."

syllables of the Greek stand on better or more constant authority. Meyer solves the difficulty by the hackneyed thought that Paul forgot himself.* It is easier to take the one manuscript (B) and throw out the ᾧ altogether. The slovenly apology for the Holy Ghost has never in one instance prospered (2 : 20, 21 ; 5 : 12 ; 15 : 24, 25) ; and it is better to imagine the very best MSS. to have strayed, than that Paul, flushed by his work, has forgotten one single particle. We come, therefore, to a solution which we are surprised that no scholar should suggest, and which is really the only way to give absolute grammar to the expressions. We may flatter the syntactic speech, but we hardly writ it down before we imagined purpose in it beyond the more commonplace ascription. Paul says. " *To him who is able ;* " and we have explained the "*able*" as meaning *in consistency with truth*. Paul paraphrases it as meaning "*according to my gospel ;*" and, therefore, very naturally at the last, makes all that he is to ascribe to God possible "**through Jesus Christ.**" And, therefore, it would range with other profoundnesses in Paul to pause a little in the expression, till he can imagine the thing to be praised, to be actually achieved. Look in this light at the ᾧ in the sentence. It destroys the more commonplace reading, " *To the only wise God be glory* " (E. V.). It makes unnecessary the ungrammarly sentence, " *To the only wise God through Jesus Christ, to whom be the glory forever* " (Re.) ; and actually adds point to Paul by making Divine Providence win the honor before receiving it ; for we put it all in the strictest grammar by saying, " *Unto him who is able to establish you, etc., etc., unto an only wise God, be that through Jesus Christ to which there shall be glory forever. Amen.*" Such pregnancy of ὅς is of course notorious. It rules through all the Greek (Lu. 9: 36 ; 23: 14 ; Acts 8: 24 ; 22: 15; Rom. 14: 22; 15: 18; 2 Cor. 12 : 17), but it is especially Paulinian. We have expounded

---

* The Revisers must have agreed in this, for they have adopted a sentence which cannot be parsed, and which in the true Meyer sense loses itself in its own confusion.

it at length under another sentence (5 : 12). If no one is attracted to it by preference, our notion is that he must be forced upon it by the grammar. And Paul has an especial fondness, when he has worn out a more forth-right text (3 : 20), to put a pebble in it like this (see Gal. 2: 16, ἐὰν μή, "*save*," *Re.*), and to turn it from a common rut, and make a reader pause for a profounder meaning.

EXCURSUS

ON THE

FAMOUS PASSAGE IN JAMES

(JAS. 2 : 14–26).

A shock of apparent discomfiture attended our work when we discovered that Jas. 2 : 14–26, in its actual Greek, did not bear out the rendering of any of our versions. It was a great surprise to us. The plain words, "*Was not Abraham, our father, justified by works?*" (E. V. & Re., v. 23), and then, most deliberately repeated, "*In like manner, was not also Rahab, the harlot, justified by works?*" (E. V. & Re., v. 25), and, plainer yet, "*A man is justified by works, and not by faith only*" (E. V. & Re., v. 24) seemed a God-send to our particular view. It was a stroke of amazement that upset the whole of this, and confronted us with a Greek which honesty of search made us believe could not submit to any such translation.

Place the Greek before your eye and judge whether James, or any one else, has fallen upon such an order, if he meant the two earlier texts to imply a question.

"**Abraham, our father, was not justified by works**" is the plain artless order of the speech. "**Likewise also Rahab was not justified by works.**" What are we to do, therefore?

An immediate search into the whole of James not only revolutionizes the epistle, and saves it from the attacks of Luther and from the bickerings that have lent it fame, but actually, on a deeper look, rids it of contrariety with Paul, and learns from it, better than from Paul, that faith itself is incipient holiness.

14. What is the profit, my brethren, if a man say he has faith, but have not works? Can the faith save him?

This by itself is very striking. "**The faith.**" The Revision says "*that faith.*" The article warrants some attention to its influence. We start, therefore, with the idea that there are two kinds of "**faith;**" and James agrees with Paul that one kind is "**dead**" (vs. 17, 26) and that the other kind is **saving**, and that this saving kind **has works**; as we have been laboring to expound it, is moral or is the faith of the conscience; as the Roman Catholics declare, is "*fides formata*," or, by their strangely perfect, because original or patristic specification, a "faith infused with love;" as Moses calls it, "a faith counted as righteousness" (Gen. 15 : 6); as Paul calls it, the "receiving of the love of the truth" (2 Thess. 2 : 10); or, in his epistle to the Galatians (5 : 6), what is perhaps the strongest testimony of all, "faith (ἐνεργουμένη, that is) made active by love;" as though faith, when saving, contained love (as the atmosphere, when vital, or able to corrode, must contain oxygen); so bringing us back to James, that "faith without works is ἀργή (Greek *a priv.* and ἐργῷ), *inoperative*, or, more literally put, *unworking*" (v. 20).

Next comes another expression, "**dead according to its very self.**" It cannot mean "*being alone*" (E. V.), for the Greek does not warrant it. This the Revisionists have seen. But then "*in itself*" (Re.) has unspeakably less *appearance* of being the sense (see Acts 28 : 16). Why did not Paul say "*in?*" "*According to*" is not only the match for κατά, but is the very edge and essence of all the thought. As the expressions," **Depart in peace; be ye warmed and filled,**" *are dead according to their very selves*, if there be the full indulgence of self, and no outcoming of food and clothes, "**so faith,**" considering its deep pretentions; taking it as a belief in hell; considering it as a profession of God and Christ and sin and grace and pardon and eternal life, if it be not under the impression of any of these things by the light of a new conscience and by the token of some obedience to their claims, "**is dead,**" just as those speeches are,—"*dead*" in the very light of the things pretended, that is, "*dead*" as these three verses illustrate it, "*according to its very self.*"

15. If a brother or sister become naked, and be destitute

of daily food, 16. And one of you say unto them, Go in peace, be ye warmed and filled, but give them not the things needful for the body; what is the profit? 17. Even so faith, if it have not works, is dead according to its very self.

18. "*Yea, a man may say*" (E. V. & Re.). This is one of those numerous cases where a sense is dashed at the very crisis of a passage. James is made to introduce by the word ἀλλά, which means "**but**" with wonderful steadiness, a sentence in which he is to appear to agree; in fact, two verses (vs. 18, 19), which are to be read as lying in unity with his whole idea. How queer if, for the course of whole centuries, these verses, like scores of others in Scripture, should have been read as just the opposite of the thing intended.

18. But a man will say,—

Surely that sounds like an objector. And all the Greek agrees. And the twentieth verse sounds like the taking up of a reply.

James seems to imagine that "**a man**" may push the Jamesian idea too far. He means to hold on to Paul in Paul's exact teaching, that "**faith**" is everything. Nevertheless he must exalt the "**works.**" But he means now to guard "**works**" on the gospel side, and keep them from displacing "**faith.**" This is the gist of the two verses (18, 19). "**But a man will say,**"—

18.—Thou hast faith, and I have works. Show me thy faith by thy works, and I will show thee by my works my faith. 19. Thou believest that God is one; thou doest well; the devils also believe and tremble.

That is, "**faith**" in any degree, even to that, rare among the Pagans, of acknowledging the unity of God, is, by your confession now "*dead if it have not works.*" And how true that is, is made incontestable in the cases of the demons, who, with the brightest kind of faith, learn only to "**believe and tremble.**" "*Works*," therefore, are the test, and we need less care for "*faith*." This is the mistake which James suffers to expound itself in these two verses.

"*But a man will say,* **Thou hast faith."** There is no doubt about that. But then the demons believe, too, the highest truths. "**Works**" are the real token. So, when all comes to all, you have to prove your "*faith*" by "*works.*" Now why need I bother about the question of "*faith*" at all? If "*works*" are the vital thing, and you have to exhibit your "*faith*" by "*works,*" why may not I show that I have "*faith,*" without being really conscious of it or in any wise doctrinally possessing it, if only I have "*works?*"

Nothing could be more aptly looked into. If you, who notoriously have faith, nevertheless are not sure of safety till you have demonstrated its saving character by its element in works, why may not I, who notoriously have works, or to express it more truthfully, may be *imagined* for the sake of argument to possess the works, ignore the faith, inasmuch as that is a thing which the demons have, and that in the higher shape of the unity of the Almighty?

20. How finely now comes in the character, "**O vain man.**" It is an awful platitude if ἀλλά means "*yea*" (E. V. & Re.) and the two hinging verses (vs. 18, 19) are all on the side of the apostle. But if it is the address of a *reply*, behold how perfect it is! James would argue, Faith is not to be given up. It is all that the Scriptures demand. "**Abraham, our father, was not made righteous by works.**" (v. 21). Nor was "**Rahab**" (v. 25). Men must seek God if they would be saved. But the faith of seeking does not mount up to being saving till it becomes moral; *ex origine* till it is of the Spirit; consequentially till it is of the conscience; till it sees the beauty of Christ (Jo. 17 : 3); till it is "made active by love" (Gal. 5 : 6); till it can be "reckoned" as holy (Rom. 4 : 3); or, as James expresses it, till it "*have works;*" for he does not carry his point by acceding to the caviller that faith need not be noticed, but simply that faith is everything, nevertheless that that faith is nothing that does not show itself by the works of the Gospel.

20. But wilt thou know, O vain man, that faith without works is idle? 21. Abraham, our father, was not made

righteous by works in that he offered Isaac, his son, upon the altar. **22. Thou seest that faith worked with his works, and by works was faith made to answer its end.**

It will be seen how utterly shapeless the next verse would be if the usual versions were admitted. If we are to read, " Was not Abraham justified by works?" (E. V. & Re.), how absurd to add (v. 23), "**And the Scripture was fulfilled that saith, Abraham believed God.**" But if it is a recoil from unbelieving "*works*," and James is thoroughly Pauline, and means to insist on faith, and faith made moral, and **working with works**, then the summing is in place :—

23. And the Scripture was fulfilled that says :—Abraham believed God, and it was accounted to him for righteousness, and he was called the Friend of God.

Let us return now to a few verbal intimations. "**Idle**" (v. 20) is a various reading, acknowledged in our day (see Re.). The word is ἀργή (from *a priv.* and ἐργῷ, *without work*); a fine description of its being "*dead*" (vs. 17, 26) "*Faith without works is unworking ;*" and that, in all the things to which it could be applied, came to mean "*idle*," and gradually came to mean *null* or just nothing at all (see, in the verbal shape, Rom. 7 : 2, 6). "**Worked with**" (v. 22). That astounding act of **offering Isaac** was, at bottom, faith (see Heb. 11 : 17, *material dative*) ; but it was a faith working with works ; that is, a faith with which love, which is the essence of good works, is incorporate ; or, more profoundly still, a faith which "*has works ;*" that is, a faith which is a case of love ; just as, in another case, love repines at sin, or is or actuates true repentance. "**Accounted**" (v. 23) ; not strictly. Abraham's real state was positive sinfulness. But "*accounted ;*" as an earnest ; as a covenanted condition ; as a promise of more ; as a condition of less sinfulness than he once submitted to ; as the beginning of a perfect "**righteousness**" in Augustine's sense (*Migne, vol.* 5 : pp. 790, 867) ; incipient here, but growing, from this advancing germ, into a perfect "*righteousness*" in the Garden of the Lord.

24. Do ye really see,* then, that a man is made righteous by works, and not rather by faith only; 25. In like manner as Rahab, the harlot, was not made righteous by works when she had received the messengers, and sent them out another way?

This translation (vs. 24, 25) serves as a sufficient summing up.

26. For as the body without a spirit is dead, so faith without works is dead also.

Luther, therefore, was rash about his "straw epistle." The whole idea of James is, that salvation is alone by "**faith**;" but that, as an unworking "*faith*" is null or ἀργή, "**works**" must be an ingredient of the "*faith*," or, more philosophically stated, *love*, which is what is moral in "*works*," must be the ingredient of "*faith*," in order that it be saving.†

---

* The *seeing* in the twenty-fourth verse (ὁράω), is different from that in the twenty-second verse (βλέπω), as meaning to *see* intimately or down to the very bottom.

† This is the sound averment of the Papists, that "*fides formata* (saving faith) is faith infused with love." What a pity they trample their own definition by perfectionism and supererogatory excellence!

THE END.

www.ingramcontent.com/pod-product-compliance
Lightning Source LLC
Chambersburg PA
CBHW032028220426
43664CB00006B/407